GRAPHIC WAR
NAVY

GRAPHIC WAR NAVY

The Secret Naval Drawings and Illustrations of World War II

DONALD NIJBOER

FIREFLY BOOKS

A FIREFLY BOOK

Published by Firefly Books Ltd. 2024

First printing

Library of Congress Control Number: 2024935019

Library and Archives Canada Cataloguing in Publication

Title: Graphic war navy : the secret naval drawings and illustrations of World War II / Donald Nijboer.
Names: Nijboer, Donald, 1959- author.
Description: Includes bibliographical references and index.
Identifiers: Canadiana 20240343131 | ISBN 9780228104841 (hardcover)
Subjects: LCSH: World War, 1939-1945—Art and the war. | LCSH: World War, 1939-1945—Pictorial works. | LCSH: World War, 1939-1945—Naval operations. | LCGFT: Illustrated works.
Classification: LCC VA42 .N55 2024 | DDC 359—dc23

Published in the United States by
Firefly Books (U.S.) Inc.
P.O. Box 1338, Ellicott Station
Buffalo, New York
14205

Published in Canada by
Firefly Books Ltd.
50 Staples Avenue, Unit 1
Richmond Hill, Ontario
L4B 0A7

Cover and interior design: Stacey Cho

Printed in China | E

Canada

We acknowledge the financial support of the Government of Canada.

For Hendrik Jan Boer, my uncle Henry. Back in 1998 Henry was the first person to buy my first book well before it was published. Whenever I wrote something new, he would buy multiple copies for friends and family. He was my biggest fan. Thank you, Henry. I will never forget.

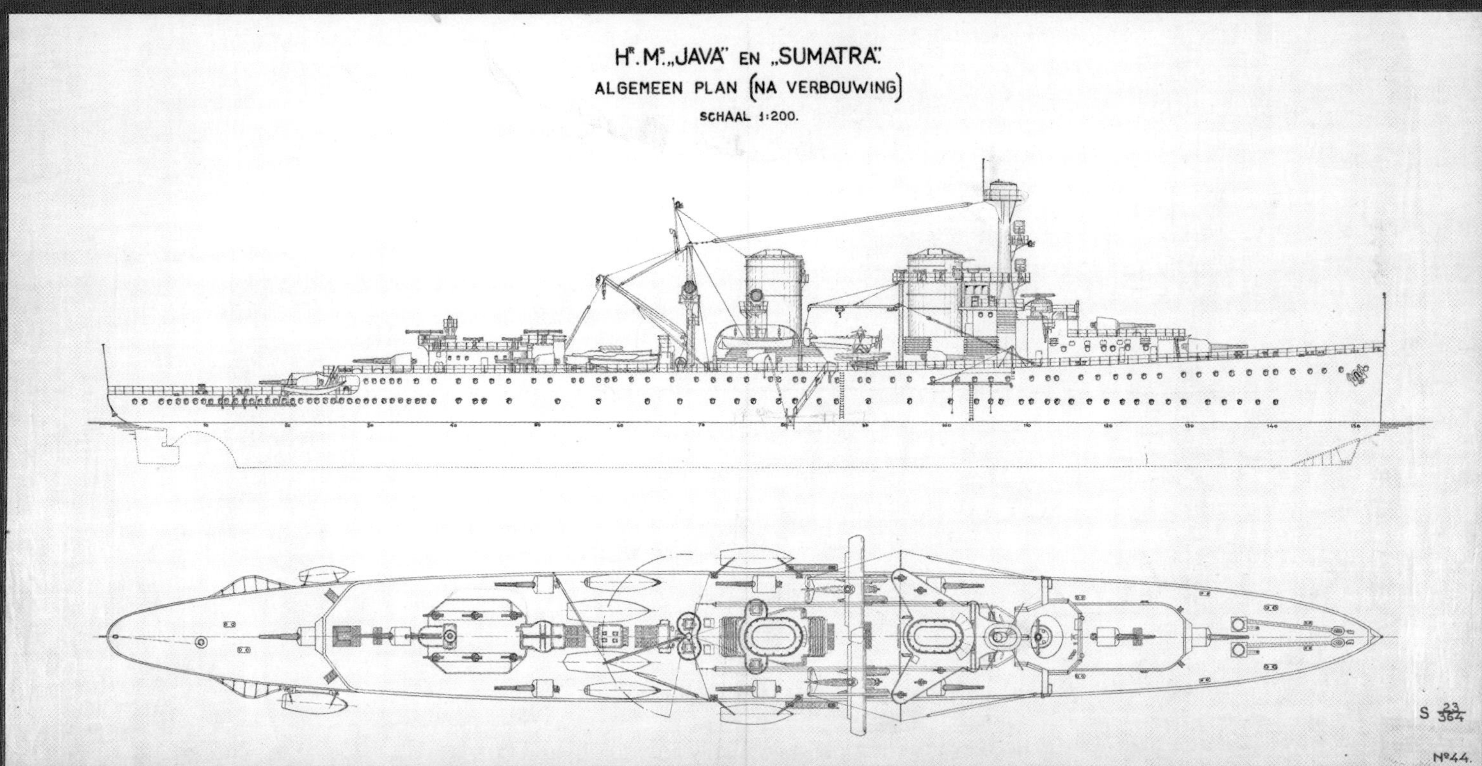

Types of TARGETS and ATTACK

Air targets

The Computer Mark 1 is primarily designed for use against air targets.

It computes accurate gun orders for Continuous Fire against nearly all types of air targets, such as:

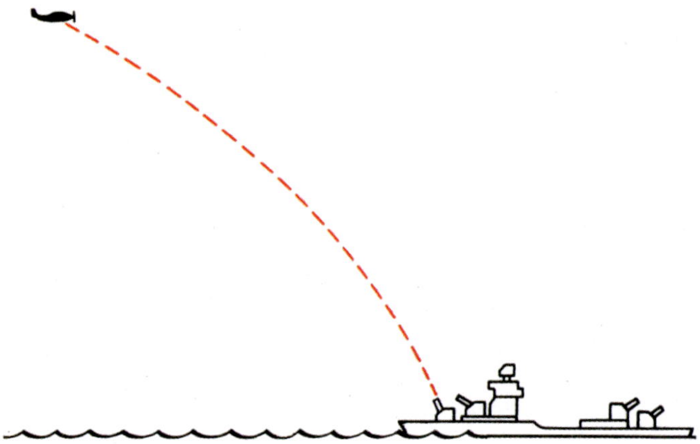

1 High-level Horizontal Bombers

2 Low-level Torpedo Planes

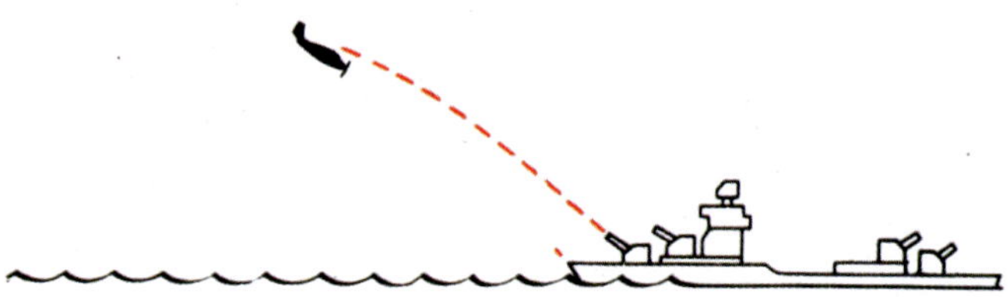

3 Dive Bombers attacking Own Ship

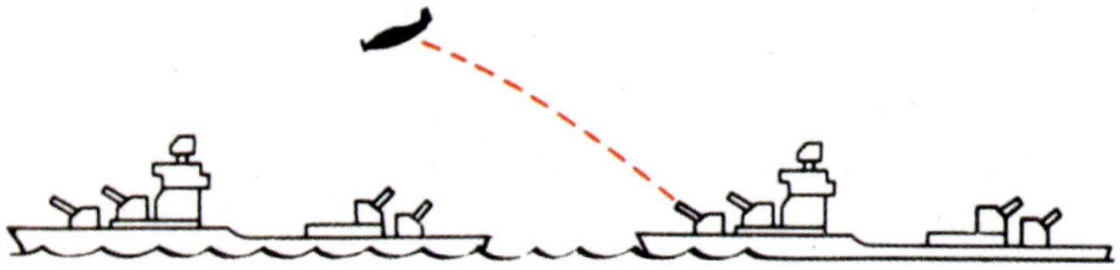

4 Dive Bombers attacking other ships (when the vertical component of Target Speed does not exceed −250 knots).

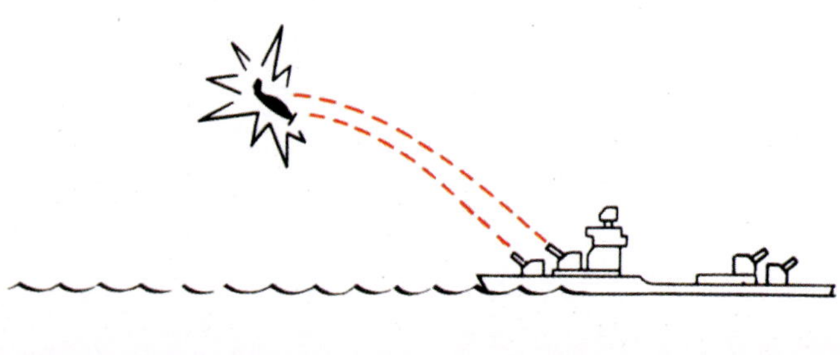

The Computer may also be used for antiaircraft barrage fire by the 5″ guns, or by the main battery guns.

Contents

TORPEDO RELEASED UNDER WATER

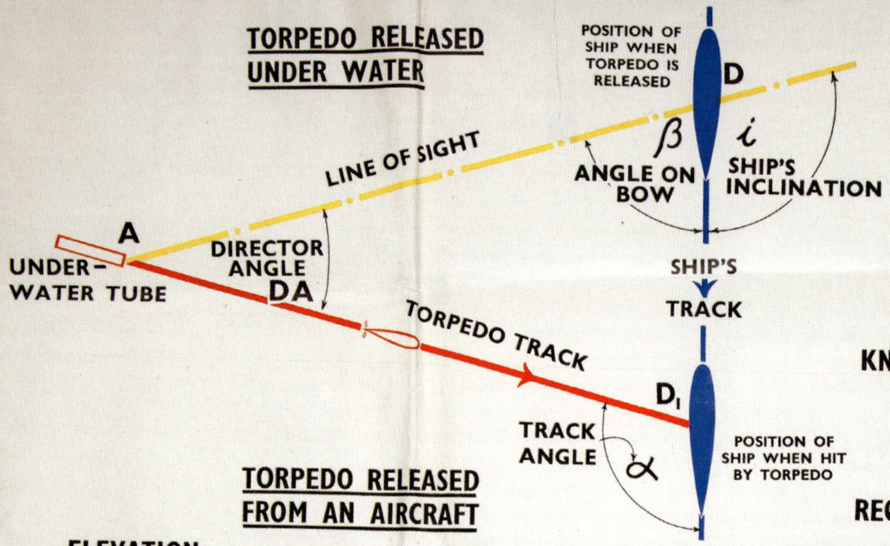

SOLUTION OF SIGHTING PROBLEM

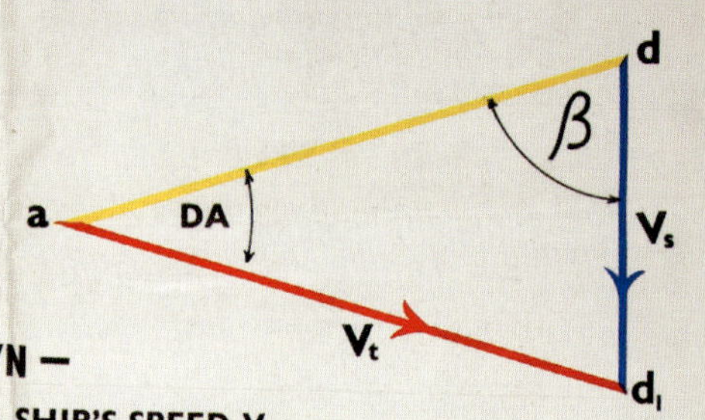

KNOWN –

(I) SHIP'S SPEED V_s
(II) TORPEDO WATER SPEED V_t
(III) ANGLE ON BOW β

REQUIRED –

DIRECTOR ANGLE DA

TORPEDO RELEASED FROM AN AIRCRAFT

ELEVATION

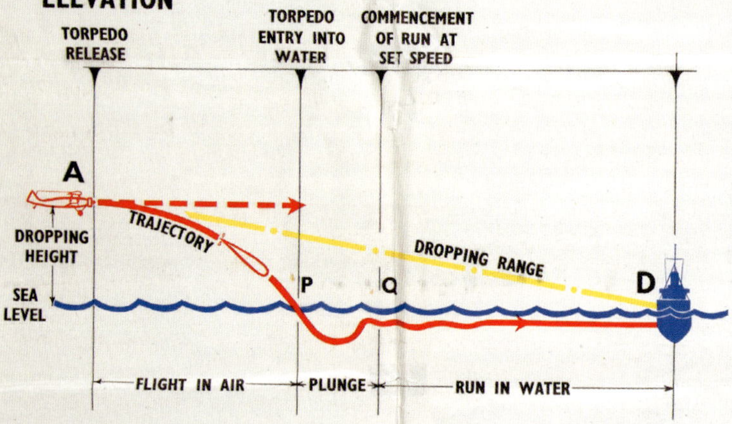

FLIGHT IN AIR

TORPEDO AIRSPEED IN HORIZONTAL DIRECTION = AIRSPEED V_a
WITH STANDARD DROPPING HEIGHT = 100 FT.
AIRSPEED = 160 KNOTS
THEN LENGTH OF FLIGHT IN AIR = 225 YDS.

PLUNGE

TORPEDO COMPLETES INITIAL DIVE AND DECELERATES FROM AIRSPEED TO WATER SPEED
LENGTH OF PLUNGE = 30 YDS. (APPROX.)

IN SIGHTING PROBLEM TREATED AS AN EXTENSION OF FLIGHT IN AIR COVERED AT AIRSPEED V_a

RUN IN WATER

COVERED AT PRESET WATER SPEED V_t

PLAN

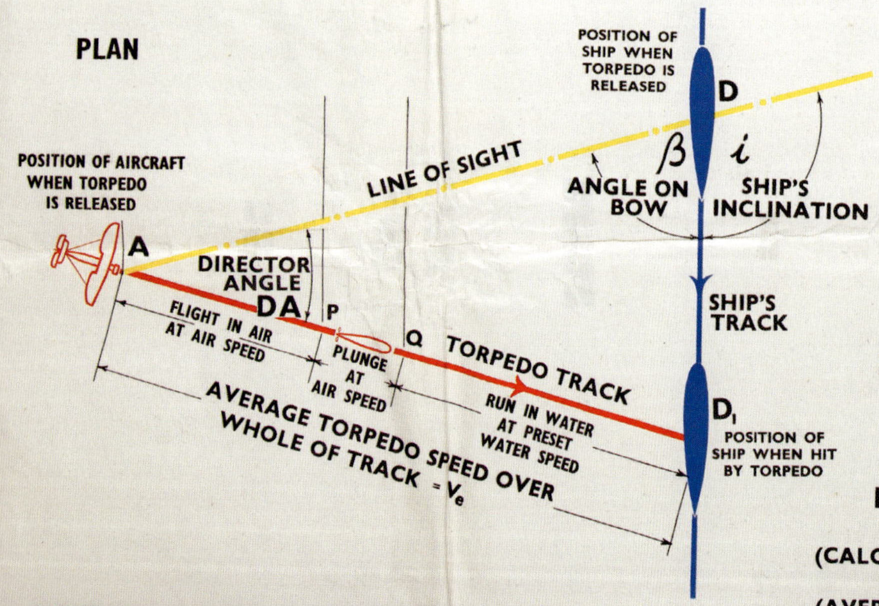

SOLUTION OF SIGHTING PROBLEM

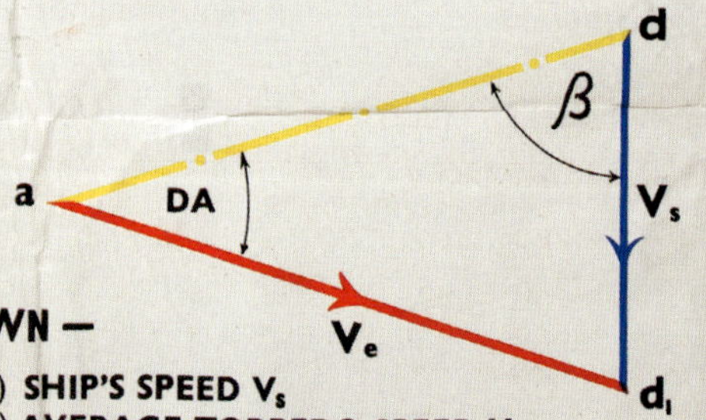

KNOWN –

(I) SHIP'S SPEED V_s
(II) AVERAGE TORPEDO SPEED V_e
(III) ANGLE ON BOW β

REQUIRED –

DIRECTOR ANGLE DA
(CALCULATED AND INDICATED BY DIRECTOR)

(AVERAGE TORPEDO SPEED V_e IS SUBSTITUTED FOR TORPEDO WATER SPEED V_t)

AIRCRAFT TORPEDO SIGHTING—

BASIC CONDITIONS OF TORPEDO RELEASE

See also A.P. 1730C, VOL. I, CHAP. I

AIR DIAGRAM 2184 | SHEET No 1 | No. OF SHEETS 1 | AIR MINISTRY PREPARED BY MINISTRY OF AIRCRAFT PRODUCTION | ISSUE No 1 | DATE 31/3/42

RTP

X001-4512

Foreword

When I was a boy, my dad, a draughtsman and engineer, had two old pocket watches. He challenged me to take one apart and then reassemble it. It wasn't long before I was faced with many small parts. What to do next? My father took the second watch apart, but this time he sketched the components' locations as he went.

My father's exercise taught me how visuals can explain complex mechanisms and processes. This is writ large in this magnificent book of diagrams that Donald Nijboer has painstakingly collected. Its content engages my enthusiasm for history, engineering, illustration and design.

Conflict is a catalyst for innovation, and naval warfare's development in World War II was no exception. Sea campaigns saw widespread use of coordinated submarine warfare, aircraft carrier operations, sophisticated air-dropped weapons and shipborne weapons to defend against them, plus radar, electronic aids, countermeasures and myriad other devices to give an edge in the deadly game of cat and mouse that defined the conflict. With those innovations came urgent requirements for visual aids to help personnel, often young conscripts with little prior knowledge of sophisticated weaponry. My own father-in-law, at age 20, found himself a lead navigator in a USAAF B-24 bomb group only three years after leaving his previous job in a New Jersey bowling alley. The gifted technical artists and designers of 1939–45, many of them anonymous, were more than up to this challenge.

What I find fascinating when browsing the following pages is how artists used all styles to communicate. I can well imagine how daunting creating detailed breakdowns of a Royal Navy fire control computer must have been, but the result is a superbly and clearly rendered example of technical illustration at its best. In my opinion, pieces such as the intricate Gato-class submarine and USS *Enterprise* cutaways transcend functionality and are fine works of art in their own right. Possibly the most striking approach of all is where artists have used humor and whimsy to communicate the soberest of topics, such as avoiding friendly fire incidents. Finally, there are pieces that just give a stark, unfiltered glimpse into combat realities, such as the diagram illustrating damage sustained by the submarine USS *Kingfish* during a seven-and-a-half-hour ordeal when over 40 depth charges were dropped in her vicinity.

Congratulations to Donald for assembling this splendid collection of work — a fitting tribute to the artists, so often unsung, who toiled for long hours to help naval personnel use their weapons.

Ian Bott, Chief Technical Artist
The Aviation Historian

Basic Conditions of Torpedo Release (Opposite)
Torpedoes were the true ship killers during World War II. Expensive and sophisticated, they required a great deal of training to be used effectively. Aircraft carriers of all nations carried about two to three torpedoes for each torpedo bomber. During the war, torpedo bombers were relatively easy to shoot down as they approached their target low and slow, making them vulnerable to AA fire and fighter attack.

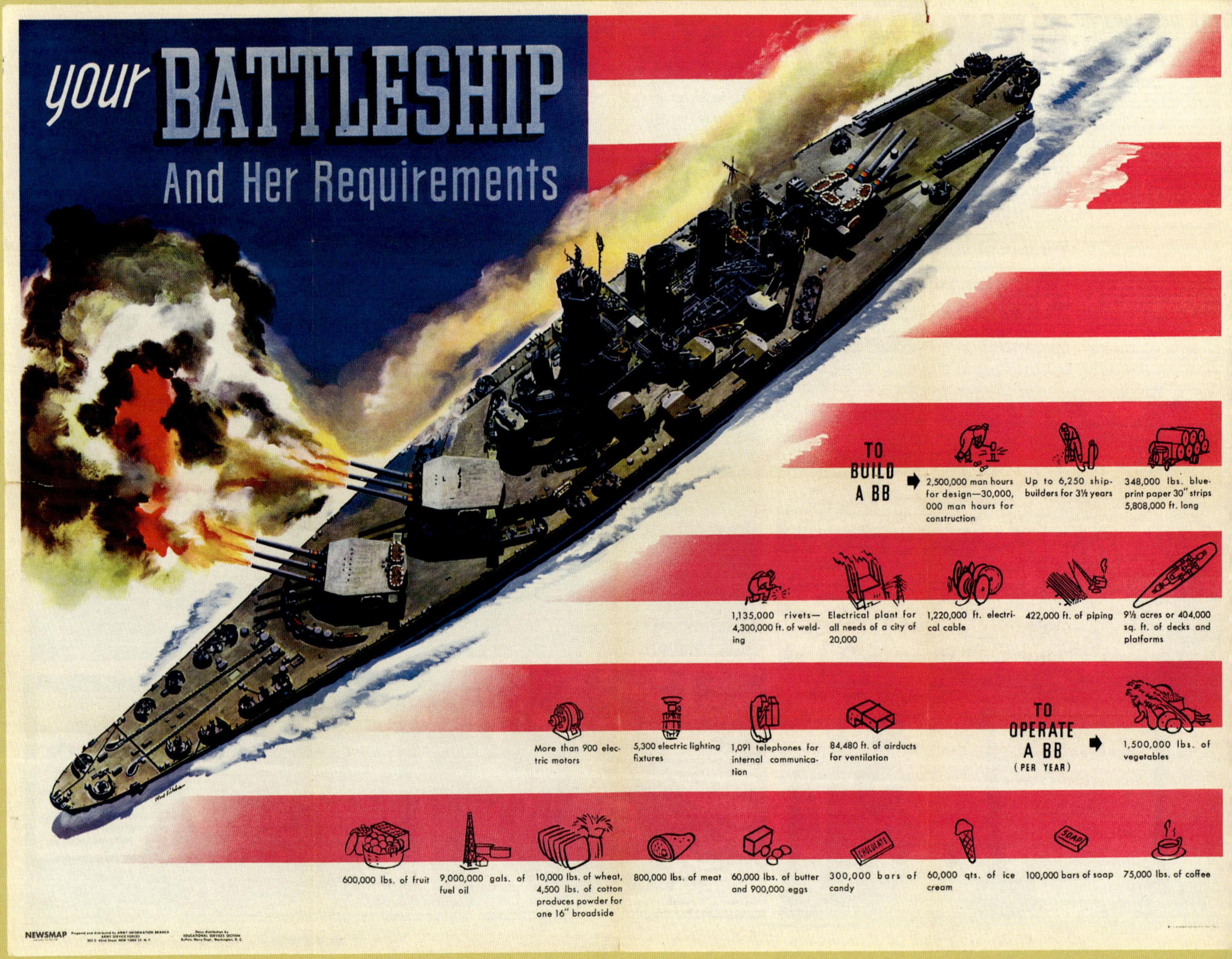
your BATTLESHIP
And Her Requirements
TO BUILD A BB
2,500,000 man hours for design—30,000,000 man hours for construction
Up to 6,250 shipbuilders for 3½ years
348,000 lbs. blueprint paper 30" strips 5,808,000 ft. long
1,135,000 rivets—4,300,000 ft. of welding
Electrical plant for all needs of a city of 20,000
1,220,000 ft. electrical cable
422,000 ft. of piping
9½ acres or 404,000 sq. ft. of decks and platforms
More than 900 electric motors
5,300 electric lighting fixtures
1,091 telephones for internal communication
84,480 ft. of airducts for ventilation
TO OPERATE A BB (PER YEAR)
1,500,000 lbs. of vegetables
600,000 lbs. of fruit
9,000,000 gals. of fuel oil
10,000 lbs. of wheat, 4,500 lbs. of cotton produces powder for one 16" broadside
800,000 lbs. of meat
60,000 lbs. of butter and 900,000 eggs
300,000 bars of candy
60,000 qts. of ice cream
100,000 bars of soap
75,000 lbs. of coffee
CHOCOLATE
SOAP
NEWSMAP
ARMY SERVICE FORCES
EDUCATIONAL SERVICES SECTION

Introduction

"This problem is with us daily and hourly. The carrying capacity of our shipping is a controlling factor in all our strategic plans upon which equipment and other items are based."

—U.S. Army Chief of Staff General George Marshall

The long history of the Second World War is too often characterized by the great land and air battles that raged in Europe and the Pacific. Thousands of books and documentaries describe Germany's unstoppable "Blitzkrieg" in the West and Russia in 1939–1941. The great land battles at El-Alamein (1942), the Battle of Stalingrad (1942–43), the huge tank battle at Kursk (1943), the D-Day landings in June 1944, the battle for Normandy and Hitler's ill-fated Ardennes offensive, known as "The Battle of the Bulge," are all described as decisive battles that shaped the outcome of World War II. Aircraft like the Supermarine Spitfire, the North American P-51 Mustang, the Boeing B-17 Flying Fortress and the Avro Lancaster are portrayed as "war-winning" machines and their pilots are considered among the bravest of the brave. However, with the exceptions of the sinking of the German battleship *Bismarck* and the famous carrier battle at Midway in June 1942, the great sea battles of World War II have not received as much attention.

Countless books have described these famous land battles in detail, and new ones appear every year. Films like *12 O'Clock High, Saving Private Ryan, The Longest Day, Memphis Belle, The Battle of Britain,* and *A Bridge Too Far* and series such as *Band of Brothers* have shaped a collective conception of World War II as a war characterized by land and air battles. While many books and films have portrayed some of the most famous naval battles of the war, their resonance is not as deep. Maybe that is because towns and villages were not liberated. Maybe it is because there were fewer military and civilian witnesses. Sea battles were short and often occurred at night on vast stretches of open water. Destroyed ships simply sank and disappeared. There was no trail of destruction visible, and no cheering crowds to welcome the victors — no obvious place for a graveyard, monument or plaque to honor the fallen.

The three most important naval campaigns of the war and the greatest Allied victories were the Battle for control of the Mediterranean (1940–42), the Battle of the Atlantic (1939–45) and the U.S. Navy's island-hopping missions in the Pacific (1942–45). For the Allies to liberate Europe and defeat the Japanese in the Pacific, they needed thousands of ships. The Allied armies were an expeditionary force and had to be transported to the battlefield by ship. One of the first Allied amphibious landings was

Your Battleship and Her Requirements (Opposite)
One of the best postings was to be assigned to a battleship. While still cramped, creature comforts were pretty good. Each ship had a doctor and dentist. Haircuts were available, along with ice cream, fresh vegetables and chocolate bars. The USN lost only two battleships during the war, both during the Japanese attack on Pearl Harbor.

Operation Watchtower, the invasion of Guadalcanal by U.S. Marines in August 1942. The liberation of Europe began with Operation Torch, the amphibious landing of American and British troops in North Africa in November 1942. This was followed by Operation Husky, the invasion of Sicily in July 1943, and culminated in the most famous amphibious landing of all: D-Day, June 6, 1944.

All of these operations were only possible with strong naval power. Allied ship construction during the war was unprecedented, and American President Roosevelt and British Prime Minister Churchill knew it was one of the keys to victory. In order of priority, the Allies chose aircraft production and expansion, followed by ship construction, over fielding a large land army. In early 1942, the U.S. Army planned to field two hundred divisions. A short time after, that number was cut in half.

Both Adolf Hitler and Admiral Karl Dönitz, head of the German submarine fleet, knew that the Battle of the Atlantic was the most important of the war. It was the most modern campaign Germany would fight against Anglo-American power. If Germany's U-boat arm had been able to sever the supply links between the U.S. and the UK, they might have won a European war — or at least forced a negotiated peace.

At the beginning of the war, Churchill maintained that control of the Atlantic was the dominating strategic consideration. The early success of German U-boats forced the Allies to devote a large share of their naval forces and national wealth to fighting and winning the campaign. Victory in the Atlantic led directly to the strategic bombing of Germany and the D-Day landings in June 1944.

The Japanese were also clear in their objectives. To defeat the United States and its Allies in the Pacific, the Imperial Japanese Navy (IJN), with its battleships and aircraft carriers, had to defeat the U.S. Navy in one or two decisive battles. This led directly to the carrier attack on Pearl Harbor on December 7, 1941.

Naval warfare during World War II was unique. It was fought on the surface, in the air, on the beaches and below the waves. It also saw the ascendancy of air power and the dominance of the aircraft carrier, in the form of the U.S. Fast Carrier Task Force.

Victory for the Allies depended on control of the seas. This meant more ships of all types. Even before war broke out, rearmament plans were already in place. The Naval Expansion Act of Congress, passed on May 17, 1938, led to the construction of the carrier USS *Hornet* and the order for the first of the new *Essex*-class carriers. In July 1940, three more were ordered, followed by nine more in September. This was just the beginning. Over the course of the Second World War, U.S. shipyards alone produced almost 100,000 vessels. These included 8 battleships, 13 heavy cruisers, 2 large cruisers, 33 light cruisers, 17 fleet aircraft carriers,

9 light aircraft carriers, 114 escort carriers, 349 destroyers and more than 85,000 smaller vessels, from landing craft to destroyer escorts. British and Canadian shipyards also contributed with 2 battleships, 6 aircraft carriers, 15 cruisers, 141 destroyers and 111 submarines.

All these ships had to be manned. A typical fleet carrier like the Royal Navy's HMS *Victorious* had a complement of 1,229 men, all with specific roles. The *Victorious*'s 1940s-era technology of steam-powered machinery, mechanical computers and vacuum tube electronics was extremely labor-intensive. When war broke out in September 1939 and enlistment exploded, the task of training thousands of young men and women began in earnest.

That's the Spot to Hit!
Admiral Chester W. Nimitz, USN, World War II Poster. (Artist: John Falter, USNR)

Training courses were already established for the world's navies, but these were designed for peacetime. As shipping losses mounted and more ships were built, training was accelerated. Most of the training involved visual aids, including posters, illustrations found in manuals and instructional films. These would include cutaway drawings, cross-sectional illustrations, how-to posters and schematics. These items were produced in the tens of thousands by artists, illustrators, technical artists, graphic illustrators, cartographers, draftsmen and women, many of whom have long been forgotten.

Many illustrators and graphic artists, classified as vital for war production, were spared from military service, and continued their work illustrating for the large shipbuilders and aircraft production companies. Others with artistic skills who enlisted or were drafted were pulled from the ranks and fought their war with pen and ink instead of being assigned to a destroyer or aircraft carrier. Many illustrations were listed as "classified, restricted, secret, top secret and most secret," with orders to destroy these documents in danger of capture.

The illustrations in this book offer a brief glimpse into the enormity of the task faced by the thousands of sailors, naval aviators and merchant seamen who risked their lives on the high seas.

CHAPTER 1

Steel Waves — The Lines of Battle

Ship Identification Silhouette: *Schleswig-Holstein*
Completed in 1908, the Schleswig-Holstein was the last of five pre-dreadnought battleships built for the German Navy. Obsolete by World War II, she was used as a cadet training vessel.

On the morning of September 1, 1939, the German pre-dreadnought *Schleswig-Holstein* unleashed a full broadside of her four 11-inch guns at the Polish ammunition depot in Danzig harbour. These were the opening shots of World War II. The final Japanese surrender ceremony aboard the battleship USS *Missouri*, 2,194 days later, officially ended humanity's bloodiest conflict. That the war's opening shots were fired by a ship and that the war ended on the deck of one of the world's most powerful battleships is a testament to the fact that the Second World War was largely a naval campaign. While many great land and air battles were fought, Allied

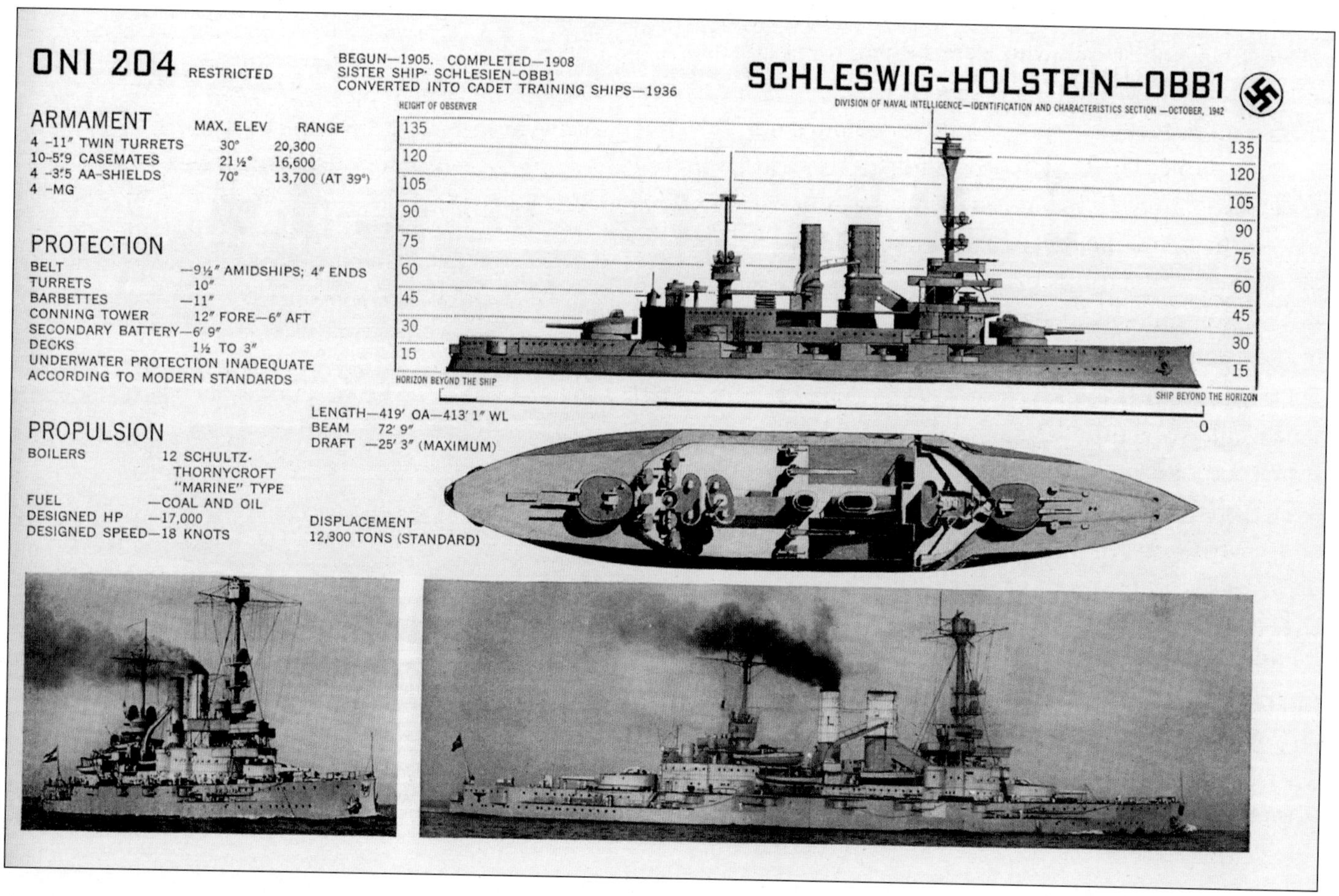

victory was never certain without control of the seas.

At the outbreak of World War II, the United Kingdom's Royal Navy was the largest and most experienced navy in the world, as well as the largest merchant marine with close to 10,000 vessels. In terms of size, it was followed by the U.S. Navy, the Imperial Japanese Navy, the French Navy, the Italian *Regia Marina* (Italian Navy) and Germany's *Kriegsmarine*. For the British, Americans, French, Japanese and, to a certain extent, the Italians, their fleets were designed and built to ensure freedom of commerce on the high seas and the protection of their colonial assets. Not only did the Royal Navy have to worry about the Germans in the Atlantic, but also the Japanese in the Pacific, who were a direct threat to their Asian interests. The U.S. Navy's primary focus was the Pacific and the ever-expanding IJN. The French and Italians also had their colonial outposts, but theirs were closer to home. The French concentrated their battleships in the Atlantic, while the Regia Marina focused on dominating the Mediterranean. As for the Germans and the Kriegsmarine, they had just five modern battleships (compared to the Royal Navy's 15) and 65 U-boats (half of which were small vessels intended for use in coastal waters) at the outbreak of war.

Spoiler
"Spoiler, the Original Flight Deck Dope" shows the "tools" of his trade: his mind is on anything but his job, his cap is unbuckled and he wears no life belt while the ship is underway, leaning on the propeller of an SBD. His lack of care wrecks equipment, damages planes and gets him hurt. Posed on board a training escort carrier, circa 1943–45.

The global war on the high seas touched every corner of the world's oceans. From the North Atlantic to the South Pacific, warships of every type would see action. It was also a battle of high technology that saw the introduction of radar, homing torpedoes, sonar buoys, VT fused anti-aircraft shells (a shell with a miniature radar that exploded when close to an aircraft), sonar, magnetic anomaly detectors and the seemingly mystical art of code breaking. It was also a battle of steel over flesh. With the horrors of the First World War still fresh in the minds of the public and Allied politicians, the idea of large land armies slugging it out on the battlefield was replaced by the ascendancy of air and sea power.

From the beginning, Britain, Germany, Japan and the United States devoted between 65 percent and 80 percent of their economic output to constructing warships and aircraft.

America's entry into the war on December 7, 1941, saw armaments production focused on shipbuilding. By April-May 1942, the U.S. Navy's allocation of steel surpassed that of the Army's and the Air Force's. Not surprisingly, Germany's allocation of resources for military production prioritized naval vessels and aircraft (the vast majority being U-boats) over Panzer tanks and armoured fighting vehicles. It was a clear indication that Germany had to win the Battle of the Atlantic to achieve victory over the U.S. and Britain.

While steel and aluminum were being allocated for ship production, the procurement of well-trained personnel to crew the new ships began. Thousands of young men and later women volunteered, while others waited for conscription. Not surprisingly, most volunteers and conscripts chose the Navy or Air Force over the Army. Every navy required their recruits to be in good health and intelligence. These new recruits would work on familiar ships like the battleship, cruiser and destroyer. As the war progressed, the ascendancy of the aircraft carrier

Dilbert

Above: These two illustrations are but two of the thousands created by Osborn during the war. Humor was often mixed with a serious message. As the crew of a German U-boat sun themselves, one says, "Don't move it's only Dilbert."

Right: Dilbert's absent-mindedness has once again compromised his mission. With his gunner napping in his turret, the aircraft comments in exasperation, "I'm the only one who works out here! I think I'll quit."

required the training of thousands of specialized naval aviators (fighter, dive bomber, and torpedo bomber pilots, along with radio/gunners, radar men and navigators).

The naval war that was to come was in many ways like the First World War. Submarines, convoy escorts and anti-submarine vessels would demand the most resources, but change was rapidly coming. The expansion of air power, the dominance of the aircraft carrier and the emergence of the U.S. Navy's Fast Carrier Task Force changed the nature of naval warfare. The war also introduced several new types of vessels. The escort carrier, the destroyer escort and landing craft of every shape and size were built in huge numbers. Not only were men trained to crew these ships, but they were also schooled in new naval tactics and ways of fighting, often learned from past battles.

Young men like American Robert Osborn were eager to join the fight against fascism, but Osborn himself was soon disappointed. Turned down by the Royal Canadian Air Force due to a persistent ulcer, Osborn had to wait until the Japanese attack on Pearl Harbor to try again. Two days after the attack, Osborn enlisted in the U.S. Navy, hoping to obtain his flying wings. Unfortunately for him, the Navy recognized his artistic talents. Born in Oshkosh, Wisconsin, on October 26, 1904, Osborn attended the University of Wisconsin and studied fine art at Yale University. To further his painting career, he travelled to Europe and studied art in Rome and Paris. For several years, he travelled back and forth between Europe and the United States. He lived in Europe until he had the unpleasant experience of seeing the rise of fascism and adulation of Adolf Hitler. Osborn was quick to recognize the threat and was determined to do his part.

In February 1942, he was sent to Washington, DC, and ordered to report to Navy Commander A.K. Doyle, who was in the Training Literature Division. During their meeting, Doyle received a phone call from Admiral Ernest King's office and was asked, "Have you got an artist down there

Spoiler dropped so many fuses and bombs around the

Spoiler found out all by himself why you park planes

Spoiler

Spoiler was the ground-bound version of Dilbert. For every naval aviator, numerous ground crew had to be trained to keep an aircraft flying. Their skill and attention to detail were critical for the safety of both pilots and ground crew.

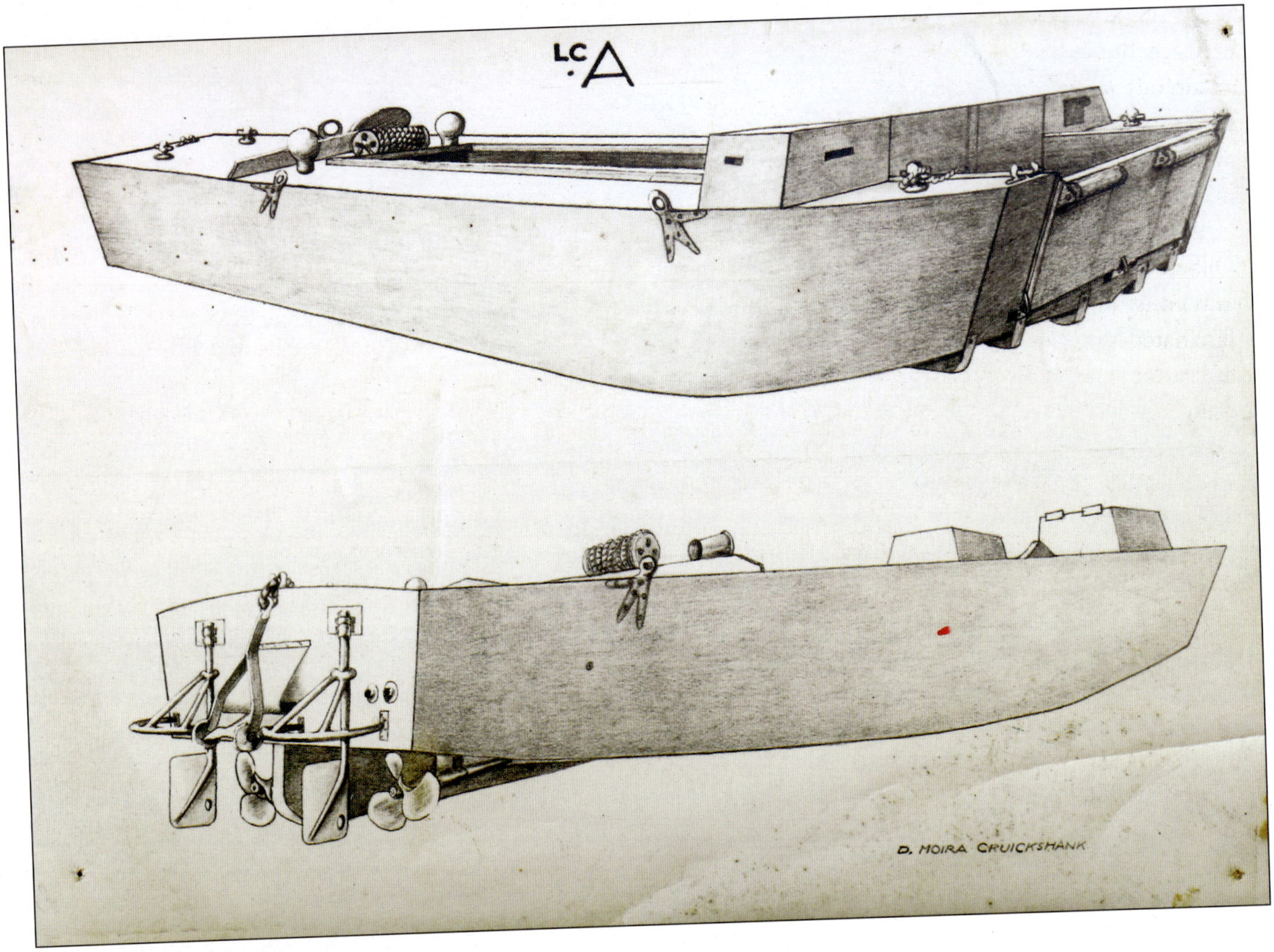

Moira's Final Drawing of a Landing Craft Assault Boat
The LCA was the only serviceable British landing craft at the beginning of World War II, and nearly 2,000 were built. Capable of carrying 35 fully equipped infantry men, the LCA saw action during operations in Norway, Dunkirk, Crete, Africa, Sicily, Italy and Normandy.

who could color the admiral's wall map?" Armed with a box of children's crayons and grease pencils, Osborn soon set about coloring a 5.5 x 9-meter map (18 x 30 feet). He later explained to Doyle that this wasn't what he wanted to do in the Navy. Doyle assured him that his future assignments would be more constructive.

Osborn thought his talents were best suited to the art of camouflage. The samples he brought to the meeting with Doyle soon found their way to the office of Commander Luis de Florez, head of Training Devices during the war. Florez liked what he saw, and Osborn received an unexpected commission. Soon after, he was sent to the old Main Navy/Munitions Building complex, adjacent to the Lincoln Memorial on the Mall. The place was somewhat in shambles, with no chairs for the desks and no sense of organization. There, Osborn met famed photographer Edward Steichen and writers Robert Louis Taylor and Roark Bradford.

As the training of new recruits ramped up, a major problem soon materialized. Young naval airmen were suffering considerable losses due to the unprecedented accident rate. Teaching young men to fly took time and patience. But in the first year of the war, time was at a premium. Mastering an aircraft was a complicated task — ignorance of standard procedures, such as switching fuel tanks or responding to engine problems, caused many fatalities. Maintenance crews were also to blame. Careless, repeated mistakes often led to unsafe aircraft and dangerous working environments.

Working together, Doyle and Osborn came up with two characters, Dilbert the pilot and Spoiler the mechanic. Both were dumb, but a cheerful and constant menace to those around them. Osborn, who had been fascinated by aircraft since he was 12, was familiar with flight operations, and after four or five hours of work and seven or eight preliminary drawings, Dilbert was born. To gain firsthand experience and get a close

Two-view Drawing of a Landing Craft Mechanized (LCM)
LCMs were used extensively in World War II. Designed originally to transport a light tank, the LCM was later used to ferry vehicles and supplies. Crew consisted of six men and it was armed with two Lewis machine guns.

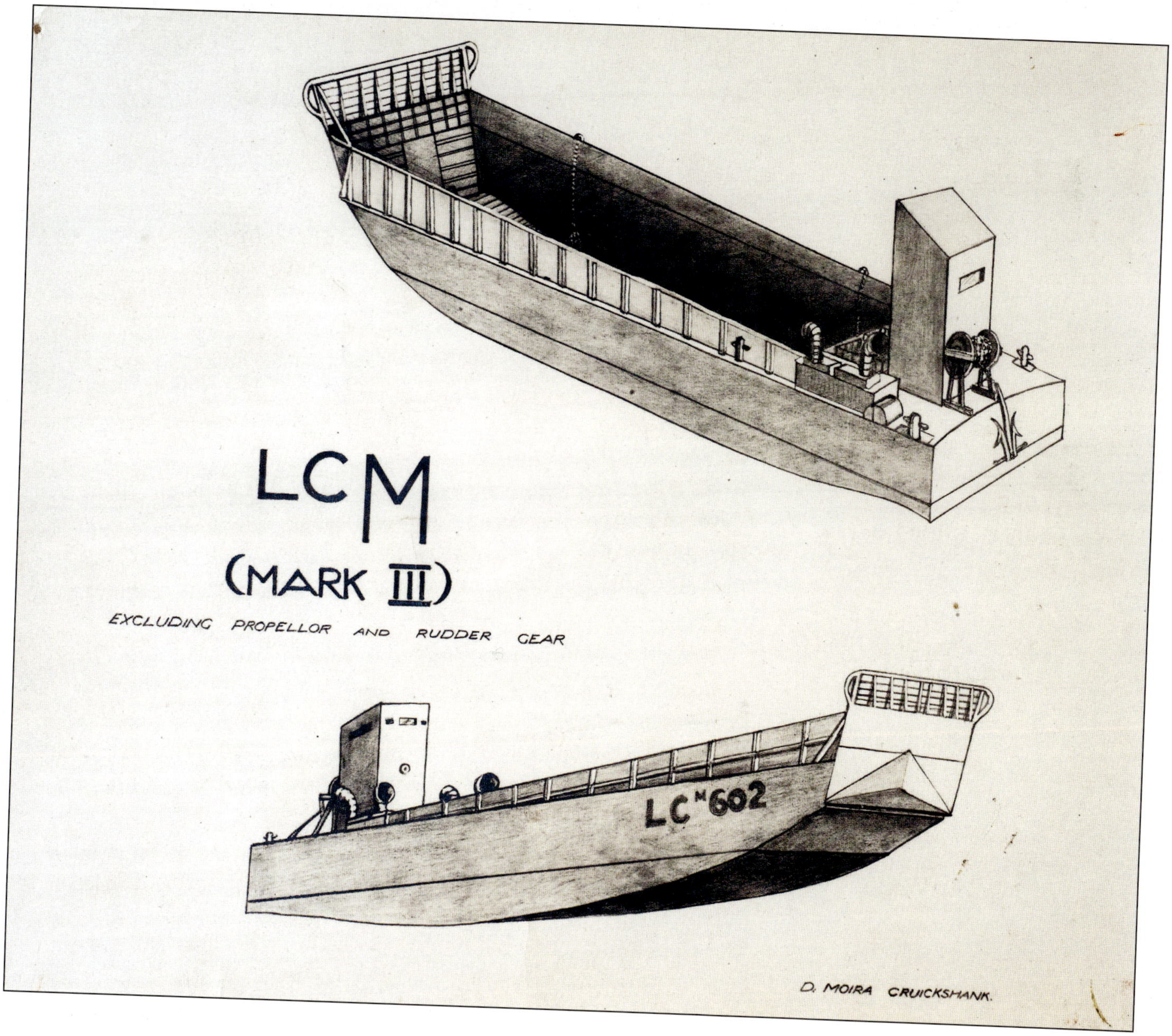

look at pilot and mechanic training, Osborn headed to the Naval Air Station in Atlanta. There, he spoke with everyone he could and took elaborate notes. He spoke to student pilots, instructors, crew chiefs and maintenance personnel. Osborn's job was to transpose their problems into helpful, quickly understood drawings with Dilbert and Spoiler as the main characters. Hopefully, these gently encouraging illustrations would reduce the accident and death rate. Osborn would go on to produce 2,000 Dilbert and Spoiler posters.

Osborn also put himself in harm's way. In the Pacific, he joined the new carrier USS *Essex* and was there for the "Marianas Turkey Shoot" on June 19–20, 1944. Over three days, Osborn, with little chance to sleep, had a close look at carrier combat operations and came away with a deep and lasting impression of the men who risked their lives there.

For Osborn, the work was exhausting. Translating a safety message into a drawing with dialogue took many hours. Osborn knew that even with the thousands of safety posters, young pilots, mechanics and seamen would still make the most basic of mistakes, stating, "We won't eliminate the wheels-up landings, but we can certainly decrease their number." He also felt that if he could save one crewman from making a thoughtless error, it was "certainly worth it."

From time to time, Osborn would hear from pilots firsthand about how Dilbert or Spoiler bailed them out. One pilot told him, after being shot down a half-mile off a Japanese-held island, "Enemy soldiers were shooting at me, and I was about to inflate my life raft when I vividly recalled a poster of Dilbert caught in a similar situation. The lesson on the poster was: Don't inflate the raft and make a bigger target of yourself. I didn't, and I was eventually rescued."

After the war, Osborn continued his work as an artist and exceptional satirist. His work appeared in *Life, Look, Fortune, The New Republic, Harper's, Horizon, The New York Times, Esquire* and many other top magazines.

Not all who volunteered for naval service were men. At the outbreak of war, the Royal Navy reformed the Women's Royal Navy Service (WRNS) branch. The WRNS was an all-volunteer service, and for Moira Cruickshank, it provided an avenue of work she could only have dreamed of. At just 17, Moira entered a new world, one where the restrictions of civilian life were cast aside. "It was a great life, freedom for me because I'd been released from a girl's school, which was very strict and was able to do things that I was unable to do." Unlike Robert Osborn, Cruickshanks's artistic talents were discovered by happenstance. As Moira recalled, "Someone saw me drawing them (landing craft) and I got the job." Moving forward, Moira was assigned to draw and sketch the various landing craft and their inner workings. Her new title was "Wren Artist." Not only did she spend her time drawing these craft, but she was trained to pilot them and recalled them as "pretty nifty boats." Using old chart paper, Moira would spend close to two days to complete a drawing, and it wasn't always easy: "Sometimes it was difficult because there would be people in them or being used for training. I was very often marooned out in the estuary somewhere, drawing another landing craft, it was dreadful when they forgot me, as happened."

Like many young volunteers, Moira found a purpose in her work, valuing the part she played in the larger, collaborative endeavor. After the war, Moira attended art school in London, but she found peacetime drawing a challenge: "I found it very difficult to occupy the right niche."

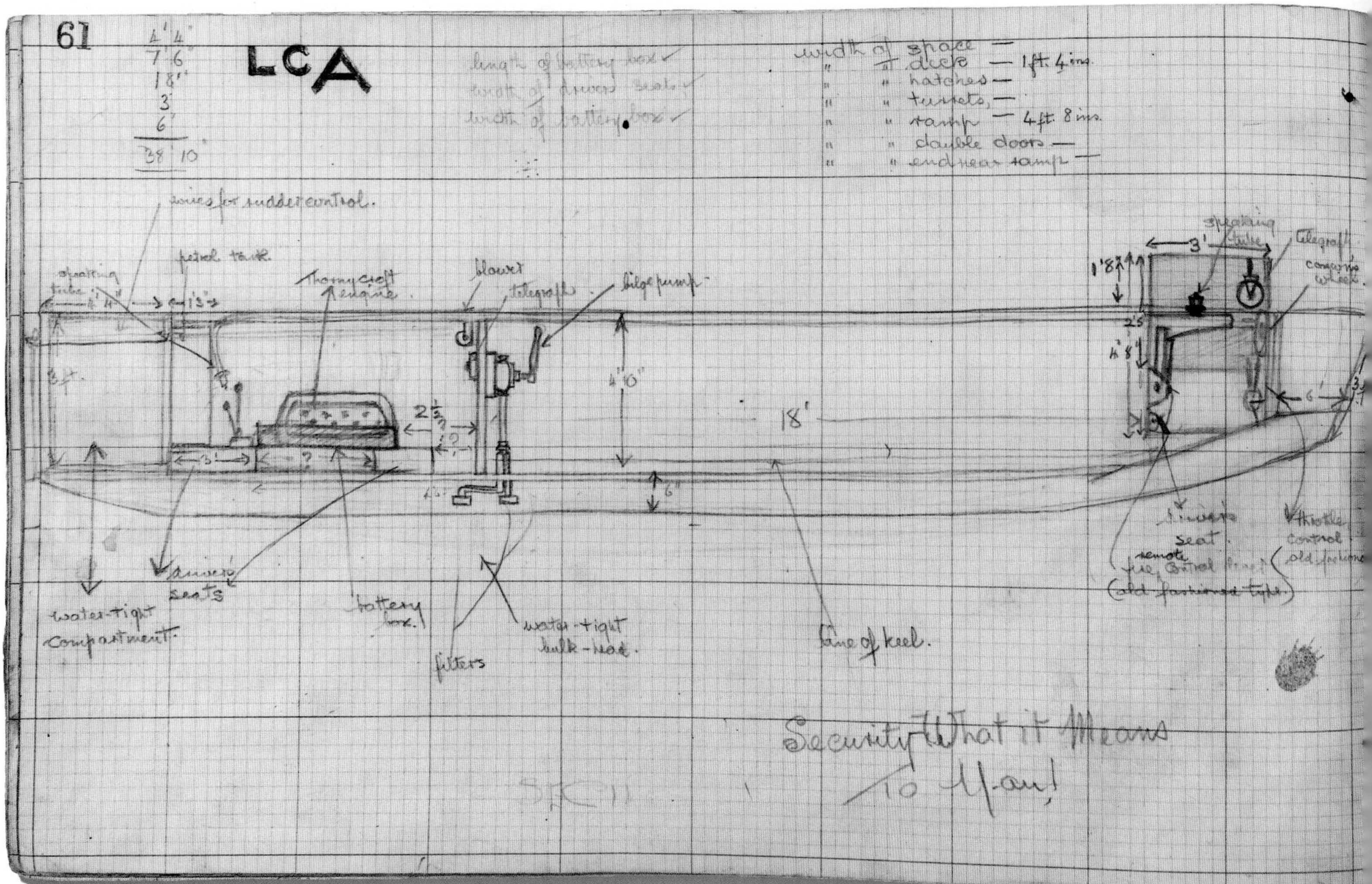

Moira's Preliminary Drawing of the Inner Workings of the LCA
This drawing could have been for her own use while training to drive these craft. LCAs had no armament and were commanded by a rating rather than an officer. Interesting to note what Moira might have been thinking when she wrote, "Security. What it means to you!"

CHAPTER 2

All Hands on Deck

The epic sea battles of World War II transformed naval warfare. The emergence of the aircraft carrier and new submarine tactics proved to be the primary instruments of offensive operations. Carrier airpower would dominate and replace the battleship as the capital ship of the sea. The Japanese doctrine of concentrating their carriers into a single unit (the *Kido Butai)* meant they could launch massive air strikes and supply the fleet with good fighter defence. The surprise attack on Pearl Harbor, mounted by six carriers, was a prime example of the Kido Butai at work. By mid-1943, the U.S. Navy had learned some hard lessons and created the Fast Carrier Task Force based on the Japanese Kido Butai. By 1945, the Fast Carrier Task Force comprised 14 fleet carriers and nine light carriers and was divided into individual task groups capable of independent offensive operations. Each task group was made up of three to four heavy and light carriers and was escorted by three battleships, five cruisers and 12 destroyers.

In the Atlantic, the rise of Germany's U-boat 'wolf packs' pressured Allied naval assets to the limit. In response, the Allies were forced to increase the number of escort ships, everything from corvettes to destroyer escorts, destroyers and escort carriers. Escort and hunter-killer groups were formed, and new technologies were introduced. It was a five-year battle that covered both the North and South Atlantic, the Mediterranean, the Caribbean and the Indian Ocean. In the Pacific, the U.S. Navy's often-overlooked submarine campaign was far more successful than the Kriegsmarine's campaign in

Concentration of Japanese Air Strength
At the beginning of the Pacific War, the IJNAF was the best trained and equipped navy. Many pilots had combat experience, and in the first months of the war, Allied aircrew paid a heavy price. By late 1943, that advantage was in rapid decline, forcing the Japanese to revert to suicidal kamikaze attacks.

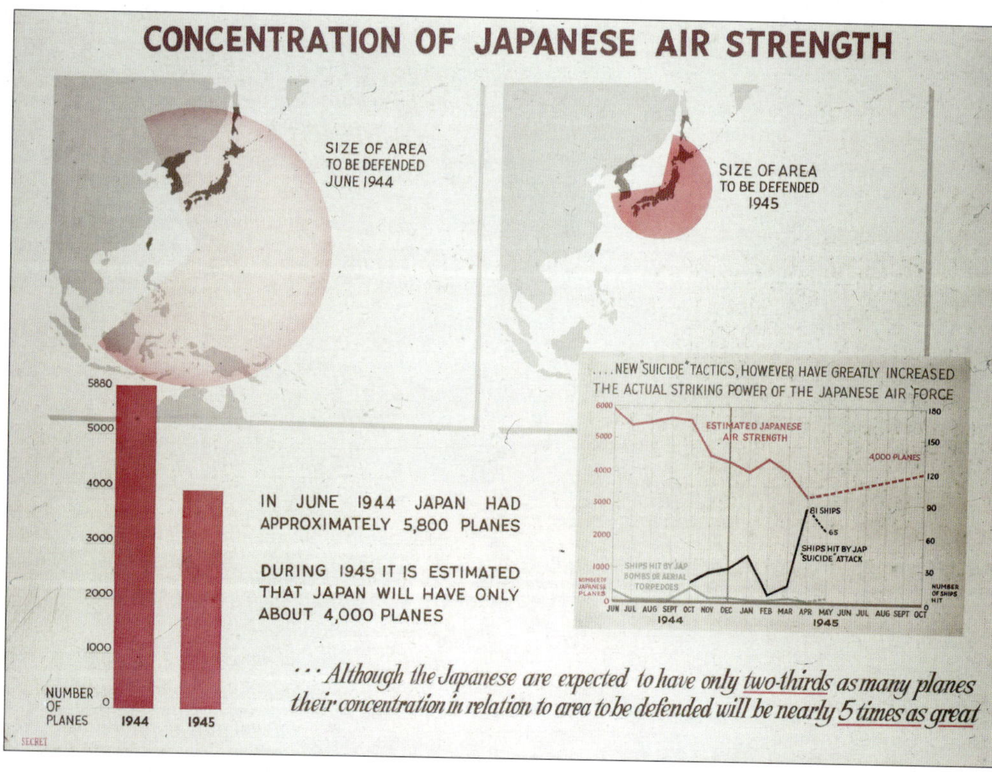

the Atlantic. By 1944, the unrestricted submarine warfare was so complete that the flow of resources from Southern Asia to Japan had virtually ceased, one of the major reasons for Japan's ultimate surrender.

It was total war on, above and below the high seas. And a war that quickly developed into a technological arms race.

It was also a war of industry and education. While more and more ships left the slipways, they were nothing without a crew, and the navy demanded the best and brightest. As Allied enlistment and conscription increased, the demand for training centers, visual aids, manuals and experienced instructors, and the need for new courses, caused a great deal of strain and, in some cases, wasteful duplication. The Bureau of Naval Personnel, or BUPERS, was at the center of the American training effort. Compared to the Royal Navy's First Sea Lord's office at the Admiralty, BUPERS had direct control of naval training centers. Prior to the Japanese attack on Pearl Harbor and America's entry into the war, BUPERS had the advantage of attracting some of the most promising officers. Chester W. Nimitz, future commander-in-chief in the Pacific, was chief of its predecessor, the Bureau of Navigation, right up until one week after Pearl Harbor.

The *Kido Butai* During the Indian Ocean Operation of April 1942

This photo clearly shows the power of this formation. *Akagi* is leading the column that includes, in order, *Soryu*, *Hiryu*, all four *Kongo*-class battleships, and the two *Shokaku*-class carriers. By April, the IJN carrier force had reached the zenith of its success. From December 7 to April 9, Japanese naval air power, using land-based torpedo bombers, sank five U.S. battleships, one British battleship and one battlecruiser, the British carrier *Hermes,* along with two heavy cruisers and two destroyers.

The Royal Navy had some clear advantages of its own when it came to training and recruitment. Unlike the army, the Royal Navy was able to attract and keep a good voluntary element. There were always enough men and women to choose from. When it came to training, the Royal Navy faced several difficulties compared to the U.S. Navy. Working in a war zone, the Royal Navy struggled with the unexpected speed of expansion, a lack of instructors and the over-stretching of industrial assets and personnel, plus the threat of invasion and the constant threat of aerial and U-boat attack.

When the U.S. Navy began hostilities, it numbered just 203,000 men. By 1945, the number had ballooned to an astonishing 3,408,000 men and women. This number includes Coast Guard personnel, naval aviators and Marines. By the end of the war, the Royal Navy had just over a million people in service, with 923,000 men and 86,000 women.

As both Allied navies expanded, so did their roles. To achieve victory, command of the seas was essential. The ascendancy of the aircraft carrier and anti-submarine forces, combined with the mastery of amphibious operations was the cornerstone of victory.

In sharp contrast to the Royal and U.S. Navies, Germany's Kriegsmarine was forced to fight a sea war for which it was woefully unprepared. Germany's surface fleet was too small to pose any real threat to the Royal Navy, and to have any hope of success, they had to repeat their World War

Four-barrel Two-Pounder Pom-Pom

The name 'pom-pom' came about because of the sound it made when firing. This drawing shows the quadruple two-pounder (40 mm) on a Mk VI mounting. The 'pom-pom' was found on almost every RN ship in single, double, quadruple and octuple mountings.

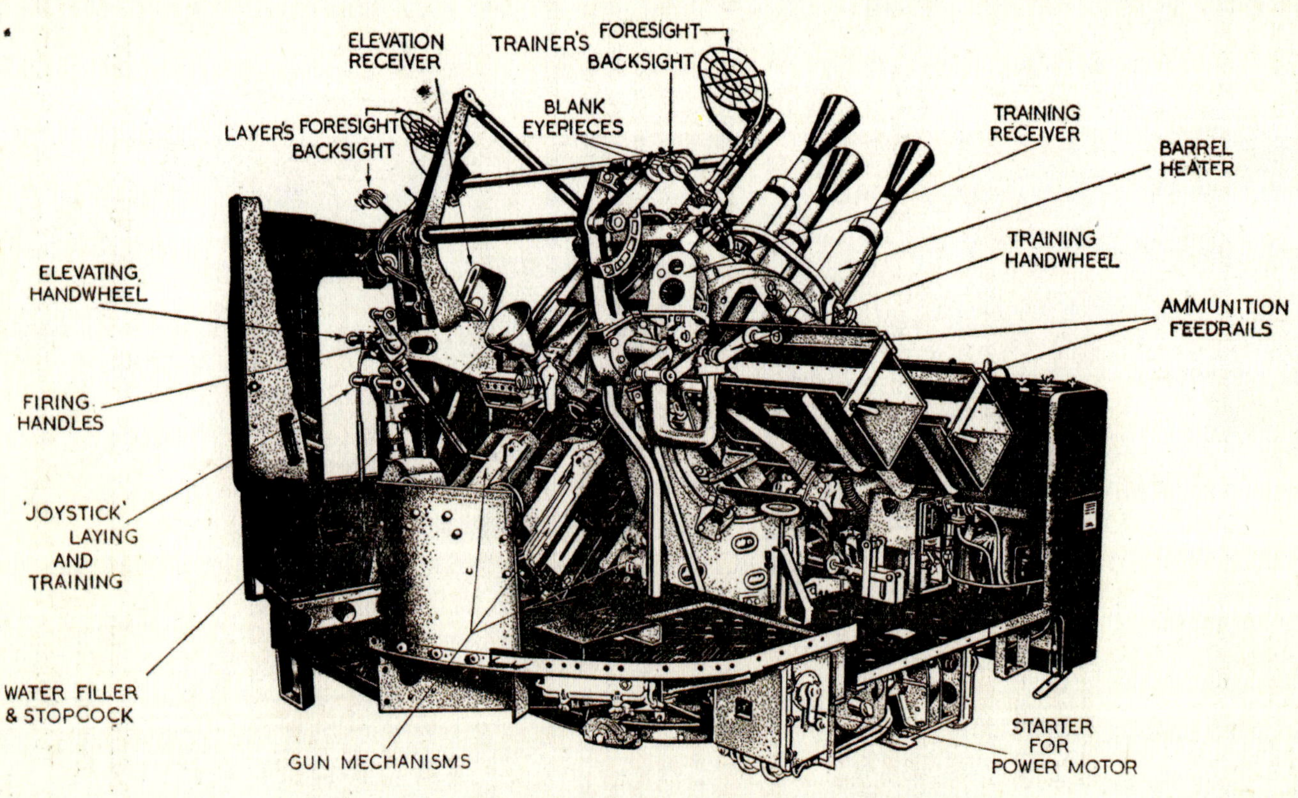

Diagram 34.—2-Pdr. POM-POM MARK VII MOUNTING.

I anti-commerce. Grossadmiral Raeder knew his navy was too small and underequipped: "As far as the Navy is concerned, obviously it is in no way adequately equipped for the great struggle with Great Britain by autumn 1939. It is true that in the short period since 1935, the date of the fleet treaty, it has built up a well-trained, suitably organized submarine arm, of which at the moment about 26 boats are capable of operations in the Atlantic; the submarine arm is still much too weak, however, to have any decisive effect on the war."

This would change. By November 1941, the Kriegsmarine had 220 U-boats in operational service. The increase in production also meant the need for well-trained crews. One of the greatest assets the Kriegsmarine possessed was its manpower. Kriegsmarine training was first-class and rigorous and produced seamen of the highest quality. For those in the U-boat arm, they

AA Officer Scanning the Horizon
This dramatic image depicts a square-jawed USN officer scanning the horizon as muscular AA crewmen man their guns.

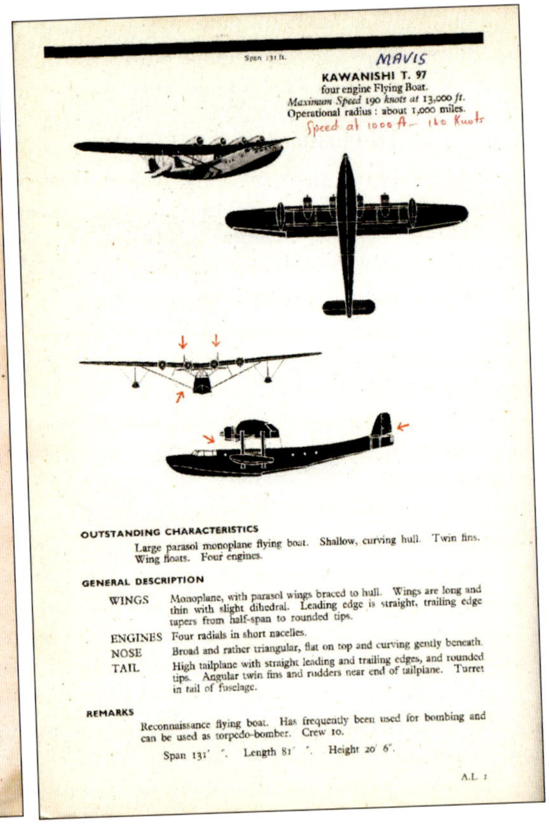
Span 131 ft.

MAVIS

KAWANISHI T. 97
four engine Flying Boat.
Maximum Speed 190 *knots at* 13,000 *ft.*
Operational radius : about 1,000 miles.
Speed at 1000 ft – 160 Knots

OUTSTANDING CHARACTERISTICS

Large parasol monoplane flying boat. Shallow, curving hull. Twin fins. Wing floats. Four engines.

GENERAL DESCRIPTION

WINGS Monoplane, with parasol wings braced to hull. Wings are long and thin with slight dihedral. Leading edge is straight, trailing edge tapers from half-span to rounded tips.

ENGINES Four radials in short nacelles.

NOSE Broad and rather triangular, flat on top and curving gently beneath.

TAIL High tailplane with straight leading and trailing edges, and rounded tips. Angular twin fins and rudders near end of tailplane. Turret in tail of fuselage.

REMARKS

Reconnaissance flying boat. Has frequently been used for bombing and can be used as torpedo-bomber. Crew 10.

Span 131′ ″. Length 81′ ″. Height 20′ 6″.

A.L. 1

Naval Manual of Aircraft Recognition

These three illustrations come from the "British Manual of Aircraft Recognition." New gunner recruits were drilled constantly in the art of aircraft recognition. It was an extremely difficult task, considering many Allied aircraft resembled those of Germany, Italy and Japan. Spotting an aircraft at a distance, in bad weather or in the sun's glare was a major challenge for most AA gunners.

themselves to be the 'Elite within the Elite of the Kriegsmarine.'

As the war progressed, it was clear that with the strike capability of the aircraft carrier, shore-based aircraft and submarines would come to dominate the sea war. This resulted in the rapid expansion and need for capable naval aviators, followed by more anti-aircraft (AA) gunners and well-trained submariners.

This next section will look at the training required for each of these specialized roles.

Royal Navy AA Gunner

"The mode of operation is similar say, to throwing a boot at a cat running along the top of a wall. To allow for movement of the target during the time of the flight of the bullet, the gun has to be pointed ahead of the target at some position along its future path."
— *Gunnery Pocket Book*, 1945

The naval battles and the projection of naval power during the Second World War centered on the submarine (Battle of the Atlantic) and the fleet aircraft carrier (five major carrier battles were fought in the Pacific between 1942–44). Naval aircraft played a dominant role in the destruction of both surface ships and submarines. Ships without air cover or adequate anti-aircraft (AA) defences were often sunk or heavily damaged. In December 1941, just three days after the Japanese attack on Pearl Harbor, the Royal Navy suffered a humiliating defeat with the destruction of the battleship HMS *Prince of Wales* and the battlecruiser HMS *Repulse*. With no air cover from fighters and inadequate anti-aircraft defences, both ships were overpowered by a force of eighty land-based Imperial Japanese Navy Mitsubishi G3M "Nells" and G4M "Bettys." Armed with torpedoes and bombs, the attack lasted just over an hour, with four torpedoes striking the *Prince of Wales* and five hitting the *Repulse*. The post-action statement by the gunnery officer of the HMS *Prince of Wales* stated, "The tracer fire from the Bofors guns and Oerlikons was definitely seen to make some attacking aircraft jink. The pom-poms, although they were seen to hit the enemy, did not frighten him during his approach due to a lack of tracer." It was clear that more AA guns on every ship were needed, and well-trained gunners were needed to operate them.

Prior to the outbreak of war, the Royal Navy's Anti-Aircraft Gunnery Committee concluded that air attacks against ships by dive bombers were an unlikely threat. Many believed that the best defence against aerial-launched torpedo or dive-bombing attacks was maneuvers at sea, and the number of anti-aircraft guns aboard the large surface vessels was more than adequate. Not everyone agreed. In 1932, Rear Admiral, Aircraft Carriers, Sir Reginald Henderson warned that "the primary defence of the fleet against air attack (by gunfire) is not justified by data or experience. No realistic firing against aircraft has taken place since the last war and, in my opinion, the value of our own High Angle Control System Mk I is rated too high. In common with others, we are apt to over-rate the capabilities of our own weapons in practice."

As the sea war unfolded, new technology and the training of anti-aircraft gunners became a top priority for both the Royal and U.S. Navies. The Royal Navy's gunnery school was HMS *Excellent*, located on Whale Island on the eastern side of Portsmouth Harbour. By the outbreak of World War II and under the command of Captain Arthur F.E. Palliser, HMS *Excellent* was soon churning out well-trained AA gunners. The approach to training AA gunners was 'user'-based, and *Excellent's* mission

How to Use Your Gun Sight
During 1945, at the height of the Japanese kamikaze attacks, the 20 mm guns of the U.S. fleet would expend 1,308,370 rounds and shoot down 297.5 aircraft for a 'rounds per bird' of 4,398.

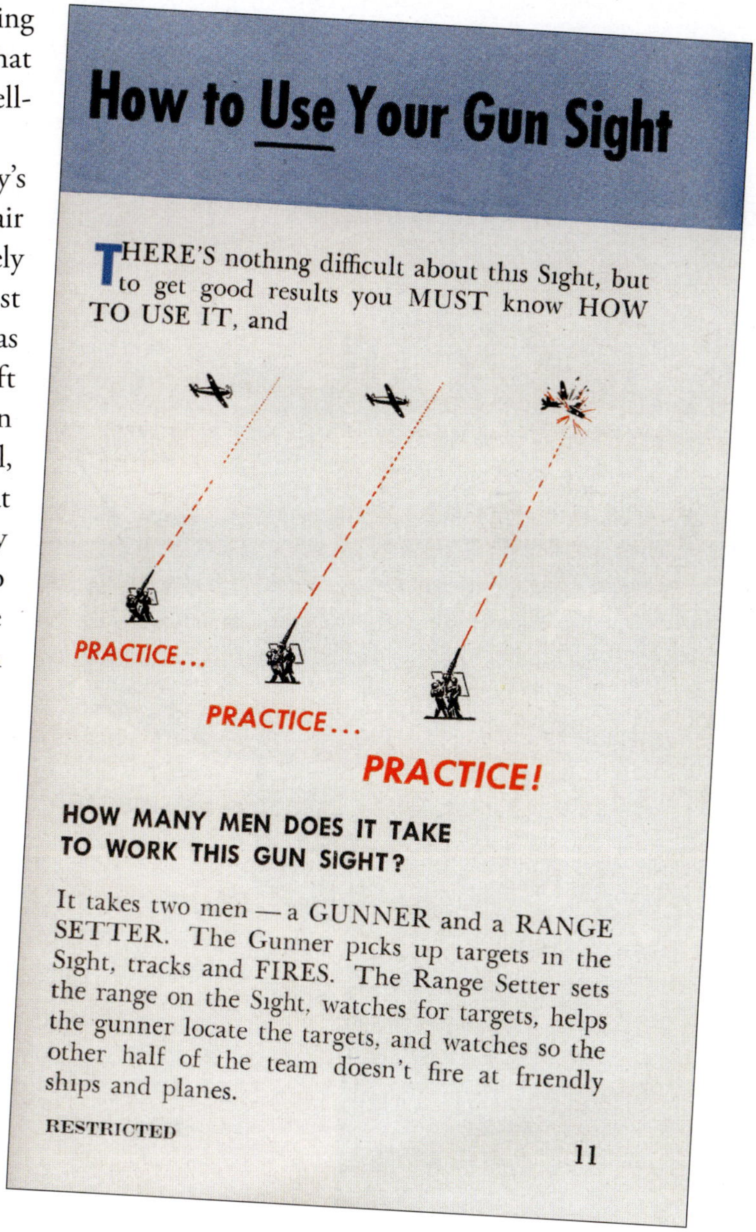
How to Use Your Gun Sight

THERE'S nothing difficult about this Sight, but to get good results you MUST know HOW TO USE IT, and

PRACTICE... PRACTICE... PRACTICE!

HOW MANY MEN DOES IT TAKE TO WORK THIS GUN SIGHT?

It takes two men — a GUNNER and a RANGE SETTER. The Gunner picks up targets in the Sight, tracks and FIRES. The Range Setter sets the range on the Sight, watches for targets, helps the gunner locate the targets, and watches so the other half of the team doesn't fire at friendly ships and planes.

RESTRICTED

11

Gunners Training
Anti-Aircraft Training Center Waianae, Oahu, Hawaii. Sailors on the AA gunnery range prepare for another round of training. Guns present are: 20-mm, .30 cal., and 40-mm single mount guns. Note the ammunition handling area behind the guns.

statement was clear: "To ensure that the development of naval gunnery proceeds on lines dictated by sea experience rather than office expediency."

For new trainees, the training course lasted eight weeks and was extremely disciplined and intense. They quickly learned that their gunnery skills were vital for the safety of a warship, and practice was the key to success. The Admiralty's *Gunnery Pocket Book* was clear and to the point:

> "You must practise again, again and again. In the same way as a professional boxer goes through an intensive course in training before fighting his adversary, so it is necessary for you, the gunnery men of the ship, to get yourselves into training for fighting the enemy. The only difference between you and the professional footballer, cricketer, or boxer, is that whereas they are going to enter a contest for which they get prize money, you are going into fight an enemy who, if you are not fully efficient, well trained, and in practice, will kill you.

Remember this: when you are in the day's gunnery order to close up at your gun, your director, or your telephone, be there punctually. You may meet the enemy at any time and in any weather. You may not have had long to practice; see that you do not curtail that time by being adrift. Your own life and the lives of your shipmate may depend on you."

The anti-aircraft guns of *Excellent* comprised .303-inch machine guns, 20 mm Oerlikon, quadruple and octuple two-pounder pom-poms and 40 mm Bofors. These guns were set up in brick-lined pits along the shore. Gunners' accuracy would be assessed by shooting at aircraft-towed sleeve targets.

One key area of focus for all new gunners was aircraft recognition. Not only did gunners and lookouts have to quickly identify an incoming aircraft, but also estimate its speed, range, height and when to begin firing.

Former officer trainee John Carter recalled one exciting night:

"One evening the air raid sirens sounded and we all took up predetermined positions at the various guns. Shortly after, a lone German aeroplane flew along the coast right in front of the range; we let fly with everything, but the aeroplane passed immediately in front of us apparently unscathed. Clearly more practice was needed! At the end of the course, I qualified as an AA3, meaning I was able to handle smaller calibre anti-aircraft guns and entitled to wear the appropriate badge on my sleeve. I also received an additional three pence per day to add to my two shillings per day!"

N3N
Nicknamed the "Yellow Peril," the Naval Aircraft Factory N3N served as the primary training facility for the U.S. Navy and U.S. Marine Corps from 1936. It shared this role with the more common Stearman NS/N2S.

Slow Flying

Before their final assignment to a carrier-based squadron, new navy pilots received further instruction at the Advanced Carrier Training Group (ACTG). Here, pilots had to complete their carrier qualification by performing eight carrier landings flying the SNJ Texan.

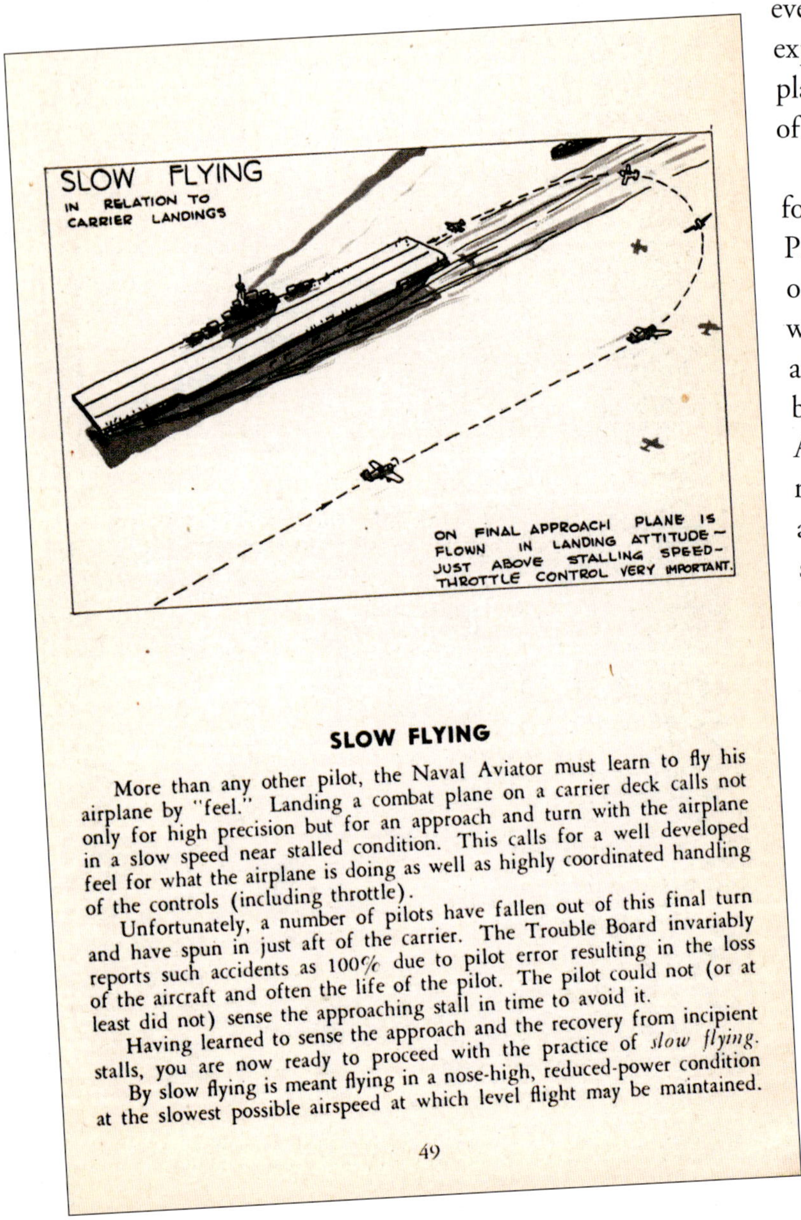

SLOW FLYING

More than any other pilot, the Naval Aviator must learn to fly his airplane by "feel." Landing a combat plane on a carrier deck calls not only for high precision but for an approach and turn with the airplane in a slow speed near stalled condition. This calls for a well developed feel for what the airplane is doing as well as highly coordinated handling of the controls (including throttle).

Unfortunately, a number of pilots have fallen out of this final turn and have spun in just aft of the carrier. The Trouble Board invariably reports such accidents as 100% due to pilot error resulting in the loss of the aircraft and often the life of the pilot. The pilot could not (or at least did not) sense the approaching stall in time to avoid it.

Having learned to sense the approach and the recovery from incipient stalls, you are now ready to proceed with the practice of *slow flying.*

By slow flying is meant flying in a nose-high, reduced-power condition at the slowest possible airspeed at which level flight may be maintained.

49

U.S. Navy AA Gunner

"There was a lot of sky out there too, so the question was, How do you get hits? Early on, gunners would aim tracers like a stream of water or use metal sights with concentric rings to achieve some sort of lead, or what the British called 'aim off.' But these efforts were unsatisfactory."

— **Robert R. Wallace, automatic weapons officer, U.S. Navy**

In most of the major naval engagements during the war, U.S. Navy and Imperial Japanese enemy fleets never saw each other. The largest battles were fought with aircraft carriers and their attack aircraft. For every attack by a Japanese ship, U.S. Navy crews experienced hundreds of air attacks by Japanese planes, culminating in the mass kamikaze attacks of 1944–45.

Unlike the British, the Americans put more focus on fleet and ship anti-aircraft protection. Prior to the outbreak of hostilities, the Bureau of Ordnance (BUORD) and the General Board worked on the development of both heavy anti-aircraft guns and automatic weapons. One of the biggest proponents of fleet AA defence was Rear Admiral J. King. As a naval aviator, King quickly realized how unprepared the U.S. Navy was for air attack, commenting that it was "the most serious weakness in the readiness of the navy for war." To rectify the situation, King personally reviewed each type of navy ship and dictated what installations would be removed to make room for more guns. It was "ruthless surgery" but would pay huge dividends in the months and years ahead.

When Admiral King became Commander in Chief, United States Fleet (COMINCH) a few days before Pearl Harbor, fleet AA defences remained one of his top priorities.

One week after the Japanese air attack on Pearl Harbor, the prototype for the first Anti-aircraft Training Center (AATC) was established at Dam Neck, Virginia. During the war, 20 AATCs were established. In addition

to the stateside locations, AATCs were established in Guantánamo, Bermuda, Guam and Guadalcanal. All followed the basic syllabus and the same plan: a firing line mounting all calibers of AA guns, facing the open sea to offer an unobstructed field of fire for towed sleeve targets. The need for AA gunners during the war was constant. Attack from the air was the greatest threat, and the policy of installing as many guns as space, weight and personnel limitations allowed on both fighting and merchant ships was followed. American AA gunners on merchant ships alone accounted for an estimated 200 German and Japanese aircraft during the war.

As more AA gunners entered the fleet, they were well-equipped and ready for the fight. During the carrier battles of 1942, the impact of U.S. Navy shipborne defences was evident. At the Battle of Santa Cruz in October 1942, AA gunners from carriers and their escorts decimated Japanese air strikes. A staff officer aboard the Japanese carrier *Junyo* recalled: "The planes lurched and staggered onto the deck, every single fighter and bomber bullet holed. Some planes were literally flying sieves. As the pilots climbed wearily from their cramped cockpits they told of unbelievable opposition, of skies choked with anti-aircraft shell burst and tracers."

NH 71374

German Type IX U-boat based in Norway. After the occupation of Norway, the Kriegsmarine quickly established several U-boat bases from which to operate in the North Atlantic and Arctic oceans.

In 1944, the Japanese introduced a new and terrifying weapon, one the young AA gunners had not been trained for. In October 1944, the first Japanese suicidal kamikaze attack was mounted. The idea of a pilot deliberately crashing his aircraft into a ship was foreign to the Western mentality and had a dramatic impact on the typical American sailor. The threat of a kamikaze attack exacted both a physical and psychological toll. The AA gunners and lookouts required a new level of awareness. Ships in the combat zone were on constant alert, with gun crews at battle stations or close to their guns. The threat seemed random, and too often, the first indication of an attack was the visual report of a diving Japanese aircraft.

As the kamikaze threat increased, reaching its peak during the Okinawa campaign, the morale of the men aboard ships never wavered. The U.S. Navy's training, logistical support, equipment and tactics proved capable of dealing with the largest threat it faced during the war.

Naval Aviator

"Carriers are like two blindfolded men armed with daggers in a ring — there is apt to be sudden destruction to one or both."

— Rear Admiral Henry V. Butler, Commander-in-Chief, Aircraft Squadrons, Battle Force, U.S. Navy

The role of the naval aviator during World War II was one of the most important in naval history. The ability to find and destroy an enemy fleet well over the horizon required flying skills that separated them from their landlocked Air Force brothers. In many ways, naval aircrew were considered elite airmen. Not only did the naval aviator have to master his aircraft and learn how to use it effectively in combat, but he also had to land and take off from a small floating flight deck in the middle of the ocean.

At the outbreak of war in 1939, both the U.S. Navy and the Imperial Japanese Navy Air Force (IJNAF) were numerically and technically superior to the Royal Navy's Fleet Air Arm (FAA). U.S. and Japanese aircraft carriers were also bigger. The USS *Saratoga* could carry up to 80 aircraft with a mix of fighters, dive bombers and torpedo bombers. In contrast, Britain's largest carrier, HMS *Ark Royal,* carried between 50 and 60 aircraft, the majority being the fabric-covered 'Fairey Swordfish' torpedo bomber.

In terms of training, the U.S., British and Japanese navies followed similar training syllabuses with ground school, elementary flight training, primary flight training, intermediate flight training and finally operational training. In the final phase, pilots had to complete eight successful carrier takeoffs and landings.

In the U.S. Navy, Operational training consisted of three phases: mastery of the service type aircraft they would fly in combat; intensive instruction in combat skills, including gunnery, dive bombing, torpedo bombing, navigation, night flying and combat tactics; and a complete overview of carrier deck operations and landings.

Training was rigorous, and many young aspiring pilots washed out, unable to master the art of carrier landings. After completing Operational training, a young U.S. Navy pilot would have 350 flying hours. Once assigned to a carrier air group (CAG) squadron, the trainee would receive more intensive training and enter combat with close to 400 flying hours.

NH 71411
Loading a torpedo on board a German Type VIIC U-boat at Narkil, Norway, during World War II.

Once assigned to a CAG, training continued. As the carrier moved closer to the war zone, the pace of training for all hands increased. Full-scale air strikers were planned and launched, gun crews were given ceaseless drill, and target practice, aircraft spotting and damage control drills were conducted by all hands.

Amazingly, in 1940, a carrier like the USS *Enterprise* had a complement of close to 2,400 men. Of that 2,400, just 100 were pilots. They represented the ship's offensive strike capability and were the reason for the ship's existence.

One of the key differences between U.S./Royal Navy and Japanese training was the use of combat veterans as instructors. Unlike their Japanese counterparts, Allied naval aviators served tours of duty and were sent home after a set time. The Japanese did not have that luxury. While some did serve as instructors, the vast majority remained on the front lines until they were either killed, wounded, or succumbed to exhaustion or mental collapse.

The IJNAF entered the war with around 3,000 well-trained pilots and was considered the most skilled and best equipped. Remarkably, once the war started, the IJNAF did little to expand pilot and aircrew training. The IJNAF's training system could not keep pace with the high attrition rate during the carrier battles of 1942.

"When we began in August 1942, most of our pilots were very well trained, with more than 500 hours flying time. But by January 1, 1943, only about 15 per cent were left, and we were receiving pilots fresh from school. They only had about 100 flying hours in combat aircraft, maybe 200 overall," said IJN Fleet staff officer Toshikazu Ohmae.

By 1944, new U.S. Navy and FAA pilots began combat operations with 500 or more flying hours, while their IJNAF counterparts entered squadron service with 300 flying hours or less.

Between 1940 and 1945, the U.S. Navy alone trained 65,000 naval and marine aviators and significantly contributed to the final victory over the Axis forces in the Atlantic and Pacific.

Kriegsmarine U-Boat Crew Training

"First of all, I put the U-boat menace. This, I'm sure, is our worst danger."

— Churchill, in a personal letter written to President Roosevelt, October 1942

At the outbreak of war, the Kriegsmarine U-boat arm was poorly equipped and capable of limited operations. Its crews, however — all volunteers — were well trained and motivated. It would remain an all-volunteer service until attrition and the demands of the Wehrmacht took their toll. For the most part, the Kriegsmarine's size meant it could be very selective about who it would take.

Those who joined the Kriegsmarine were young, 17 to 23 years of age, and those younger than 21 needed parental permission. Good health and physical fitness were prerequisites, along with a secondary education. Applicants were drawn from all over Germany, and those who possessed merchant fleet experience in mechanics and electricity were preferred.

New recruits went through the same basic training as infantry, after which they were posted to specialized training schools. After a year's service, trained recruits were given the rank of *Matrose* (ordinary seaman). During the U-boat's rapid expansion (1940–42), promising recruits could be offered promotion to *Matt* (petty officer) after basic training and channelled into more specialized training.

Officer training was even more vigorous, arduous and strict. Candidates went through the same three-month basic infantry training, followed by four months of practical training depending on their technical specialty.

With officer training complete, the newly promoted cadet served nine months on a training ship.

Officers earmarked for U-boat service had to complete a 12-week training course that included lectures and seagoing exercises. Once complete, they then went to sea aboard their first U-boat. There they learned basic handling, tactical theory, torpedo aiming and tactics.

As U-boat construction increased and new boats were completed, senior crew members were sent to the shipyard to examine their vessels and see them through construction. Prior to launch, they were joined by the rest of the crew.

After launch and acceptance trials, a three-week shakedown cruise was undertaken. This involved 66 surfaced and 66 submerged practice attacks. Only then were they allowed to fire their first live torpedo.

Of all the naval services, U-boat crews endured the worst the sea had to offer. Their craft were cramped, unsanitary and claustrophobic, with no ventilation and no privacy. It was an act of extreme human endurance, often accompanied by outbreaks of rashes, boils and crab lice.

But through it all, U-boat crews, more than any other vessel, knew that their individual survival depended on the man beside him doing his job. A sinking U-boat meant almost certain death. Survival was the strongest motivator, and as a result, the U-boat force maintained high morale even in the face of devastating losses beginning in 1942 until the end of the war.

Blow-in and Emergency Blow-out Device, Express Control and Underdrive Cells

German U-boat crews had to be well-versed in the various systems that ran the boat. In case of an emergency, each member could quickly assess the damage, report it and take action.

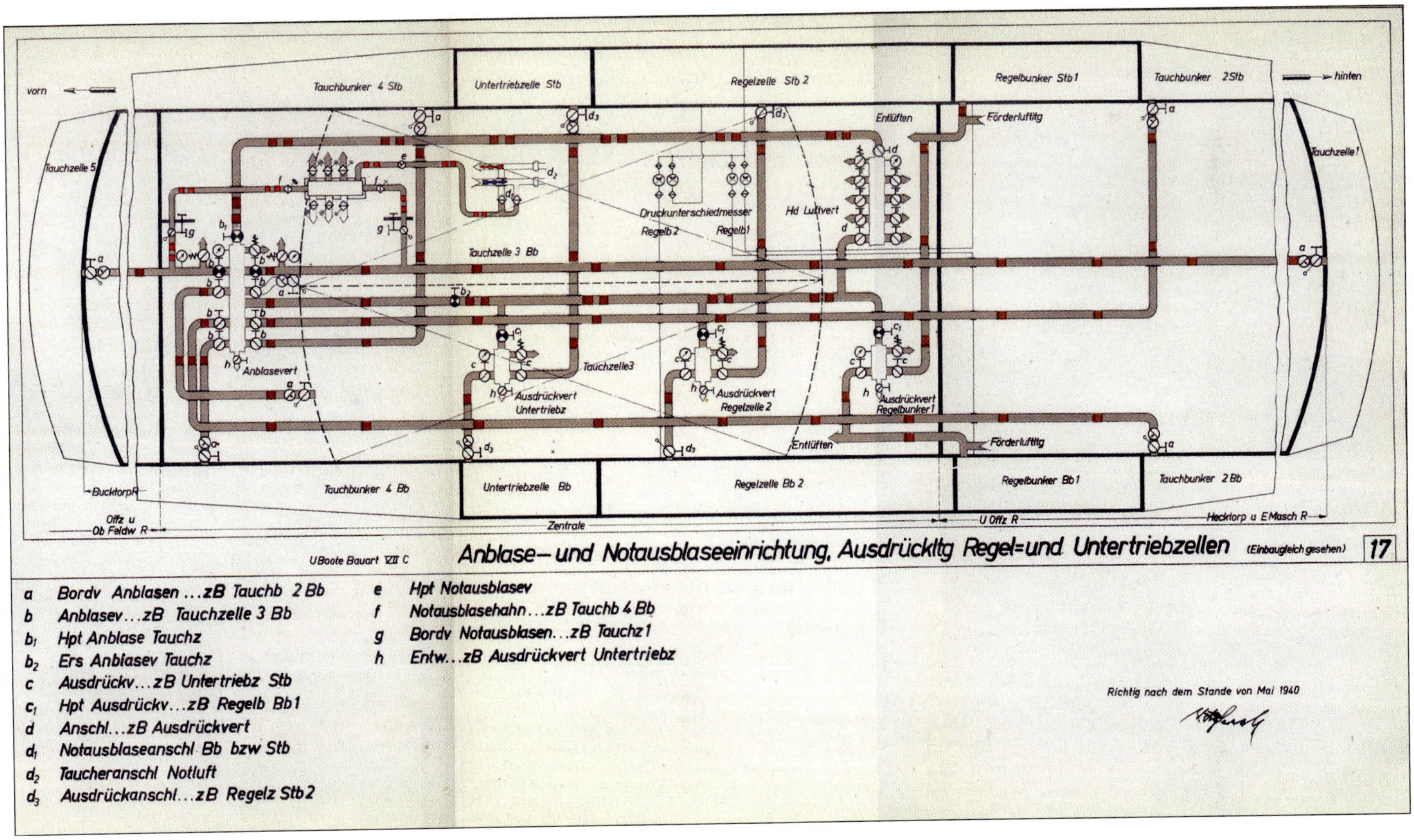

CHAPTER 3

Crossing the T — The Battle Forward

USS *Enterprise*

At Sea

November 28, 1941

BATTLE ORDER NUMBER ONE

1. The *Enterprise* is now operating under war conditions.
2. At any time, day or night, we must be ready for instant action.
3. Hostile submarines may be encountered.
4. The importance of every officer and man being specially alert and vigilant while on watch at his battle station must be fully realized by all hands.

The most pivotal year of the Second World War proved to be 1942. It was the year Axis expansion was checked, and Allied forces gained their first victories. During that year, the Allies focused on control of the sea lanes and then mounted their first successful amphibious operations.

Camouflage Measure 32, Design 11A
This drawing was prepared by the Bureau of Ships for a camouflage scheme intended for USS *Saratoga* (CV-3). Approved by Captain Logan McKee, USN, this plan is dated January 25, 1944.

For the young men about to embark on their first tour, there were many challenges. They were filled with fear and doubt, but their training was thorough, enabling them to conquer their panic when the shooting started. They would work as a team to fight and survive.

Japanese dominance in the first six months of 1942 seemed unstoppable. Kriegsmarine U-boats were gaining the upper hand in the Battle of the Atlantic, but the Allies were gaining strength. By year's end, the Allied strategy was clear. Naval dominance and air superiority over the battlespace were critical for successful amphibious operations needed for final victory.

In the Pacific, the U.S. Navy and IJN fought four carrier battles and several surface engagements. The Japanese lost four fleet carriers, one light carrier, three heavy cruisers and two battleships. The U.S. Navy lost four fleet carriers and eight cruisers.

In the Atlantic, the Royal Navy lost two aircraft carriers, one light carrier and nine cruisers to submarine and air attacks. Merchant ships sunk by U-boats amounted to an incredible 1,322. German U-boat losses amounted to just 87.

Battleship "X"
The USS *South Dakota* was one of the most successful USN battleships of the Pacific War. She was credited with shooting down 32 Japanese aircraft during the Battle of Santa Cruz on October 26, 1942.

The first half of 1942 was a crisis for Allied shipping in the Atlantic. America's entrance into the war presented the Germans with a new target-rich environment, leading to their second and last "Happy Time." It was the single greatest shipping disaster the Allies would suffer, but in the end, it was also the beginning of the greatest British and Canadian victory over the Kriegsmarine U-boat arm.

With America's entry into the war, Admiral Karl Dönitz immediately sent five Type XII U-boats to the east coast of North America. Ships travelling from the Caribbean did not sail in convoy. U.S. Admiral Ernest King, Chief of Naval Operations and Commander in Chief of the United States Fleet, refused to adopt the convoy system, insisting he didn't have enough escort vessels and naval aircraft. While the U.S. Navy was hard-pressed for warships, it had more than enough to provide a basic convoy system in home waters. His obstinacy led to a massacre. Army Chief of Staff George Marshall made his views plain: "The losses by submarines off our Atlantic seaboard and in the Caribbean now threaten our entire war effort."

Incredibly, the destruction inflicted by the Germans was caused by just a handful of submarines. There were no more than twelve U-boats operating at any one time off the U.S. eastern seaboard. In May 1942, just six U-boats sank 41 merchant vessels in the Caribbean. Between January and the end of July 1942, a staggering 360 ships were sunk.

Finally, in the summer of 1942, the convoy system was implemented, resulting in just three merchant ships sinking in July and the last sinking along the eastern seaboard. Forced to withdraw, the Germans had lost their last and best chance to alter the outcome of the war.

USS *Santee* (ACV-29)
Douglas SBD-3 Dauntless scout-bombers and Grumman F4F-4 Wildcat fighters are seen on the ship's flight deck during Operation Torch, the November 1942 invasion of French North Africa.

As horrific as these losses were, the Royal Navy was about to embark on the first amphibious operation of the war. Largely forgotten and far from prowling U-boats, Operation Ironclad was the British campaign to capture the Vichy French-controlled island of Madagascar. Fearing that the Vichy French would allow Japanese submarines to operate from the island and interdict shipping in the Indian Ocean, the British realized capturing the island was the only option. On May 5, Force 121, led by the battleship HMS *Ramillies*, along with two fleet carriers, six cruisers and 22 destroyers, successfully landed three

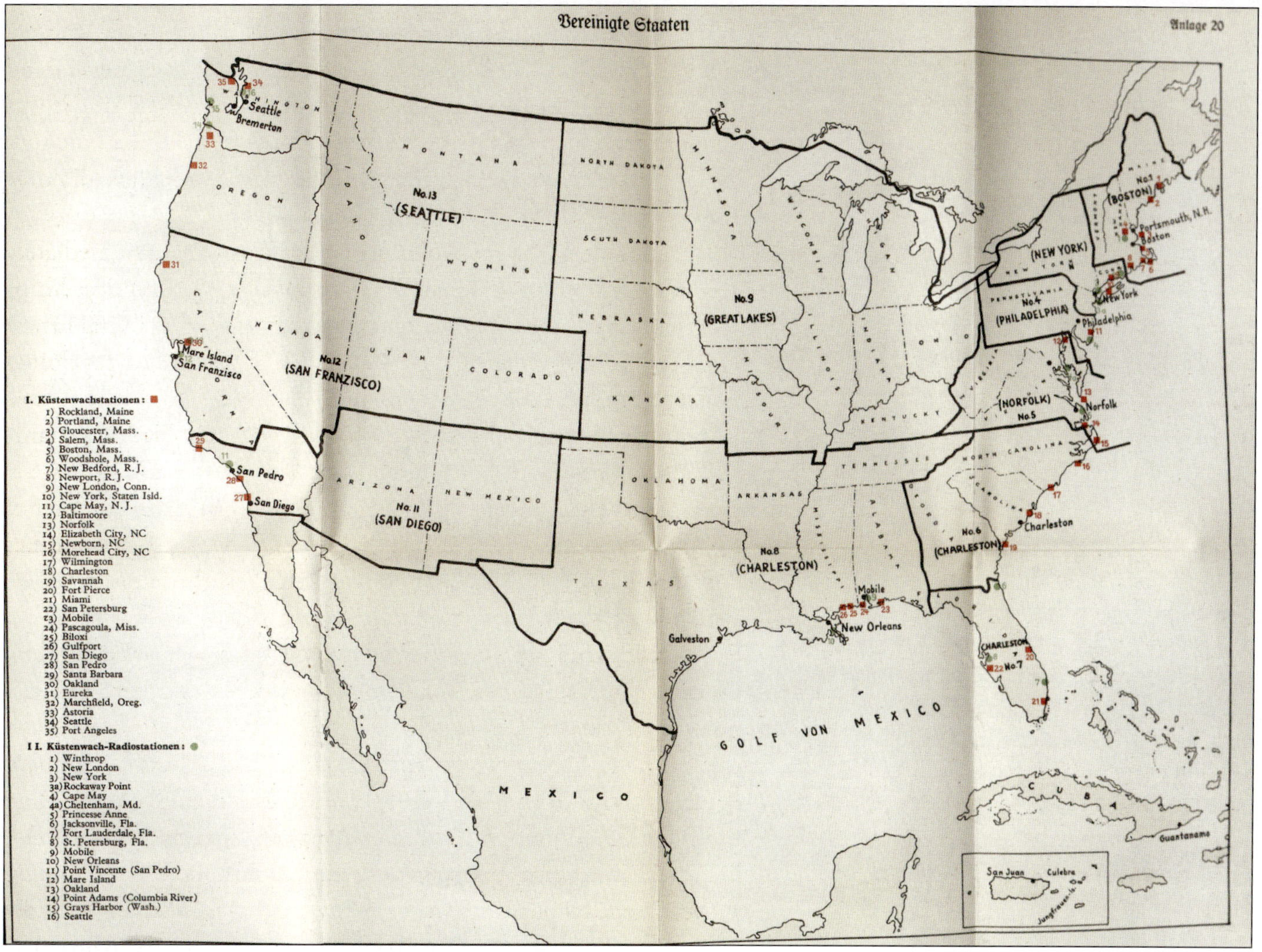

infantry brigades. The landing force was unopposed, but the tenacious Vichy defenders put up a stiff resistance until their defeat on November 6.

Just as the U-boats withdrew from the American eastern seaboard, U.S. warships and troops were at the same time preparing for their first amphibious landing of the war. Codenamed Operation Watchtower, the invasion force consisted of three fleet carriers, one battleship, nine heavy cruisers, two light cruisers, 31 destroyers and 23 transports carrying the 1st Marine Division.

On August 7, Marine troops began landing on the beaches of Guadalcanal in the Eastern Solomons. The surprise was complete, and while the Marines encountered no Japanese opposition in the early days, the battle for Guadalcanal would last until February 1943.

The objective of the operation was to capture the Japanese airstrip that was then under construction. By August 20, the airfield was in American control and ready for the first 19 F4F Wildcats and 12 SBD Dauntlesses flown from the escort carrier *Long Island.*

Kriegsmarine Officer's Map
Coast Guard radio stations (red) and Coast Guard watch radios (green). America's entry into the war in December 1941 provided German U-boats with new hunting grounds. In a few short months, losses reached crisis levels, with the Germans sinking more merchant ships than in any other six-month period during World War II (January to May). The majority were sunk along the American eastern seaboard and Caribbean.

For the next seven months, Japanese and American troops, aircraft and ships fought a grinding battle of attrition that would ultimately lead to an American victory. It was the first decisive victory over Japanese land, sea and air forces, and one that set the template for the rest of the Pacific war.

The Allies were now two for two in terms of successful amphibious operations. The two landings revealed many flaws and disorganization in the coordination of air, sea and land forces, but they had persevered. Sadly, on August 19, 237 ships and landing craft unsuccessfully attempted to land 6,050 mostly Canadian infantry and a regiment of Churchill tanks on the beaches of the French port of Dieppe. Designed as a raid, the Allies grossly underestimated the power of a well-defended port and suffered accordingly. As the troops hit the beach, they were met with withering machine gun and mortar fire. Landing craft were hit before they made the beach, and many tanks stalled on the gravel beach and were destroyed. After just ten hours of combat, 3,600 Canadian troops were killed, wounded or taken prisoner. The Royal Navy lost 33 landing craft and one destroyer.

History has claimed the raid provided many lessons for the upcoming D-Day operation, but in reality, the raid was an example of poor planning, intelligence, tactical execution and inter-service coordination. Well-defended ports were to be avoided at all costs.

"Val I" Arcs of Fire
The Aichi D3AI Type 99 Japanese dive bomber was a very effective design, being able to dive at a maximum angle of 80 degrees. Overall, it was not equal to the American SBD Dauntless dive bomber, having a weak defensive armament, no armor protection and self-sealing fuel tanks.

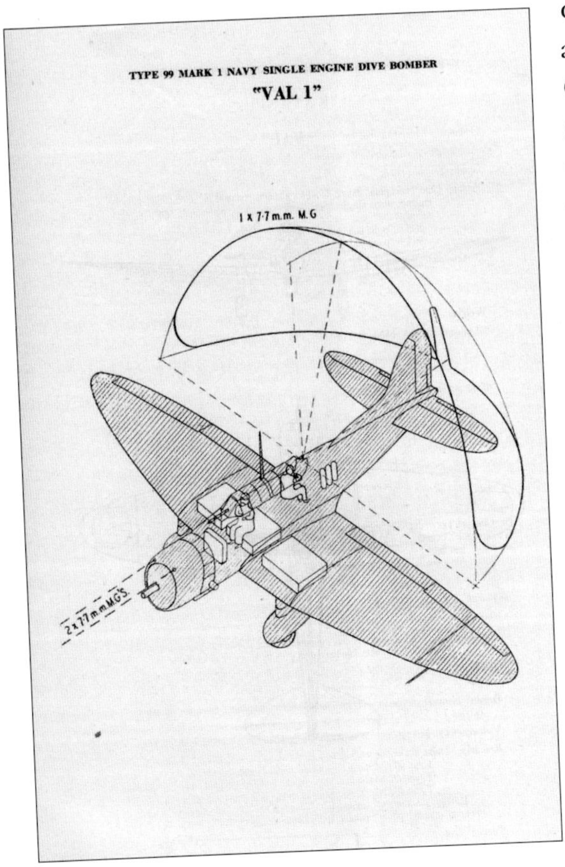

It seems incredible now, but just 11 months after America's entry into the war, U.S. and British naval power was about to embark on one of the most complex and daring operations of the war. It was also the first Anglo-American campaign undertaken. Code named Operation Torch, this was to be the invasion of French North Africa (November 7–16) with three landings at Casablanca, Algiers and Oran. The Allies organized three amphibious task forces: Western, Center and Eastern. The Western Task Force sailed directly from the United States, with the Center and Eastern sailing from the UK. In all, 350 warships provided escort, including the fleet carriers USS *Ranger*, HMS *Victorious*, HMS *Formidable*, HMS *Furious* and seven escort carriers. Over 100,000 troops in 500 transports represented the largest invasion fleet at this point in the war. The threat of German U-boat attack was considerable, but Allied naval power held most of the aces. In concert with a strong destroyer and corvette escort, carrier aircraft provided constant anti-submarine patrols over the convoys. While successful, this escort came at a price. To protect the vital troopships, the Allies stripped escorts from the North Atlantic convoys, causing the loss of 132 merchantmen. During Operation Torch, U-boats managed to sink just four warships and five transports. In the end, twenty-nine Allied ships were sunk during the invasion.

The Torch landings had been a great risk. As the official U.S. Army Air Forces' history concluded: "the purest gamble America

Type VIIC U-boat with Improved Anti-aircraft Armament (Left)
As Allied airpower grew, U-boats were forced to add more AA guns for self-defence.

HMS *Formidable* (Below)
HMS *Formidable* with Seafires from 885 NAS Squadron on outriggers during Operation Torch, November 8, 1942. This would be the Seafire's baptism of fire. Seafires claimed five enemy aircraft shot down for the loss of 21 aircraft due to operational causes.

Fairey Albacore Dinghy Drill
Designed as a replacement for the Fairey Swordfish, the Albacore did not live up to expectations, but it did have the luxury of an automatic emergency dinghy ejection system. In all, 800 were built during the war, equipping 15 FAA squadrons.

and Britain undertook during the war." Its success also led directly to the successful landings in Sicily and Italy in 1943, and the monumental D-Day landings in June 1944. In the Pacific, the victory on Guadalcanal was just the start of the U.S. Navy's island-hopping campaign toward Japan and final victory.

For the tens of thousands of young sailors, aviators and merchantmen (both volunteer and conscripts), the battle for the high seas could only be described as gruelling. The vast majority had never been to sea before. Life aboard ships was cramped, no matter the size of the vessel. Privacy was non-existent. For most, sleeping quarters consisted of a hammock, with officers entitled to a small claustrophobic room. Food, depending on which navy you served, could be described as awful. Injury was constant on a rolling, pitching ship. Broken bones, cuts and concussions were common. Storms and heavy seas meant sea sickness turned even the hardest men into puking ghosts. Standing watch on a rolling ship in stormy weather was a marathon of human endurance. Many simply disappeared, swept overboard by a crashing wave. Escape was impossible. Boredom and loneliness lurked in every corner. Many spent weeks, months, even years on the ship before returning to their home port.

There was one constant every seaman shared, however, and that was the fear of sudden death. A torpedo strike in the middle of the night. A kamikaze battling through a wall of anti-aircraft fire, crashing with sudden fury. Being depth-charged in a submarine with nowhere to hide. Ships sank with surprising speed. The battle cruiser HMS *Hood,* struck by a shell from the German battleship *Bismarck,* suffered a devastating explosion and sank within three minutes, leaving just three survivors out of a crew of 1,418 men.

For the sailors, submariners and aviators of every nation, the cost was high. The battle for the high seas took a heavy toll, resulting in the deaths of close to 500,000 men and women.

- U.S. Navy and Coast Guard: 64,531
- Royal Navy: 50,758
- Allied Merchant Marine: 36,000
- Kriegsmarine U-boat: 28,000 (75 percent casualty rate)
- Imperial Japanese Navy: 300,386

Sicily Order of Battle (Above)
Operation Husky, the invasion of Sicily, was the Allies' fourth successful amphibious operation. This 'secret' map shows the army divisions and landing areas used on July 10, 1943. Over the next three days, over 3,000 ships landed 150,000 troops covered by 4,000 aircraft. This was a clear and decisive indication of the Allies' seaborne power and the ability to land troops with air cover at the place of their choosing.

The End of the Pacific War (Left)
Japanese representatives prepare to sign the documents of surrender on September 2, 1945, in Tokyo Bay. In the photo are Japanese Foreign Ministry representatives Katsuo Okazaki and Toshikazu Kase.

GREAT BRITAIN

HMS *Mauritius*

HMS *Mauritius* was a *Fiji*-class light cruiser commissioned in January 1940. The main armament consisted of 12 6-inch guns in four triple turrets. The magazines held 200 rounds per gun. The rate of fire per gun was between five and six rounds per minute.

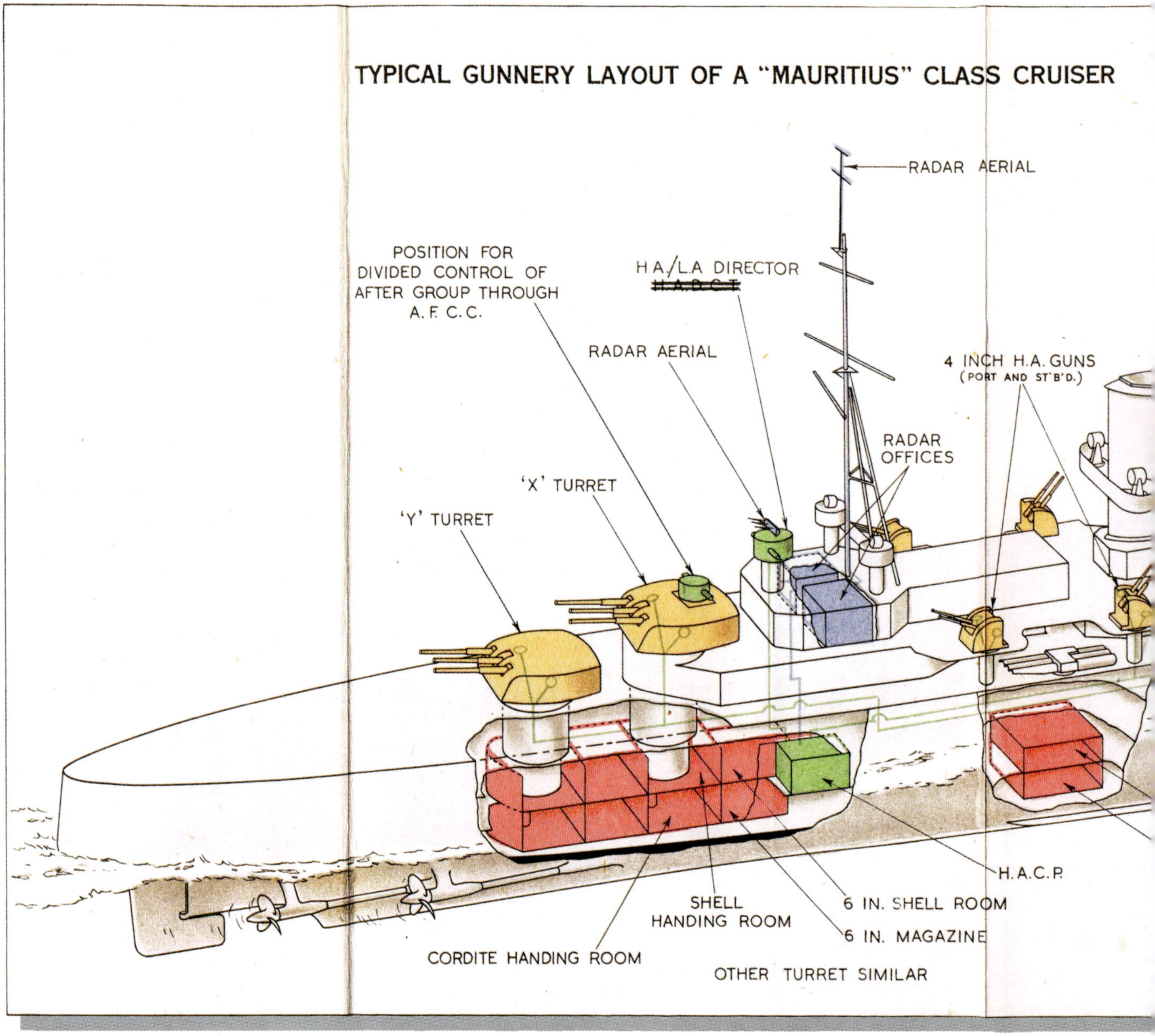

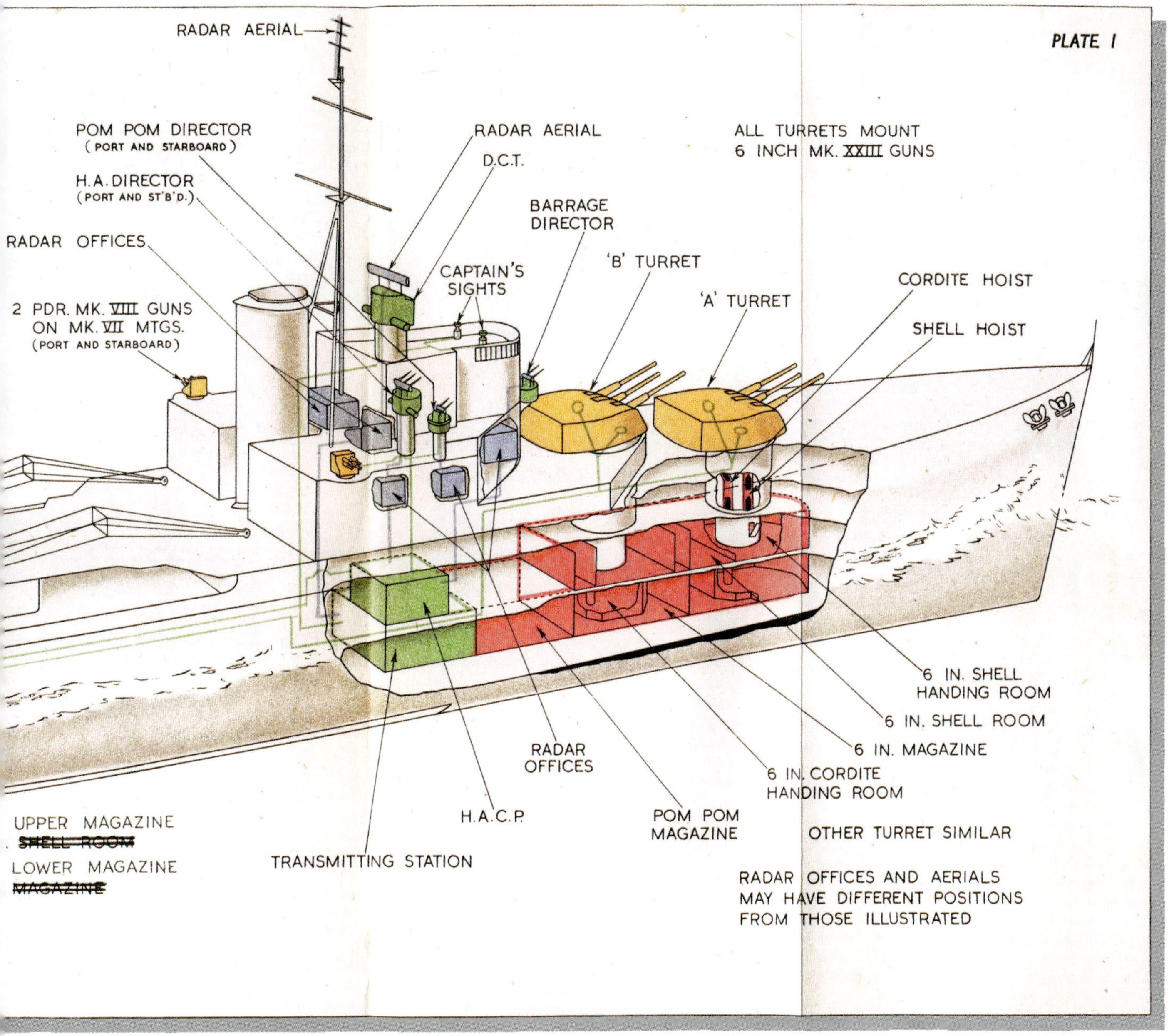
PLATE I
RADAR AERIAL
POM POM DIRECTOR
(PORT AND STARBOARD)
H.A. DIRECTOR
(PORT AND ST'B'D.)
RADAR OFFICES
2 PDR. MK. VIII GUNS
ON MK. VII MTGS.
(PORT AND STARBOARD)
RADAR AERIAL
D.C.T.
BARRAGE
DIRECTOR
CAPTAIN'S
SIGHTS
'B' TURRET
'A' TURRET
ALL TURRETS MOUNT
6 INCH MK. XXIII GUNS
CORDITE HOIST
SHELL HOIST
6 IN. SHELL
HANDING ROOM
6 IN. SHELL ROOM
6 IN. MAGAZINE
6 IN. CORDITE
HANDING ROOM
RADAR
OFFICES
H.A.C.P.
POM POM
MAGAZINE
OTHER TURRET SIMILAR
TRANSMITTING STATION
UPPER MAGAZINE
~~SHELL ROOM~~
LOWER MAGAZINE
~~MAGAZINE~~
RADAR OFFICES AND AERIALS
MAY HAVE DIFFERENT POSITIONS
FROM THOSE ILLUSTRATED

Typical Gunnery Layout of a "Dido" Class Cruiser

Sixteen *Dido*-class light cruisers served with the Royal Navy during World War II. Initially, the class was to be armed with ten 5.25-inch guns, but only HMS *Dido* was so equipped. The *Dido*-class had up to 360 rounds of ammunition for 'A,' 'B' and 'Q' turrets, 320 rounds for 'X' turrets and 300 rounds for 'Y' turrets.

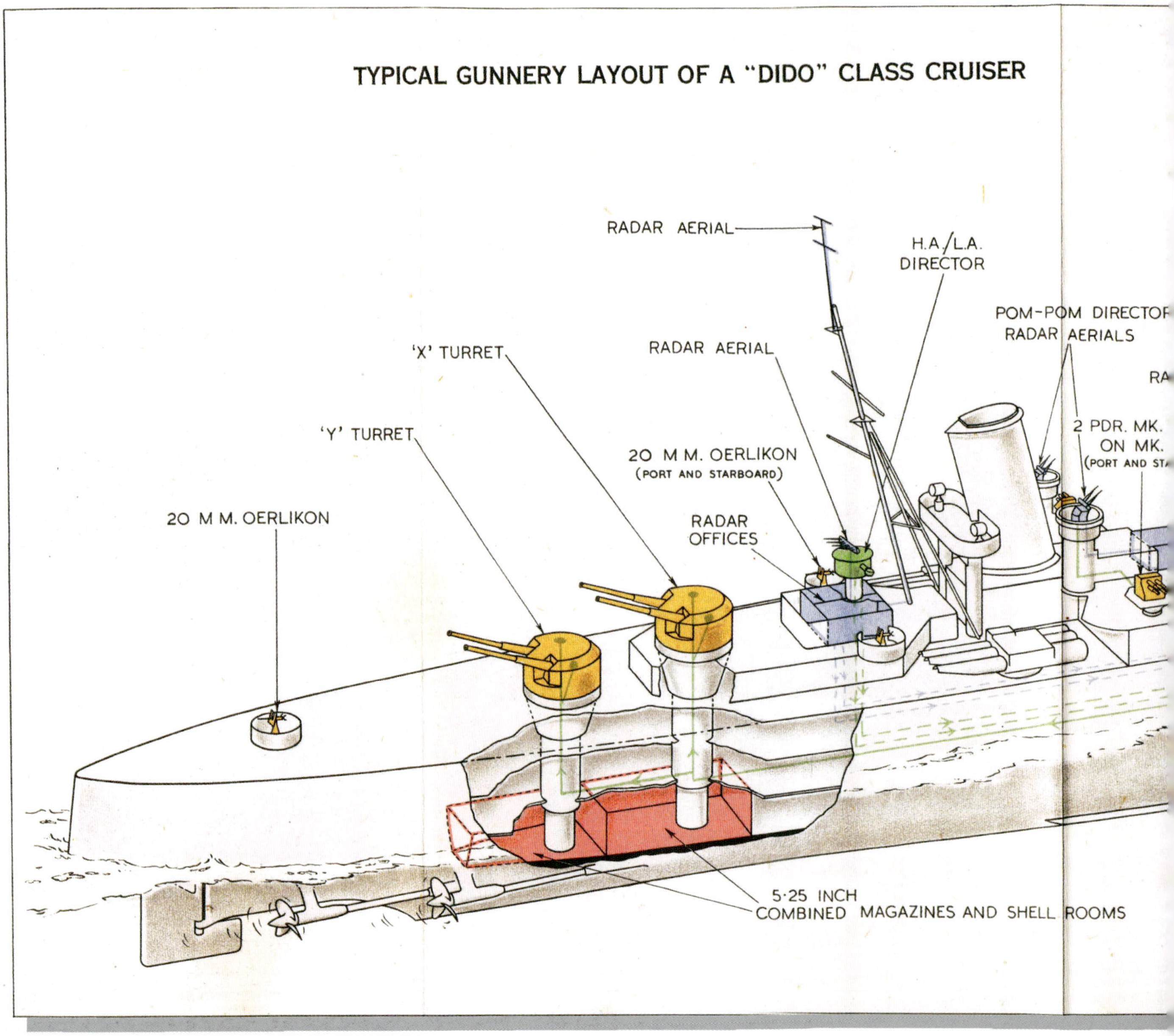

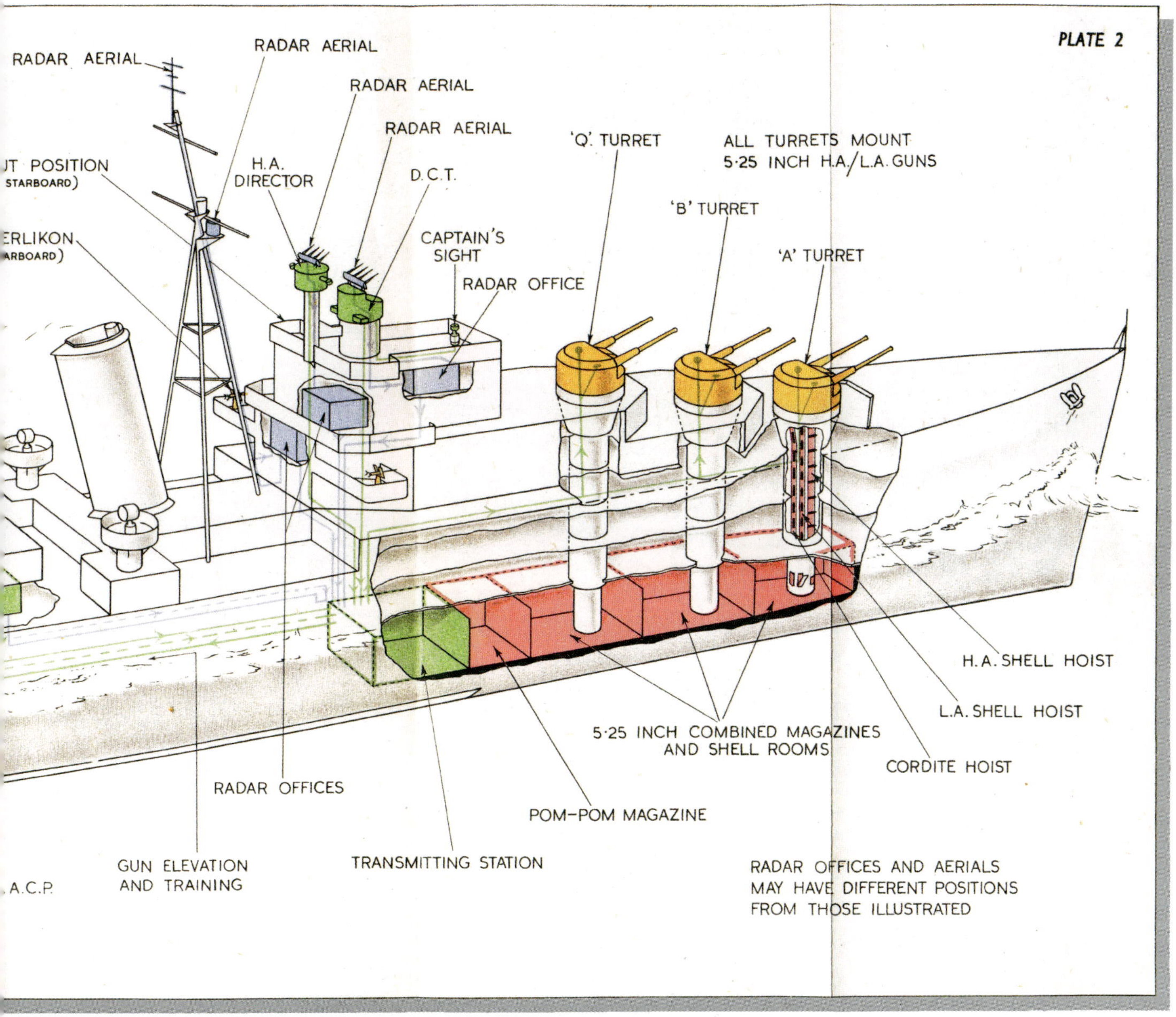
PLATE 2
RADAR AERIAL
RADAR AERIAL
RADAR AERIAL
RADAR AERIAL
H.A. DIRECTOR
D.C.T.
CAPTAIN'S SIGHT
RADAR OFFICE
'Q' TURRET
ALL TURRETS MOUNT 5·25 INCH H.A./L.A. GUNS
'B' TURRET
'A' TURRET
H.A. SHELL HOIST
L.A. SHELL HOIST
5·25 INCH COMBINED MAGAZINES AND SHELL ROOMS
CORDITE HOIST
RADAR OFFICES
POM-POM MAGAZINE
GUN ELEVATION AND TRAINING
TRANSMITTING STATION
A.C.P.
RADAR OFFICES AND AERIALS MAY HAVE DIFFERENT POSITIONS FROM THOSE ILLUSTRATED

Typical Layout of a Royal Navy Modern Destroyer

The 4.7-inch QF Mk IX gun was used on most RN destroyers built in the 1930s and 1940s. Unfortunately, the 4.7-inch gun was not a truly dual-purpose weapon, and its anti-aircraft capability was limited. This resulted in more RN destroyers sunk by air attack than by any other cause.

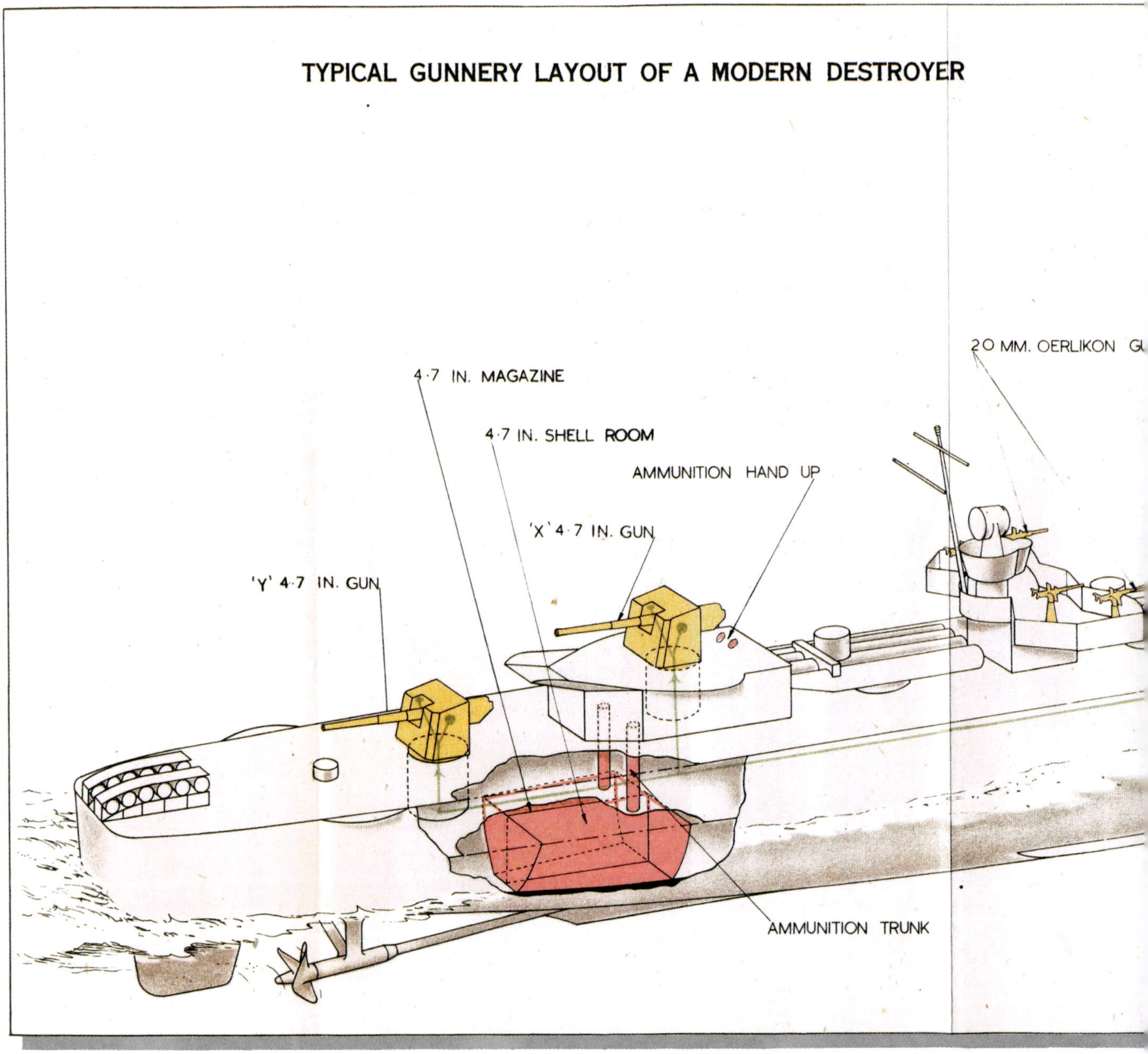

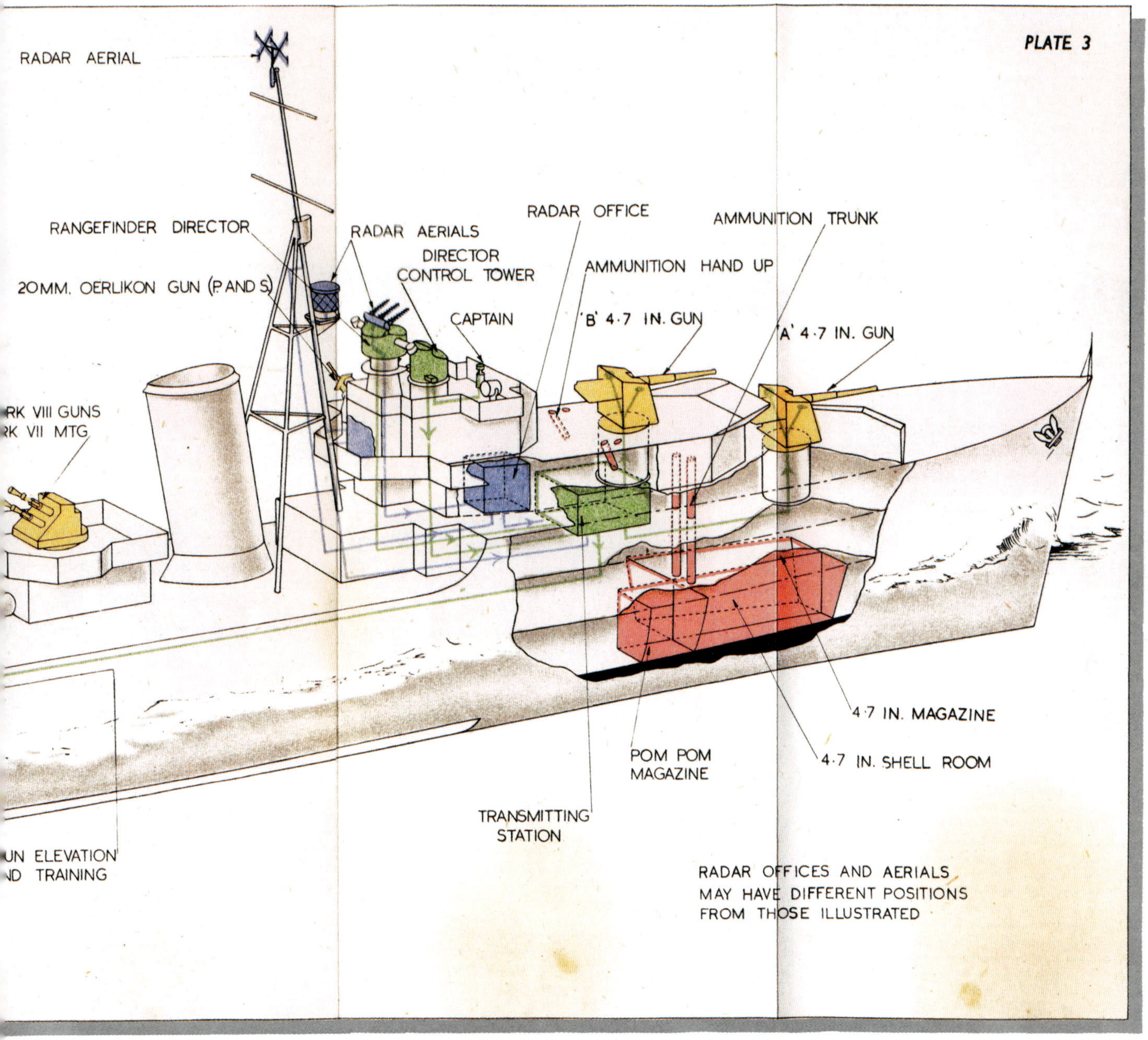
PLATE 3
RADAR AERIAL
RANGEFINDER DIRECTOR
RADAR AERIALS
DIRECTOR
CONTROL TOWER
RADAR OFFICE
AMMUNITION TRUNK
AMMUNITION HAND UP
20MM. OERLIKON GUN (P. AND S)
CAPTAIN
'B' 4·7 IN. GUN
'A' 4·7 IN. GUN
RK VIII GUNS
RK VII MTG
4·7 IN. MAGAZINE
POM POM
MAGAZINE
4·7 IN. SHELL ROOM
TRANSMITTING
STATION
UN ELEVATION
ND TRAINING
RADAR OFFICES AND AERIALS
MAY HAVE DIFFERENT POSITIONS
FROM THOSE ILLUSTRATED

Loading Tray for 4.7-inch Mark XVIII Mounting

The 4.7-inch QF Mk IX had a rate of fire of 10 to 12 rounds a minute. A typical British destroyer carried approximately 200 rounds of semi-armor-piercing rounds, plus 50 rounds of high explosive and 50 rounds of star shell per gun.

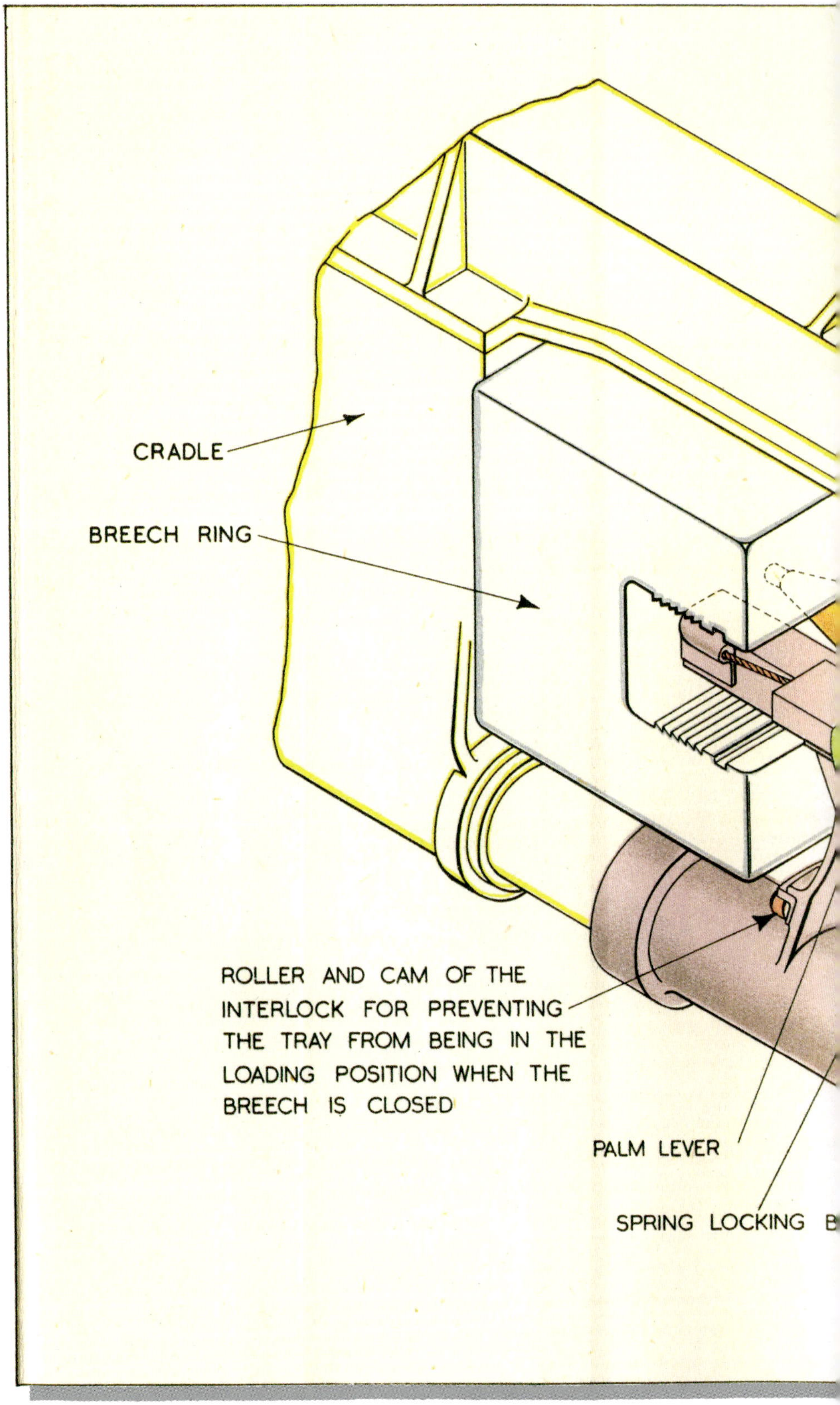

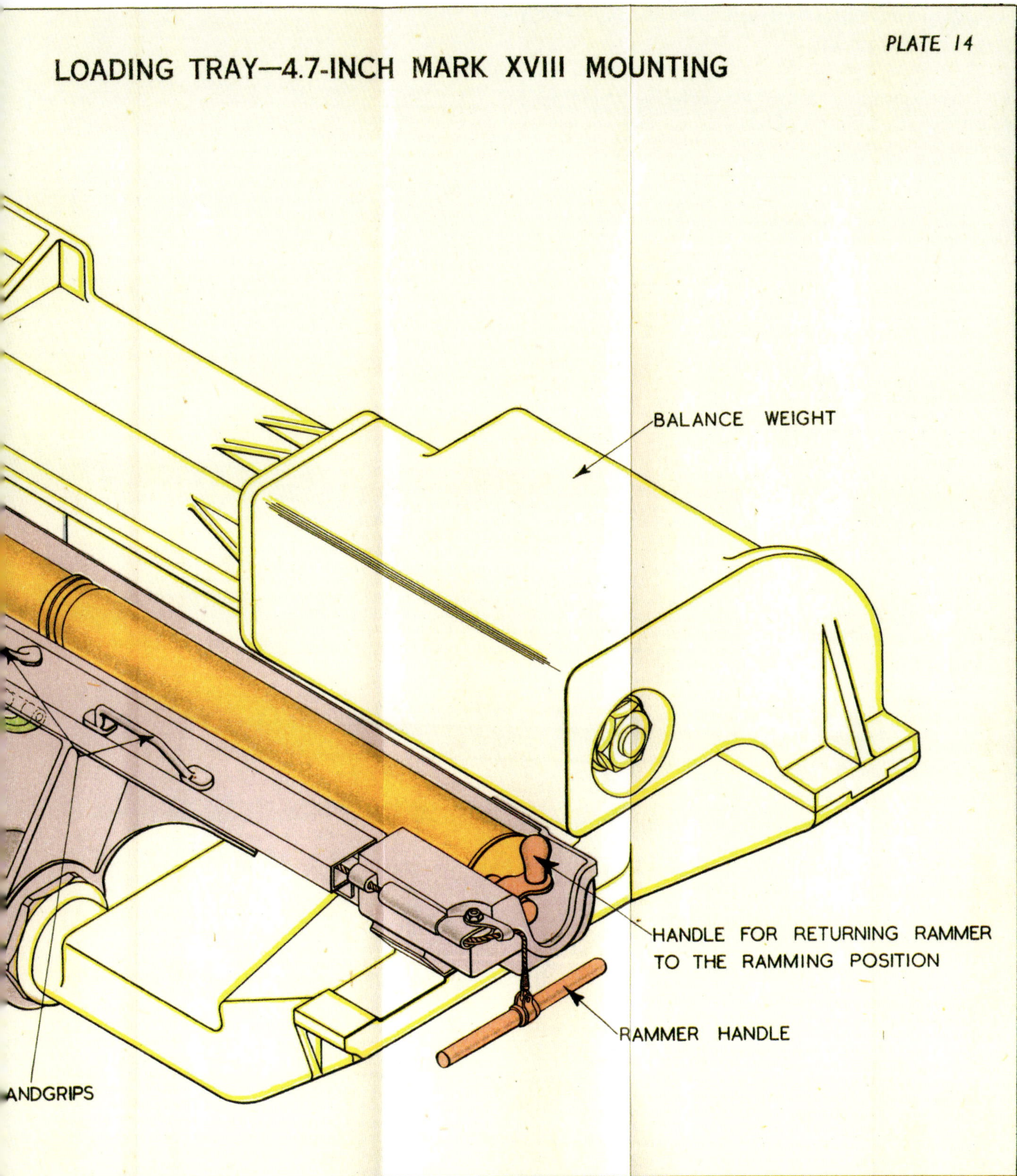

LOADING TRAY—4.7-INCH MARK XVIII MOUNTING
PLATE 14
BALANCE WEIGHT
HANDLE FOR RETURNING RAMMER TO THE RAMMING POSITION
RAMMER HANDLE
ANDGRIPS

Breech Mechanism 6-inch Mark XXIII Gun, Open and Closed

Built by the Royal Gun Factory, the 6-inch breech mechanism was somewhat obsolescent when using bag charges, manual ramming and manually operated breech mechanisms. The total weight of the gun was 6,265 kg (6.906 tons).

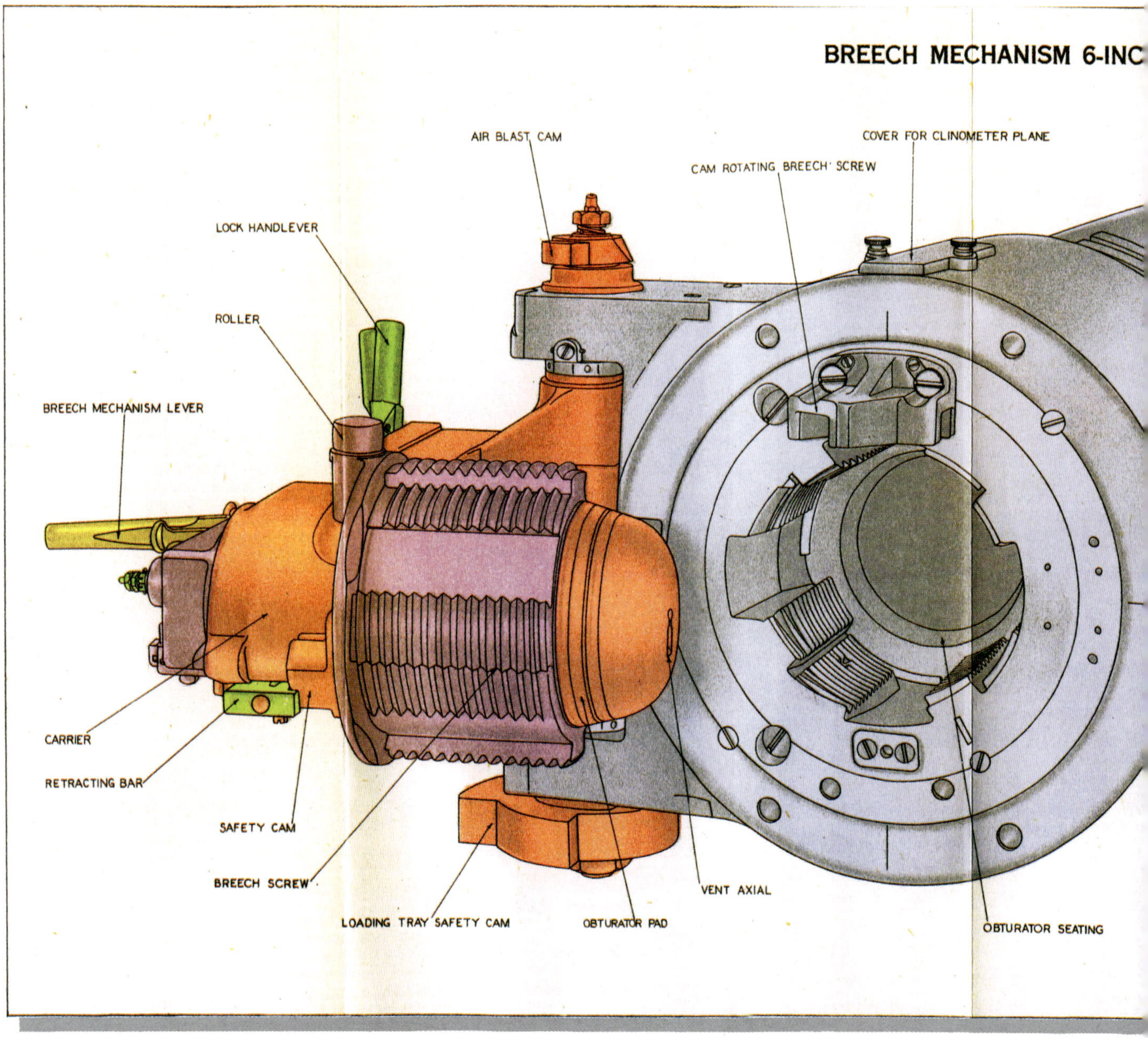

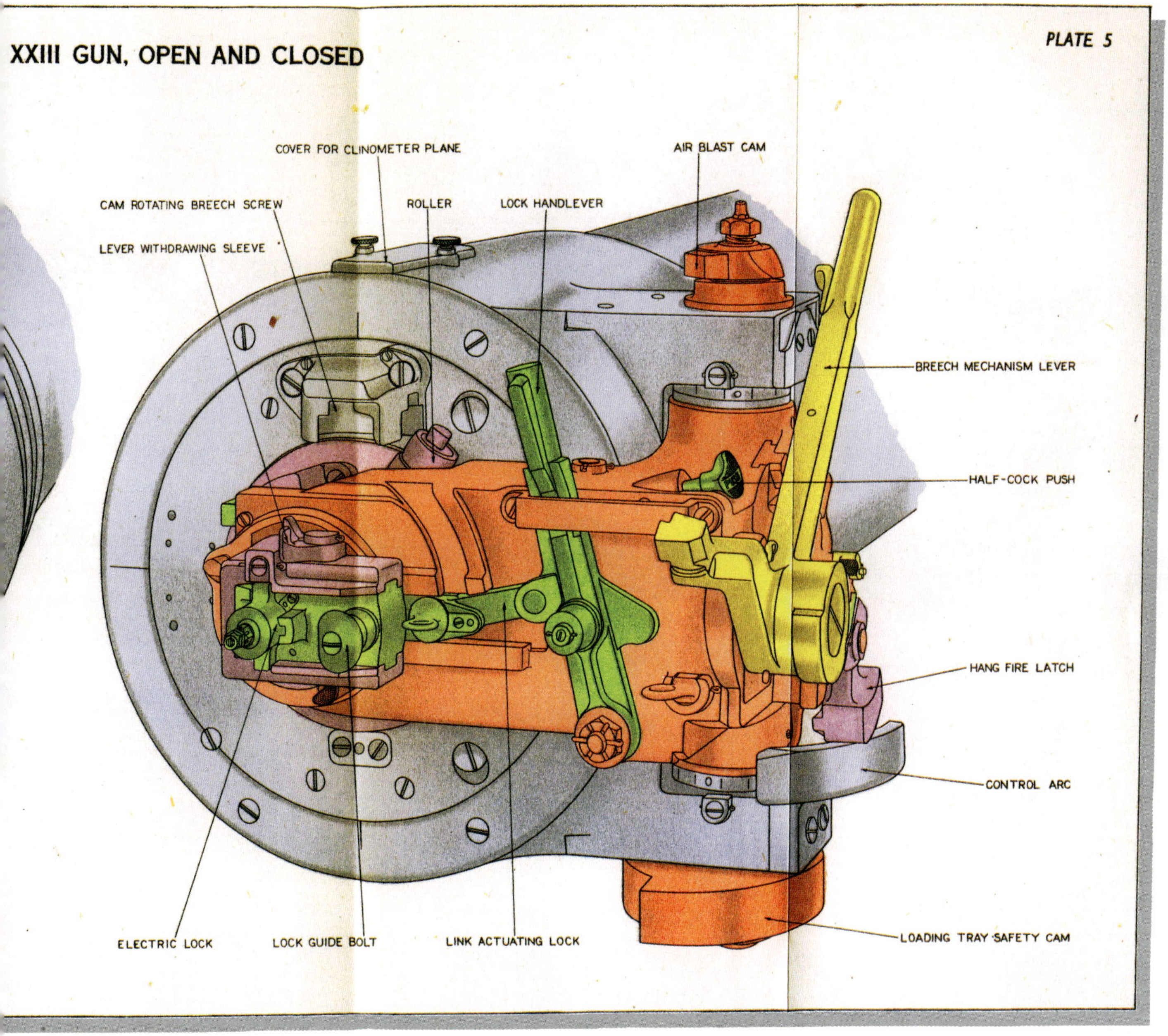
XXIII GUN, OPEN AND CLOSED
PLATE 5
COVER FOR CLINOMETER PLANE
AIR BLAST CAM
CAM ROTATING BREECH SCREW
ROLLER
LOCK HANDLEVER
LEVER WITHDRAWING SLEEVE
BREECH MECHANISM LEVER
HALF-COCK PUSH
HANG FIRE LATCH
CONTROL ARC
ELECTRIC LOCK
LOCK GUIDE BOLT
LINK ACTUATING LOCK
LOADING TRAY SAFETY CAM

Sections of 6-inch and 4-inch Guns

This illustration shows the differences between a breech-loading (BL) (top) and quick-fire (QF) gun. QF guns could use both fixed rounds and bag charges. QF guns firing fixed rounds had higher rates of fire when compared to the BL-loading guns.

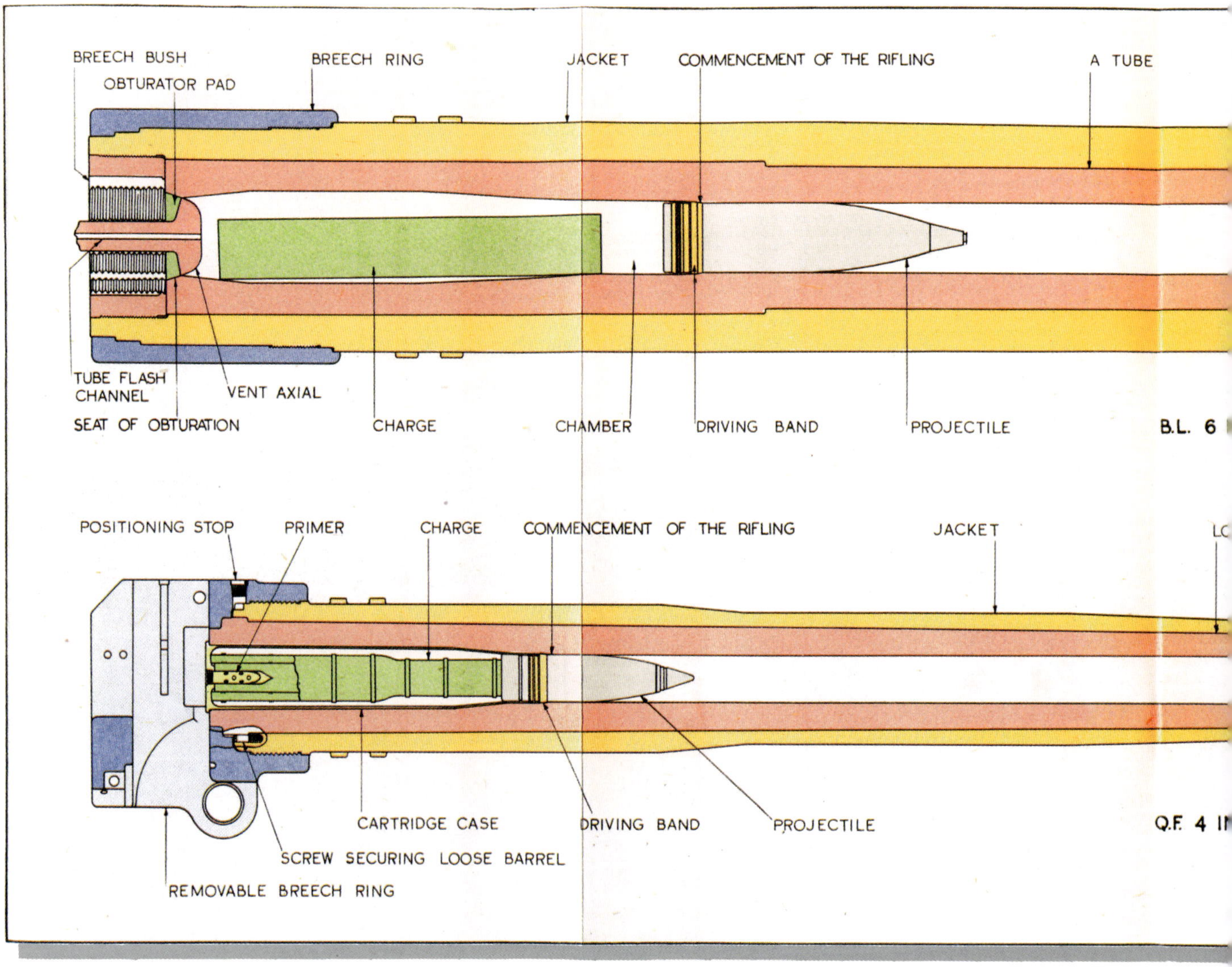

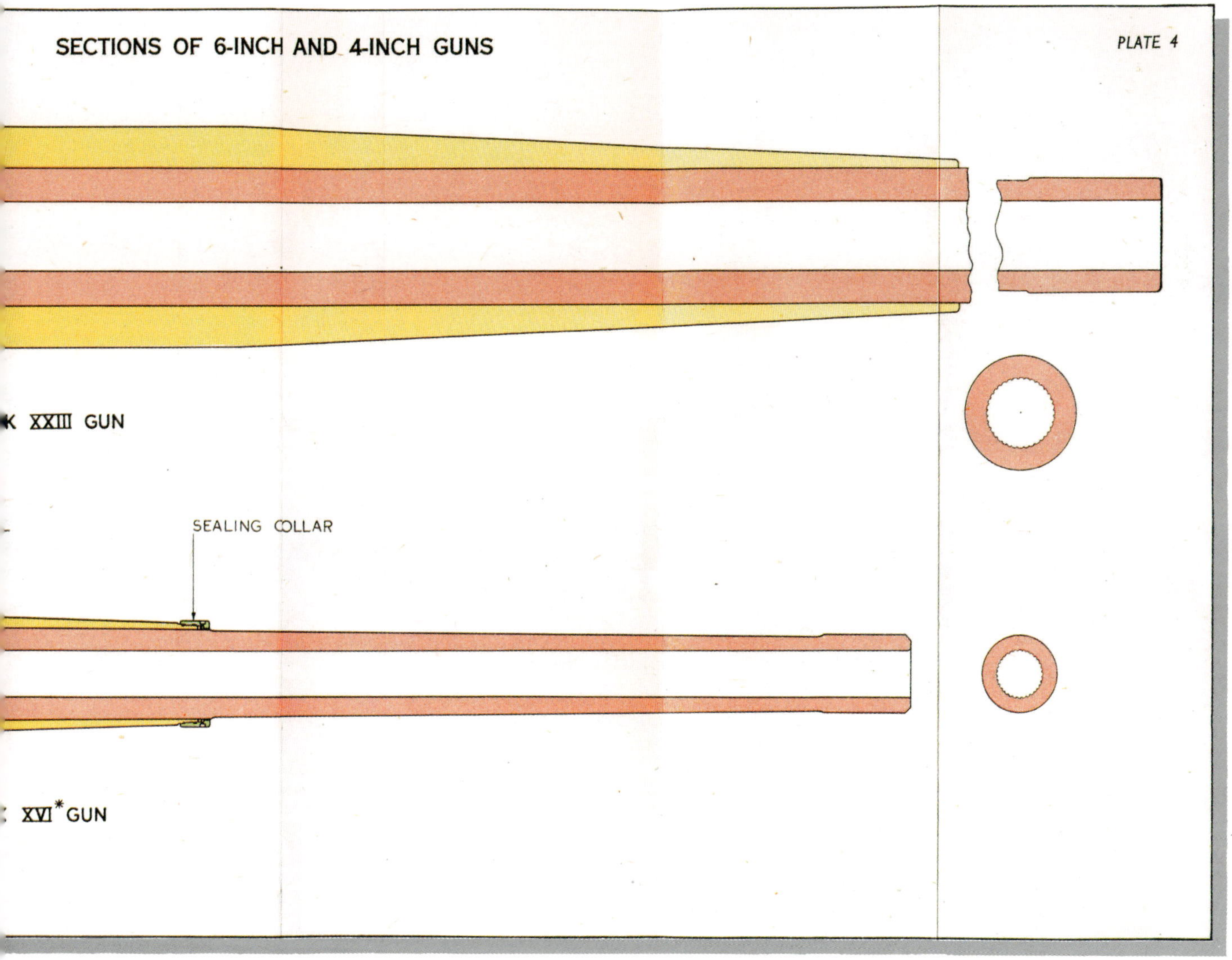
SECTIONS OF 6-INCH AND 4-INCH GUNS
PLATE 4
K XXIII GUN
SEALING COLLAR
XVI* GUN

Typical Central Pivot Mounting — 4.7-inch Mark XVIII

The Mark XVII gun weighed 8,010 kg (8.83 tons). Its range at a 30-degree elevation with high an explosive shell (HE) was 14,450 meters (15,800 yards). The range of a semi-armor-piercing round (SAP) was 5,950 meters (6,500 yards).

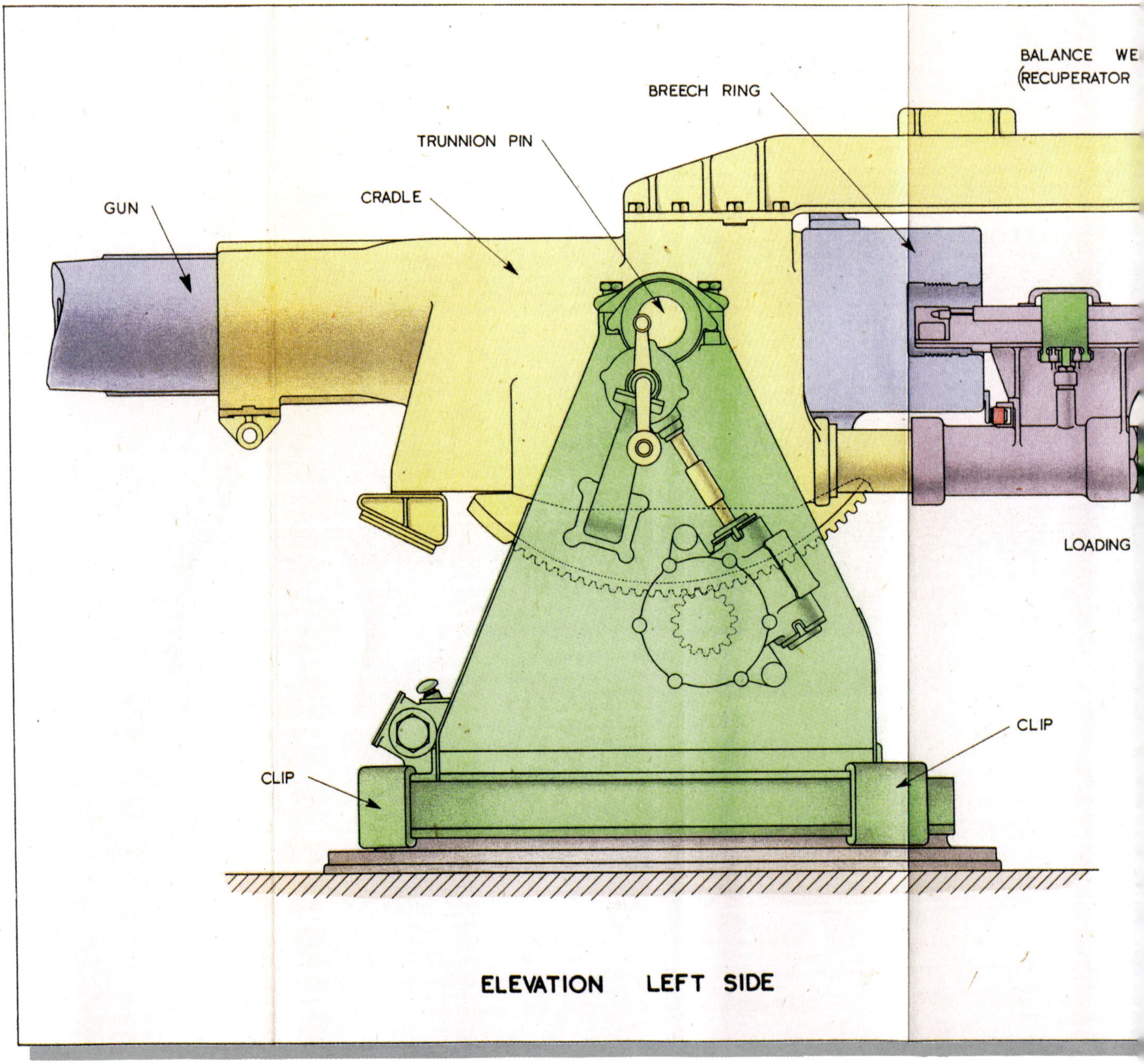

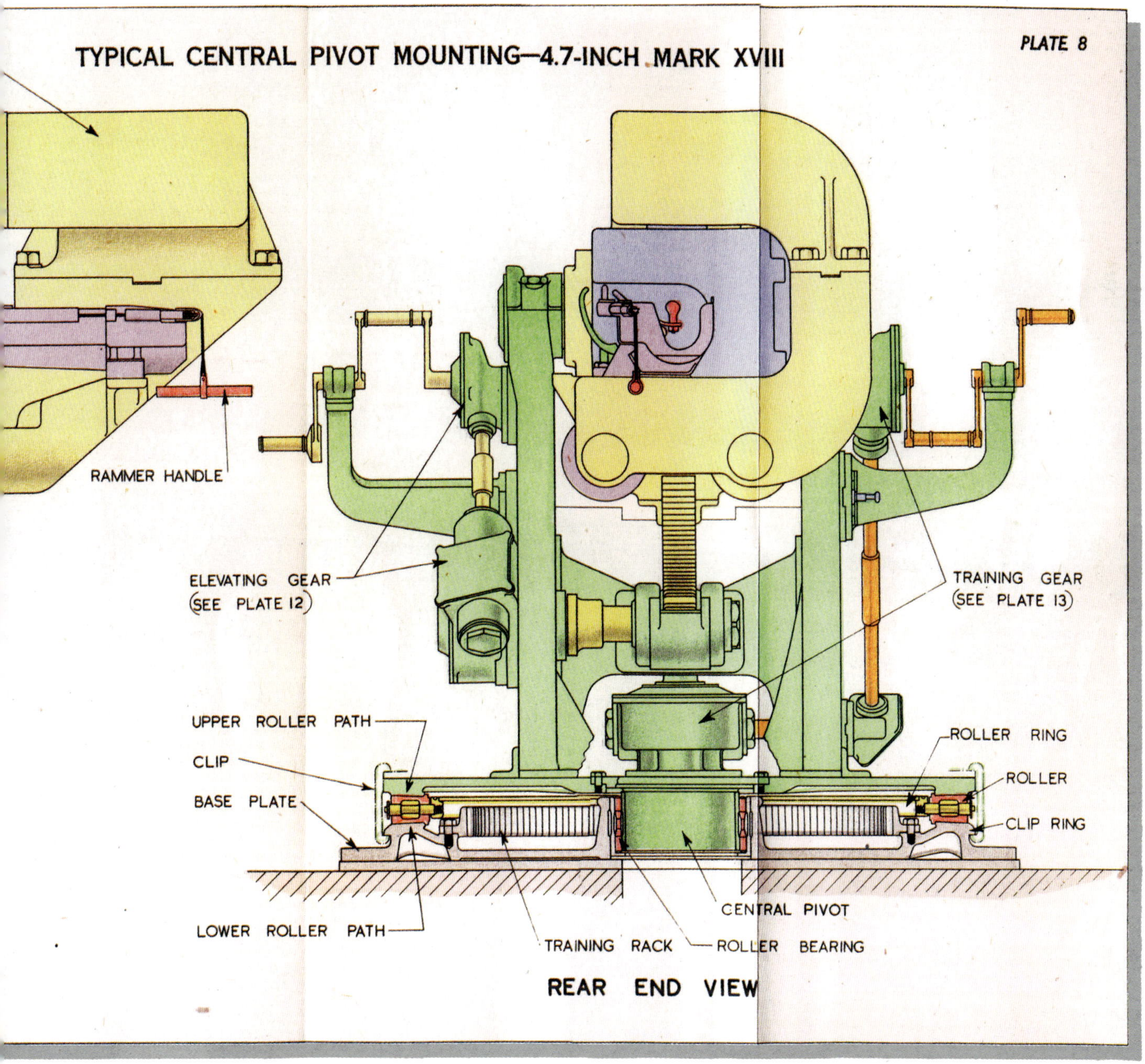
TYPICAL CENTRAL PIVOT MOUNTING—4.7-INCH MARK XVIII
PLATE 8
RAMMER HANDLE
ELEVATING GEAR (SEE PLATE 12)
TRAINING GEAR (SEE PLATE 13)
UPPER ROLLER PATH
CLIP
BASE PLATE
LOWER ROLLER PATH
ROLLER RING
ROLLER
CLIP RING
CENTRAL PIVOT
TRAINING RACK
ROLLER BEARING
REAR END VIEW

General Arrangement of 6-inch Mark XXIII Mounting

The 6-inch gun in triple turrets equipped ten of the Royal Navy's *Town*-class light cruisers built in the 1930s. Bag charges and shells had to be hoisted from the ship's magazine, located at the bottom of the ship in armored magazines with 76 mm (3 inches) of armor. The black outline of the turrets shows 100 mm (4 inches) of face armor and 50 mm (2 inches) for the roof and sides of the turret.

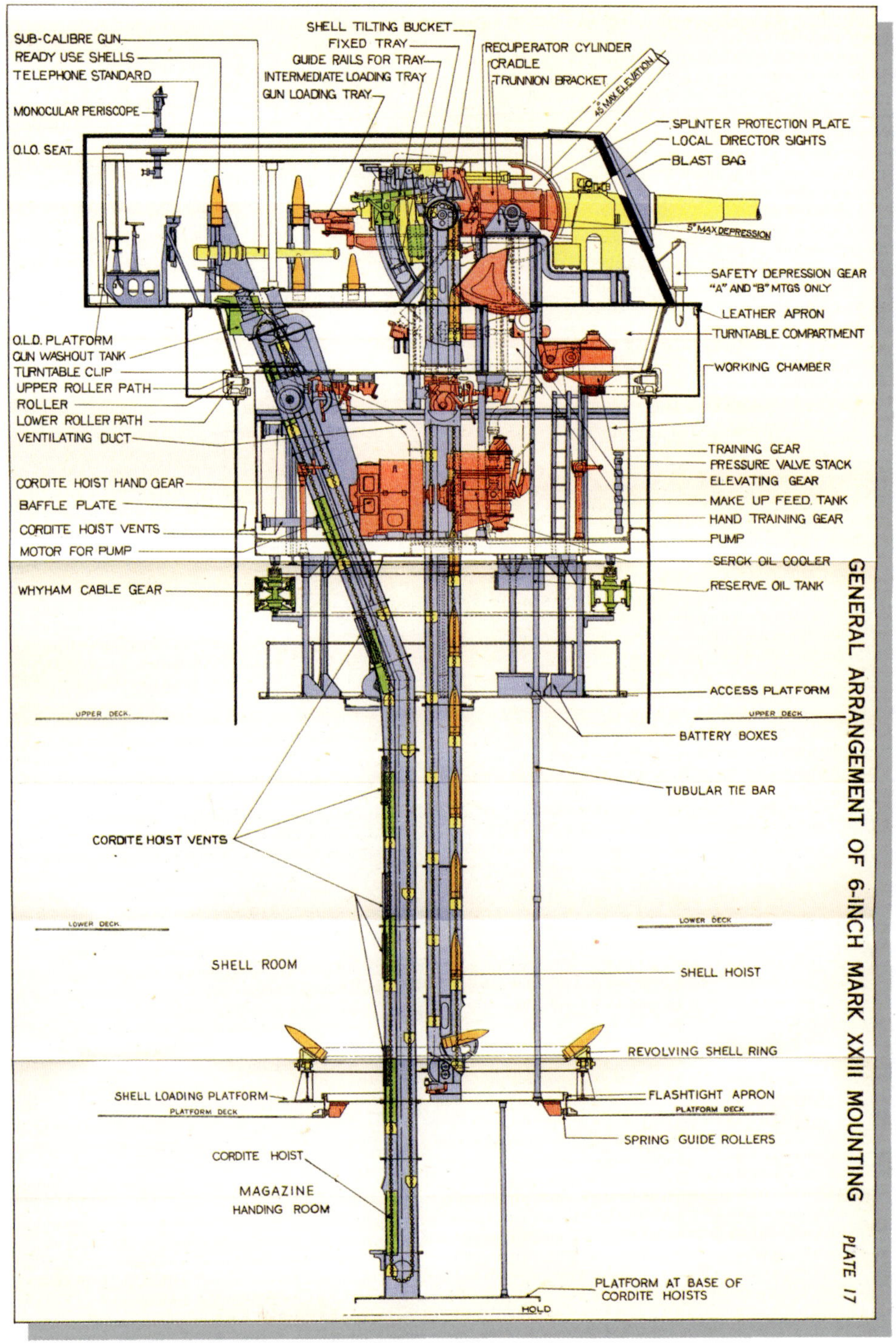

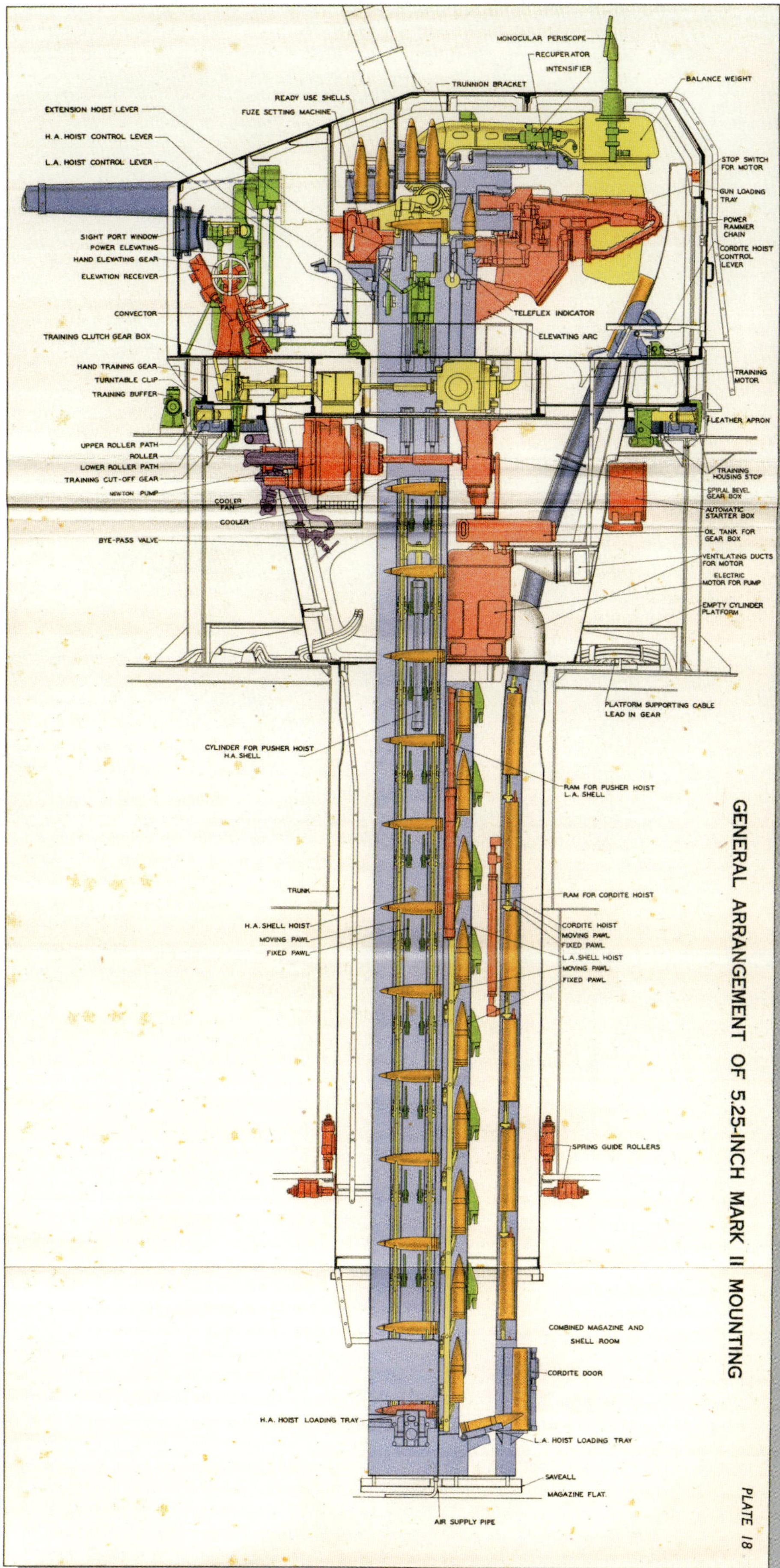

General Arrangement of 5.52-inch Mark II Mounting

The 5.25-inch gun in a twin turret was the standard dual-purpose (DP) secondary armament of the *King George V*-class and *Vanguard*-class battleships and the main armament for the *Dido*- and *Spartan*-class light cruisers. The *King George V*-classes carried 400 rounds per gun (a total of 6,400 rounds), with *Vanguards* carrying 391 rounds per gun.

15-inch General Arrangement

The Royal Navy's most successful gun design was the 15-inch Mk I main battery gun. These guns equipped the five *Queen Elizabeth*-class and five *Royal Sovereign*-class battleships, as well as the battlecruisers HMS *Hood* and *Repulse* at the beginning of World War II. The gun was reliable and accurate. During the Battle of Calabria, HMS *Warspite* hit the Italian battleship *Giulio Cesare* with a single 15-inch shell at a range of 2.4 km (26,000 yards), the longest hit ever recorded by a battleship.

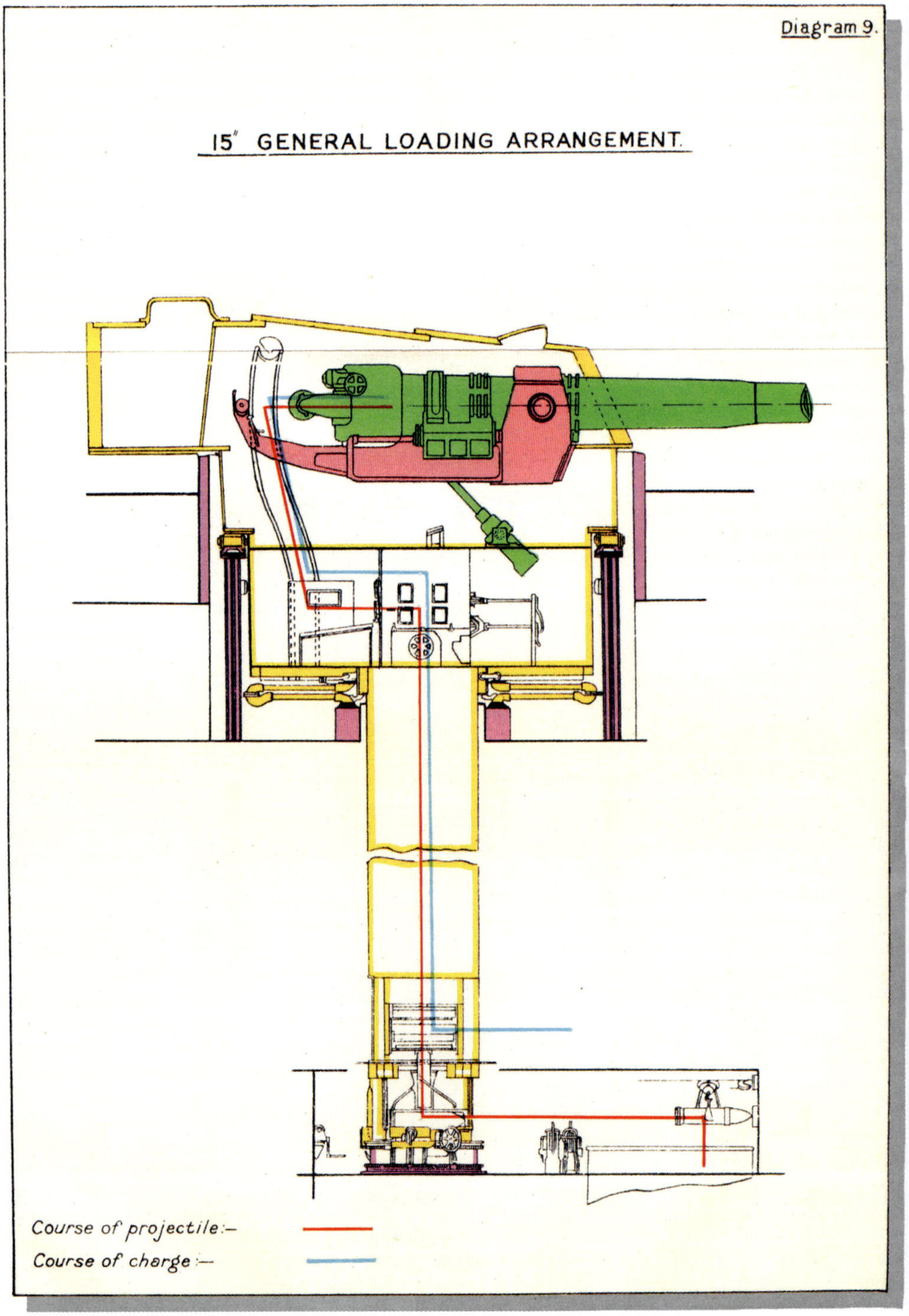

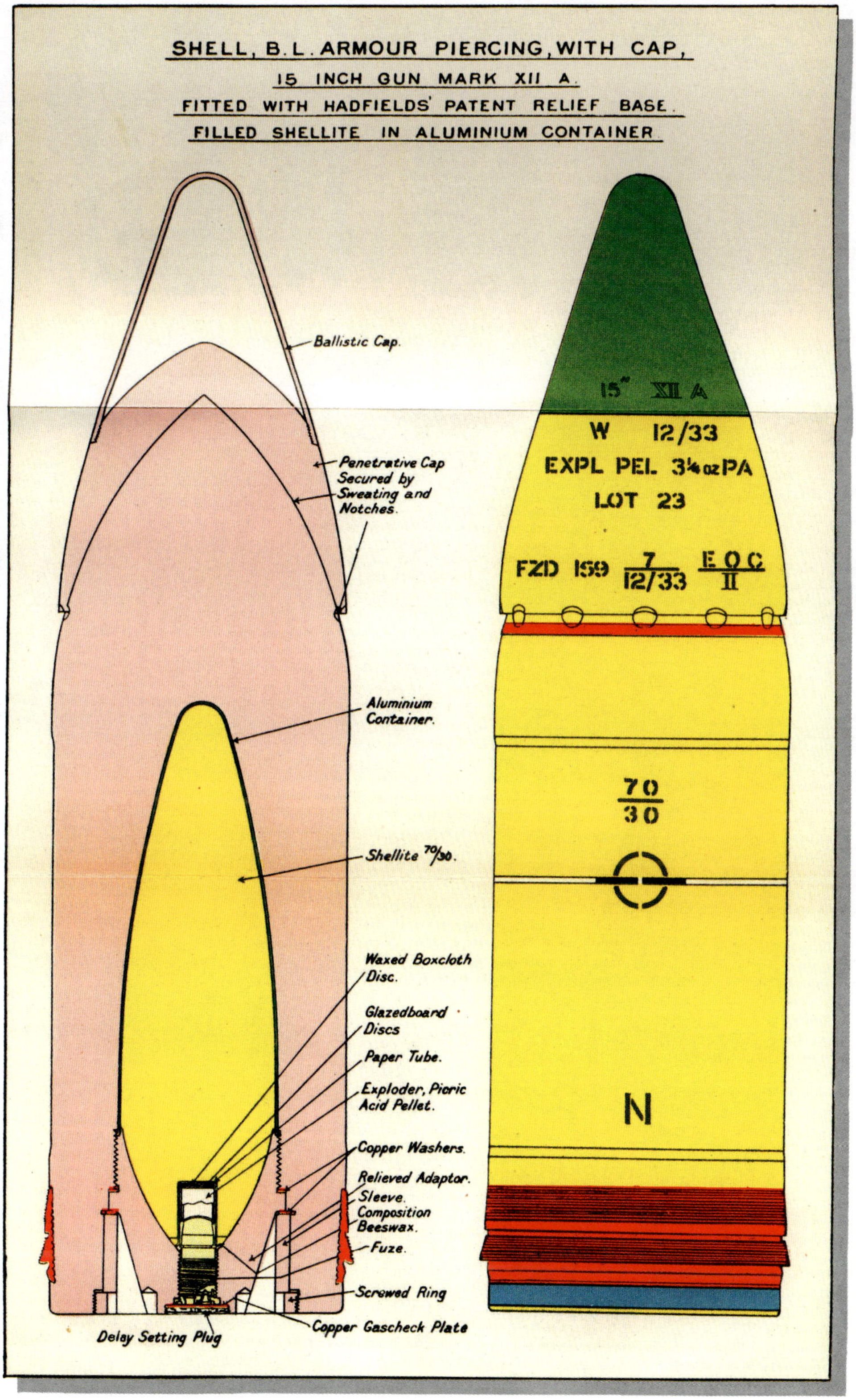

15-inch Shell Armor Piercing Round with Cap

Ammunition storage for the *Queen Elizabeth*- and *Royal Sovereign*-class battleships was 800 rounds with a mix of armor-piercing and high-explosive rounds. Each armor-piercing shell weighed 879 kg (1,938 lb). At a range of 15,730 meters (17,200 yards), a 15-inch AP round could penetrate 356 mm (14 inches) of deck armor and 52 mm (2 inches) of side armor.

Shell, Semi-Armor-Piercing, with Cap 8-inch Gun

During World War II, British heavy cruisers were armed with eight Mk VIII breech-loading 8-inch guns. The shells weighed 116 kg (256 lbs) and had a separate powder charge. The ballistic cap on the front of the shell reduced wind resistance. The shell was detonated by the base fuse after passing through a ship's deck or side plating.

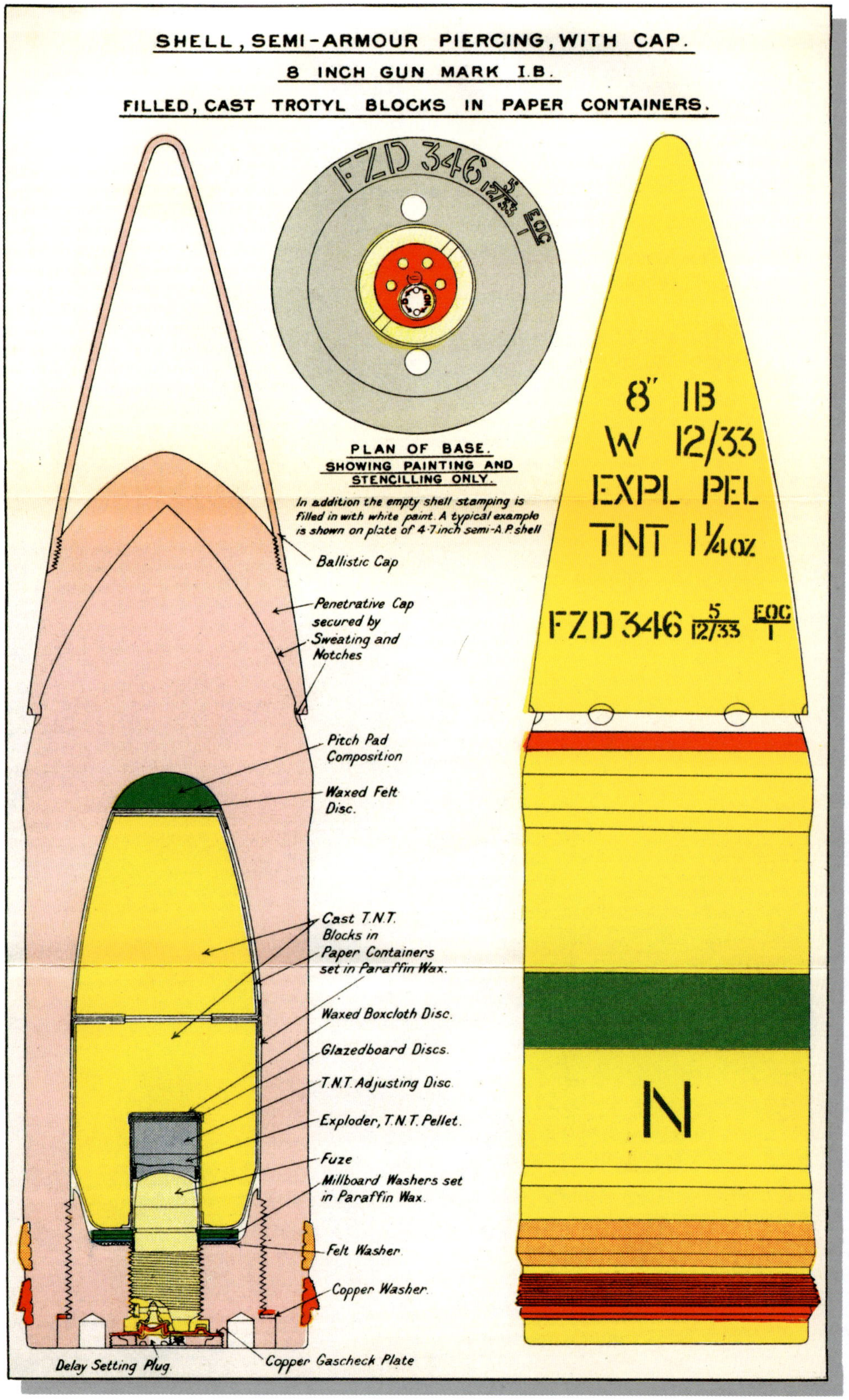

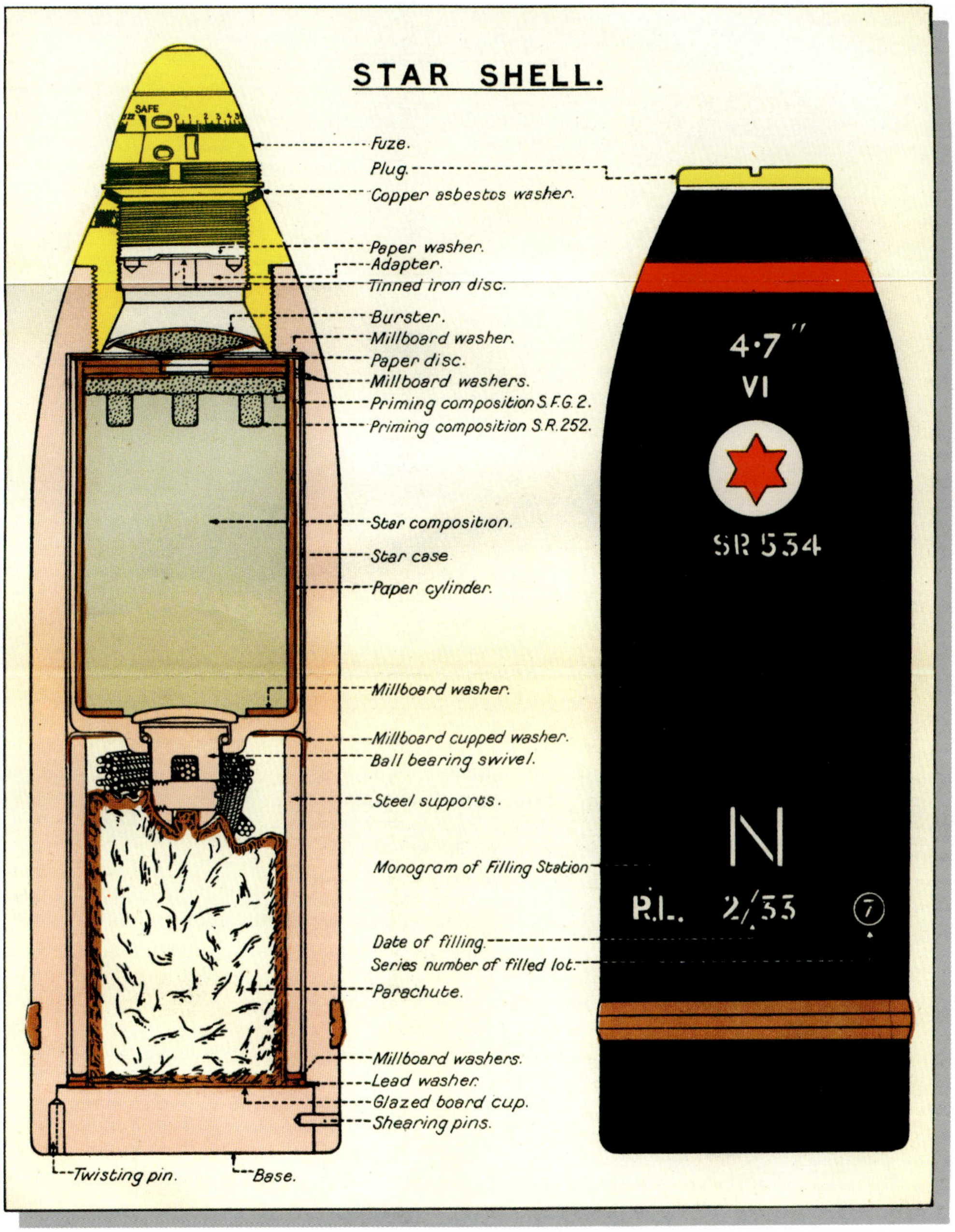

Star Shell

Star shells were used to illuminate targets at night. These shells contained brightly burning incendiary material attached to a parachute. The material was ignited when the shell burst. A 6-inch shell burned for about 60 seconds, a 4.7-inch shell for 18 seconds, a 4-inch shell for 35 seconds and a 3-inch shell for 20 seconds.

Color Markings on Shells

This illustration shows the inner workings of a 4.7-inch armor-piercing and anti-aircraft round fitted with a timed fuze. Armor-piercing rounds carried the least amount of explosive charge in comparison to high-explosive and AA rounds.

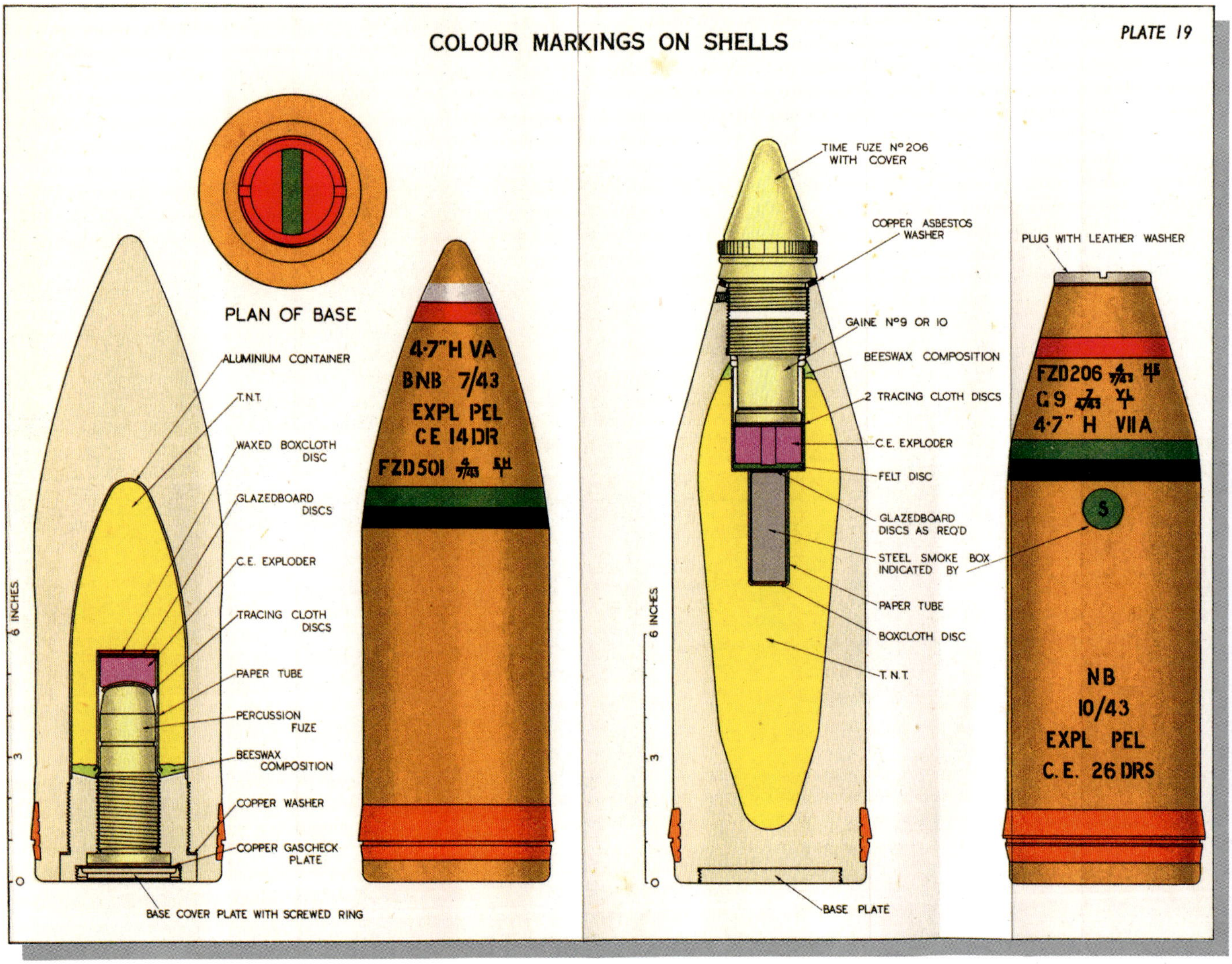

Fuze, Time No. 400 Mk I & II

The No. 400 Fuze Time was used on the star shell. Timed fuzes used either a clockwork mechanism or a powder train that burned for a specific time before setting off the main charge.

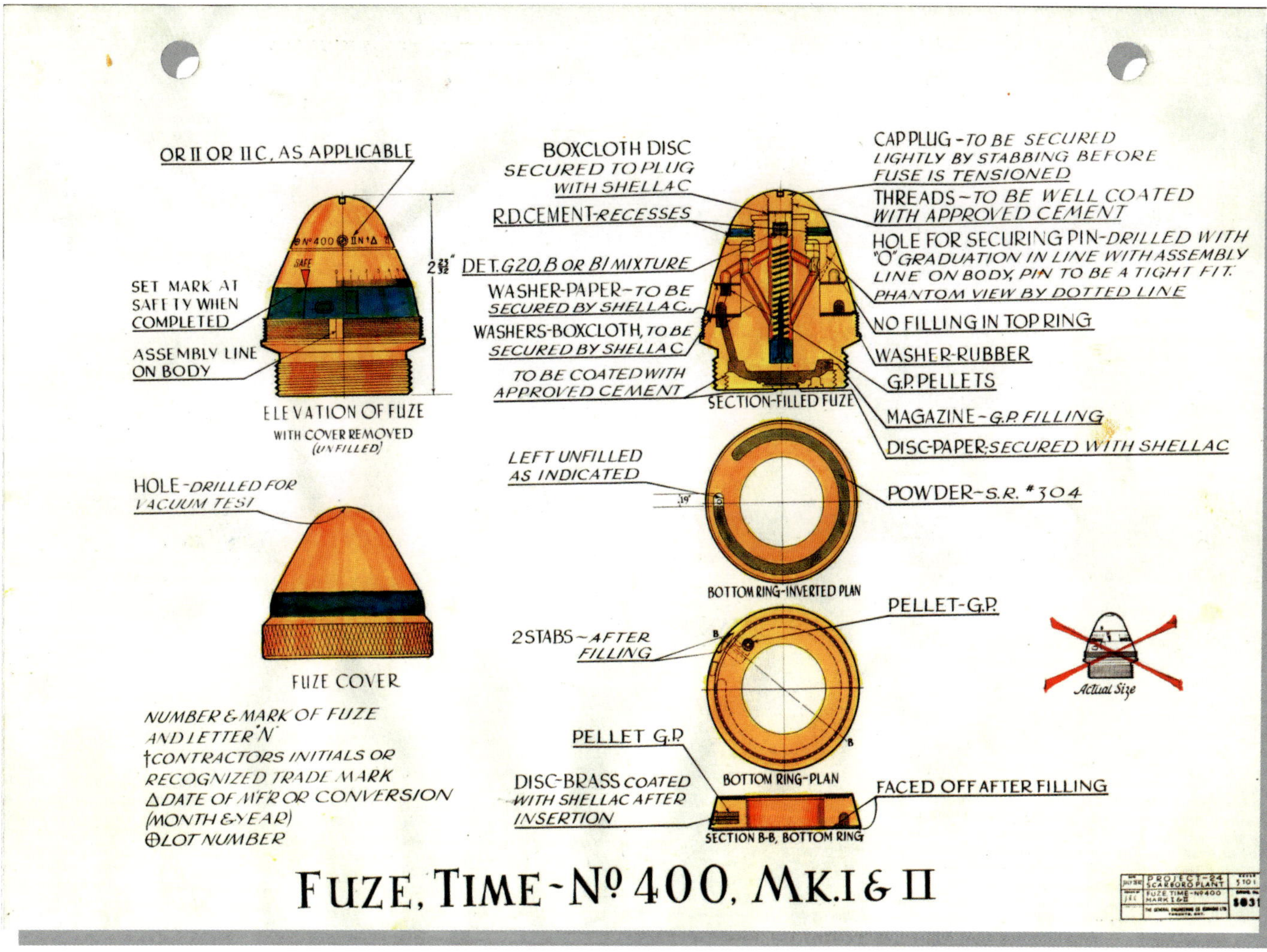

Fuze, Time No. 206 Mark I

The inner workings of a timed fuze. High-explosive shells were fuzed with a standard No. 208 mechanical fuze and used on the dual-purpose 5.25-inch naval gun, 3.7- and 4.5-inch AA guns. As described elsewhere in the manual: "These fuzes depend for their action on a clockwork mechanism consisting of a train of wheels, driven by a spring or by centrifugal weights, and controlled by an escapement. At the end of the time as set, the mechanism releases a lever which allows a striker to be driven on a detonator to fire a magazine."

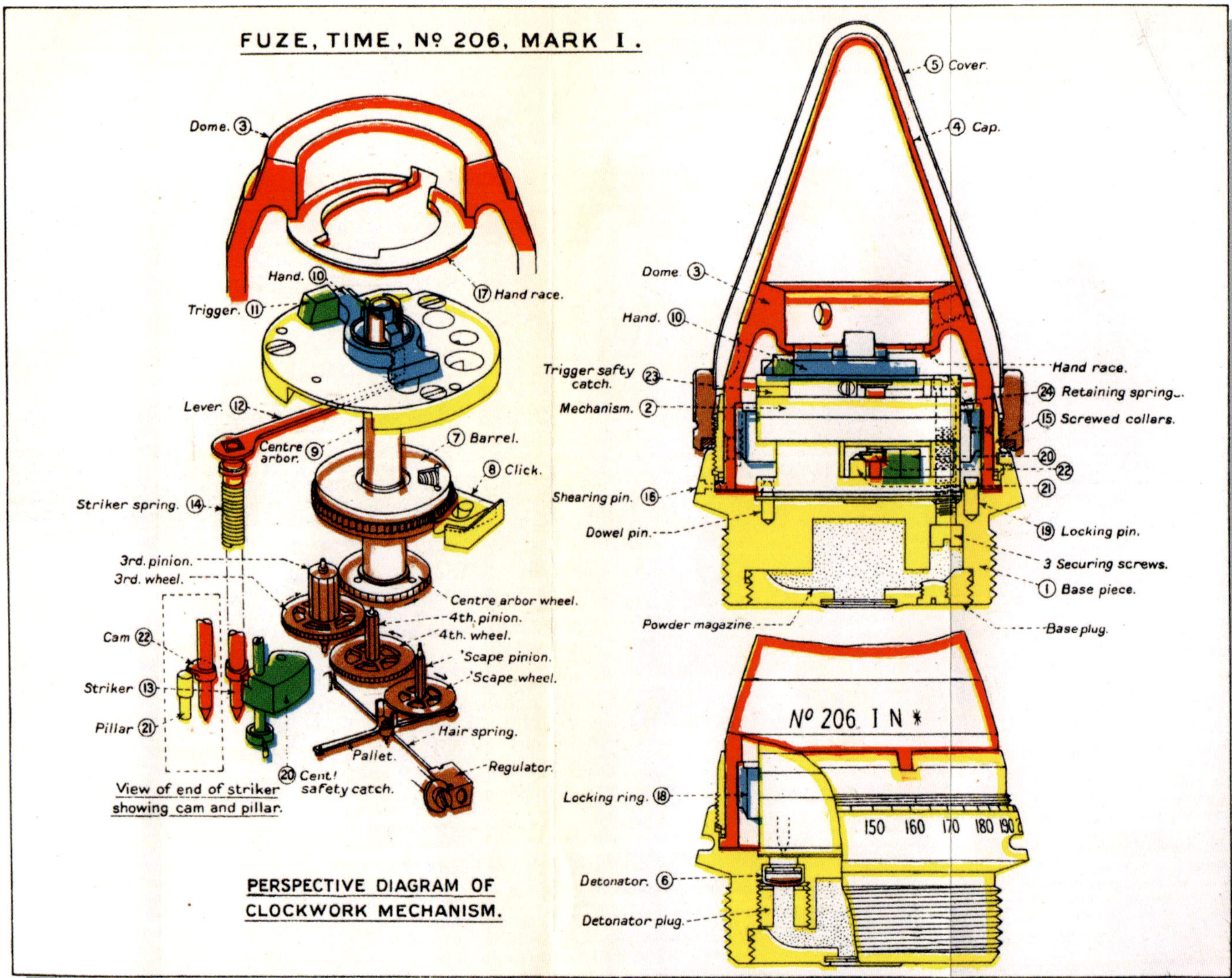

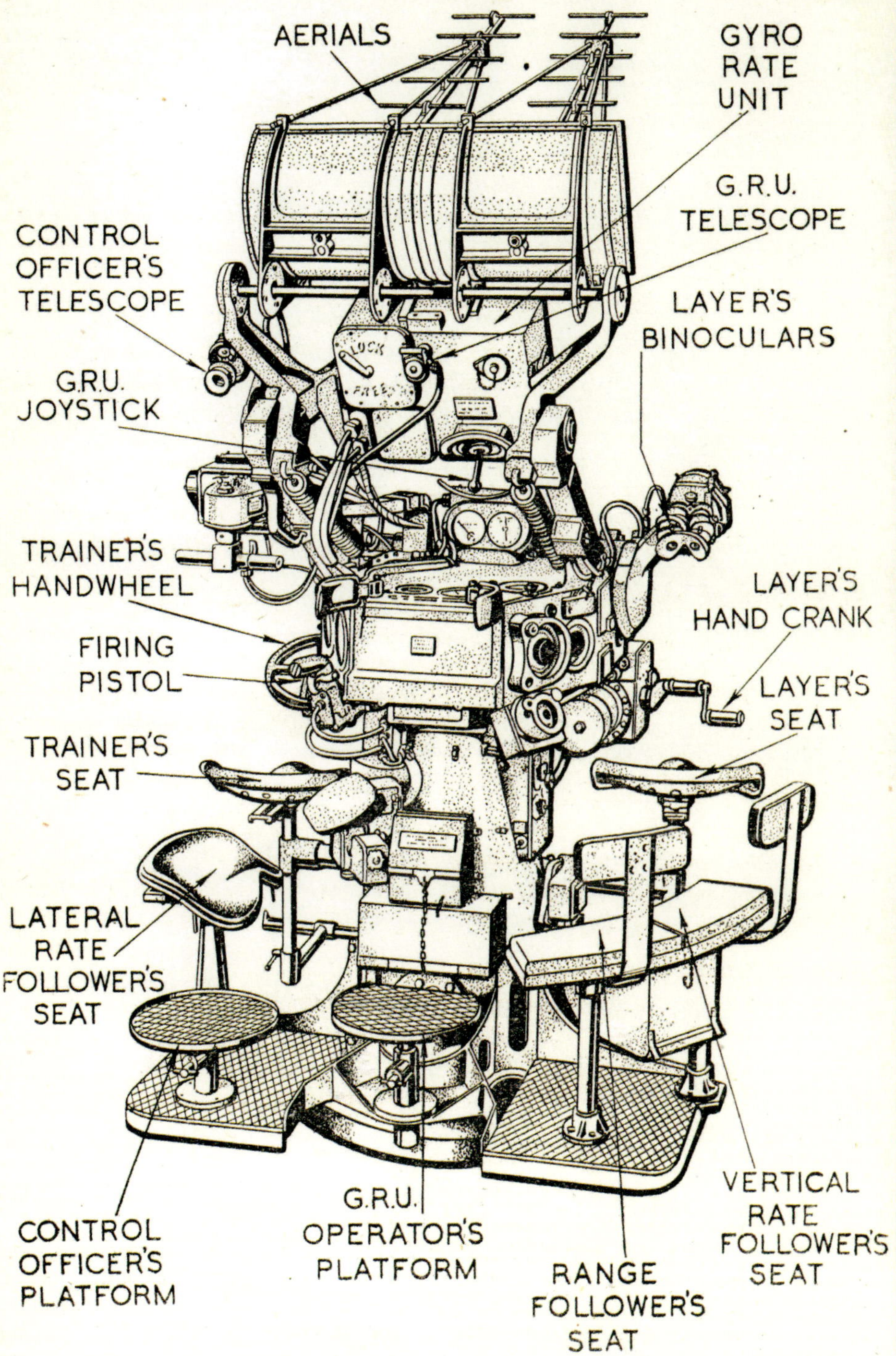

Diagram 33.—POM-POM DIRECTOR, MARK IV.

Pom-pom Director Mark IV

In the early years of the war, pom-pom gunners had to aim with open sights or the aid of any calculating instrument. This method wasted ammunition and was not efficient. The introduction of the Mk IV Director was a huge improvement. Using gyroscopes coupled with an optical rangefinder and Type 282 radar, target information was fed into an on-director computer that produced an accurate fire control solution.

Binocular Pattern 1900A

See first. Shoot first. Hit first. Spotting the enemy before he saw you gave the observer a huge tactical advantage. Binoculars and lookouts played a critical role. As radar was introduced, the role of the lookout was still vital. Radar had its limitations and wasn't always perfect. Lookouts were divided into the following classes: AA, surface and night lookouts. Surface lookouts were subdivided into far, near and fog lookouts.

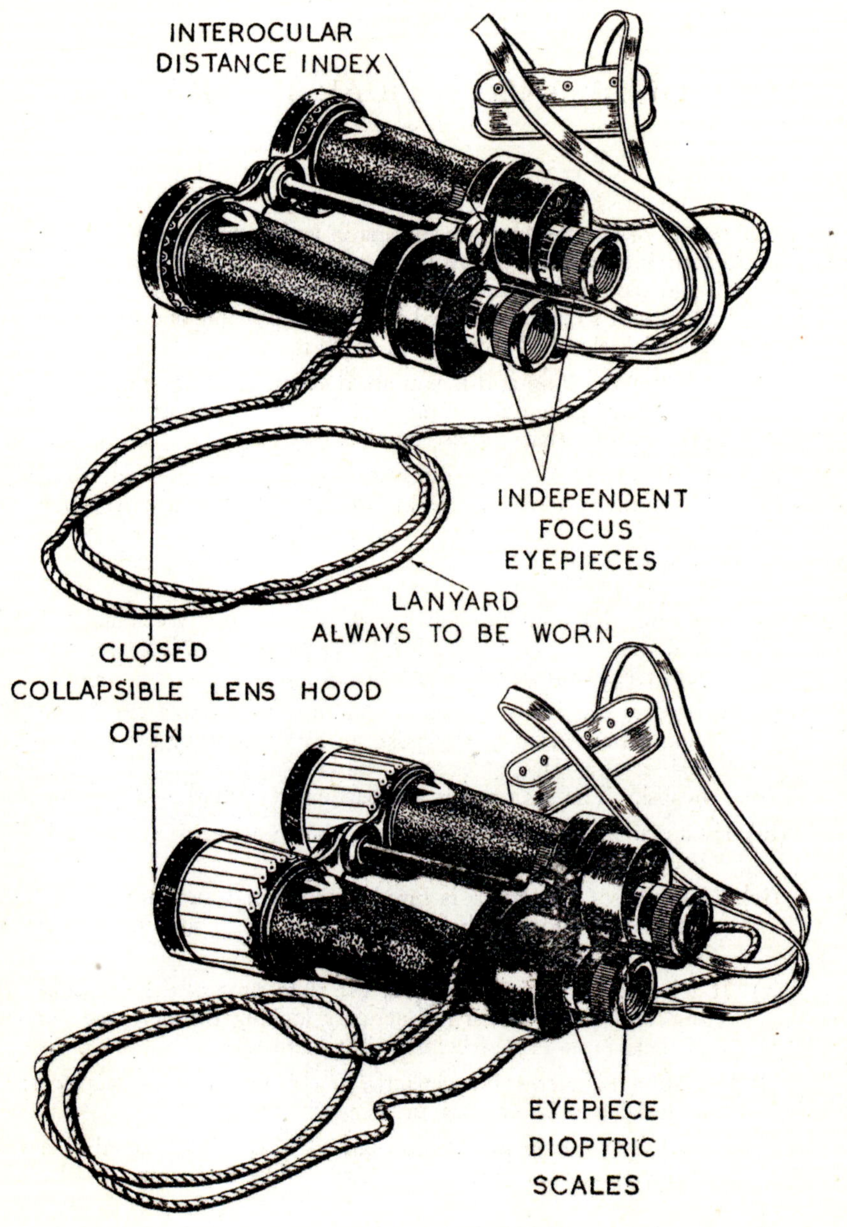

Diagram 36.—BINOCULAR PATTERN 1900A.

Diagram 9.—TYPICAL ARRANGEMENT OF D.C.T. CREW.

Arrangement of Direct Control Tower Crew

The director sight is situated in the foremost part of the director control tower and has a director layer and director trainer as its crew. The gyroscope, in the middle, is housed between the two stabilized telescopes and, besides keeping the prisms upright in the telescopes, has an attachment that will fire the guns automatically at the right moment.

Modern Fire Control Table

Hitting a moving ship from another moving warship was extremely difficult. The modern fire control table, which was fitted to RN cruisers, was an analog computer that calculated the range, speed, direction and elevation of the guns and time of flight of the outgoing shells required before the guns were fired.

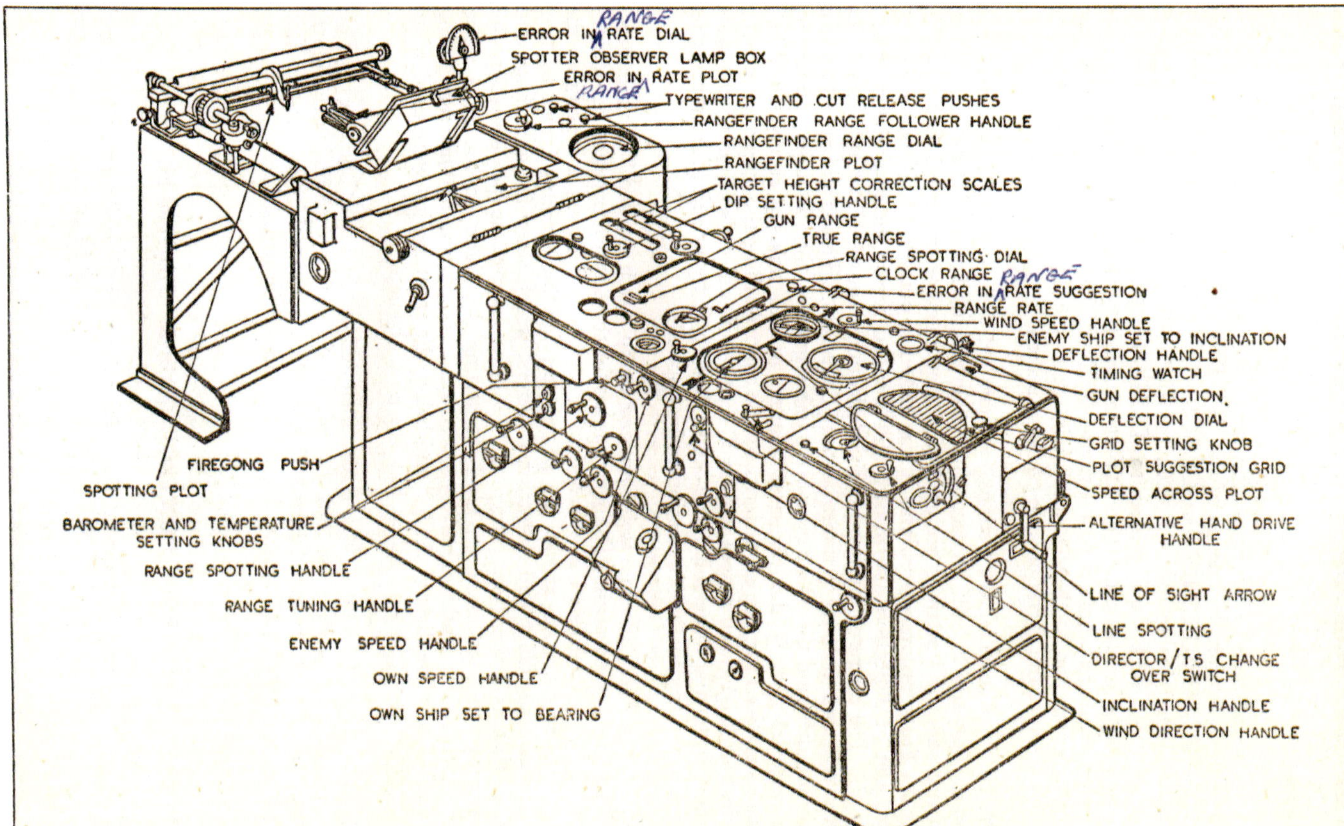

Diagram 19.—TYPICAL MODERN FIRE CONTROL TABLE.

2-Pounder Octuple Pom-Pom Mount

The last line of defence. British *Illustrious*-class carriers were equipped with six eight-barreled (octuple) two-pounder gun mounts. These were used against low-flying and dive-bombing aircraft at ranges of 2.7 km (3,000 yards) or less.

20 mm Oerlikon

This gun was the most widely produced and used by the Allied navies in World War II. It was equipped by everything from PT boats and trawlers to the largest battleships. It was a reliable and accurate weapon, but as the war progressed, its decreasing effectiveness against aircraft (especially Japanese kamikaze aircraft) revealed its limitations.

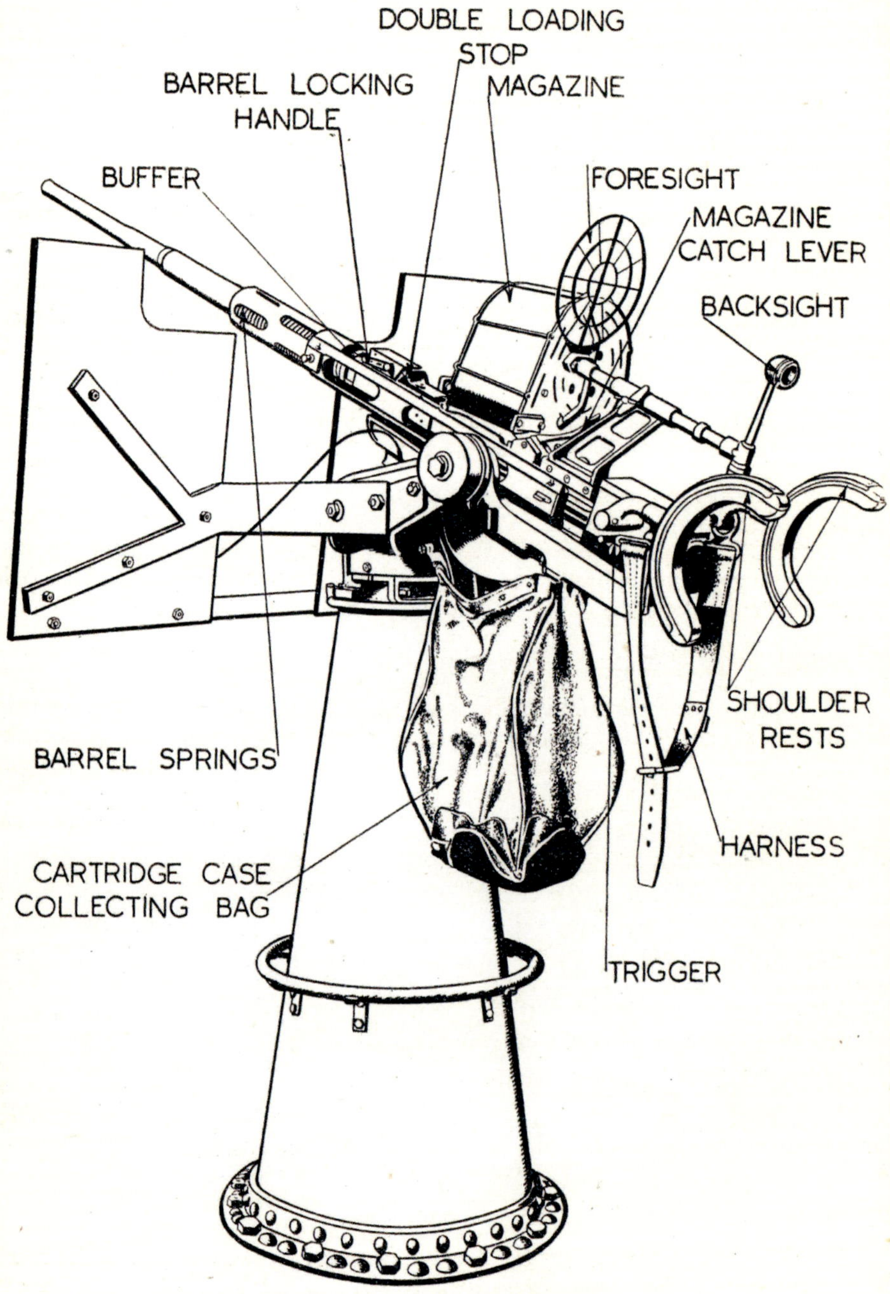

Diagram 35.—20mm. OERLIKON GUN.

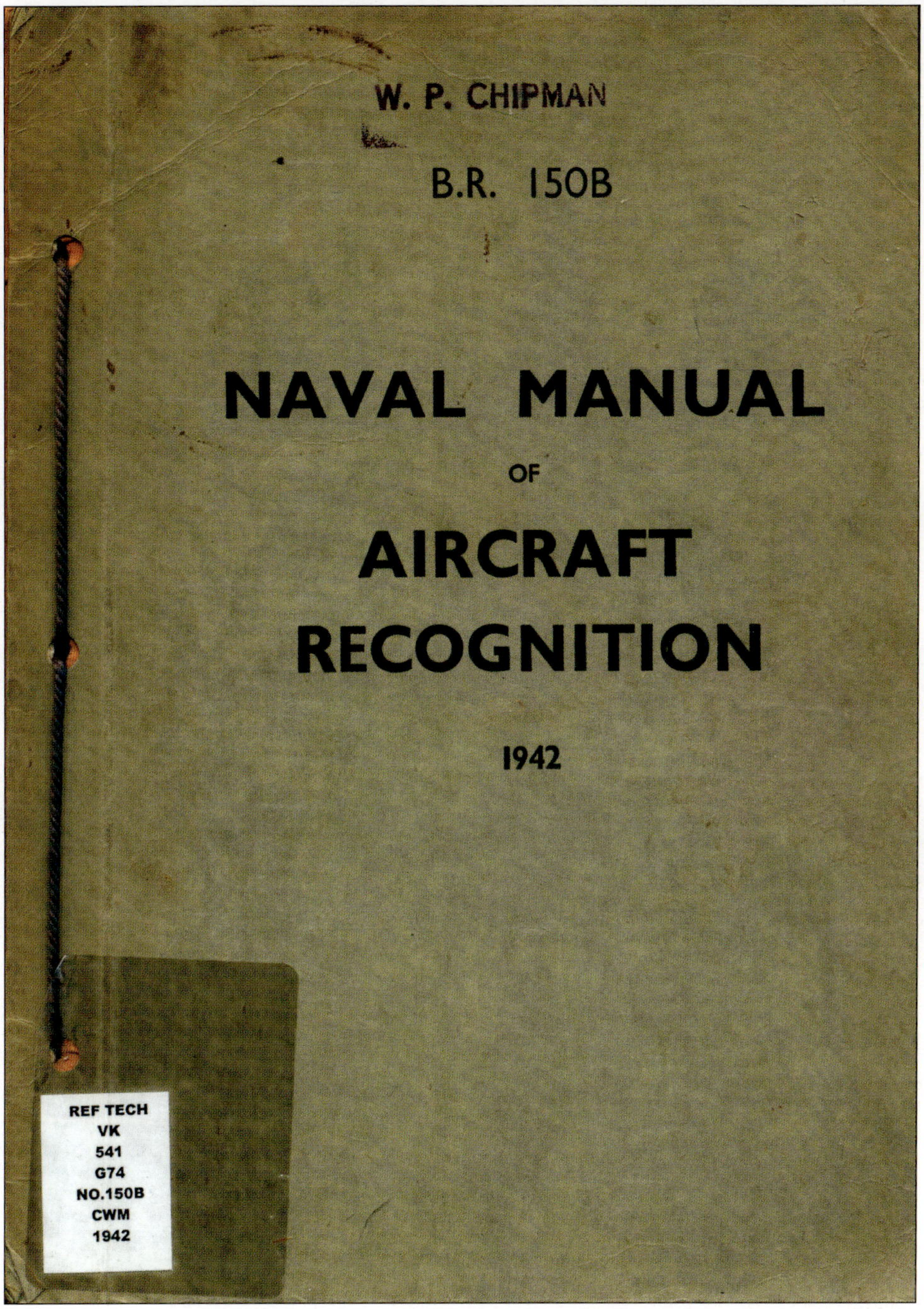

British Naval Manual of Aircraft Recognition, 1942

These manuals were continually updated as new Allied and Axis aircraft types entered service.

Anti-Aircraft Posters

These comical posters were produced to remind naval AA gunners of some very basic fundamentals. The first was aircraft identification. This skill was hard to master, and friendly fire incidents were common. An aircraft approaching a ship in a combat zone was considered hostile until identified and was often fired upon. The other skill to master was to aim and shoot where an aircraft was going to be rather than directly at it.

PERCEVAL.
"Can't you blighters see I'm on your side."

Luftwaffe Maritime Aircraft

In the early years of the war, Luftwaffe long-range maritime aircraft provided the U-boat arm with far-reaching reconnaissance and direct bombing attacks on convoys. The most famous was the Focke-Wulf Fw 200 Condor, known as the 'Scrouge of the Atlantic.' Though no more than 8 to 10 Fw 200s were in service at any one time, they managed to sink 52 ships between August 1940 and February 1941. With the introduction of the HMS *Audacity*, the Royal Navy's first escort carrier, the Fw 200's days were numbered. Between September and December 1941, fighters from the *Audacity* shot down four Fw 200s, all but ending the threat of Luftwaffe maritime aircraft in the Atlantic.

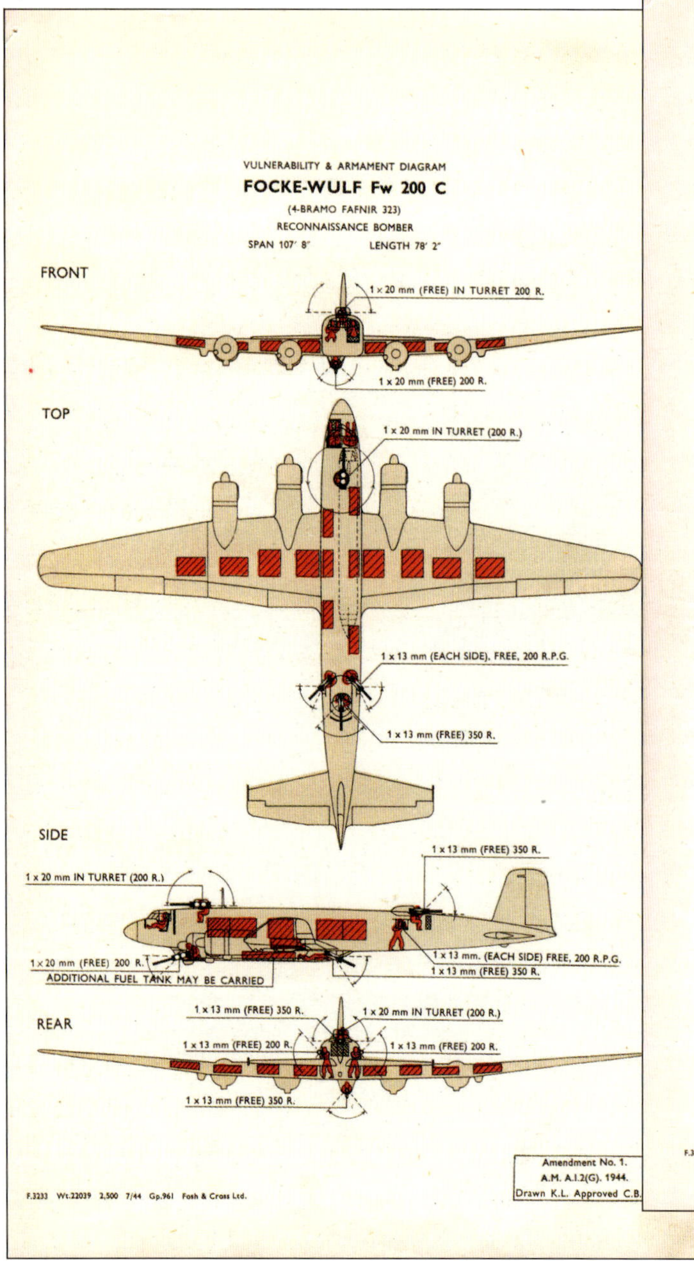

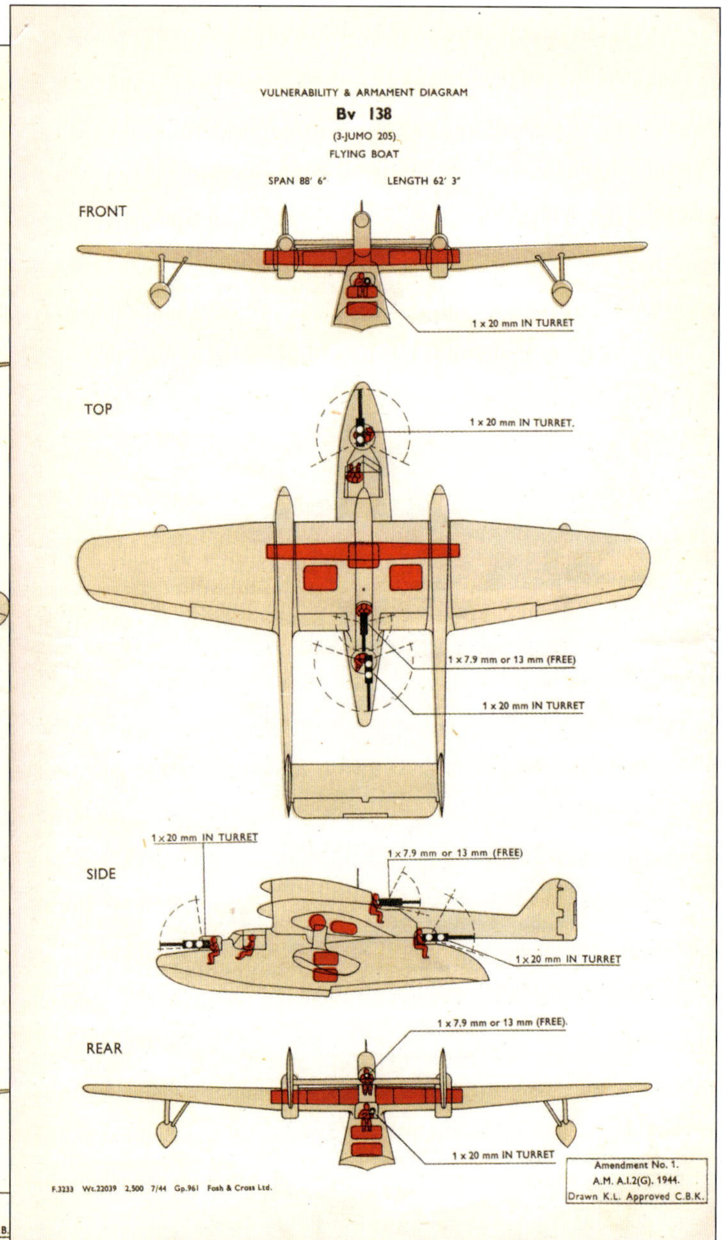

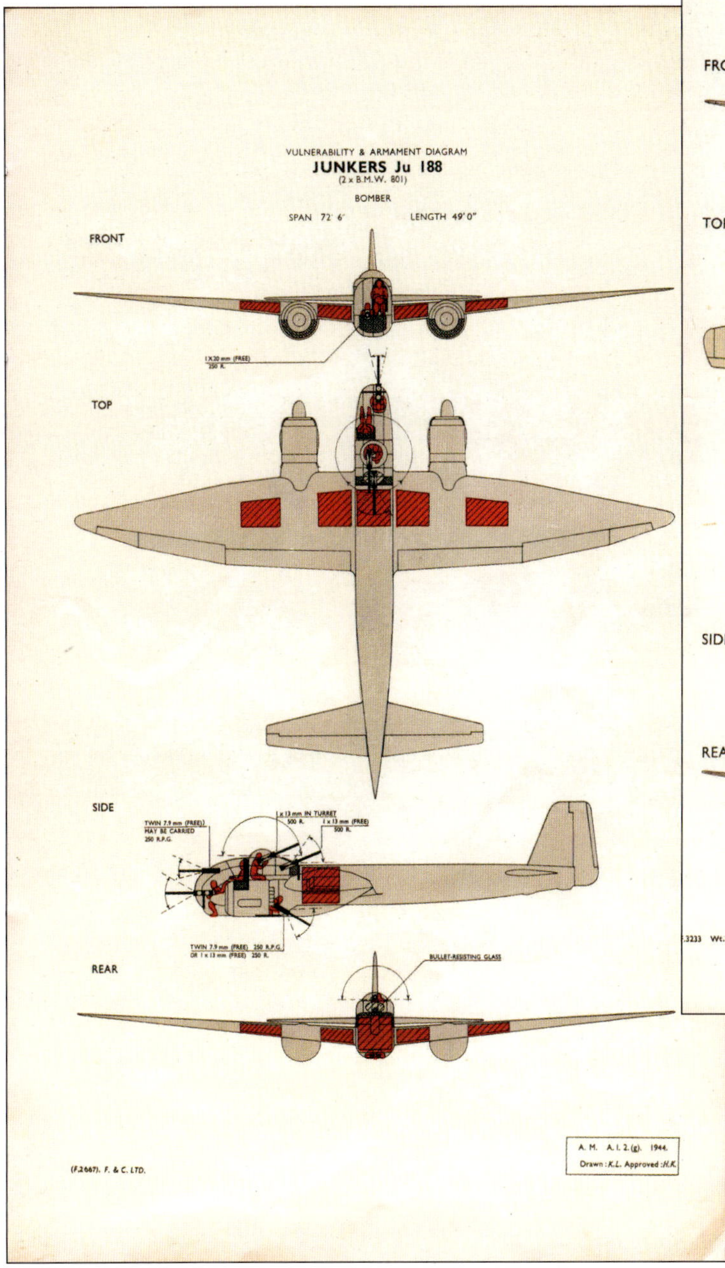
VULNERABILITY & ARMAMENT DIAGRAM
JUNKERS Ju 188
(2 x B.M.W. 801)
BOMBER
SPAN 72' 6"
LENGTH 49' 0"
FRONT
TOP
SIDE
REAR
BULLET-RESISTING GLASS
A. M. A.I.2.(g). 1944.
Drawn : K.L. Approved : H.K.
(F.2667). F. & C. LTD.

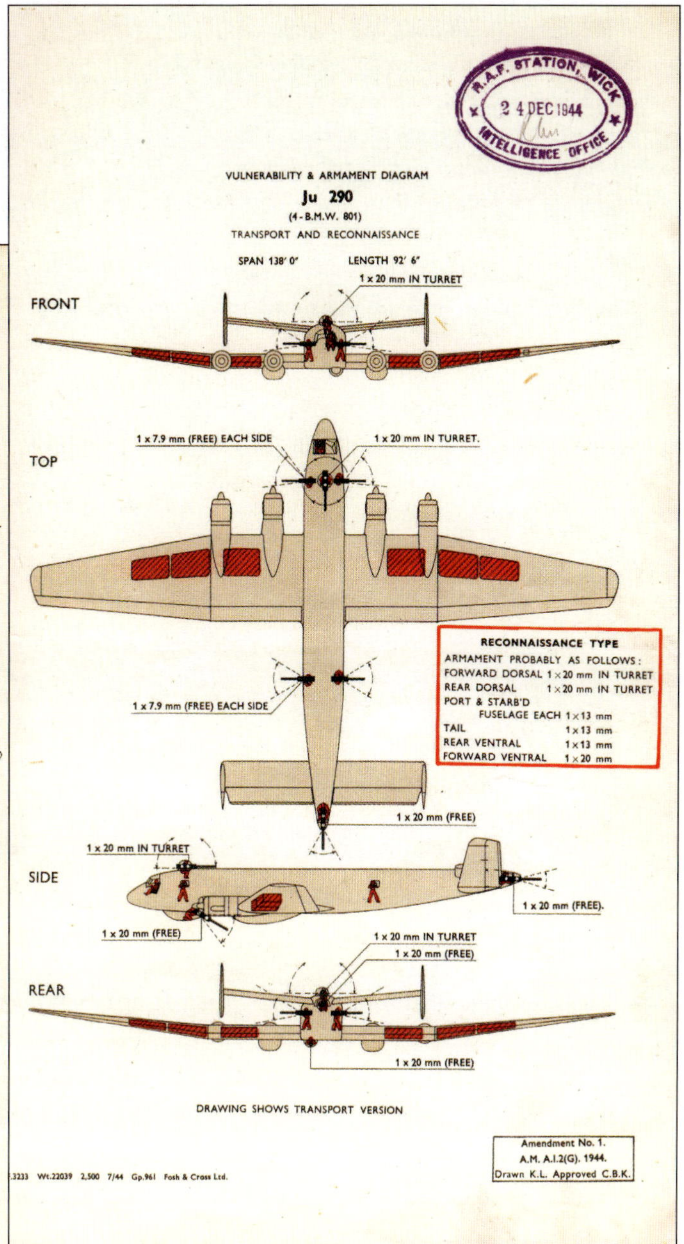
R.A.F. STATION, WICK
24 DEC 1944
INTELLIGENCE OFFICE
VULNERABILITY & ARMAMENT DIAGRAM
Ju 290
(4-B.M.W. 801)
TRANSPORT AND RECONNAISSANCE
SPAN 138' 0"
LENGTH 92' 6"
FRONT
1 x 20 mm IN TURRET
TOP
1 x 7.9 mm (FREE) EACH SIDE
1 x 20 mm IN TURRET.
1 x 7.9 mm (FREE) EACH SIDE
RECONNAISSANCE TYPE
ARMAMENT PROBABLY AS FOLLOWS:
FORWARD DORSAL 1 x 20 mm IN TURRET
REAR DORSAL 1 x 20 mm IN TURRET
PORT & STARB'D
FUSELAGE EACH 1 x 13 mm
TAIL 1 x 13 mm
REAR VENTRAL 1 x 13 mm
FORWARD VENTRAL 1 x 20 mm
1 x 20 mm (FREE)
SIDE
1 x 20 mm IN TURRET
1 x 20 mm (FREE)
1 x 20 mm (FREE).
REAR
1 x 20 mm IN TURRET
1 x 20 mm (FREE)
1 x 20 mm (FREE)
DRAWING SHOWS TRANSPORT VERSION
Amendment No. 1.
A.M. A.I.2(G). 1944.
Drawn K.L. Approved C.B.K.
Wt.22039 2,500 7/44 Gp.961 Fosh & Cross Ltd.

HMCS *Skeena*

The first destroyers built for the Royal Canadian Navy (RCN) were the *River*-class HMCS *Skeena* and her sister ship HMCS *Saguenay*. *Skeena* weighed 1,358 tonnes (1,497 tons) and was 98 meters (322 feet) long with a beam of nearly 10 meters (32 feet). Its top speed was an impressive 31 knots, and it was armed with four 4.7-inch guns, two two-pounder guns, five machine guns and eight torpedo tubes. The RCN started the war with six *River*-class destroyers. These were British-built to Canadian specifications and were fast and well-armed. By the war's end, the RCN had grown to be the third-largest navy in the world, with 270 ocean escort vessels.

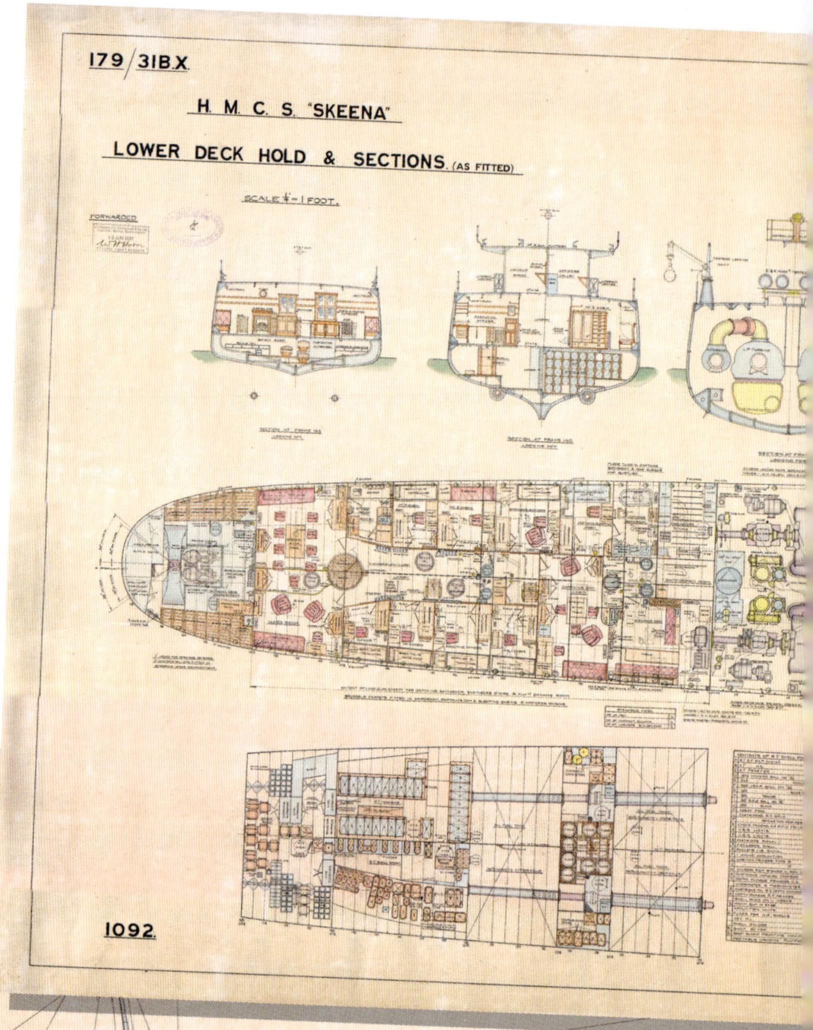

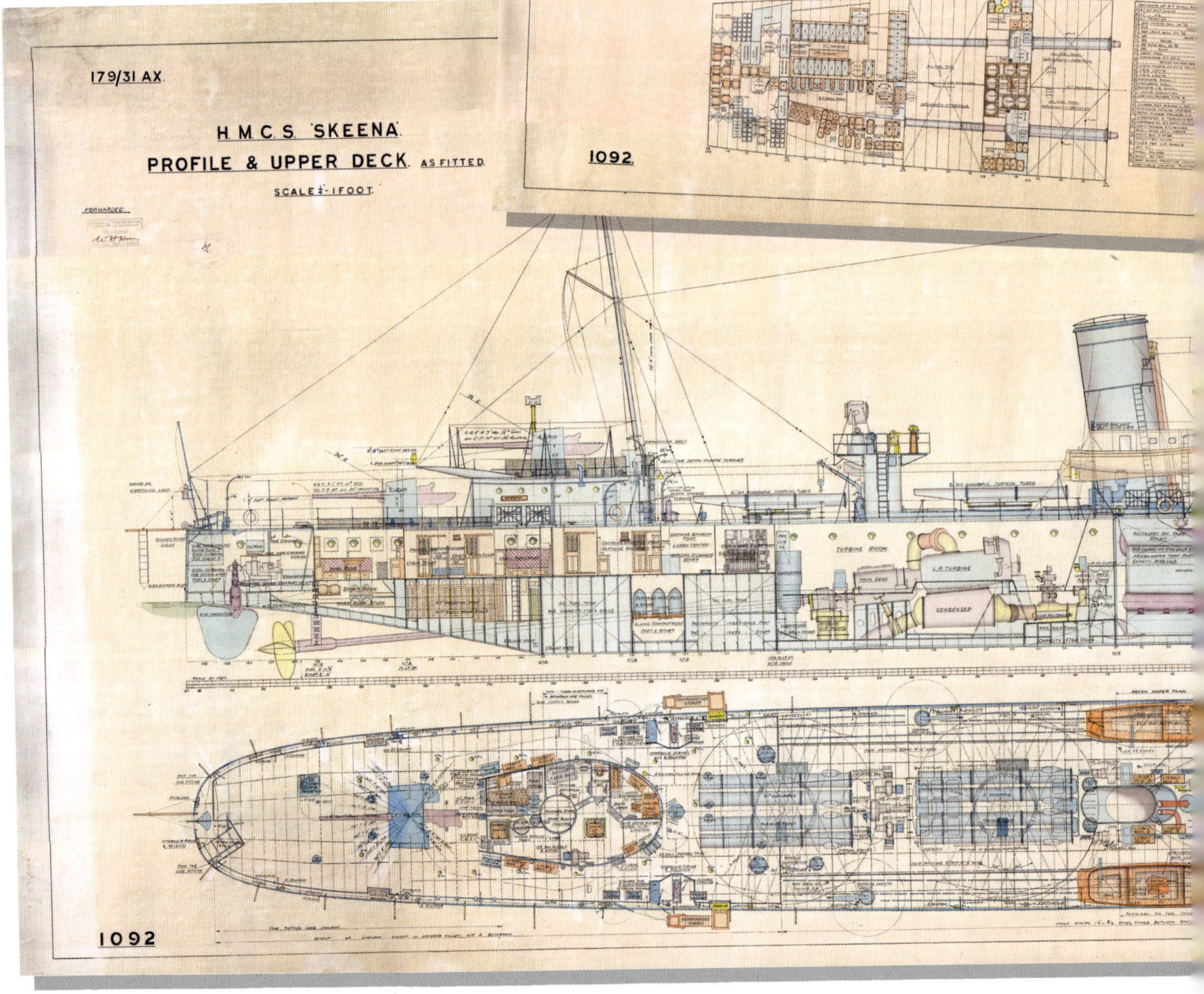

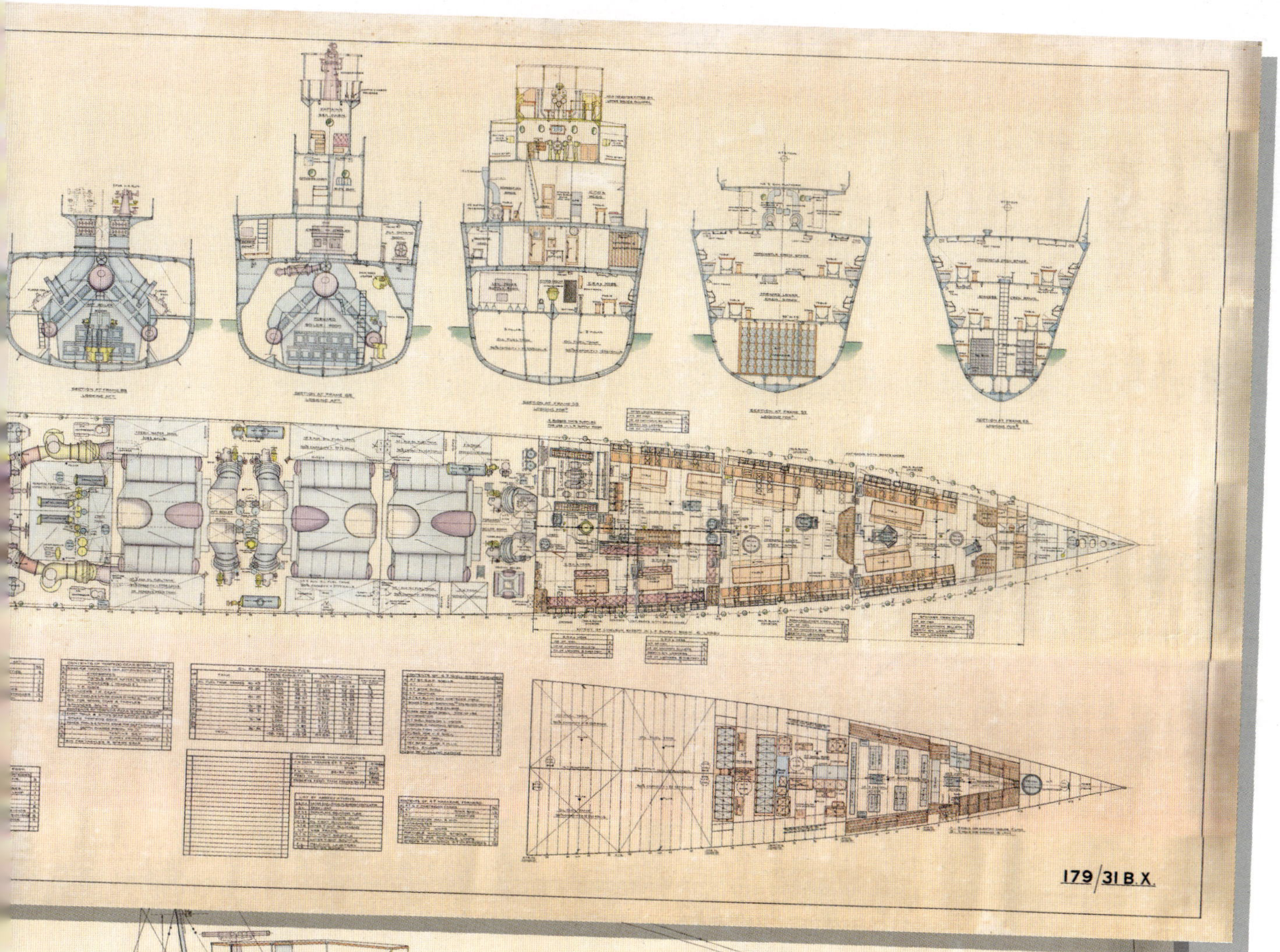
179/31 B.X.

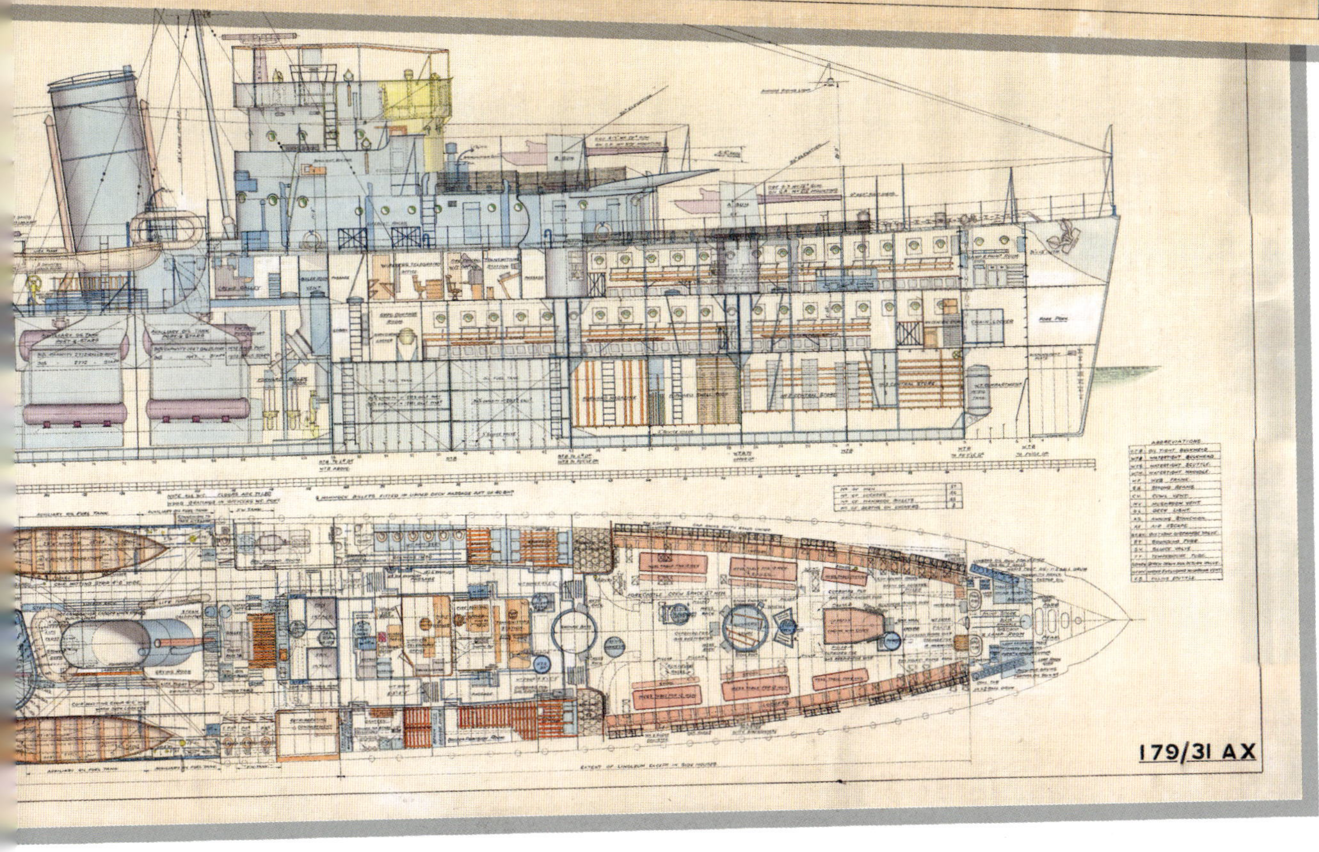
179/31 AX

HMS *Hood*

HMS *Hood* was built in 1918. The battlecruiser *Hood* is arguably one of the most famous ships in the Royal Navy. At 37,376 tonnes (41,200 tons) and 262 meters (860 feet) in length, *Hood* was for many years the largest and most prestigious warship in the world. After her initial design, some 3,130 tonnes (3,450 tons) of additional armor and protective plating were added, but the ship was still considered vulnerable to long-range plunging fire.

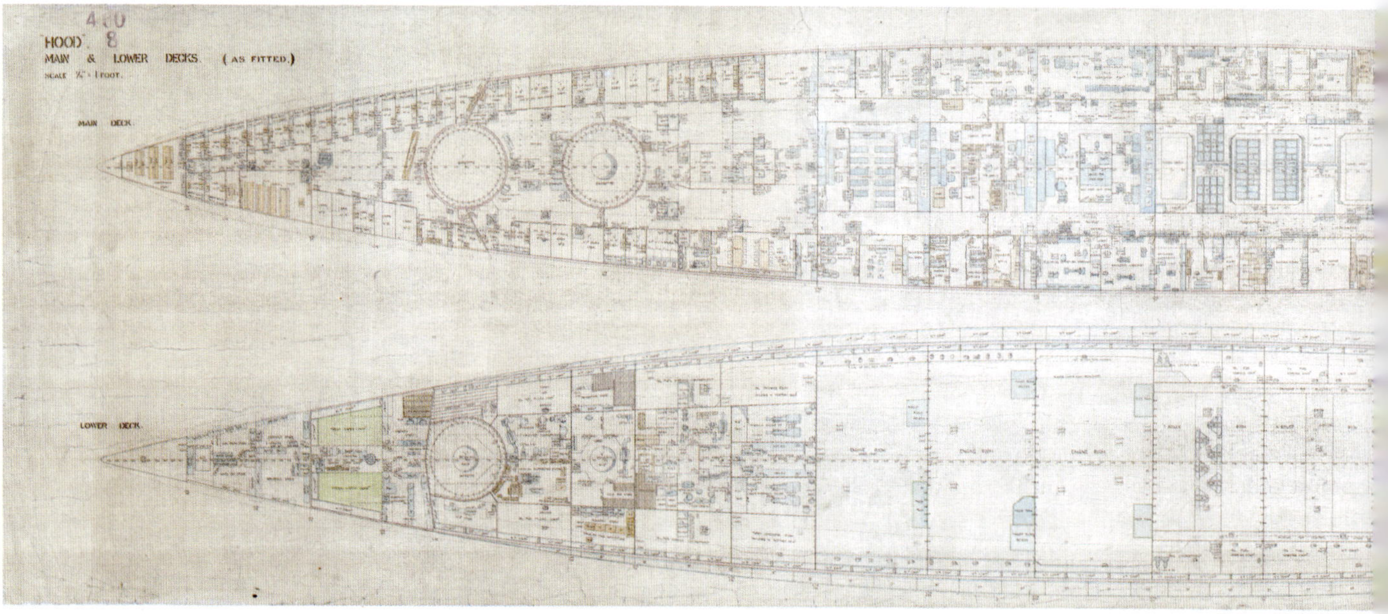

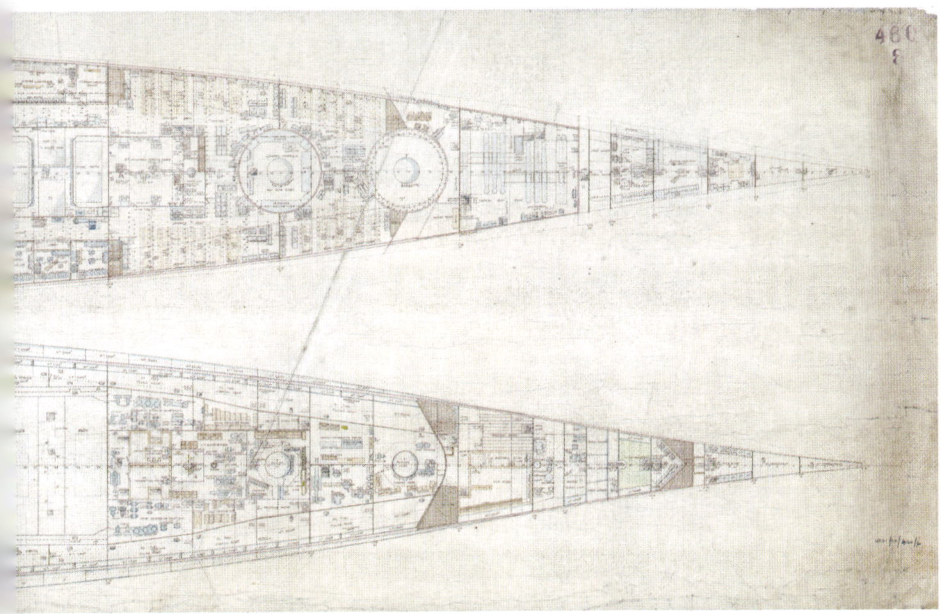

HMS *Hood* Lower Decks

The below-deck living spaces were ventilated by electric exhaust fans leading to open air and external vents. To provide heat, the air could be passed through steam-powered heaters. Many accounts describe *Hood's* ventilation as poor, leading to outbreaks of tuberculosis and other respiratory ailments.

HMS *Hood* Armament

When built, the HMS *Hood* was armed with eight 15-inch guns with 120 rounds per gun, 12 single 5.5-inch guns with 200 rounds per gun, four single 4-inch AA guns and six 21-inch torpedo tubes.

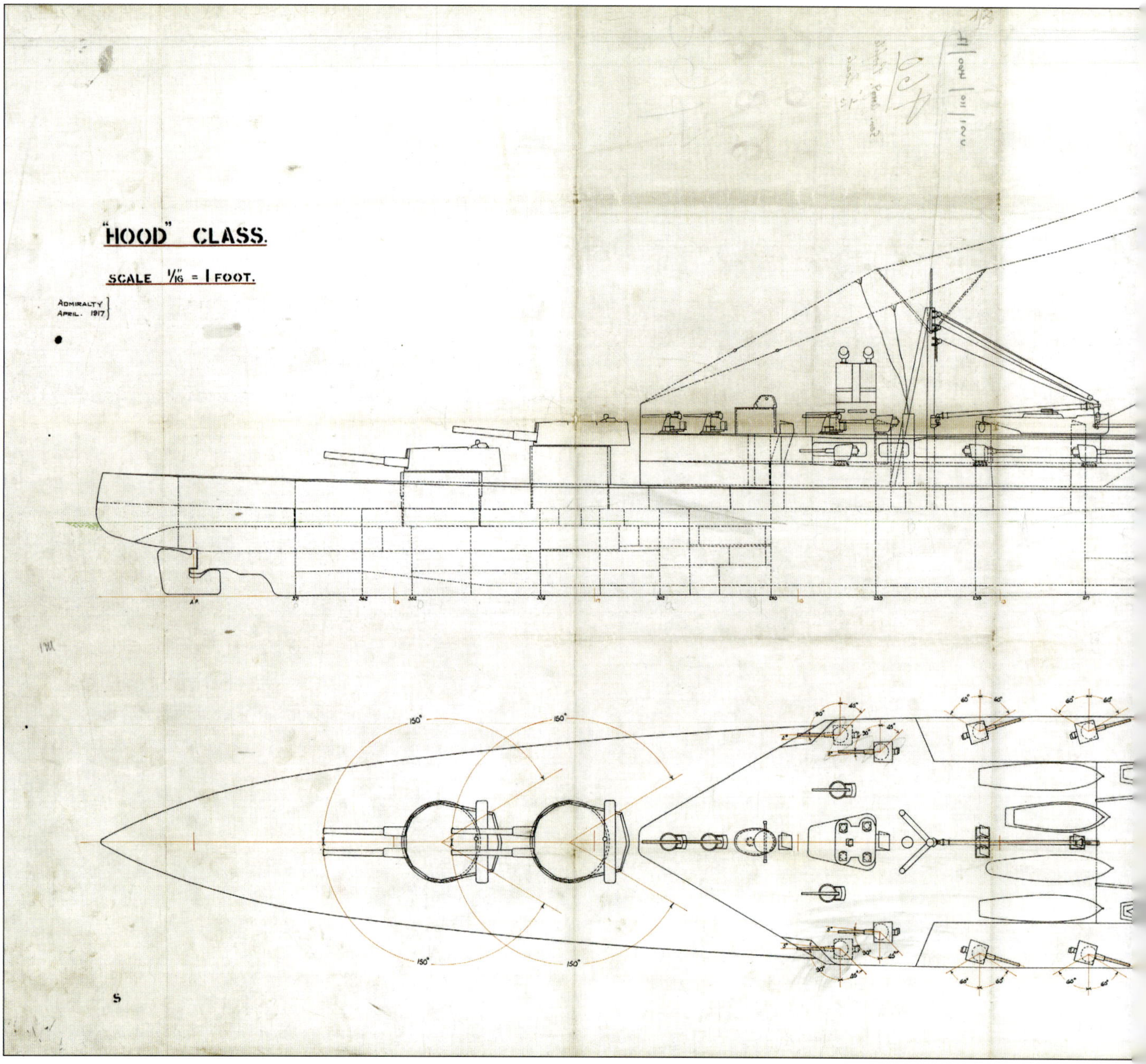

HMS *Resolution* Rigging

HMS *Resolution* was a *Revenge*-class battleship built during the First World War. She was one of the 16 RN battleships in service at the beginning of World War II. All warships carried rigging which consisted of transmitting and receiving aerials for the various radio and electronic navigation systems.

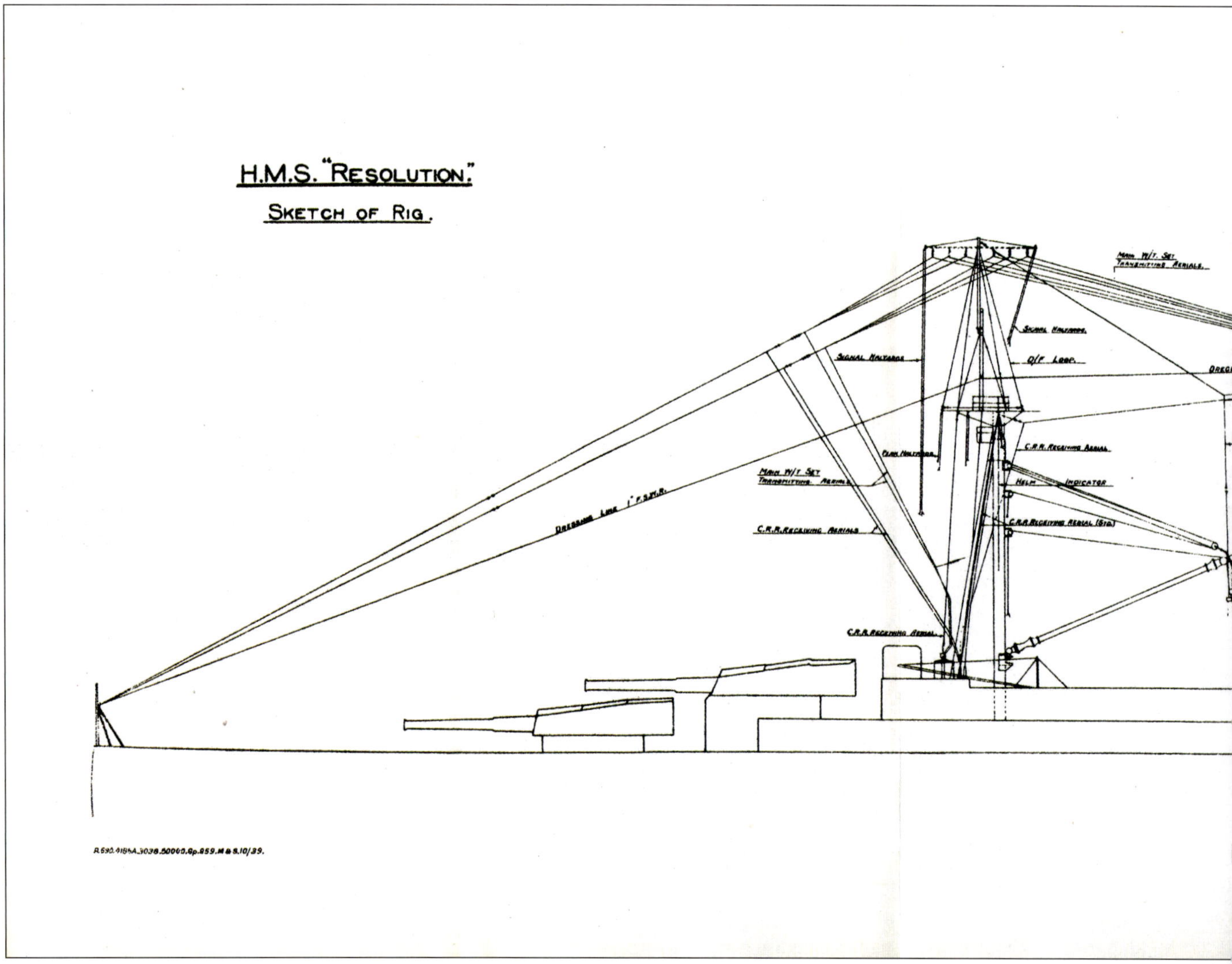

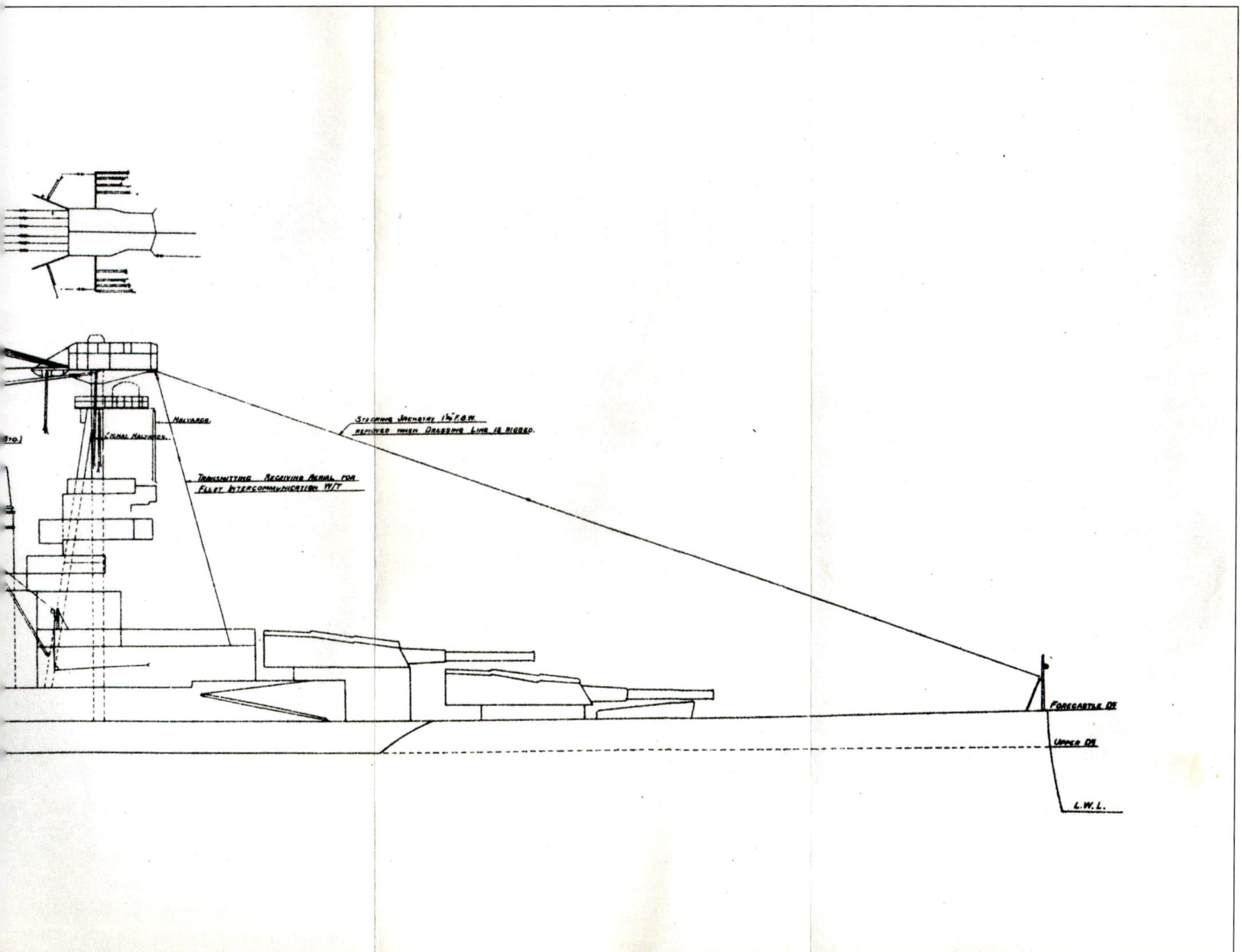
HALYARDS
TRANSMITTING RECEIVING AERIAL FOR FLEET INTERCOMMUNICATION W/T
REMOVED WHEN DRESSING LINE IS RIGGED.
FORECASTLE
UPPER
L.W.L.

British Empire Ship Silhouettes

These ship silhouettes are taken from the *War Vessels Silhouettes Identification Book: British Empire*. The escort carrier HMS *Biter* seems to be pasted in as a late addition before publication. After HMS *Audacity*, the HMS *Biter*, along with the *Avenger* and *Dasher*, were the next escort carriers to enter RN service in the early summer of 1942.

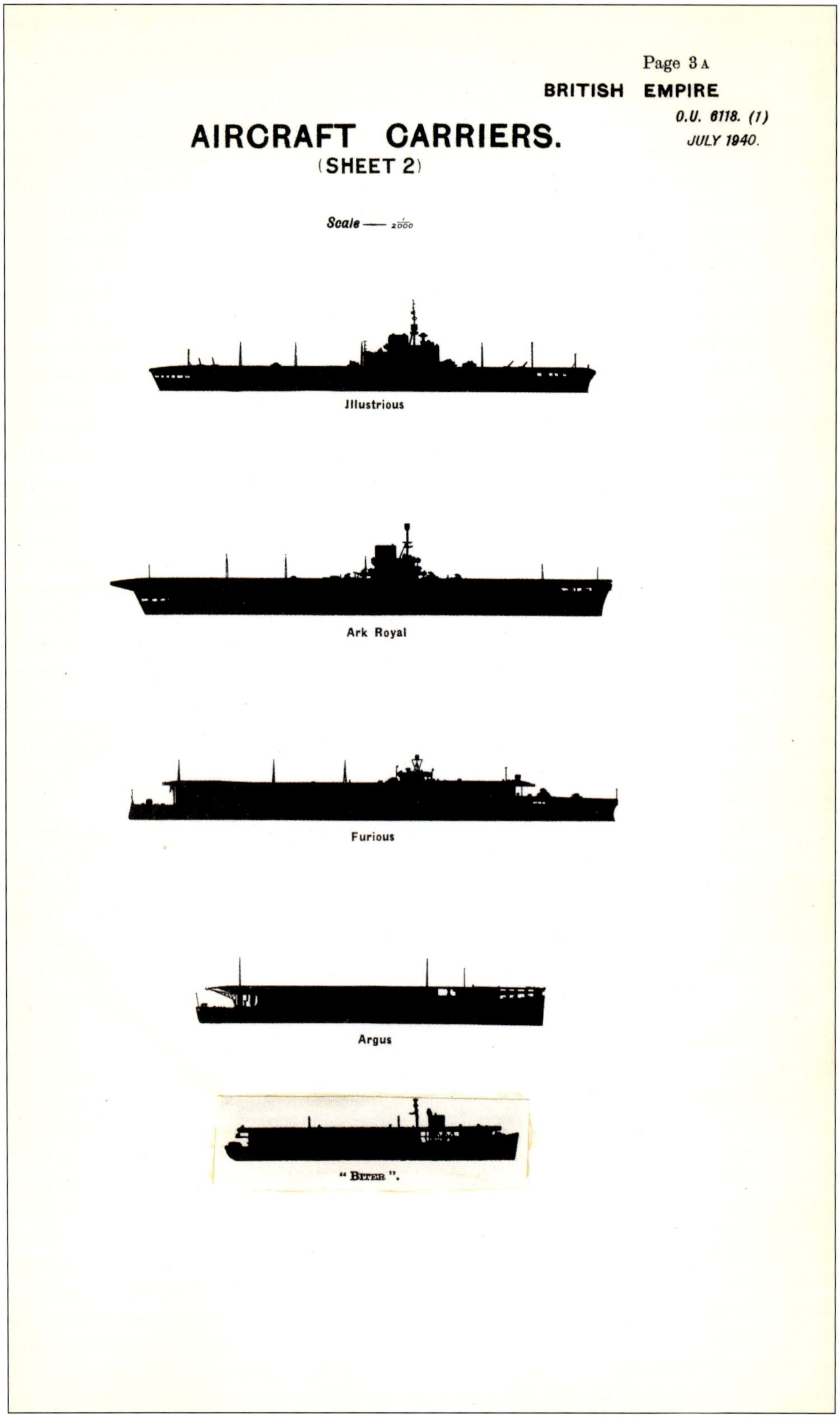
Page 3A

BRITISH EMPIRE

O.U. 6118. (1)

JULY 1940.

AIRCRAFT CARRIERS.

(SHEET 2)

Scale — 1/2000

Illustrious

Ark Royal

Furious

Argus

"BITER".

Page 1

BRITISH EMPIRE

O.U.6118.(1)
JULY, 1941.

BATTLESHIPS

Scale – $\frac{1}{2000}$

Rodney

Queen Elizabeth, Valiant
Valiant has pole mainmast

Royal Sovereign

Warspite

Revenge

Malaya

Resolution

Barham

Ramillies

British Mk XII Aerial Torpedo

This five-piece air diagram illustration is a full-size depiction of the Mk XII aircraft torpedo. The Mk XII was the standard airborne torpedo for both the RAF and Fleet Air Arm for the first half of the war. It weighed 702 kg (1,548 lbs) with a warhead of 176 kg (388 lbs). Its maximum speed was 40 knots for 1,400 meters (1,500 yards). At typical fleet carrier carried between two to three torpedoes for each torpedo bomber.

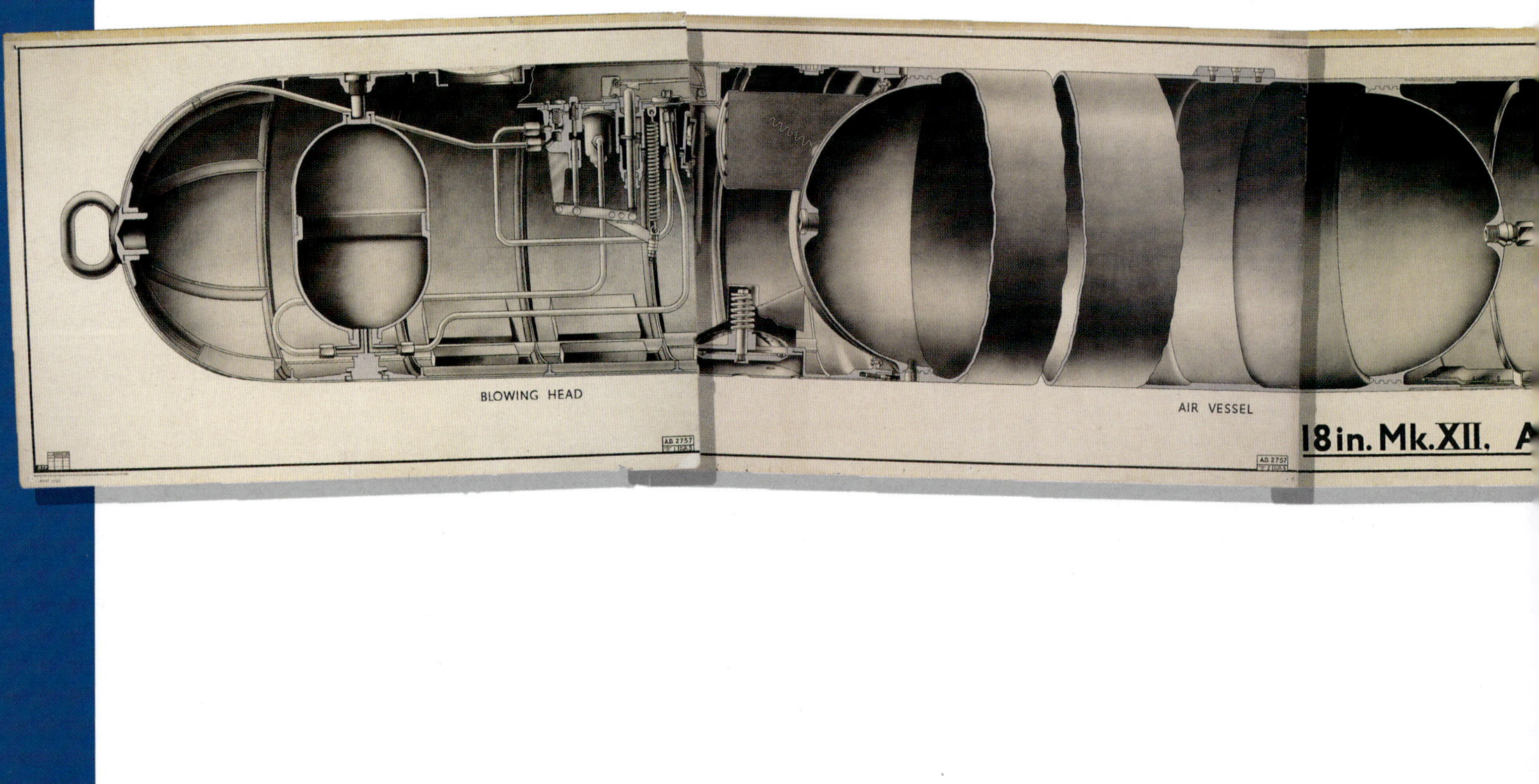

BALANCE CHAMBER
ENGINE ROOM
BUOYANCY CHAMBER
TAIL
FT TORPEDO
KEY TO SYSTEMS
HIGH PRESSURE AIR
LOW PRESSURE AIR
FUEL
OIL
AP 2757
AIR MINISTRY

Depth, Roll and Inclination Recorder

Torpedoes were sophisticated and expensive weapons. When they worked, they were true ship killers. However, there were many problems and failures, especially in the early years of the war. 'Depth, roll and inclination recorders' were inserted into torpedoes to record their depth and movement through the water. These recordings provided data which helped to determine faults and their solutions.

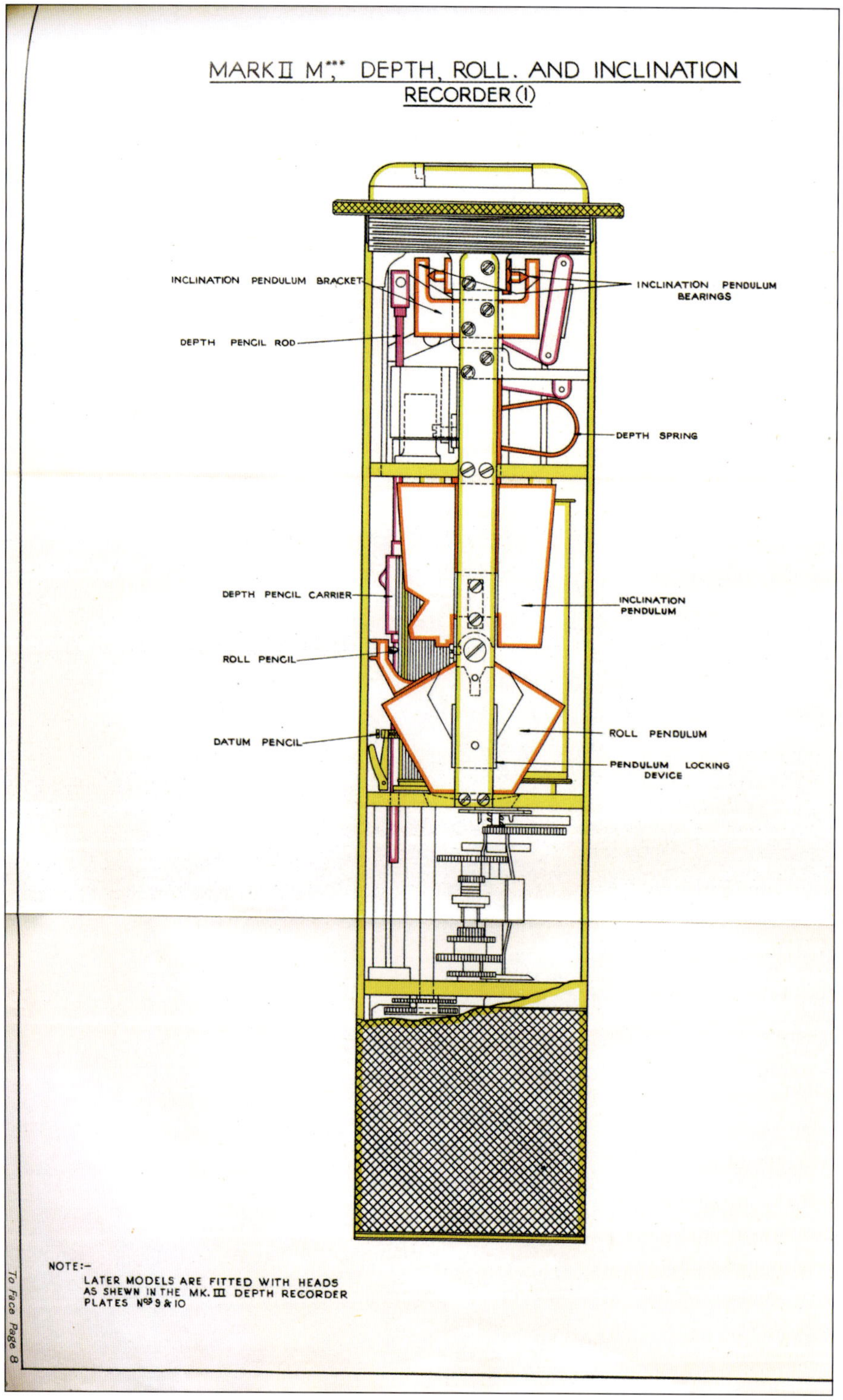

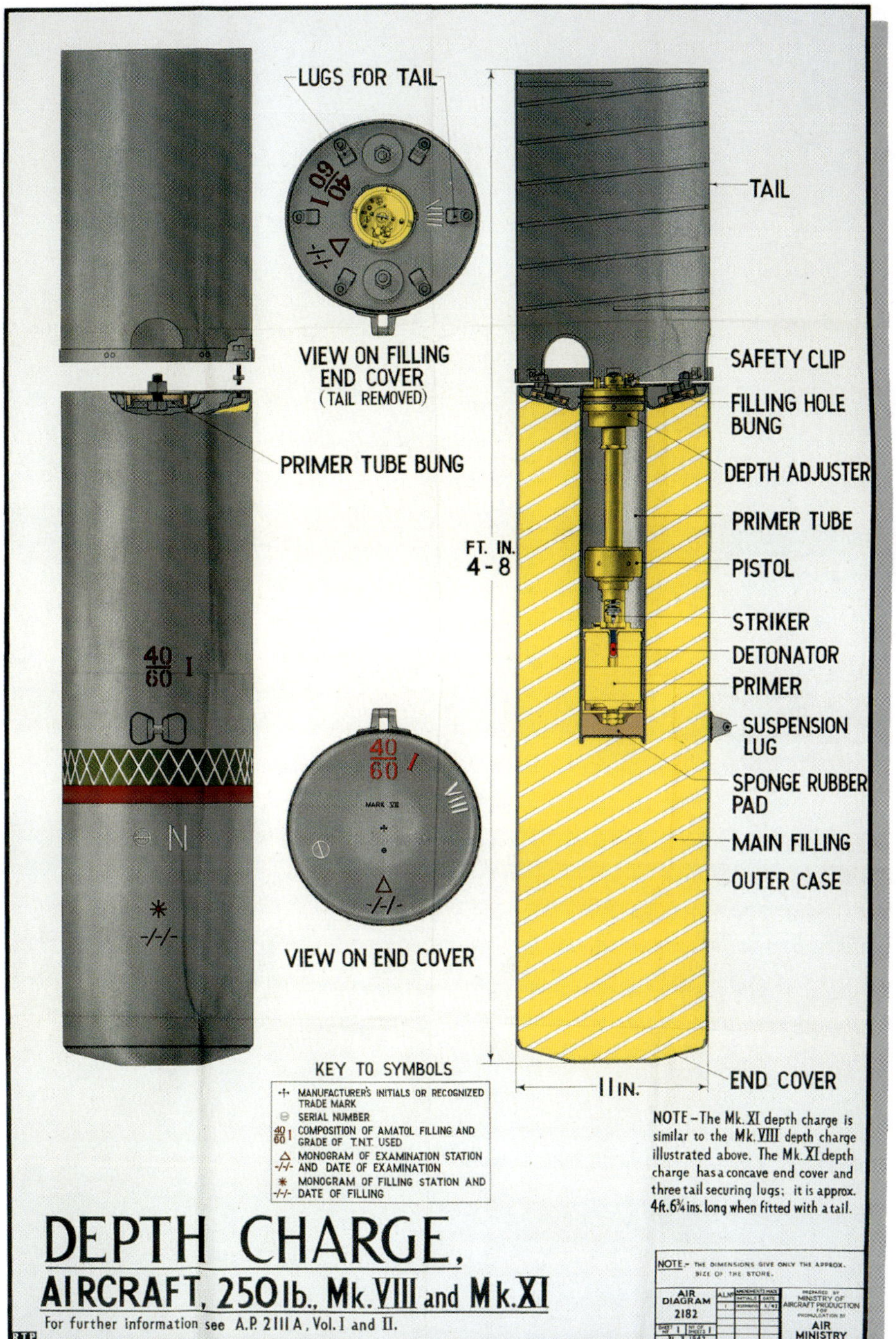

Aerial Depth Charge

One of the most effective weapons against submarines was the air-dropped depth charge. This cutaway drawing shows the British 113 kg (250 lb) Mk VIII and Mk XI depth charge. The Fairey Swordfish could carry up to six 113 kg depth charges.

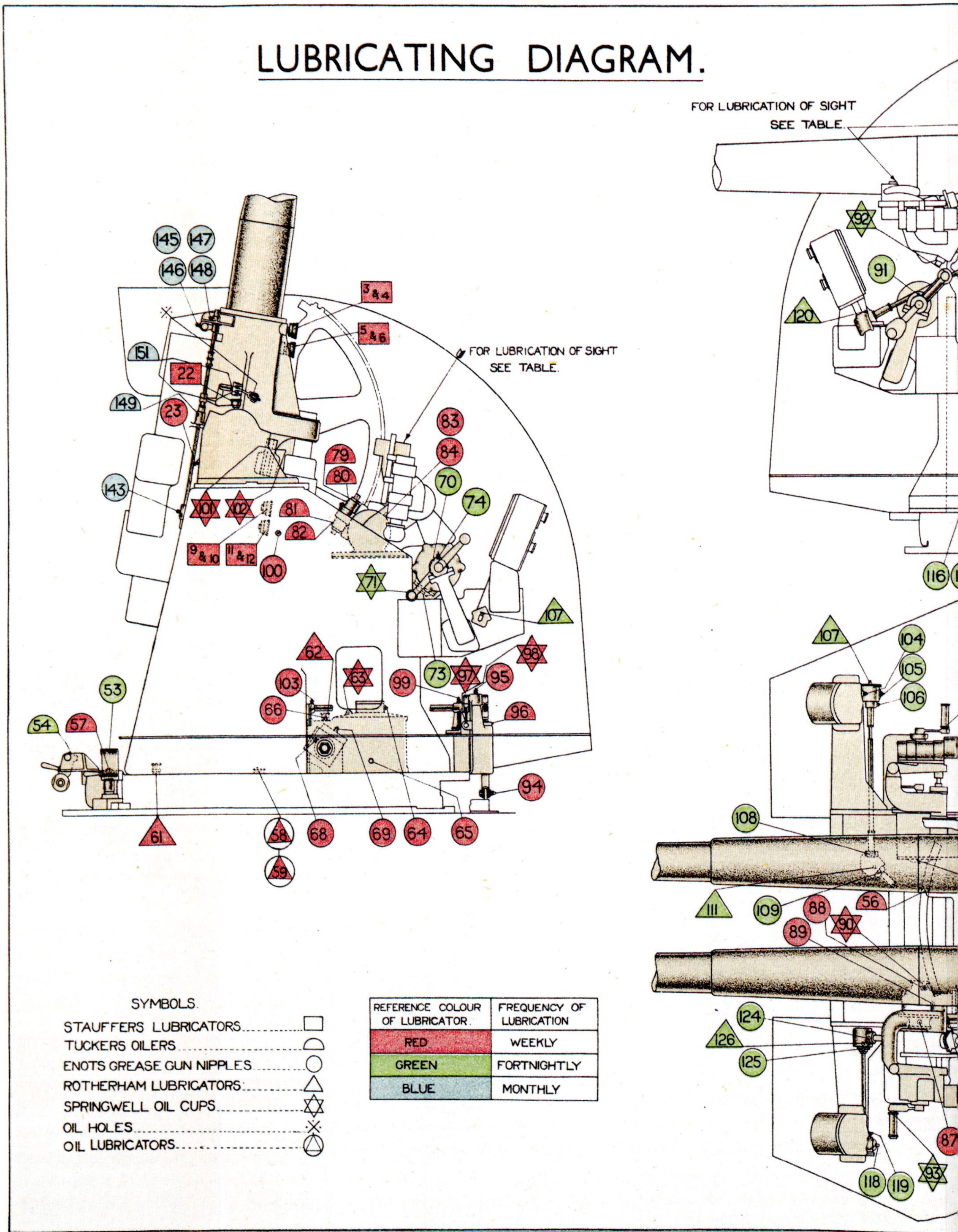

REFERENCE COLOUR OF LUBRICATOR.	FREQUENCY OF LUBRICATION
RED	WEEKLY
GREEN	FORTNIGHTLY
BLUE	MONTHLY

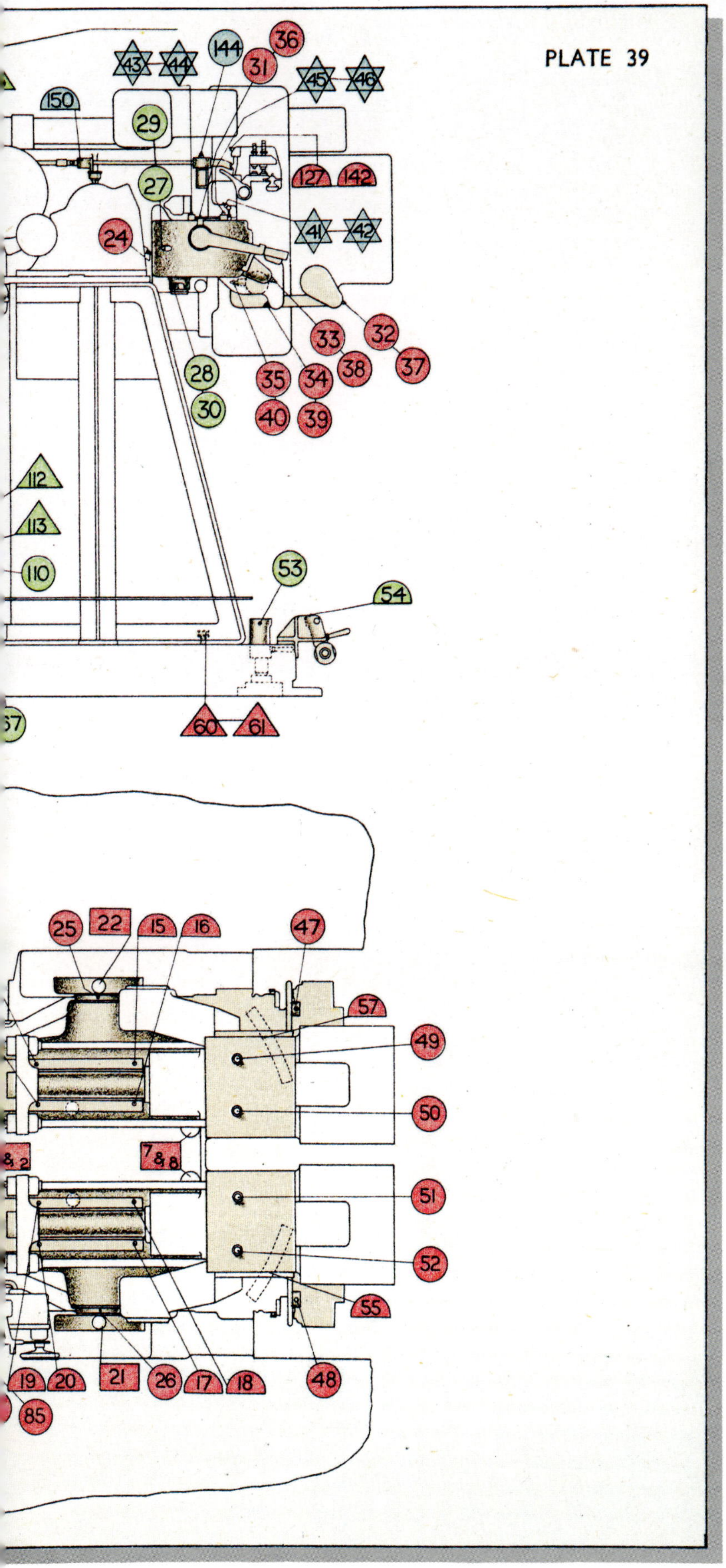

Lubricating Diagram for 4.7-inch Twin Turret Gun

Proper maintenance aboard the ship was critical, especially the guns. When not manning their battle stations, gunners spent their time training and maintaining their guns. This diagram illustrates the key points for lubrication and the maintenance schedule required for each part of the gun.

High Angle (HA) Director Sight

The HA sight was the primary anti-aircraft director sight used by the Royal Navy in World War II. Most battleships and carriers had four HA directors, while cruisers had two or three.

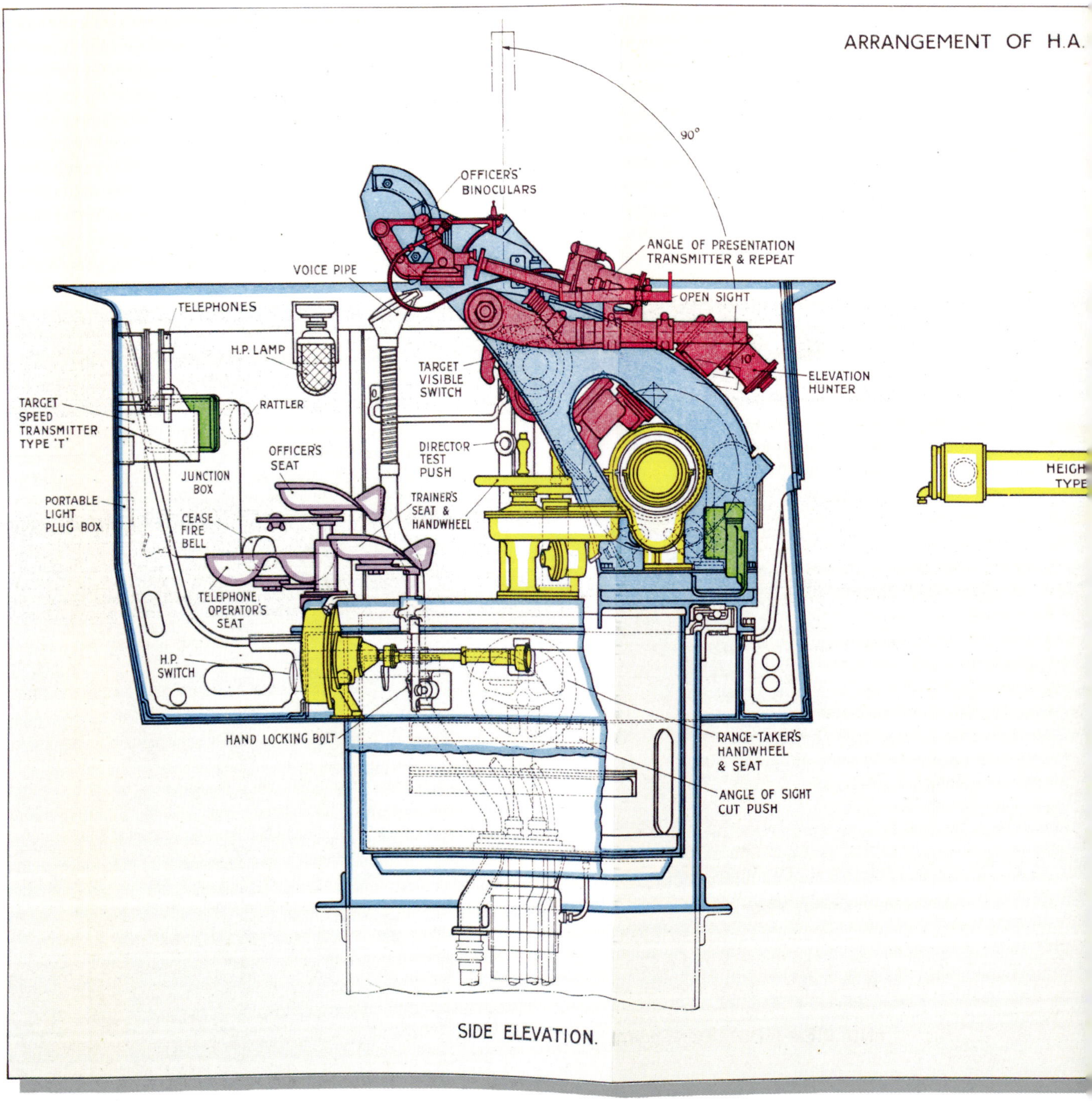

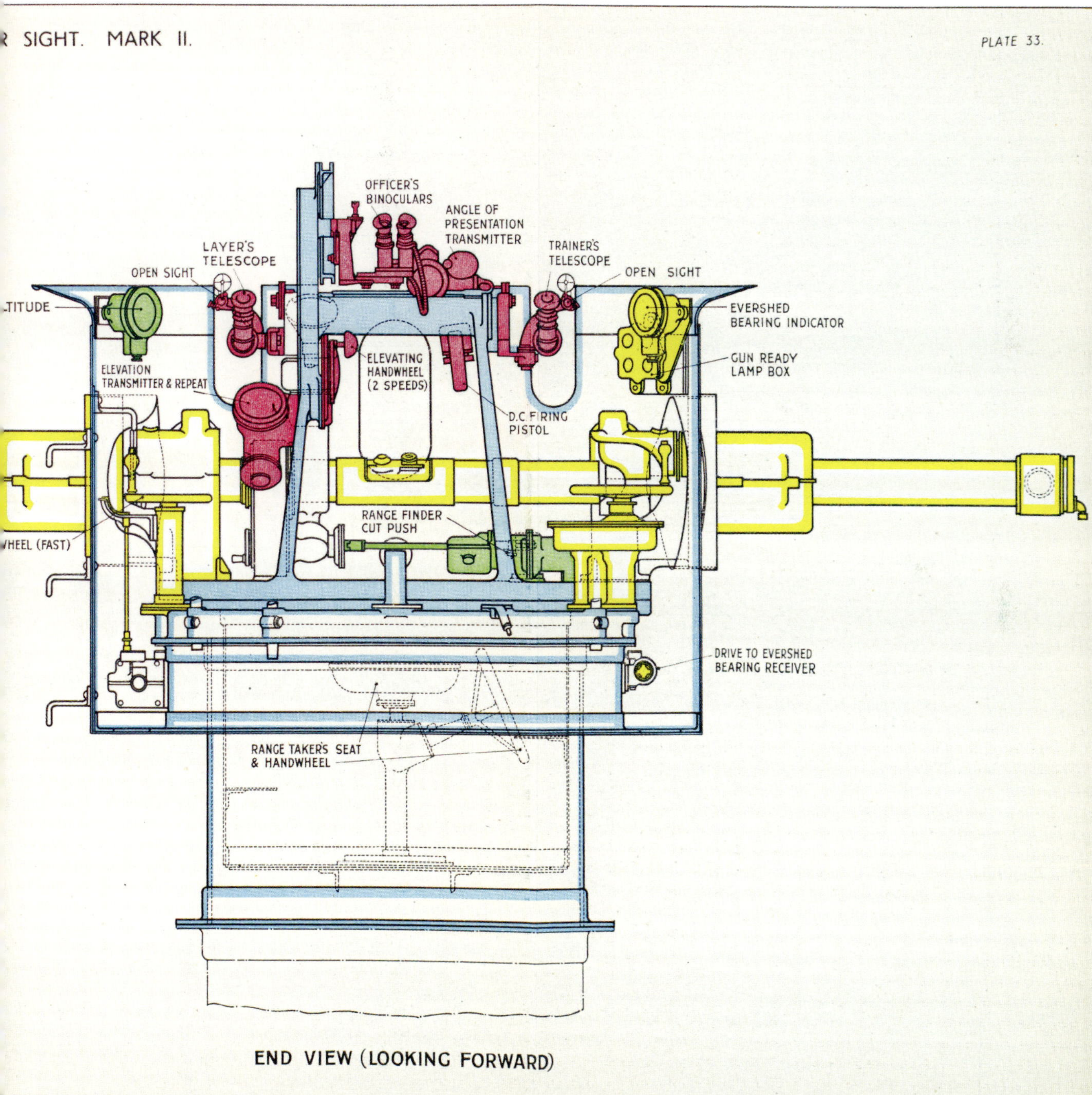
R SIGHT. MARK II.
PLATE 33.
OFFICER'S BINOCULARS
ANGLE OF PRESENTATION TRANSMITTER
LAYER'S TELESCOPE
TRAINER'S TELESCOPE
OPEN SIGHT
OPEN SIGHT
LTITUDE
EVERSHED BEARING INDICATOR
GUN READY LAMP BOX
ELEVATION TRANSMITTER & REPEAT
ELEVATING HANDWHEEL (2 SPEEDS)
D.C. FIRING PISTOL
RANGE FINDER CUT PUSH
WHEEL (FAST)
DRIVE TO EVERSHED BEARING RECEIVER
RANGE TAKER'S SEAT & HANDWHEEL
END VIEW (LOOKING FORWARD)

Top-Down View of High Angle Director Sight

This illustration clearly shows the cramped working space and positions of the four-man HA director crew. Anti-aircraft fire control required a large crew of highly trained sailors and specialized equipment. Information from the HA sight was fed into a 'high angle control system,' which calculated a firing solution and was then fed directly to the guns.

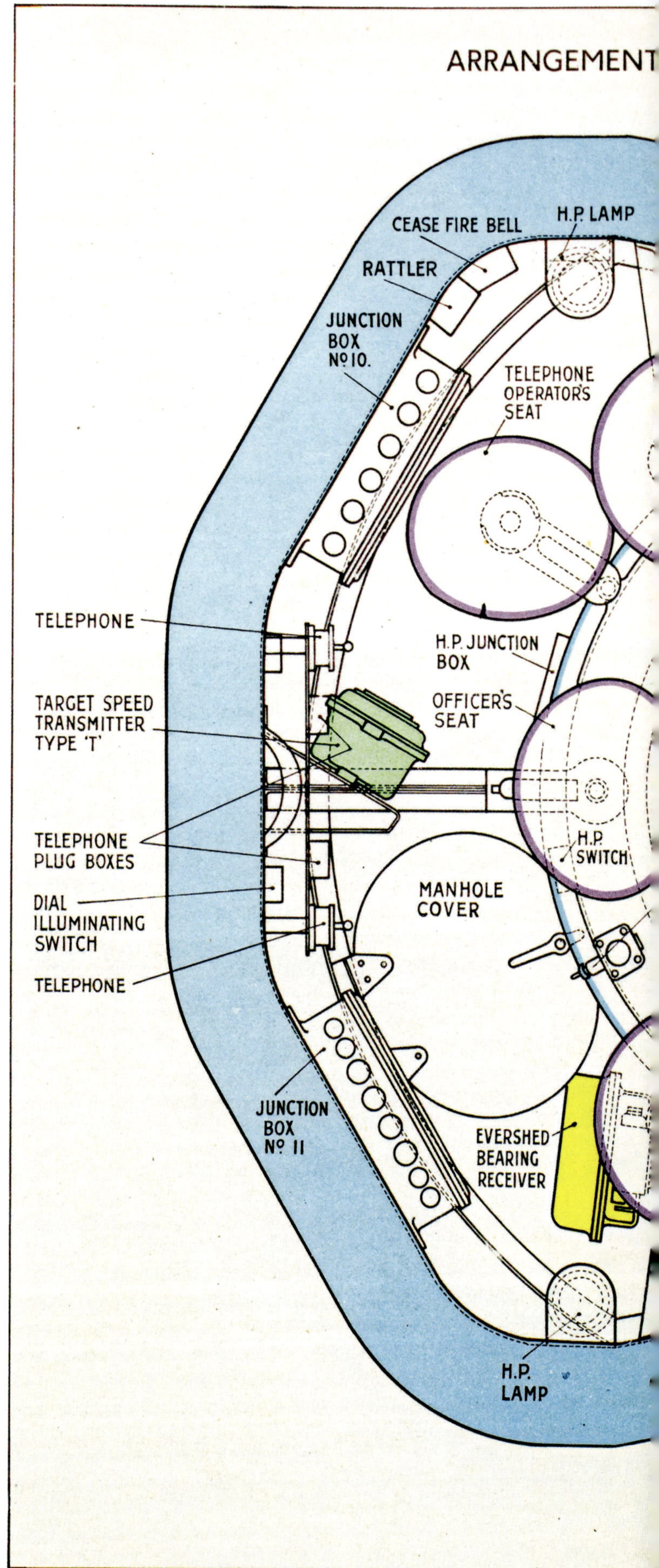

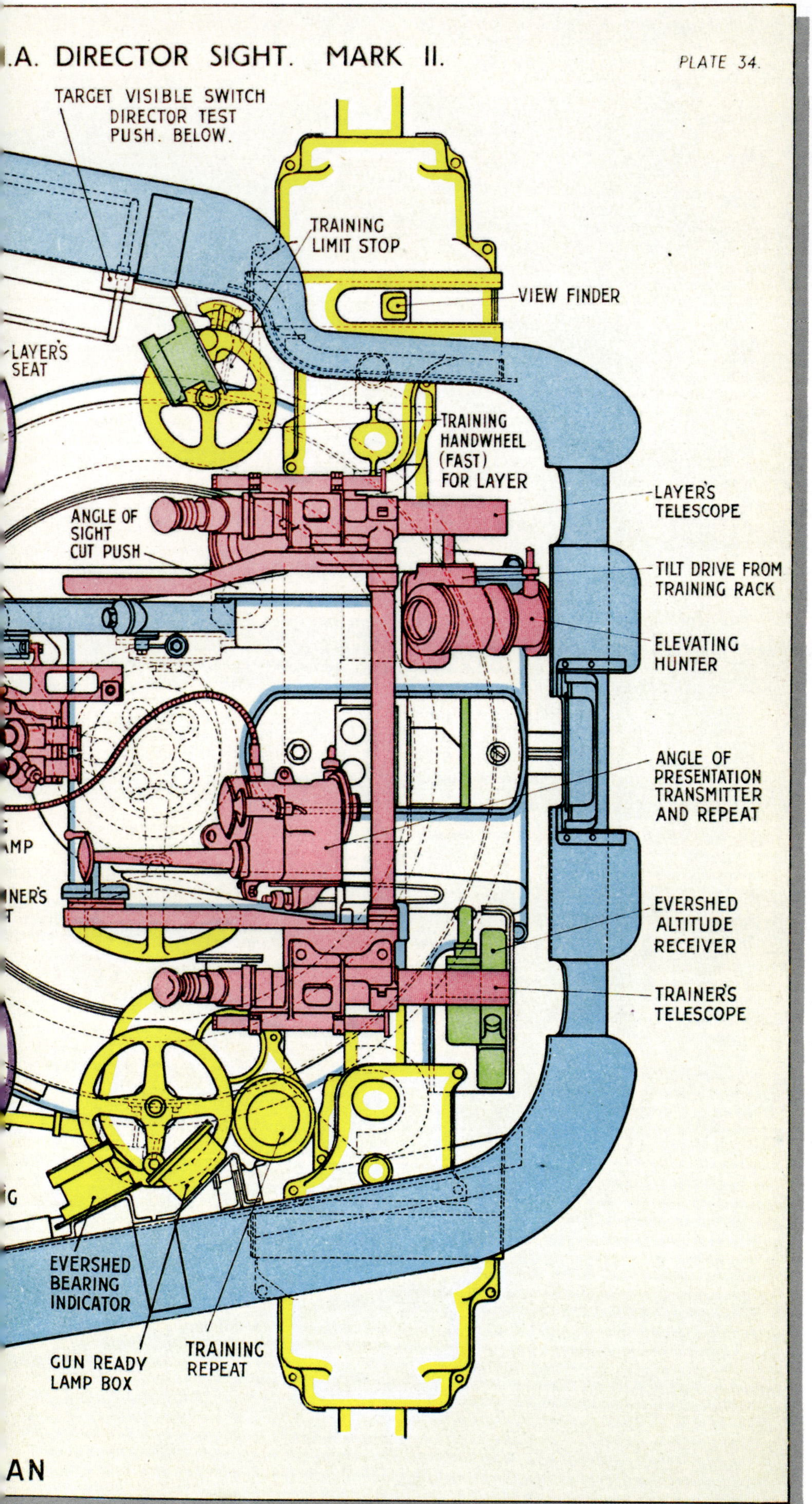

GREAT BRITAIN

Admiralty Fire Control Clock (AFCC) Mark X

The AFCC was the smaller of the two main fire control instruments of the Royal Navy in World War II. Its job was to make calculations that provided the guns with an accurate fire solution. Inputs included: deflection due to the ship, the enemy or the wind; gun training; line of sight training; gun deflection; drift and cross leveling correction; range corrections for the enemy; wind; ballistics; and tangent elevation.

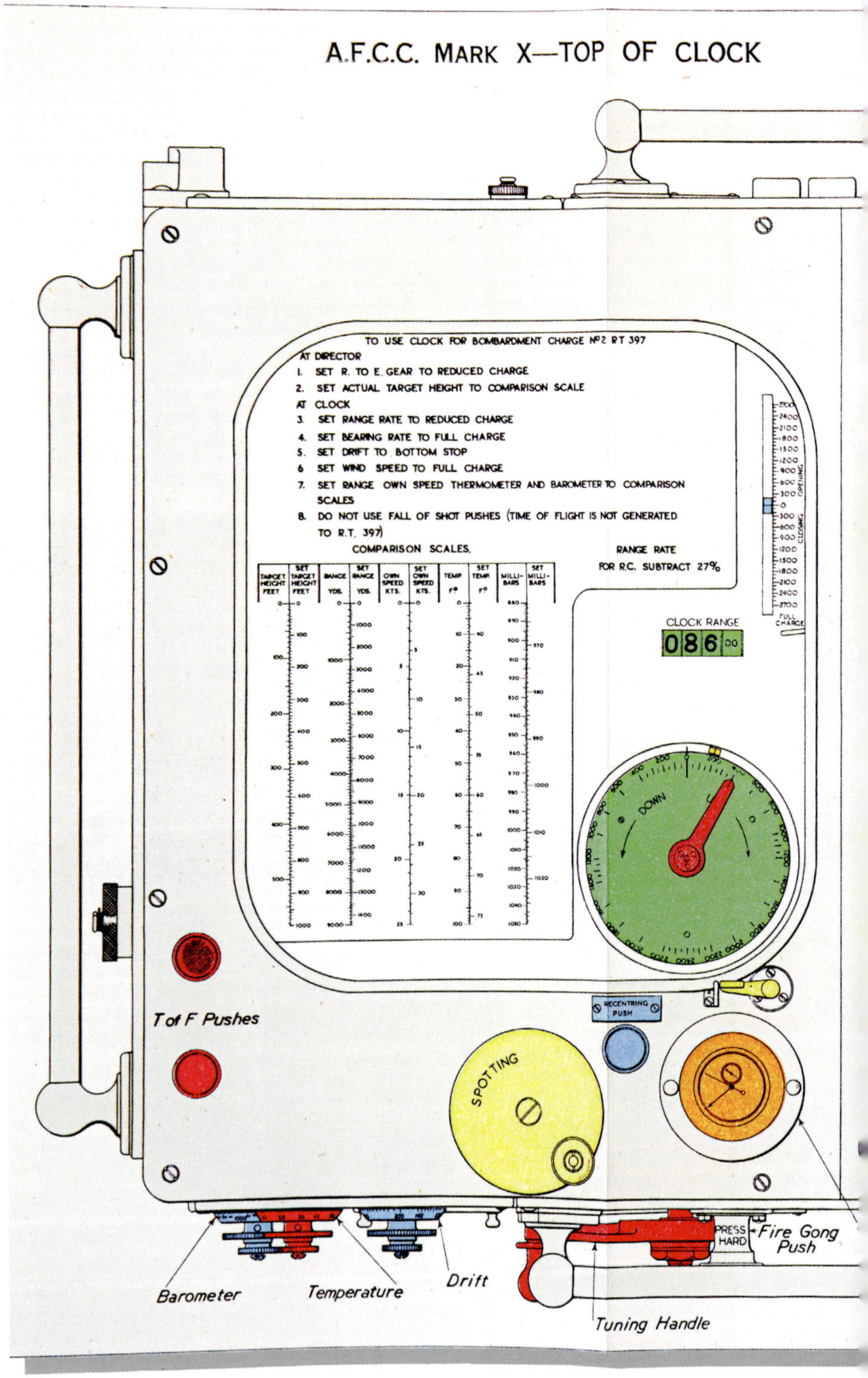

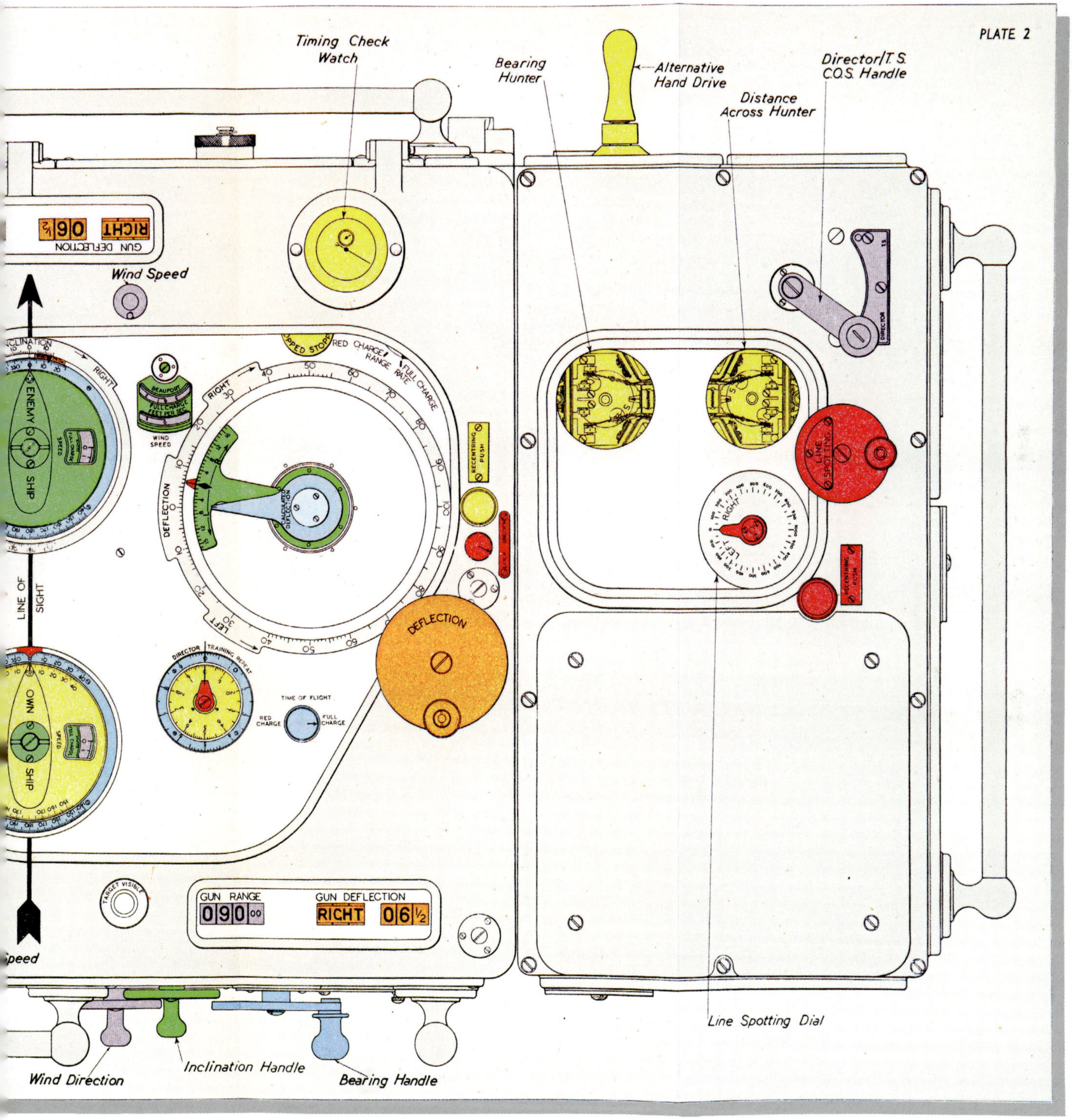
PLATE 2
Timing Check Watch
Bearing Hunter
Alternative Hand Drive
Distance Across Hunter
Director/T.S. C.O.S. Handle
Wind Speed
GUN DEFLECTION
RIGHT
LINE OF SIGHT
ENEMY SHIP
OWN SHIP
DEFLECTION
LINE SPOTTING
TIME OF FLIGHT
RED CHARGE
FULL CHARGE
GUN RANGE
090
GUN DEFLECTION
RIGHT
06½
Speed
Line Spotting Dial
Wind Direction
Inclination Handle
Bearing Handle

The Inner Workings of the AFCC

The AFCC was a complex and highly sophisticated calculator. Its inner workings were a series of gyros, cams and gears, all connected to a series of input dials and handles. Production required a great deal of precision and a highly trained workforce.

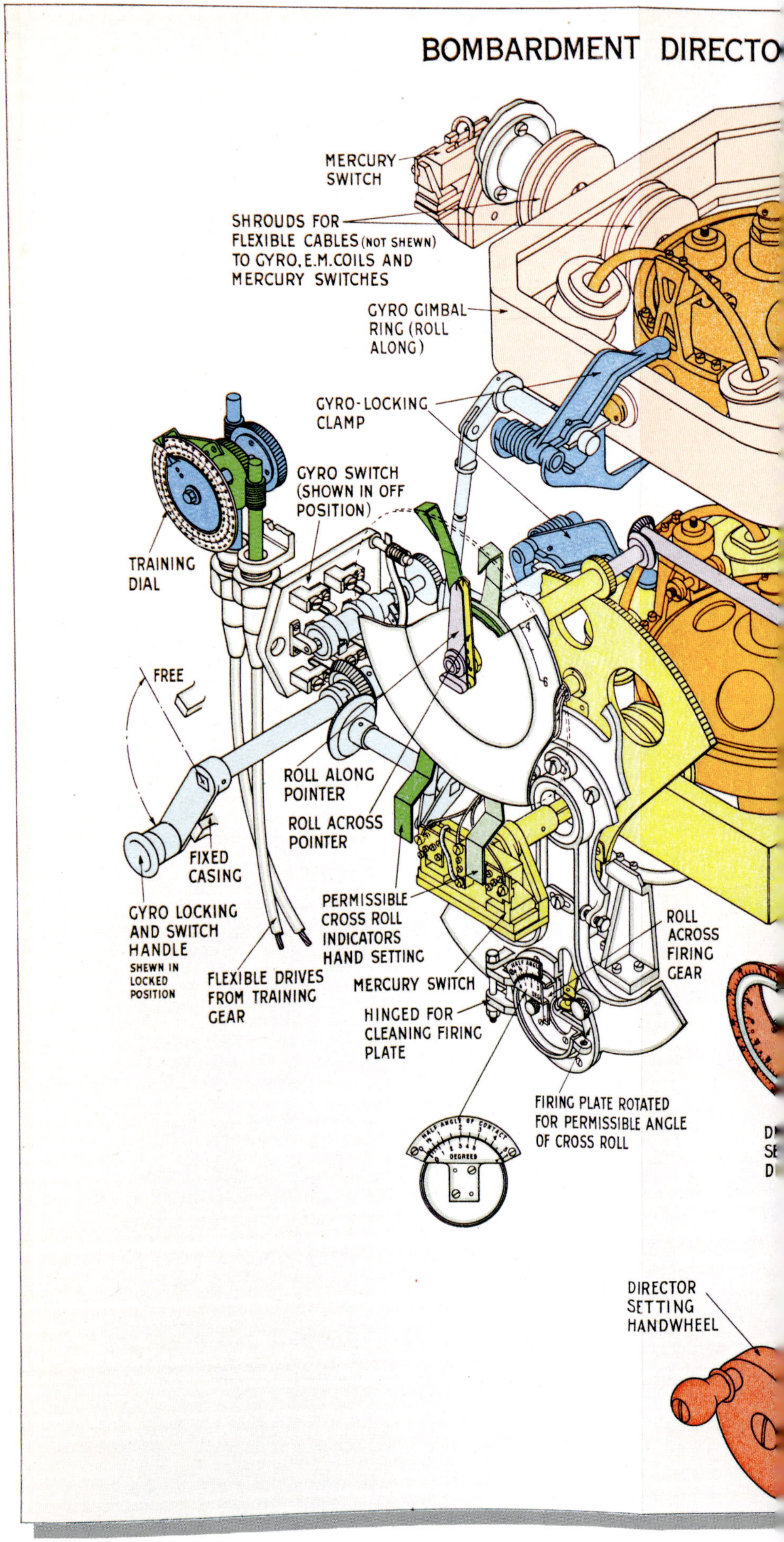

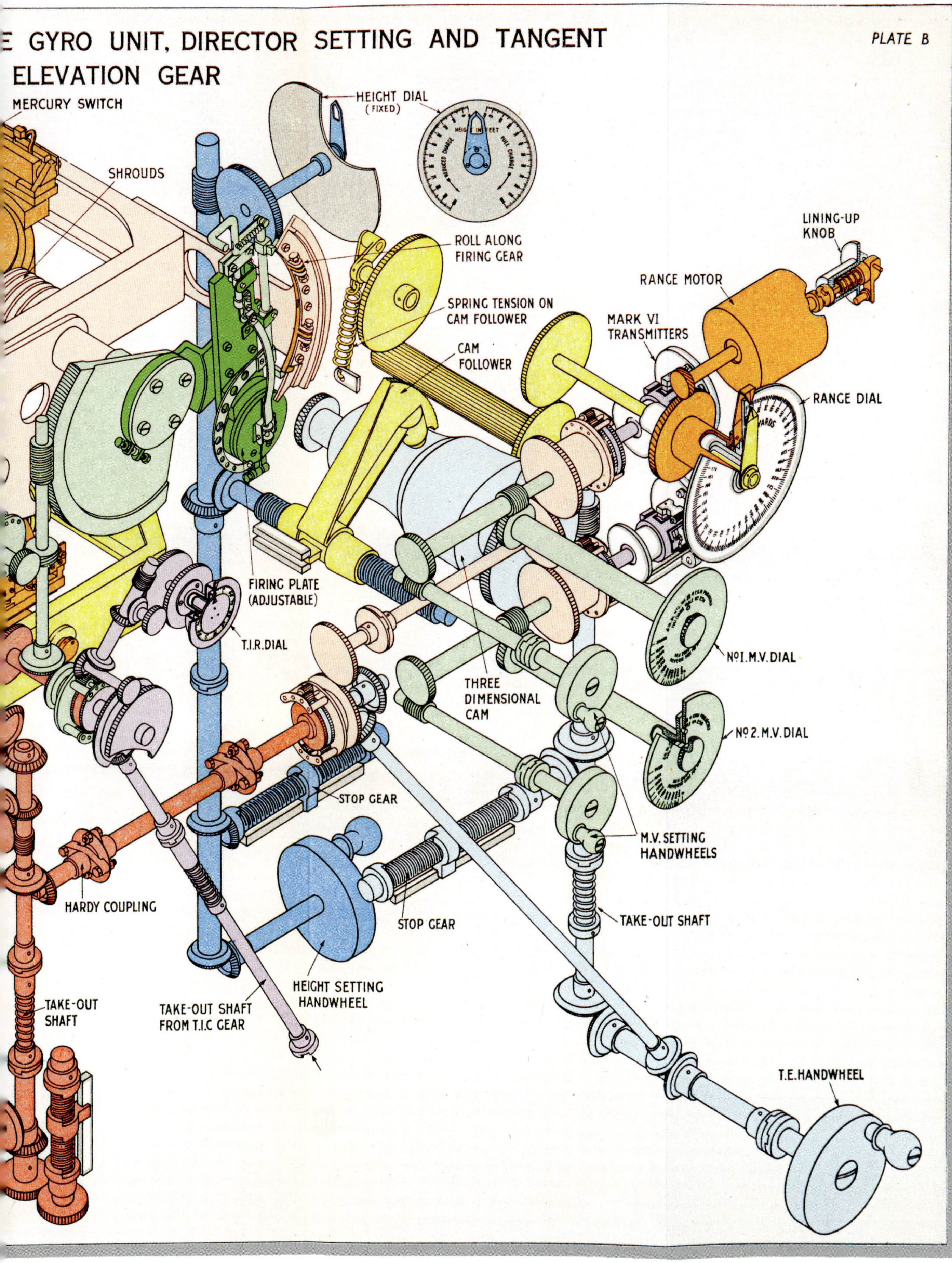
E GYRO UNIT, DIRECTOR SETTING AND TANGENT
ELEVATION GEAR
PLATE B
MERCURY SWITCH
HEIGHT DIAL
(FIXED)
SHROUDS
ROLL ALONG
FIRING GEAR
SPRING TENSION ON
CAM FOLLOWER
CAM
FOLLOWER
LINING-UP
KNOB
RANGE MOTOR
MARK VI
TRANSMITTERS
RANGE DIAL
FIRING PLATE
(ADJUSTABLE)
T.I.R. DIAL
THREE
DIMENSIONAL
CAM
Nº1. M.V. DIAL
Nº2. M.V. DIAL
STOP GEAR
M.V. SETTING
HANDWHEELS
HARDY COUPLING
STOP GEAR
TAKE-OUT SHAFT
HEIGHT SETTING
HANDWHEEL
TAKE-OUT
SHAFT
TAKE-OUT SHAFT
FROM T.I.C GEAR
T.E. HANDWHEEL

GREAT BRITAIN

Target Indication Unit (TIU)

"The object of the Target Indication Unit (TIU) is, in conjunction with Radar W.C., Types 293/M, to detect and display all gunnery targets within the range of the Radar sets, so that selected targets can be indicated to different sections of the armament."

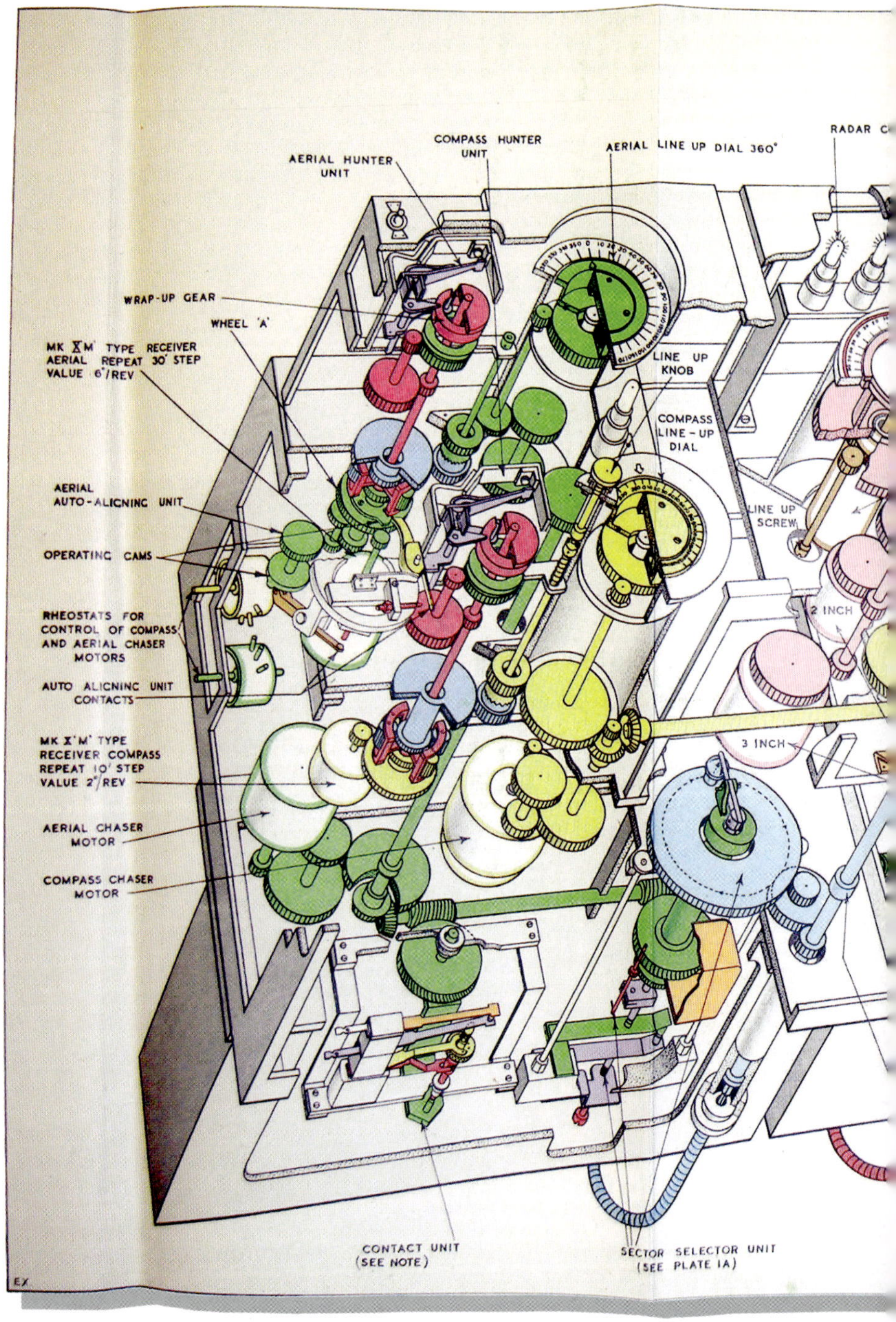

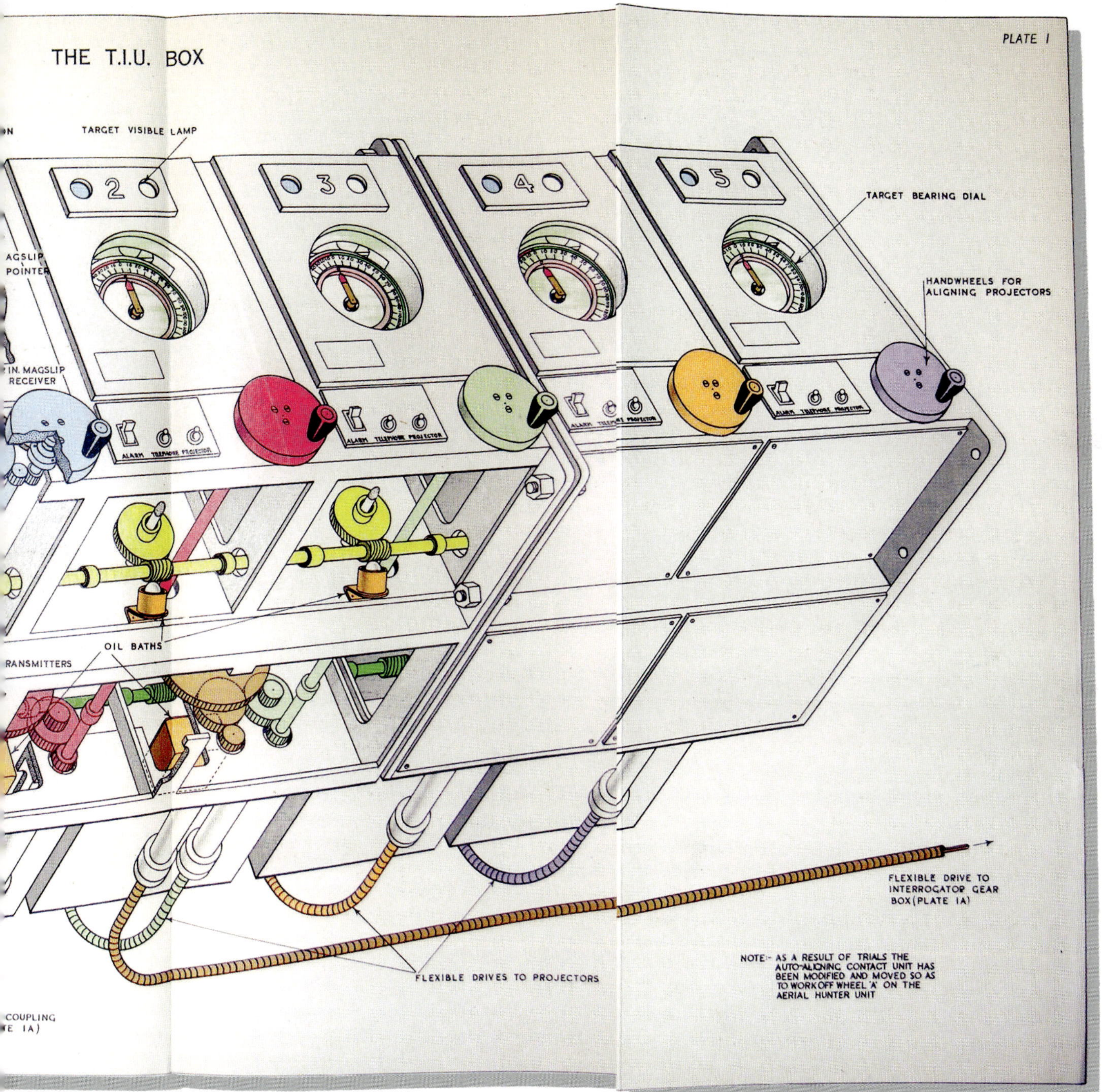
THE T.I.U. BOX
PLATE I
TARGET VISIBLE LAMP
TARGET BEARING DIAL
HANDWHEELS FOR ALIGNING PROJECTORS
ALARM TELEPHONE PROJECTOR
OIL BATHS
FLEXIBLE DRIVE TO INTERROGATOR GEAR BOX (PLATE IA)
FLEXIBLE DRIVES TO PROJECTORS
NOTE:- AS A RESULT OF TRIALS THE AUTO-ALIGNING CONTACT UNIT HAS BEEN MODIFIED AND MOVED SO AS TO WORKOFF WHEEL 'A' ON THE AERIAL HUNTER UNIT

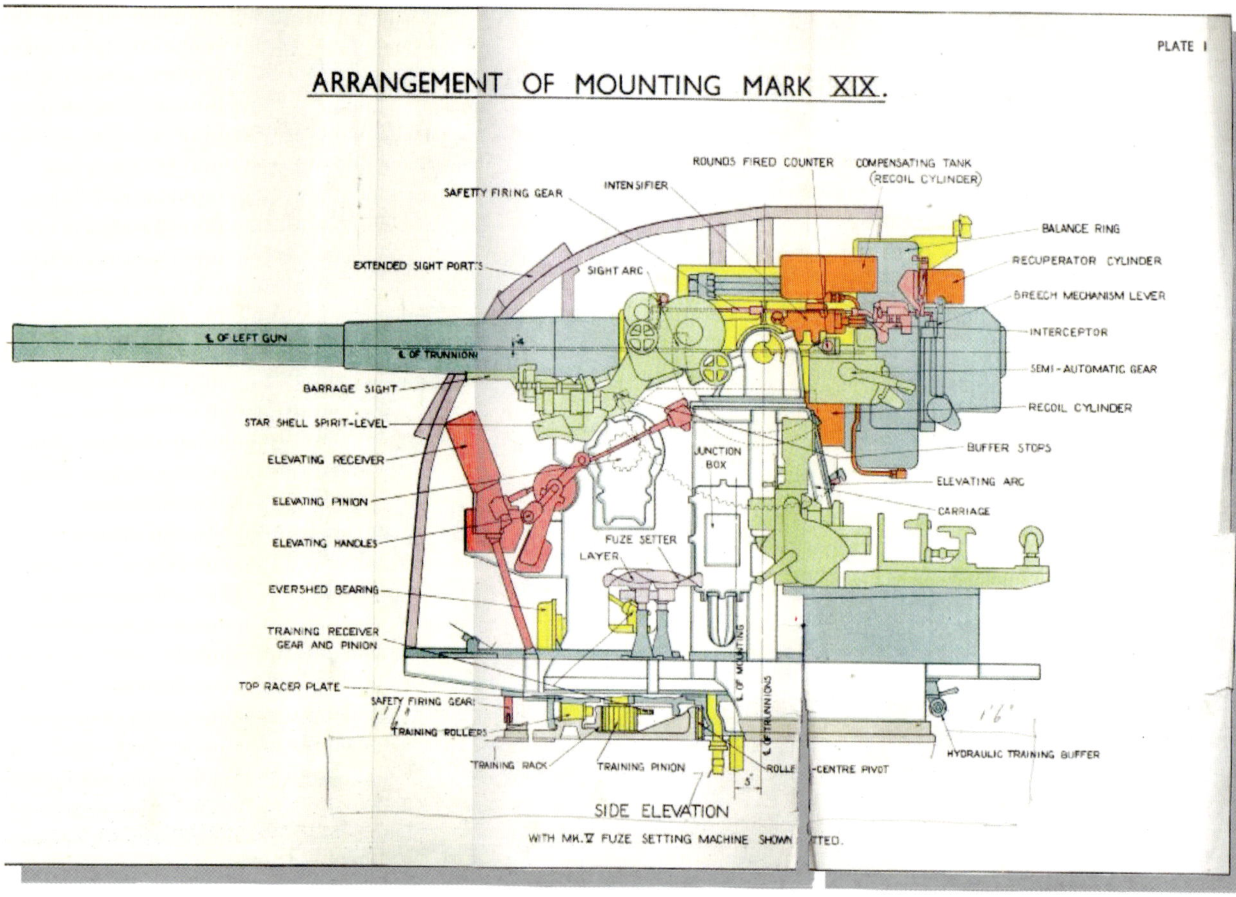
PLATE I
ARRANGEMENT OF MOUNTING MARK XIX.
ROUNDS FIRED COUNTER
COMPENSATING TANK (RECOIL CYLINDER)
INTENSIFIER
SAFETY FIRING GEAR
BALANCE RING
RECUPERATOR CYLINDER
EXTENDED SIGHT PORTS
SIGHT ARC
BREECH MECHANISM LEVER
INTERCEPTOR
℄ OF LEFT GUN
℄ OF TRUNNIONS
SEMI-AUTOMATIC GEAR
BARRAGE SIGHT
RECOIL CYLINDER
STAR SHELL SPIRIT-LEVEL
BUFFER STOPS
ELEVATING RECEIVER
JUNCTION BOX
ELEVATING ARC
ELEVATING PINION
CARRIAGE
ELEVATING HANDLES
FUZE SETTER
LAYER
EVERSHED BEARING
TRAINING RECEIVER GEAR AND PINION
℄ OF MOUNTING
TOP RACER PLATE
℄ OF TRUNNIONS
SAFETY FIRING GEAR
TRAINING ROLLERS
TRAINING RACK
TRAINING PINION
ROLLE
CENTRE PIVOT
HYDRAULIC TRAINING BUFFER
SIDE ELEVATION
WITH MK.V FUZE SETTING MACHINE SHOWN FITTED.

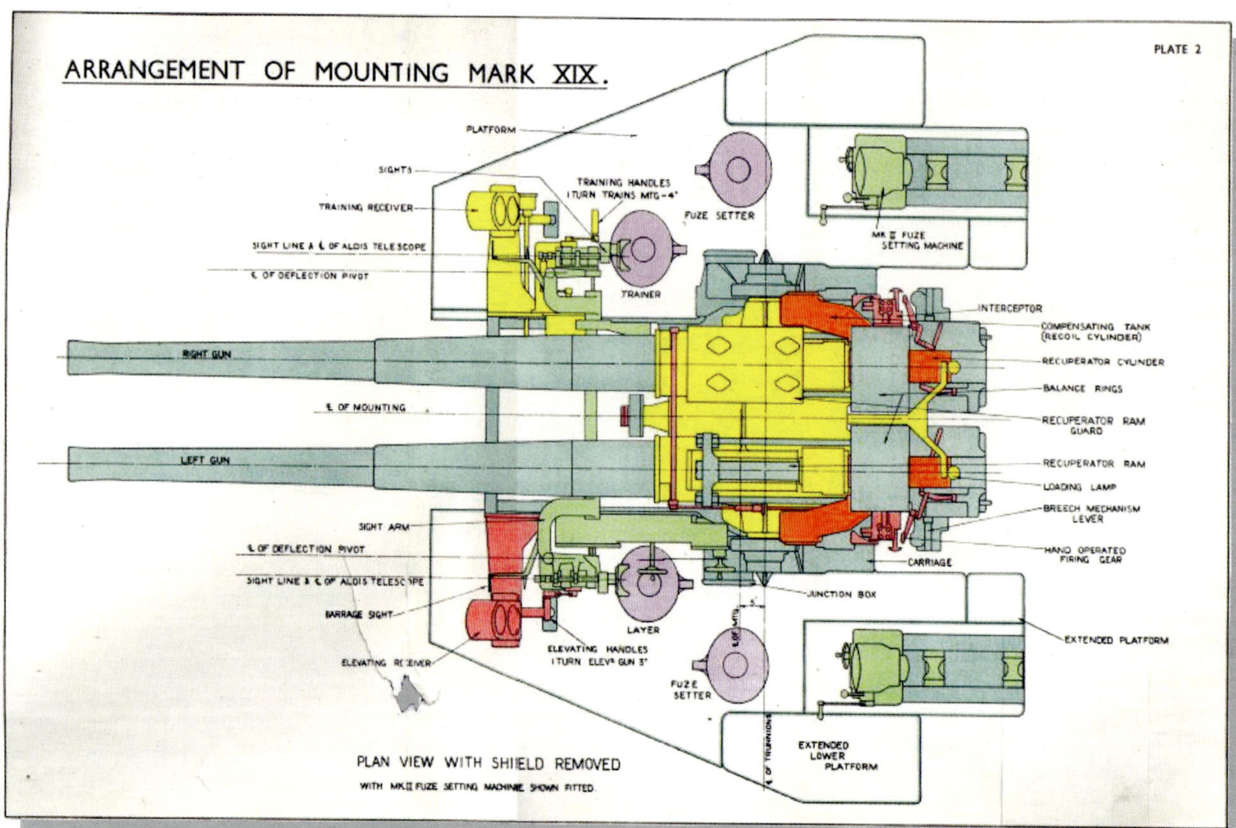
PLATE 2
ARRANGEMENT OF MOUNTING MARK XIX.
PLATFORM
SIGHTS
TRAINING HANDLES 1 TURN TRAINS MTG 4°
TRAINING RECEIVER
FUZE SETTER
SIGHT LINE & ℄ OF ALDIS TELESCOPE
MK II FUZE SETTING MACHINE
℄ OF DEFLECTION PIVOT
TRAINER
INTERCEPTOR
COMPENSATING TANK (RECOIL CYLINDER)
RIGHT GUN
RECUPERATOR CYLINDER
BALANCE RINGS
℄ OF MOUNTING
RECUPERATOR RAM GUARD
LEFT GUN
RECUPERATOR RAM
LOADING LAMP
BREECH MECHANISM LEVER
SIGHT ARM
℄ OF DEFLECTION PIVOT
CARRIAGE
HAND OPERATED FIRING GEAR
SIGHT LINE & ℄ OF ALDIS TELESCOPE
JUNCTION BOX
BARRAGE SIGHT
LAYER
EXTENDED PLATFORM
ELEVATING HANDLES 1 TURN ELEVS GUN 3°
ELEVATING RECEIVER
FUZE SETTER
EXTENDED LOWER PLATFORM
℄ OF TRUNNIONS
PLAN VIEW WITH SHIELD REMOVED
WITH MK II FUZE SETTING MACHINE SHOWN FITTED.

4-inch Twin Turret Arrangement of Mounting Mark XIX

The 4-inch gun was designed as a dual-purpose weapon and was reasonably good in the AA role, but its shell was considered too small for the anti-shipping role. During the 1930s and early '40s, many of the older RN battleships and cruisers replaced their single 4-inch guns with the Mk XIX twin mounting.

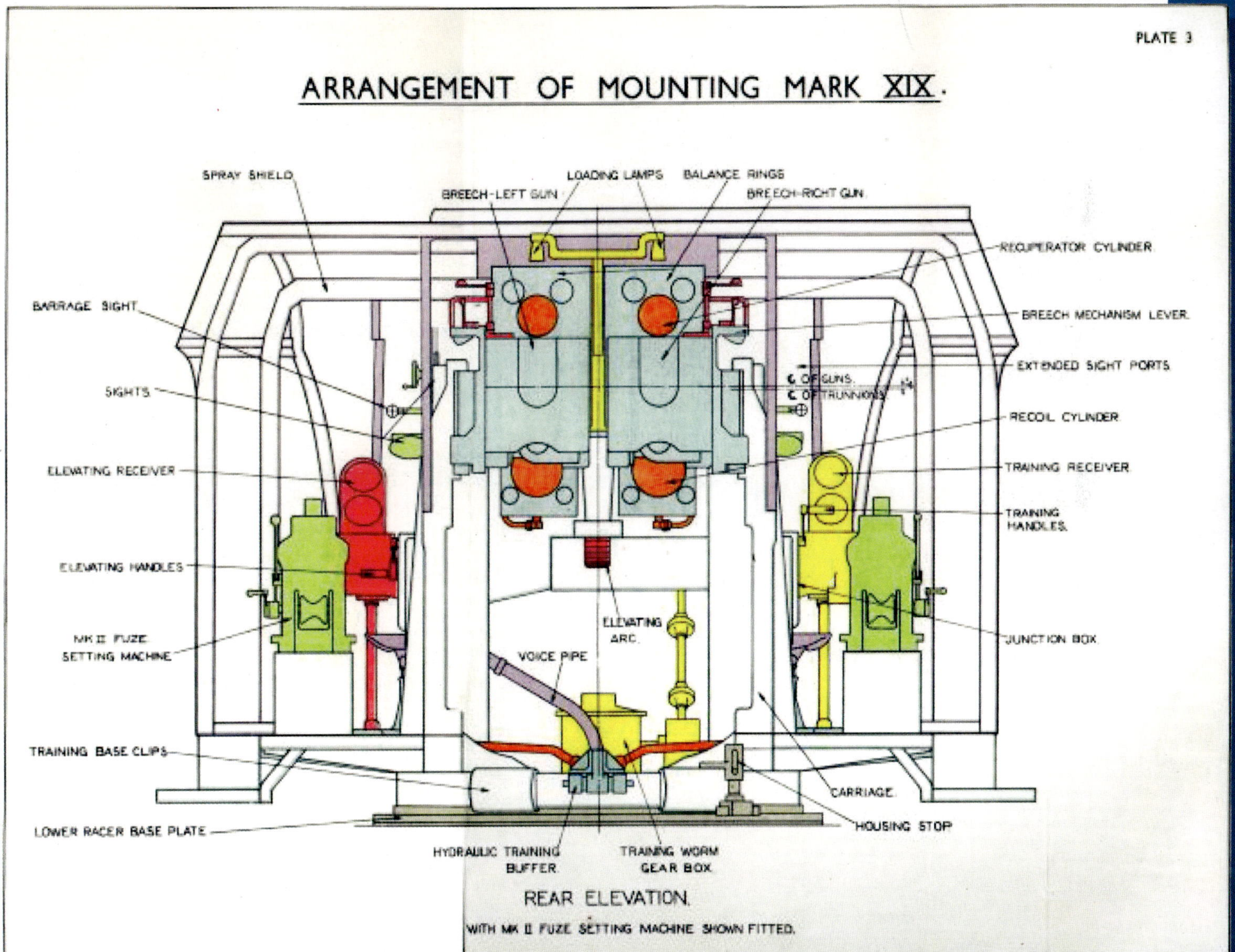

GREAT BRITAIN

Aircraft Torpedo Sight

By 1943 the Moving Mirror Torpedo Sight replaced the old Sight Bar torpedo sight found in the Fairey Swordfish and Albacore. When approaching their target, torpedo bombers flew between 5,000 feet and 7,000 feet. This altitude was needed to find their target and set up the attack formation. Typical release distance was about 1,000 yards.

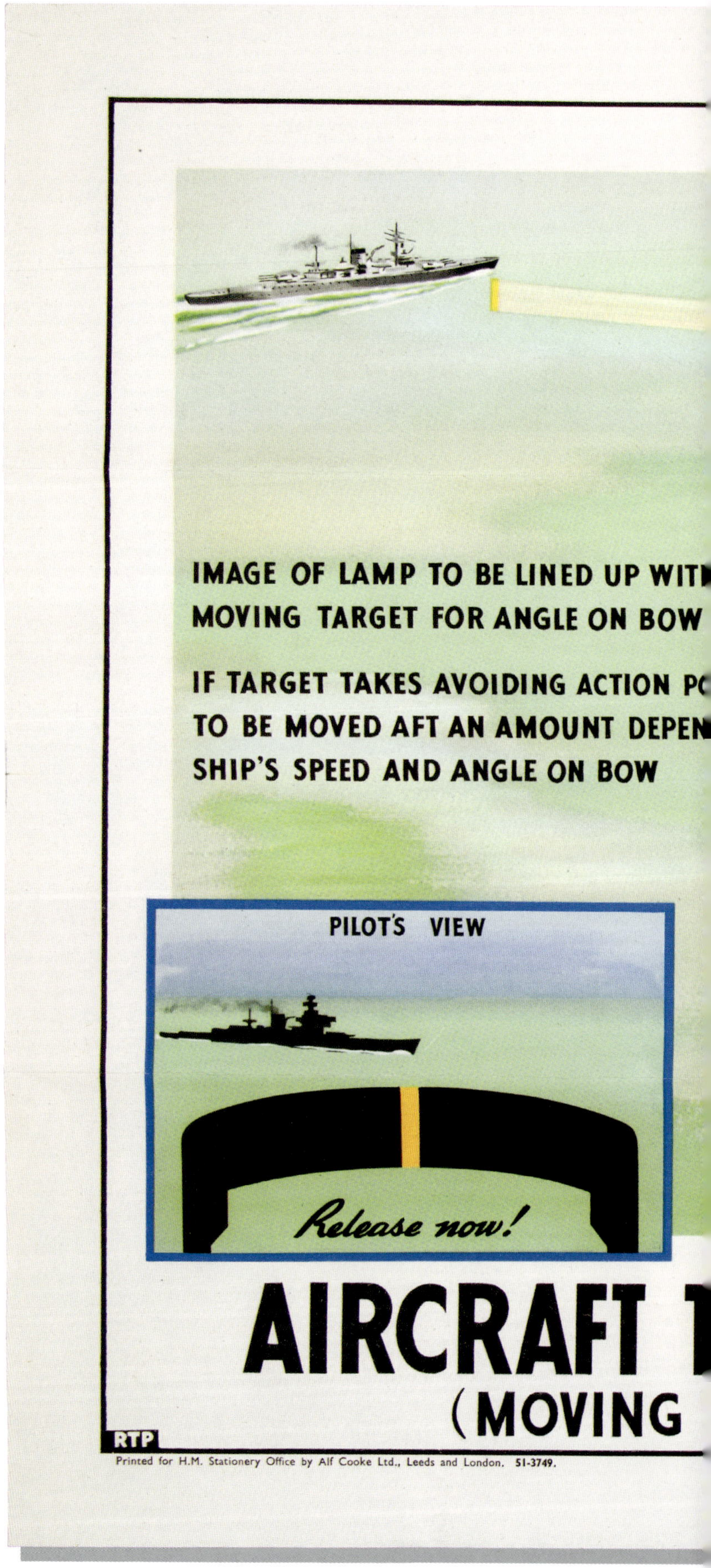

FOR OFFICIAL USE ONLY
OF
DEG.
AIM
N
ADRANT
RIAGE
STEEP ATTACK
RPEDO SIGHT
ROR TYPE)
See also A.P. 1730 C, Vol. I
AIR DIAGRAM 2385
SHEET No 1
No OF SHEETS 1
JUNE 1943
A.L.No
AMENDMENTS MADE
INITIALS
DATE
PREPARED BY MINISTRY OF AIRCRAFT PRODUCTION FOR PROMULGATION BY AIR MINISTRY

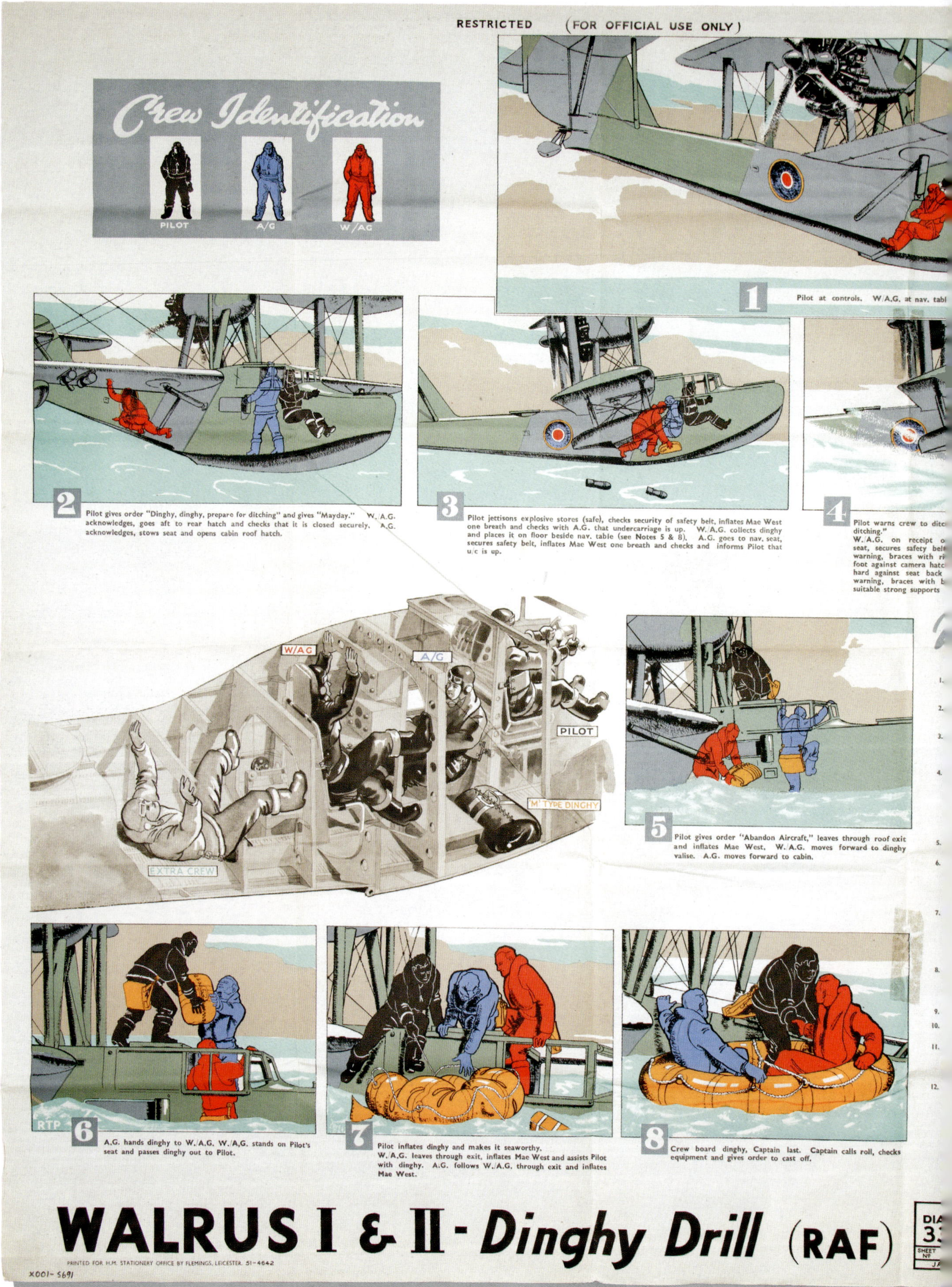
RESTRICTED (FOR OFFICIAL USE ONLY)
Crew Identification
PILOT
A/G
W/AG
1
Pilot at controls. W/A.G. at nav.
2
Pilot gives order "Dinghy, dinghy, prepare for ditching" and gives "Mayday." W./A.G. acknowledges, goes aft to rear hatch and checks that it is closed securely. A.G. acknowledges, stows seat and opens cabin roof hatch.
3
Pilot jettisons explosive stores (safe), checks security of safety belt, inflates Mae West one breath and checks with A.G. that undercarriage is up. W./A.G. collects dinghy and places it on floor beside nav. table (see Notes 5 & 8). A.G. goes to nav. seat, secures safety belt, inflates Mae West one breath and checks and informs Pilot that u/c is up.
4
Pilot warns crew to
ditching."
W./A.G. on receipt
seat, secures safety
warning, braces with
foot against camera
hard against seat back
warning, braces with
suitable strong supports
W/AG
A/G
PILOT
'M' TYPE DINGHY
EXTRA CREW
5
Pilot gives order "Abandon Aircraft," leaves through roof exit and inflates Mae West. W./A.G. moves forward to dinghy valise. A.G. moves forward to cabin.
6
A.G. hands dinghy to W./A.G. W./A.G. stands on Pilot's seat and passes dinghy out to Pilot.
7
Pilot inflates dinghy and makes it seaworthy.
W./A.G. leaves through exit, inflates Mae West and assists Pilot with dinghy. A.G. follows W./A.G. through exit and inflates Mae West.
8
Crew board dinghy, Captain last. Captain calls roll, checks equipment and gives order to cast off.
WALRUS I & II - Dinghy Drill (RAF)
PRINTED FOR H.M. STATIONERY OFFICE BY FLEMINGS, LEICESTER. 51-4642
X001-5691

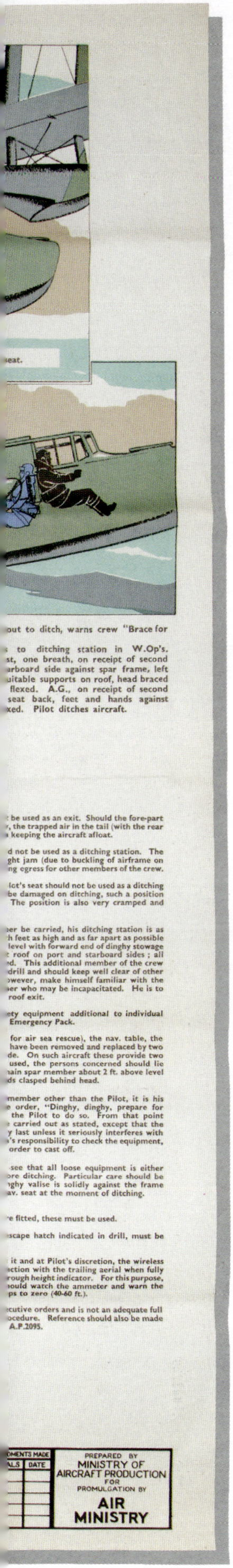

Walrus I & II — Dinghy Drill

At the outbreak of World War II, the Supermarine Walrus flying boat equipped most of the Royal Navy's battleships, battlecruisers and cruisers. Nicknamed the 'Shagbat,' the Walrus was used for ship-to-shore communication, gunfire spotting, anti-submarine patrol and air sea rescue. Its top speed was 217 km/h (135 mph).

Barracuda II & III Bailing-Out Drill (right)

Bailing out of a damaged aircraft was fraught with danger. The Fairey Barracuda was no different. Even if the crew survived and were able to inflate their life rafts, the chances of rescue were remote. Introduced in 1943 to replace the Fairey Swordfish and Albacore, the Barracuda was not a great success. With the exception of its top speed and manoeuvrability, it was not significantly better than its biplane predecessors.

Seafire I & II Oxygen System (below)

The Supermarine Seafire was simply the navalized version of the Spitfire. All World War II fighters were equipped with an oxygen system for pilots to fly above 10,000ft. When the Seafire entered service with the Royal Navy, it was not well suited to carrier operations. Mike Davey, FAA Seafire pilot, recalled, *the problems with the Seafire, were a weak and narrow undercarriage and, because of a long nose, the forward vision was very restricted, and if flown at only a few knots above stalling speed one could easily miss the wires and end up in the barrier.*

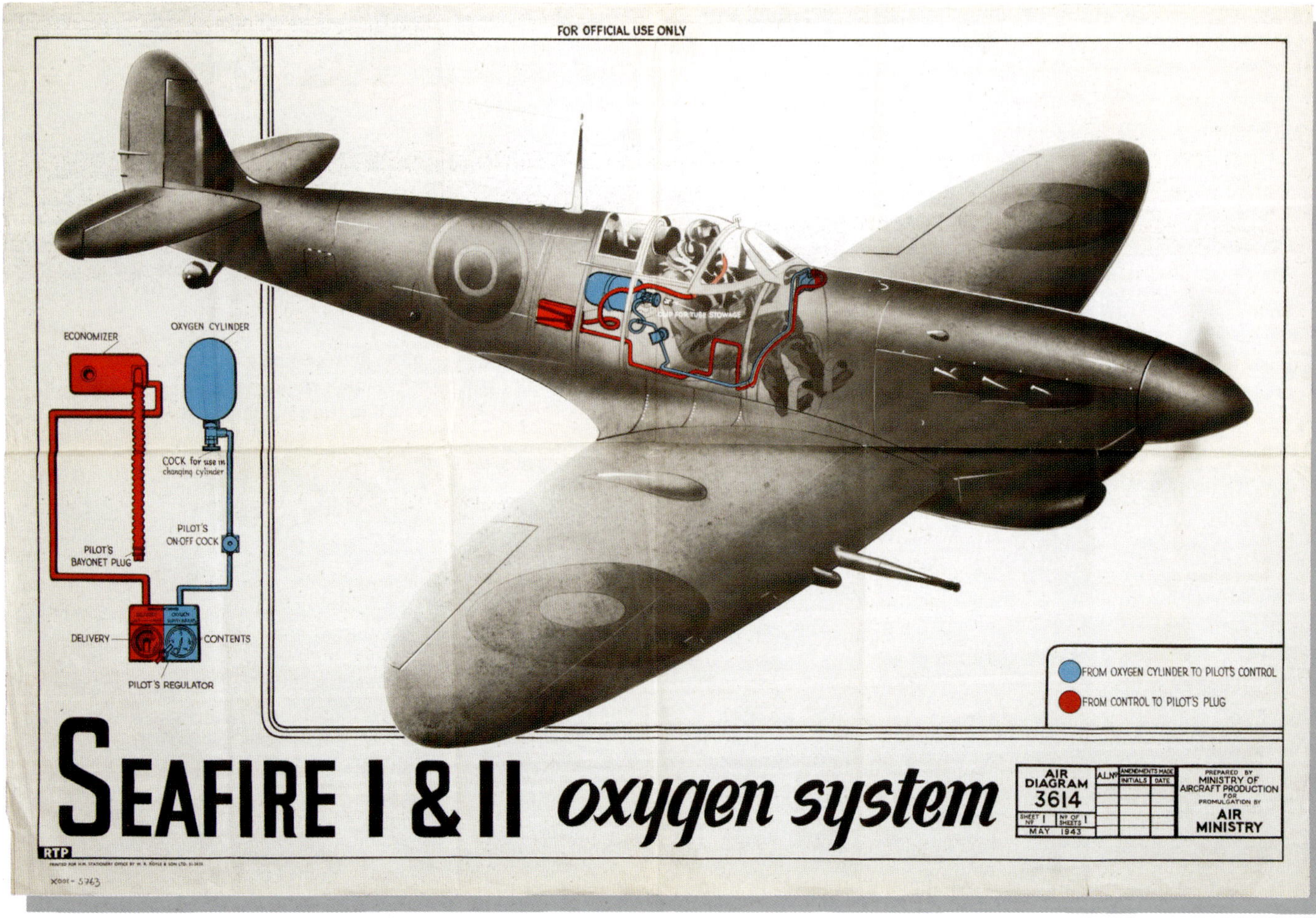

RESTRICTED
BARRACUDA II & III
BALING-OUT DRILL
ROYAL NAVY
PREPARATION FOR EXIT
PILOT gives the order "Put on Parachutes," and receives acknowledgment from Observer and Telegraphist Air Gunner. Switches I.F.F. to Emergency, opens cockpit hood, locks, and sends "Mayday" message informing position, height, and intention to bale-out. Checks security of parachute harness and K Dinghy. Makes for nearest ship or land. Inflates Mae West one breath and closes valve.
PILOT flies at minimum cruising speed; Gives order "Jump! Jump!" Receives acknowledgment from OBSERVER and T.A.G. Repeats "Mayday" message giving baling-out position and height. Ensures that OBSERVER and T.A.G. have abandoned aircraft. Releases safety harness and leaves the aircraft last; head first, facing aft, and sliding over starboard mainplane.
OBSERVER acknowledges to Pilot. Fits parachute—Attaches K Dinghy to parachute harness, and lanyard to Mae West—Checks that oxygen and W/T leads are clear of parachute. Switches I.F.F. to "Emergency," and directs Pilot on course to nearest ship or land. Prepares distress message stating intention to bale out, giving course, height, airspeed, and position. Passing distress data to T.A.G., ensures that he is prepared for baling-out order from Pilot.
OBSERVER acknowledges to Pilot. Ensures T.A.G. has received the order. Re-checks security of parachute and harness. Opens port blister and leaves aircraft head first. Note: Lift the parachute pack over the edge of the blister before putting out your head.
TELEGRAPHIST AIR GUNNER acknowledges to Pilot. Fits parachute. Releases safety belt. Attaches K Dinghy to parachute harness, and lanyard to Mae West. Checks that oxygen and W/T leads are clear of parachute. Opens hood. Transmits S.O.S. giving data received from OBSERVER, and awaits PILOT'S order to bale out. Continues S.O.S. procedure requesting a fix. Inflates Mae West one breath, and closes valve.
Notes
1. If at oxygen height take seven deep breaths before disconnecting oxygen lead.
2. Remove helmet prior to jumping. If time permits, disconnect oxygen and W/T leads, and tuck helmet into flying clothing.
3. Immediately canopy has opened, fully inflate Mae West.
4. This drill is to be studied in conjunction with A.F.O. 3369/44 and A.F.O. 917/44, Sect. 4, Para. 1.
TELEGRAPHIST AIR GUNNER acknowledges to PILOT. Clamps down W/T key. Re-checks security of parachute and harness. Leaves aircraft through rear exit by diving out head first, facing aft, over port or starboard side.
NAVAL AIR DIAGRAM 3341
R.T.P. PREPARED IN COLLABORATION WITH THE R.N. SAFETY EQUIPMENT SCHOOL
X001-5697

Handbook and Drill Book, 2-Pounder QF Mark VIII Gun

The 2-pounder was introduced into service in 1930 and was a very advanced design at the time. By 1939 the rapid improvements in aircraft design rendered it obsolete for AA use. To remedy the issue a high-velocity projectile was introduced in 1938. The 2-pounder was manufactured in large numbers in both Britain and Canada.

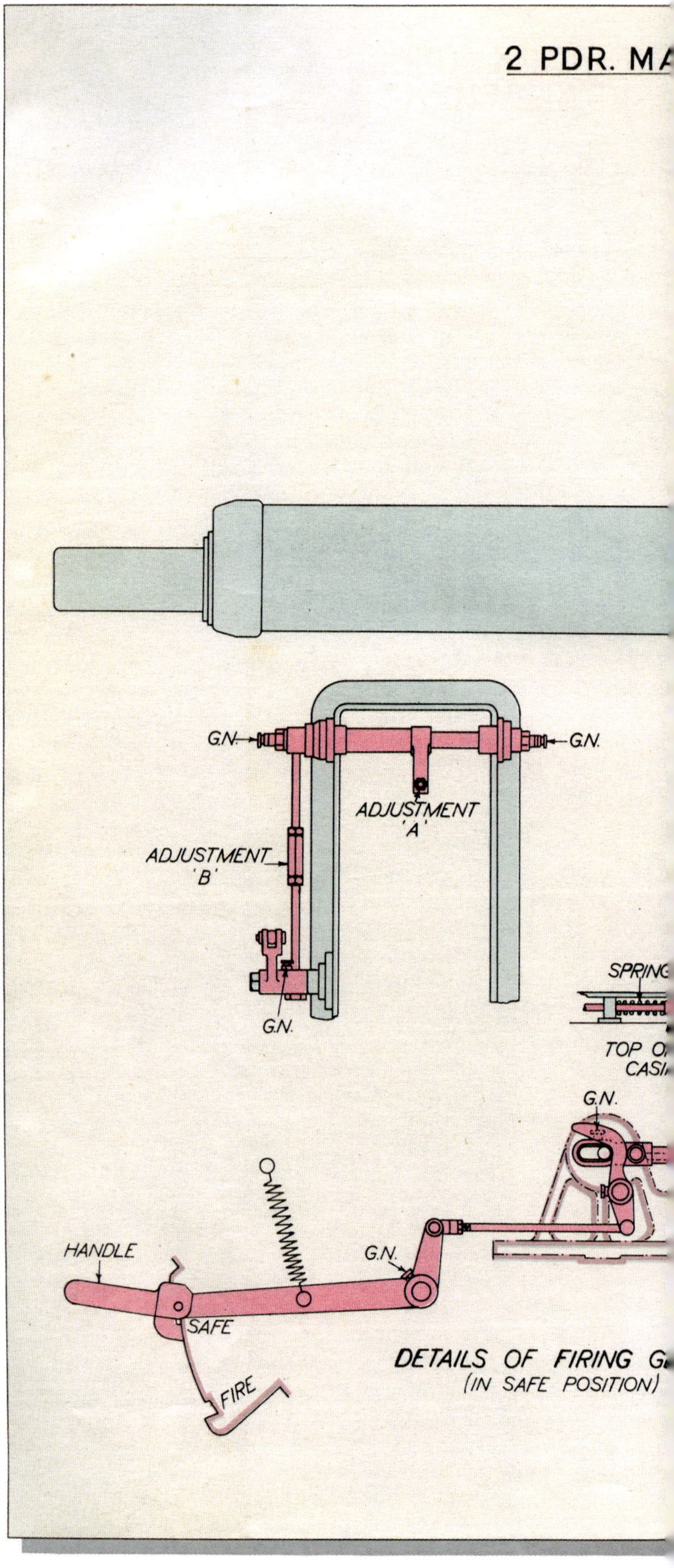

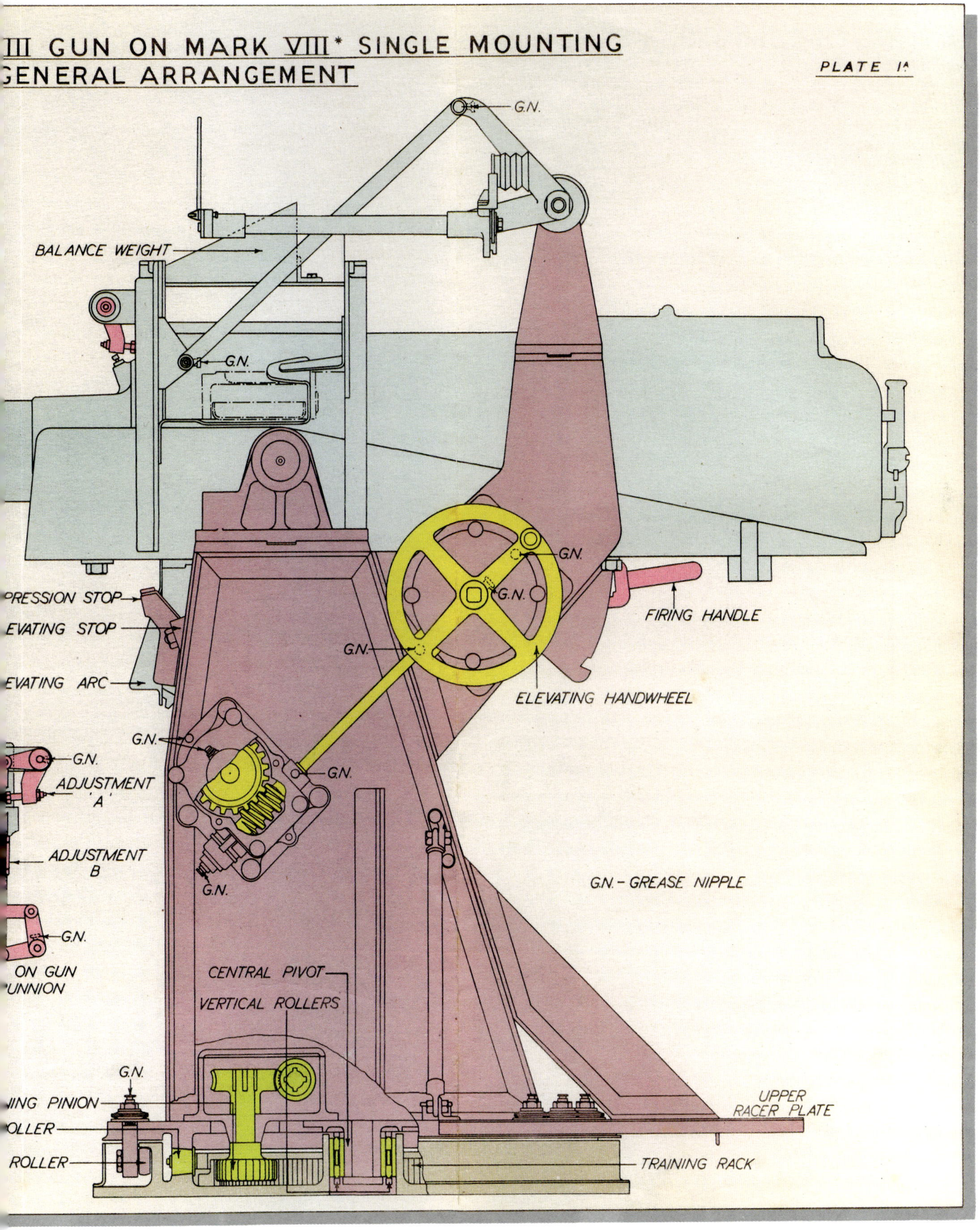

III GUN ON MARK VIII* SINGLE MOUNTING
GENERAL ARRANGEMENT
PLATE I^A
G.N.
BALANCE WEIGHT
G.N.
G.N.
G.N.
PRESSION STOP
EVATING STOP
FIRING HANDLE
G.N.
EVATING ARC
ELEVATING HANDWHEEL
G.N.
G.N.
G.N.
ADJUSTMENT 'A'
ADJUSTMENT B
G.N.
G.N. - GREASE NIPPLE
G.N.
ON GUN
UNNION
CENTRAL PIVOT
VERTICAL ROLLERS
G.N.
ING PINION
OLLER
ROLLER
UPPER RACER PLATE
TRAINING RACK

Handbook and Drill Book, 2-Pounder QF Mark VIII Gun

The 2-pounder's rate of fire was 115 rounds per minute. It could fire high-explosive, semi-armor-piercing and armor-piercing rounds. Barrel life was 7,500 rounds of high-velocity ammunition. Effective anti-aircraft ceiling was 3,960 m (13,000 ft).

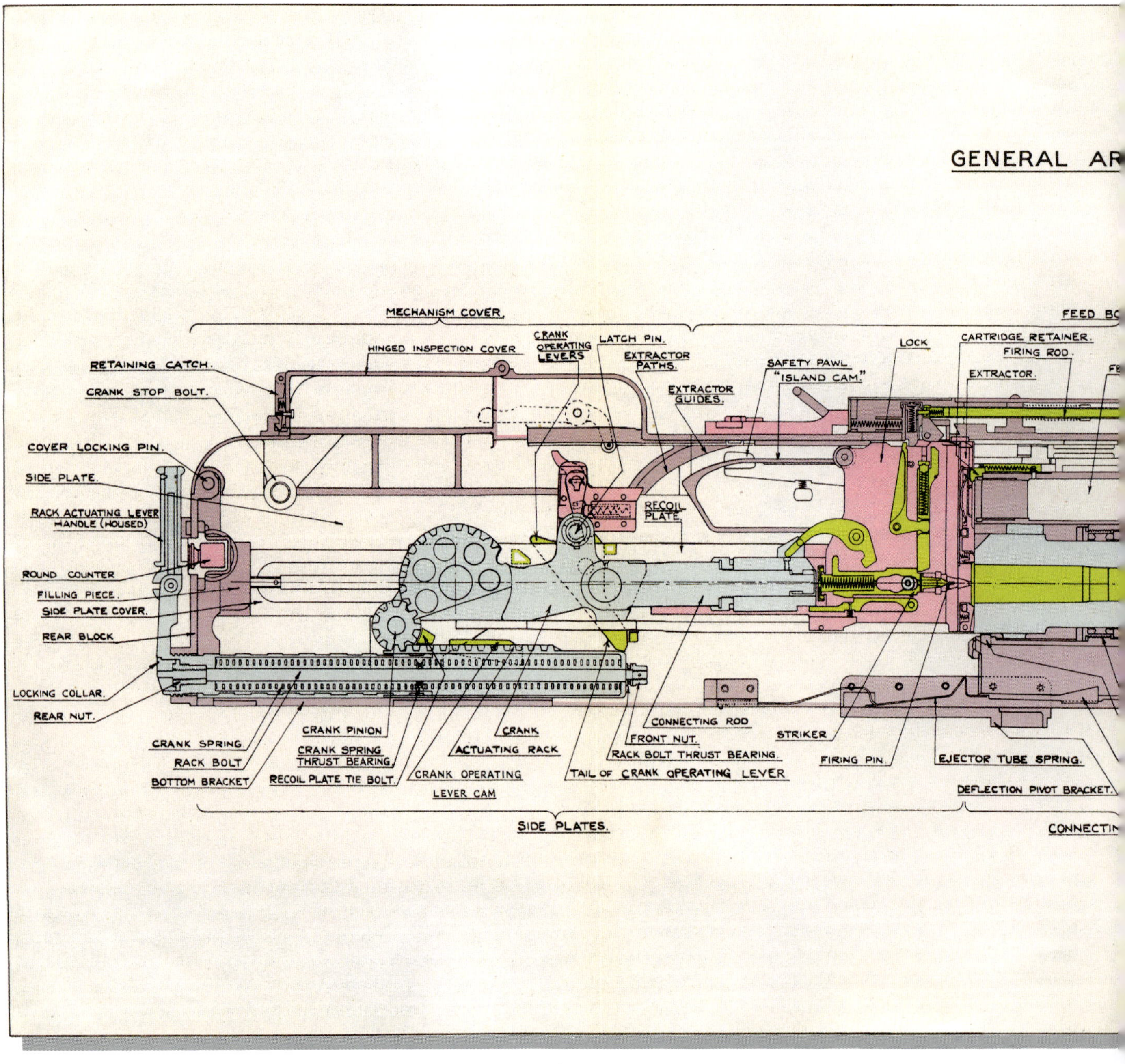

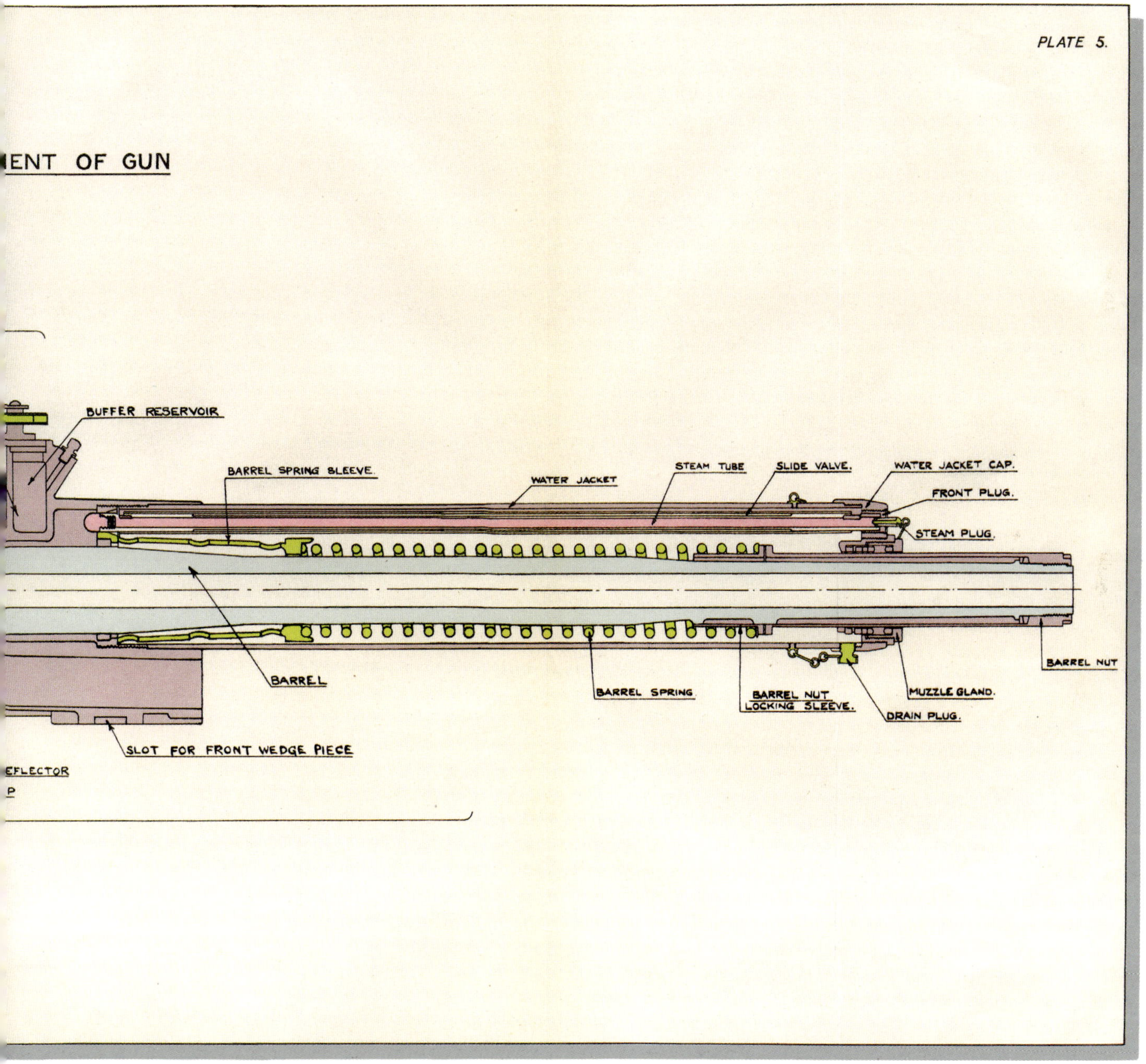
PLATE 5.
ENT OF GUN
BUFFER RESERVOIR
BARREL SPRING SLEEVE.
WATER JACKET
STEAM TUBE
SLIDE VALVE.
WATER JACKET CAP.
FRONT PLUG.
STEAM PLUG.
BARREL NUT
BARREL
BARREL SPRING
BARREL NUT LOCKING SLEEVE.
MUZZLE GLAND.
DRAIN PLUG.
SLOT FOR FRONT WEDGE PIECE
EFLECTOR
P

UNITED STATES

GO! As the plane director gives the signal a U. S. Navy Avenger torpedo-bomber starts its take-off run down the deck of the carrier.
The gun crew of a U. S. Aircraft Carrier is ready for action with a big dual purpose gun as an "alert" is sounded somewhere in the Pacific.
AMERICAN
AIRCRAFT CARRIE
By JIM RAY
A DETAILED CROSS-SECTION OF A TYPICAL MODERN FLAT-TOP
Produced with the Cooperation of the Deputy Chief of Na
Operations for Air and the Bureau of Ships — U. S. NAVY
A starboard airview of a 27,000-ton U. S. Aircraft Carrier streaking into the wind at high speed as she launches her fighter planes. The U. S. Navy has many of these big carriers that are courageously and effectively carrying the war to our enemies far from our shores.
I—ISLAND
F—FLIGHT DECK
G—GALLERY DECK
M—MAIN DECK
2—SECOND DECK
COPYRIGHT, 1944 BY GARDEN CITY PUBLISHING CO., INC., GARDEN CITY, NEW YORK
PRINTED IN THE U.S.A.
DESIGNED, PLANNED AND EXECUTED BY JIM RAY

American Aircraft Carrier

Produced in 1944, this extensive cutaway drawing of a U.S. fleet carrier appears to be the USS *Enterprise* (CV-6). The anti-aircraft gun mounts on either side of the island are a mystery. Identified as 40 mm Bofors guns, the *Enterprise* had been refitted with two twin 5-inch turrets on each side of the island in 1942.

USS *Lexington*, As Built

The *Lexington* and her sister ship *Saratoga* were large carriers, displacing 32,659 tonnes (36,000 tons). Both were armed with a hybrid armament of eight 8-inch guns in four twin turrets for engaging surface targets. Anti-aircraft armaments consisted of twelve 5-inch and 14 water-cooled .50 caliber machine guns. The *Lexington*-class were the fastest American carriers, with a top speed of 34 knots.

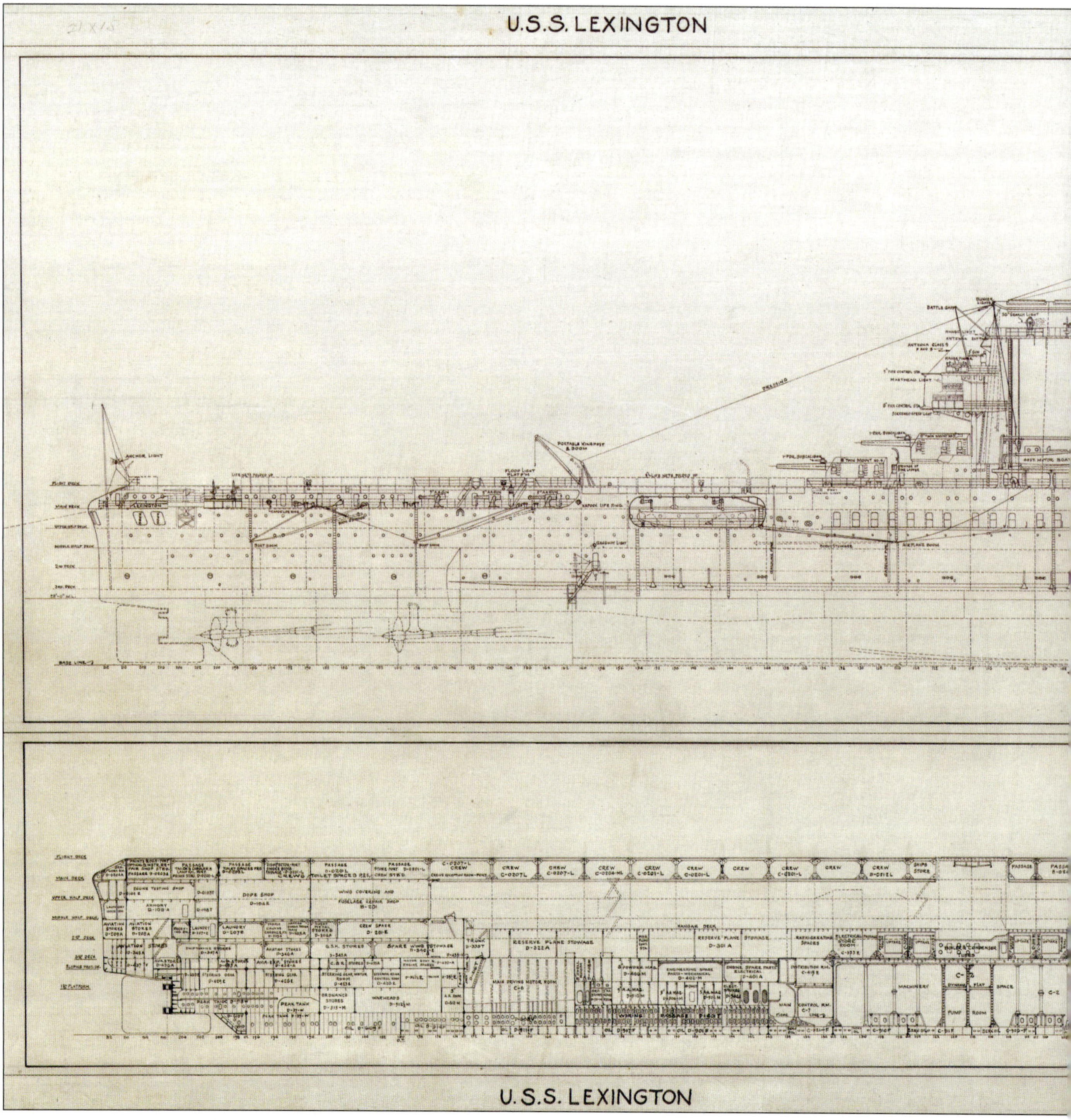

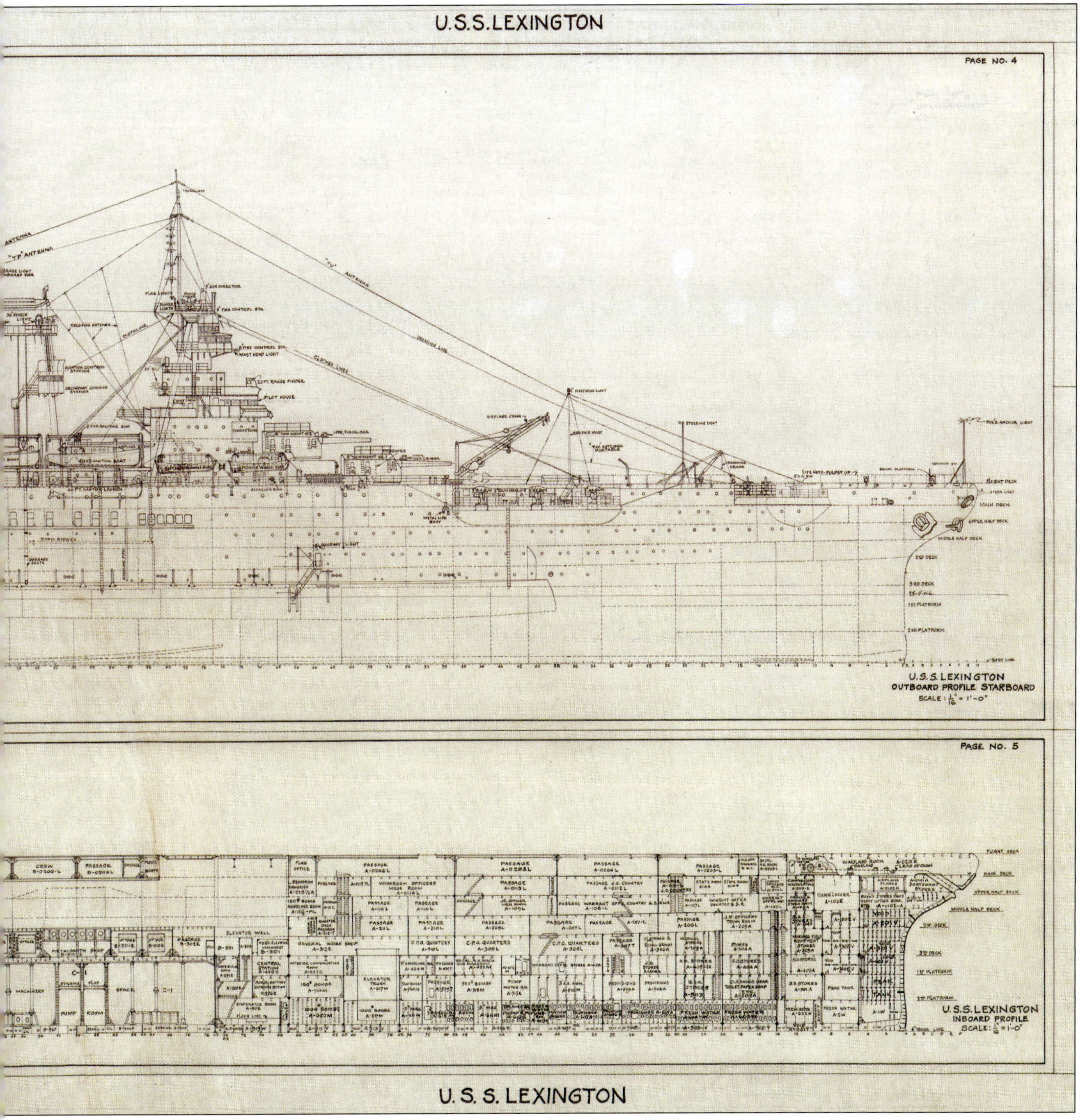
U.S.S. LEXINGTON
PAGE NO. 4
U.S.S. LEXINGTON
OUTBOARD PROFILE STARBOARD
SCALE: 1/16" = 1'-0"
PAGE NO. 5
U.S.S. LEXINGTON
INBOARD PROFILE
SCALE: 1/16" = 1'-0"
U. S. S. LEXINGTON

USS *Texas* (BB-35)

This drawing shows the areas assigned for the installation of new anti-aircraft guns aboard the USS *Texas* (BB-35). The Pearl Harbor attack demonstrated the need for more AA guns on all U.S. warships. By 1944, the Texas was fully equipped with ten quad-mounted 40 mm guns and 44 20 mm guns, along with several .50 caliber machine guns.

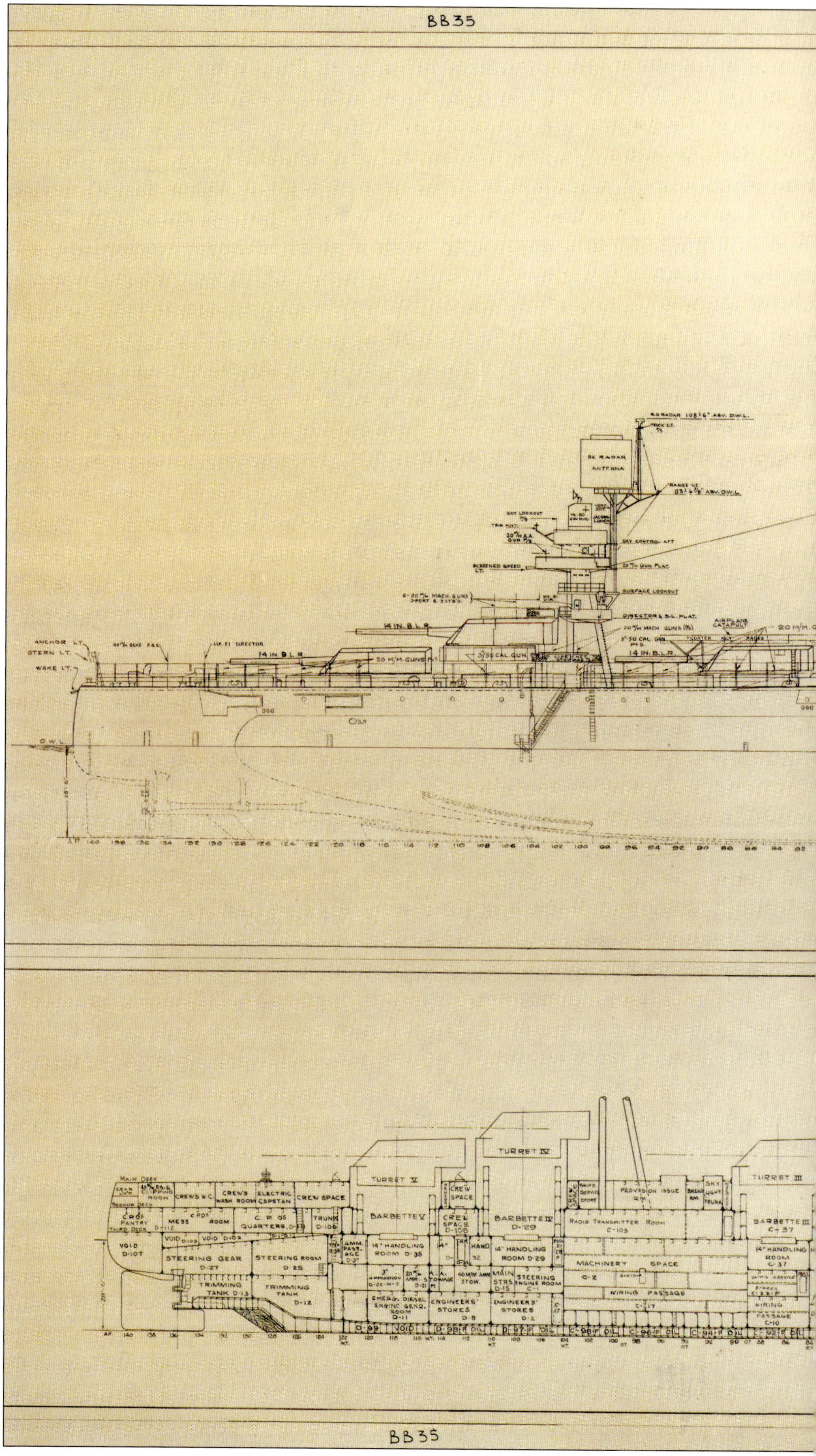

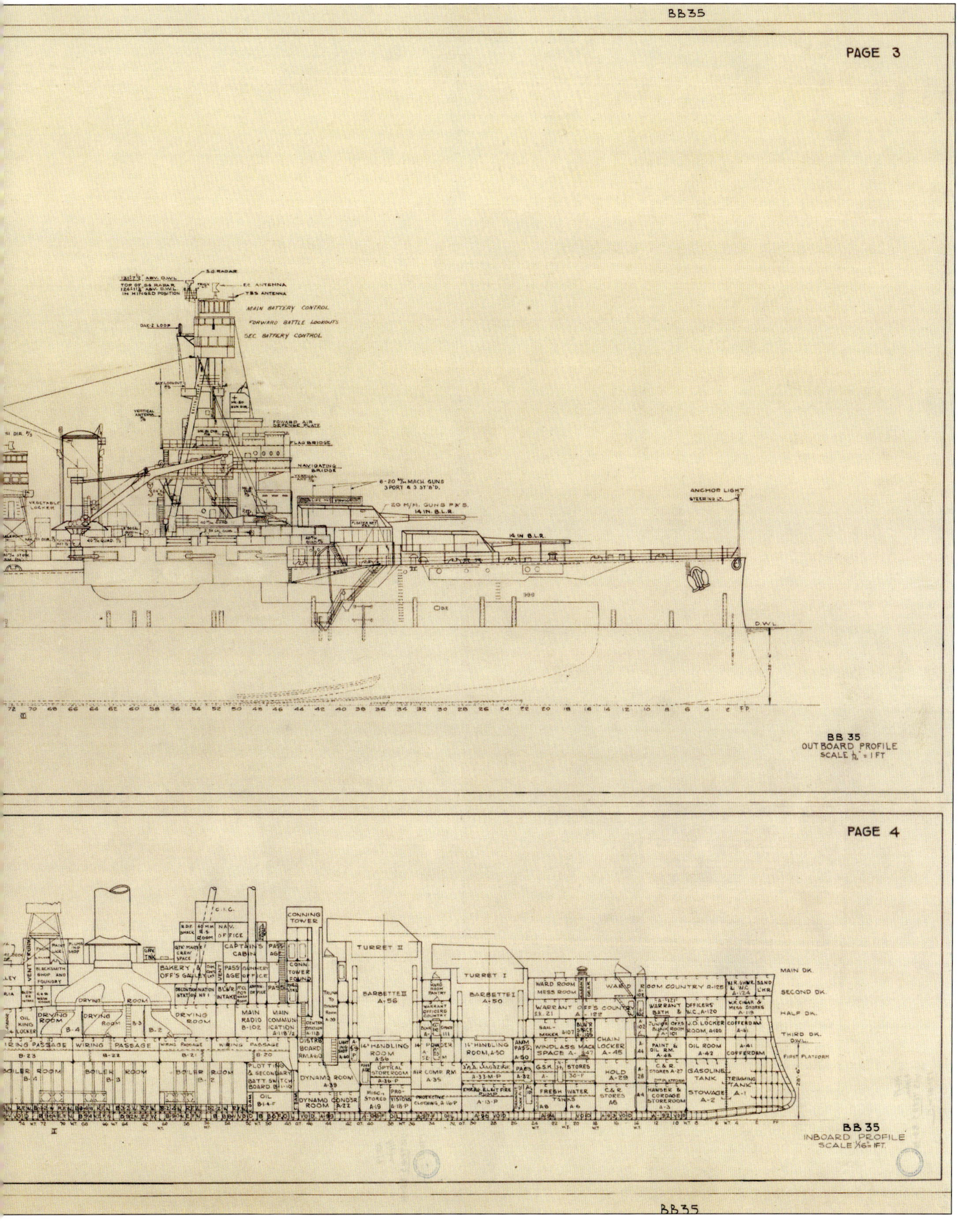
BB35
PAGE 3
MAIN BATTERY CONTROL
FORWARD BATTLE LOOKOUTS
SEC. BATTERY CONTROL
FORWARD AIR DEFENSE PLATE
FLAG BRIDGE
NAVIGATING BRIDGE
ANCHOR LIGHT
14 IN. B.L.R.
D.W.L.
BB 35
OUTBOARD PROFILE
SCALE 1/16" = 1 FT
PAGE 4
CONNING TOWER
TURRET II
TURRET I
BARBETTE II A-56
BARBETTE I A-50
CAPTAIN'S CABIN
MAIN DK.
SECOND DK.
HALF DK.
THIRD DK.
FIRST PLATFORM
BB 35
INBOARD PROFILE
SCALE 1/16" = 1 FT.
BB35

USS *Louisville* (CA 28)

Launched on September 1, 1930, the USS *Louisville* was the third *Northampton*-class heavy cruiser to be built. World War II cruisers were lightly armored, heavily armed fast ships designed for trade protection and to act as a screening force for U.S. Fast Attack Carrier groups and to scout out enemy fleets.

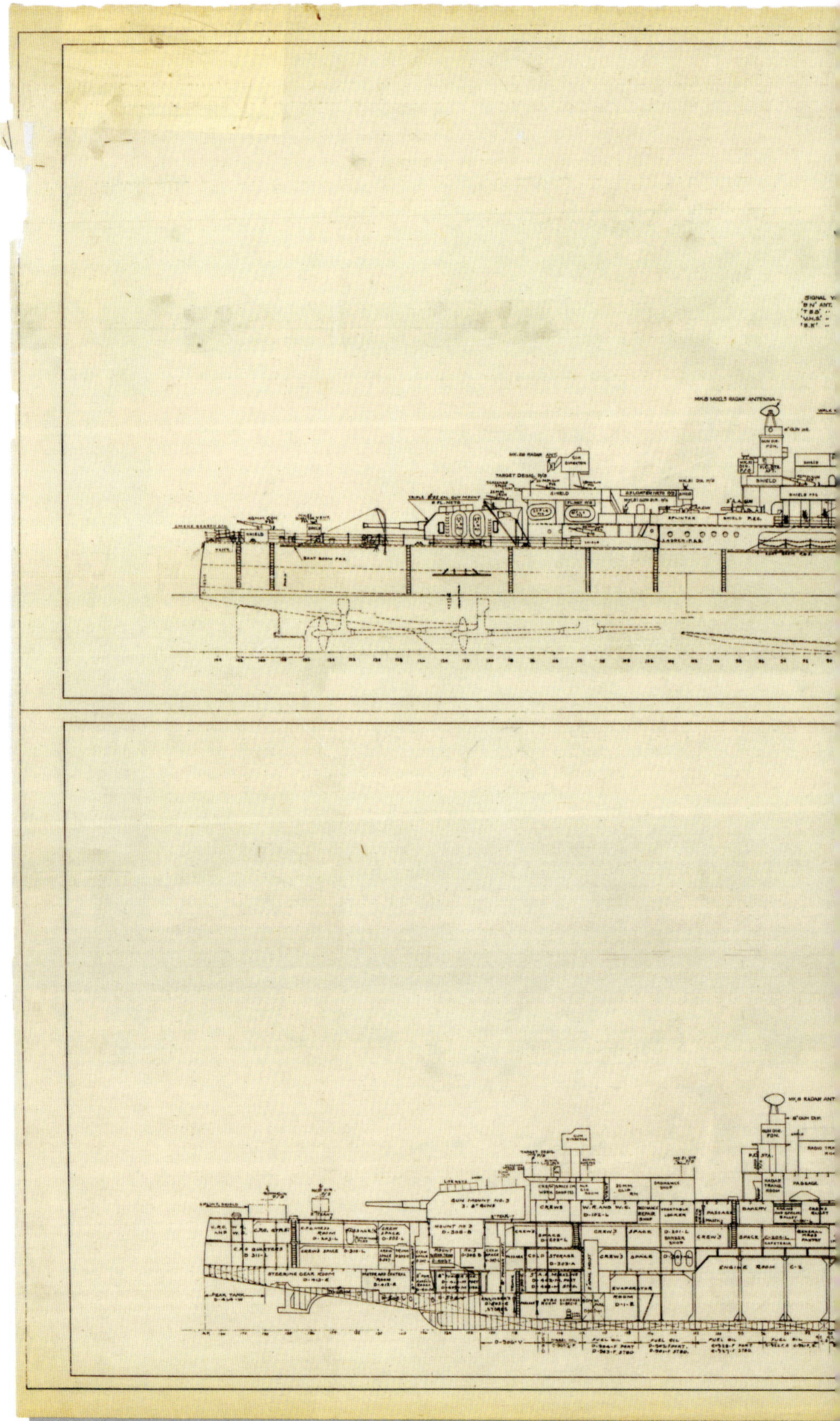

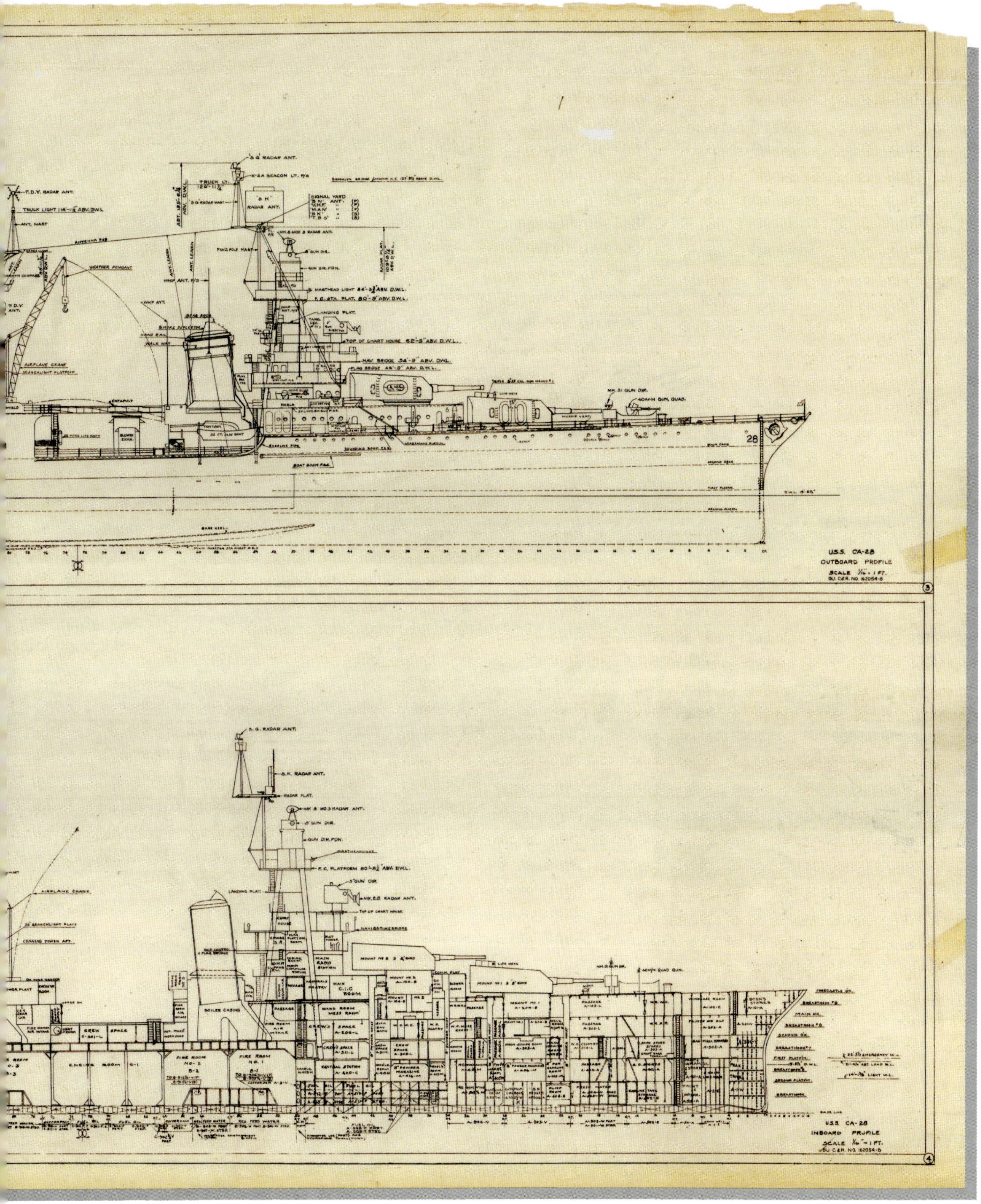

U.S.S. CA-28
OUTBOARD PROFILE
U.S.S. CA-28
INBOARD PROFILE

USS *Buck* (DD-420)

Bagley-class destroyers were externally similar to the earlier *Gridley*-class. The USS *Buck*'s armament was four 5-inch/38-caliber guns in single mounts and four quadruple mount torpedo tubes. Its speed was 38.5 knots with a crew of 158. These ships were all active in the Pacific, and during the Battle for Guadalcanal two were sunk and four damaged.

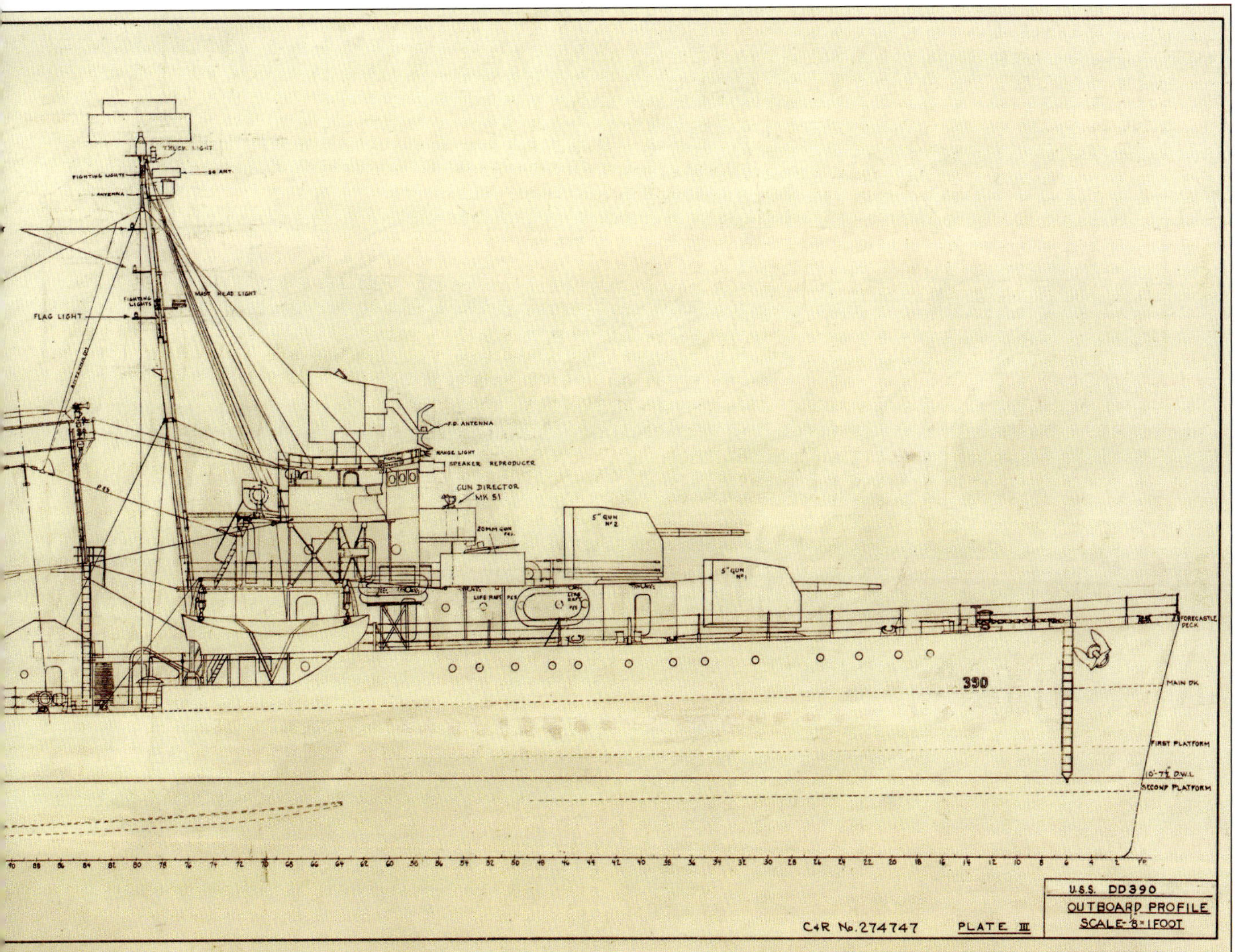
FLAG LIGHT
F.D. ANTENNA
RANGE LIGHT
SPEAKER REPRODUCER
GUN DIRECTOR
MK 51
FORECASTLE DECK
MAIN DK
FIRST PLATFORM
SECOND PLATFORM
390
U.S.S. DD390
OUTBOARD PROFILE
C&R No. 274747
PLATE III
D390

USS *Arizona* (BB-39)

The USS *Arizona* is the most famous and well-known USN battleship. During the Japanese attack on Pearl Harbor on December 7, 1941, the *Arizona* was hit by two armor-piercing bombs, one of which struck her forward magazine, causing a huge explosion. As the *Arizona* began to sink, the order to abandon ship was given. Many men were trapped below deck and did not survive. A total of 1,177 men died. Today the remains of the once mighty ship are a war grave.

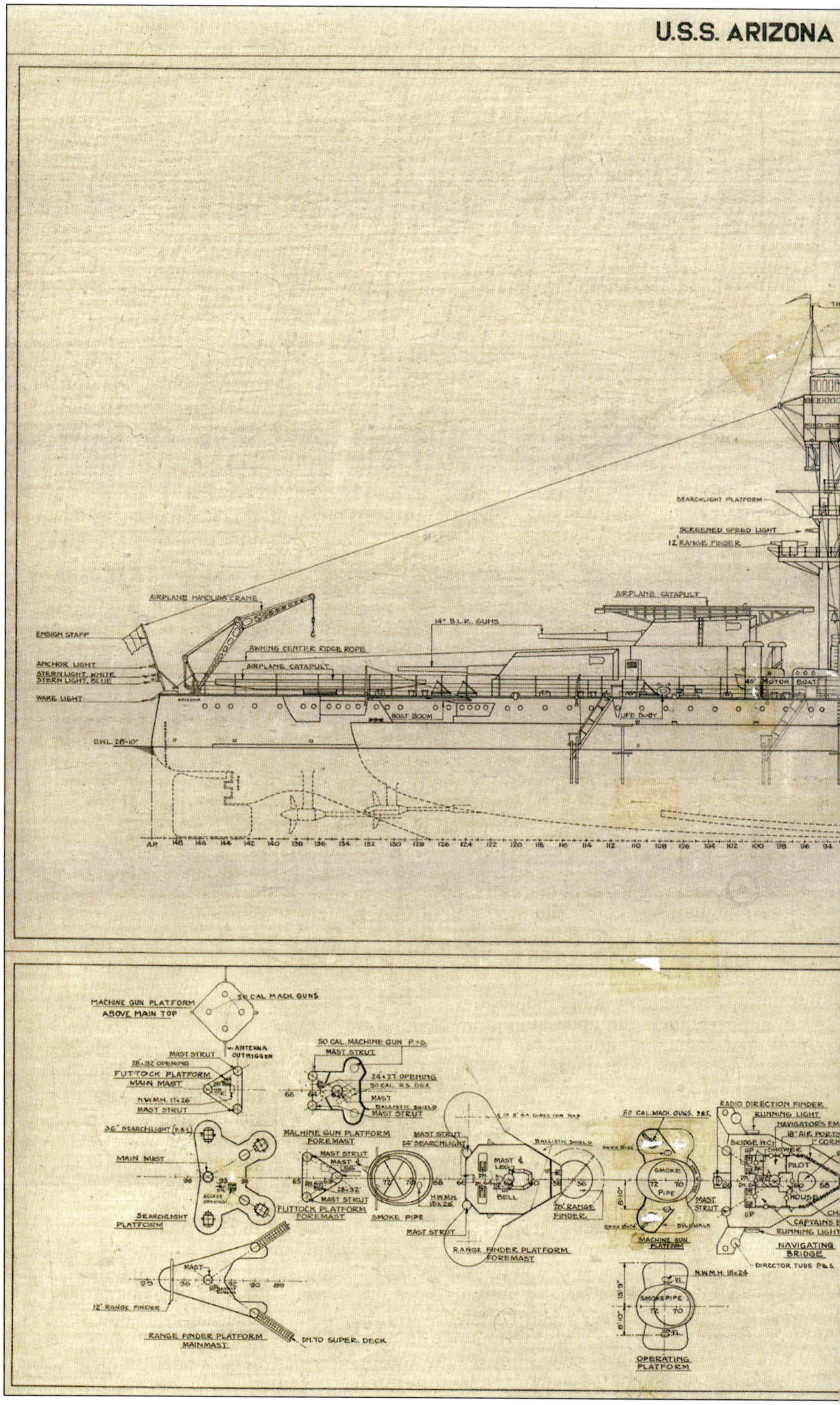

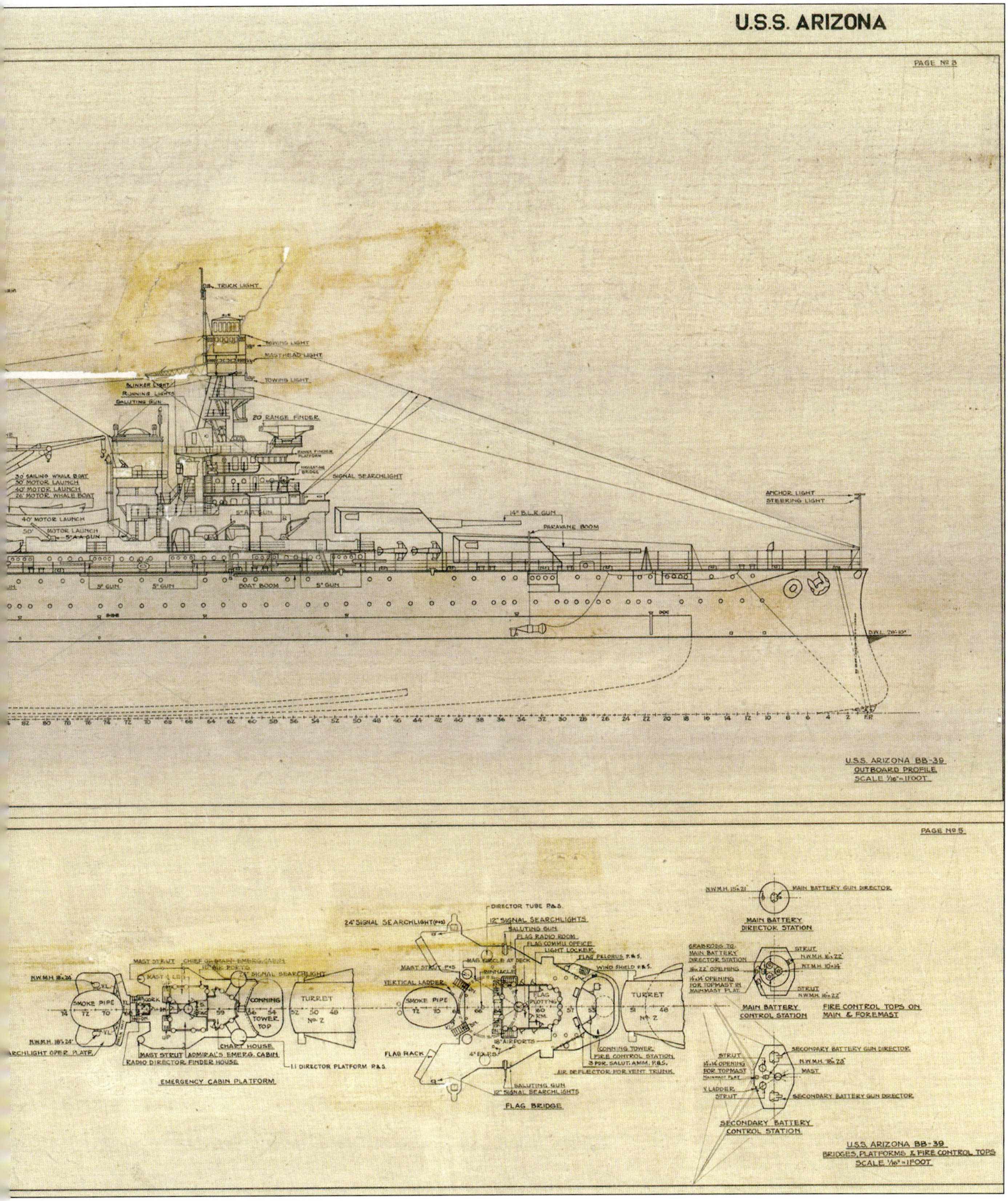
U.S.S. ARIZONA
PAGE Nº 3
TRUCK LIGHT
TOWING LIGHT
MASTHEAD LIGHT
BLINKER LIGHT
RUNNING LIGHTS
SALUTING GUN
20' RANGE FINDER
SIGNAL SEARCHLIGHT
30' SAILING WHALE BOAT
40' MOTOR LAUNCH
26' MOTOR WHALE BOAT
ANCHOR LIGHT
STEERING LIGHT
14" B.L.R. GUN
PARAVANE BOOM
5" GUN
BOAT BOOM
U.S.S. ARIZONA BB-39
OUTBOARD PROFILE
PAGE Nº 5
MAIN BATTERY GUN DIRECTOR
MAIN BATTERY DIRECTOR STATION
DIRECTOR TUBE P.&S.
24" SIGNAL SEARCHLIGHT
12" SIGNAL SEARCHLIGHTS
SALUTING GUN
FLAG RADIO ROOM
SMOKE PIPE
TURRET
Nº 2
CONNING TOWER TOP
CHART HOUSE
MAST STRUT
ADMIRAL'S EMERG. CABIN
RADIO DIRECTOR FINDER HOUSE
1.1 DIRECTOR PLATFORM P.&S.
EMERGENCY CABIN PLATFORM
VERTICAL LADDER
FLAG RACK
CONNING TOWER
FIRE CONTROL STATION
FLAG BRIDGE
MAIN BATTERY CONTROL STATION
FIRE CONTROL TOPS ON MAIN & FOREMAST
SECONDARY BATTERY GUN DIRECTOR
SECONDARY BATTERY CONTROL STATION
U.S.S. ARIZONA BB-39
BRIDGES, PLATFORMS & FIRE CONTROL TOPS

USS *Seawolf* (SS-197)

When America entered the war, the USN had 112 submarines in commission. Half of these boats, however, were of World War I vintage and too old for combat. The USS *Seawolf* was one of six boats of the *Sargo*-class. With a crew of 55, it had a range of 17,703 kilometers (11,000 miles) at 10 knots and was armed with 20 torpedoes. The *Seawolf* was lost in December 1944 for unknown reasons.

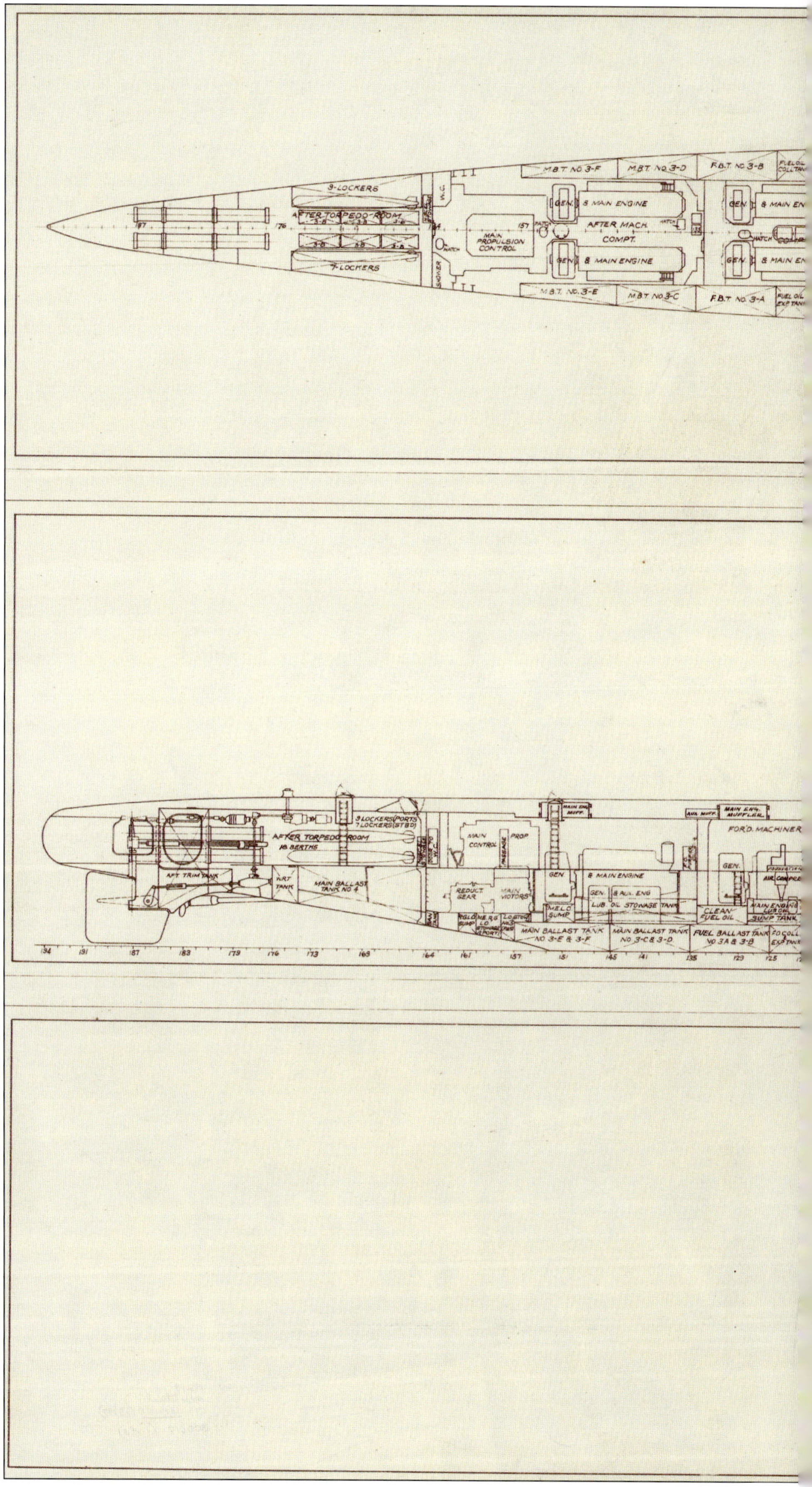

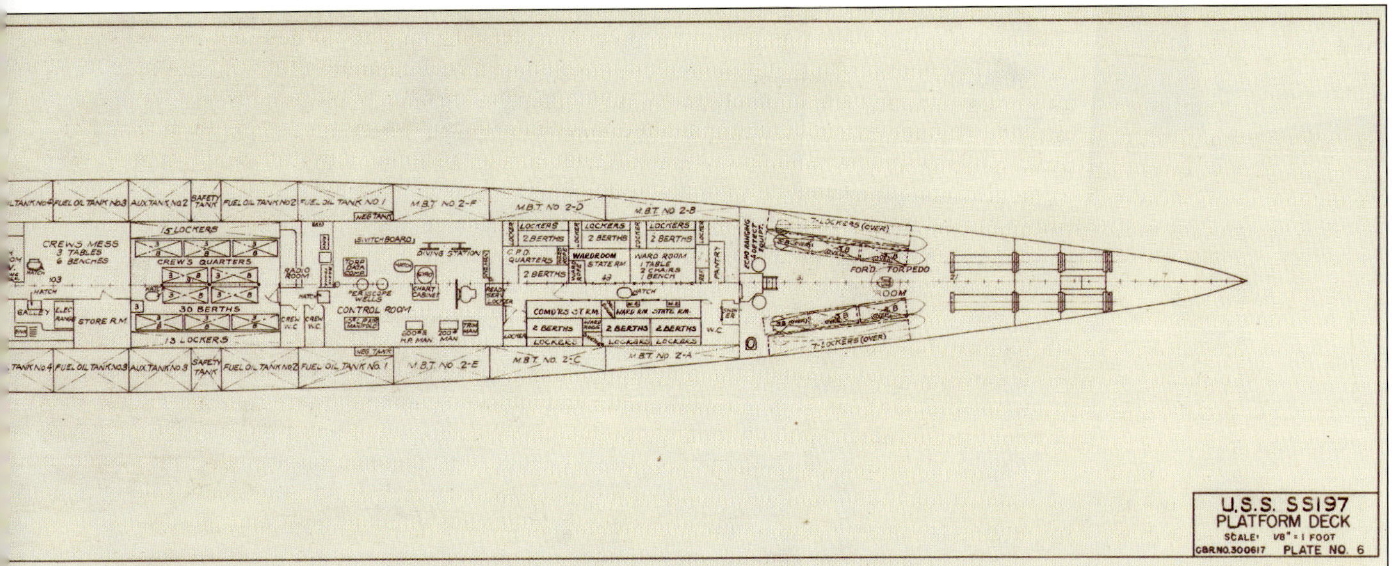
U.S.S. SS197
PLATFORM DECK
SCALE: 1/8" = 1 FOOT
CBR.NO.300617 PLATE NO. 6

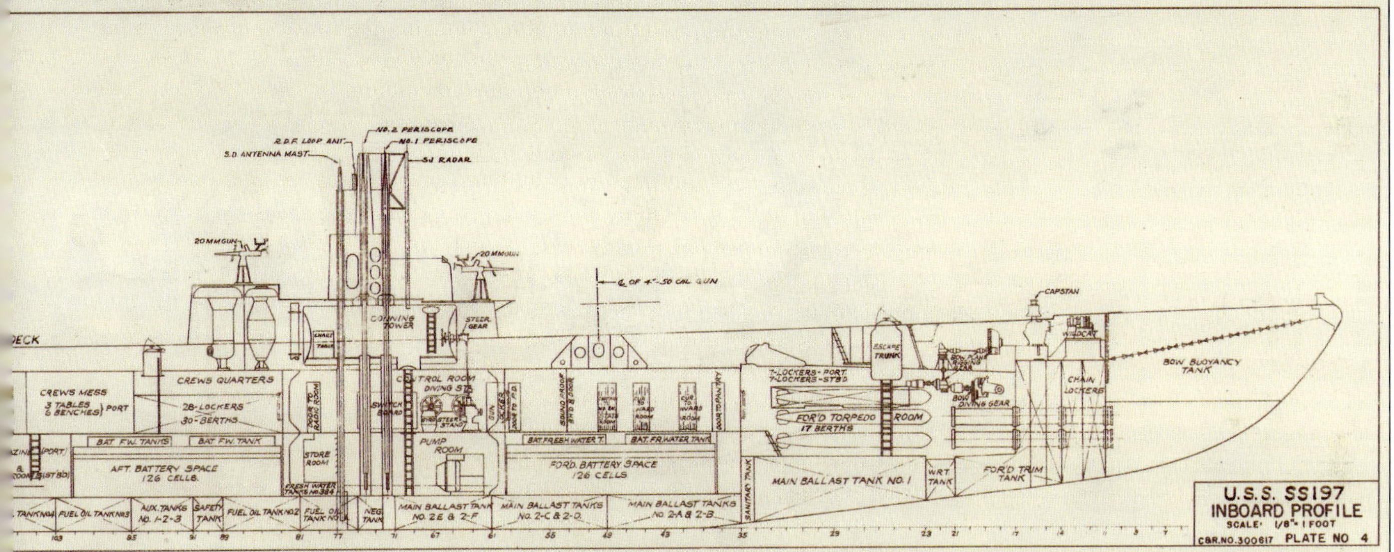
U.S.S. SS197
INBOARD PROFILE
SCALE: 1/8" = 1 FOOT
CBR.NO.300617 PLATE NO 4

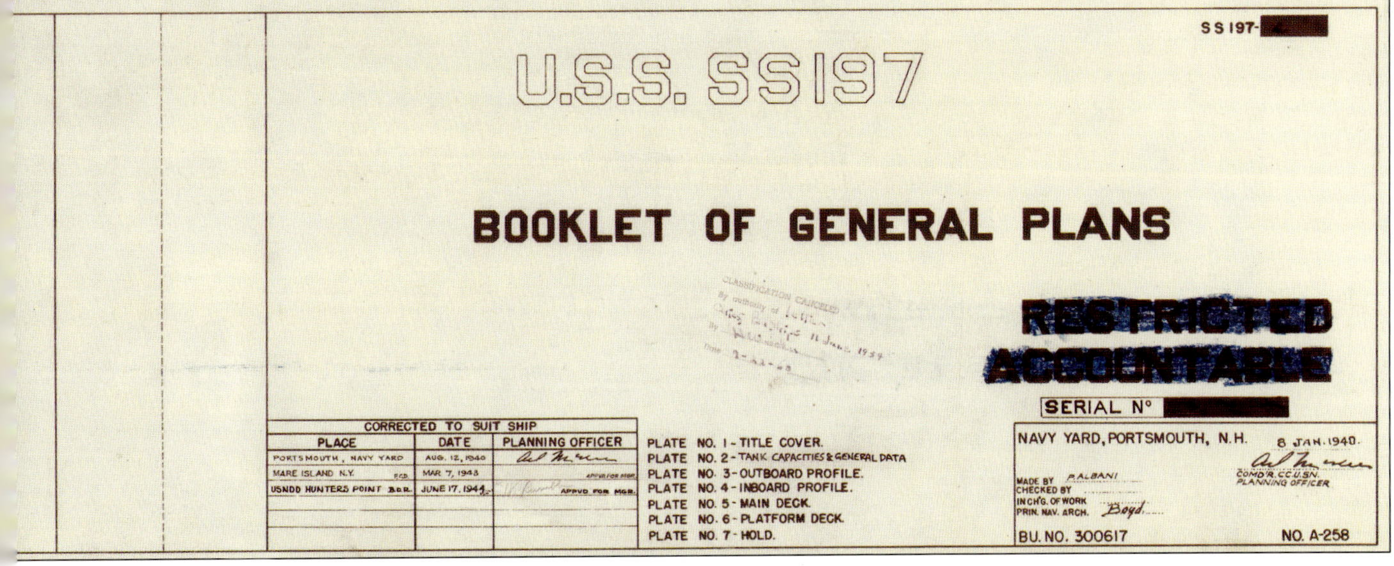
SS 197-[illegible]
U.S.S. SS197
BOOKLET OF GENERAL PLANS
RESTRICTED
ACCOUNTABLE
SERIAL N°
CORRECTED TO SUIT SHIP
PLACE DATE PLANNING OFFICER
PORTSMOUTH, NAVY YARD AUG. 12, 1940
MARE ISLAND N.Y. MAR. 7, 1943
USNDD HUNTERS POINT JUNE 17, 1944 APPVD FOR MGR.
PLATE NO. 1 - TITLE COVER.
PLATE NO. 2 - TANK CAPACITIES & GENERAL DATA
PLATE NO. 3 - OUTBOARD PROFILE.
PLATE NO. 4 - INBOARD PROFILE.
PLATE NO. 5 - MAIN DECK.
PLATE NO. 6 - PLATFORM DECK.
PLATE NO. 7 - HOLD.
NAVY YARD, PORTSMOUTH, N.H. 8 JAN. 1940.
MADE BY P. ALBANI
CHECKED BY
IN CH'G. OF WORK
PRIN. NAV. ARCH. Boyd
COMD'R. C.C. U.S.N. PLANNING OFFICER
BU. NO. 300617
NO. A-258

USS *Houston* Torpedo Damage

During World War II, a 'war damage report' was required when a ship sustained battle damage or any other type of mishap (e.g., collision, running aground, explosion, fire, heavy weather damage). At the first opportunity, a follow-up, detailed, preliminary shipboard inspection/damage assessment at sea of the affected spaces was conducted for a required, descriptive war damage report. The *Houston* was damaged by two Japanese aircraft torpedoes off Formosa in October 1944.

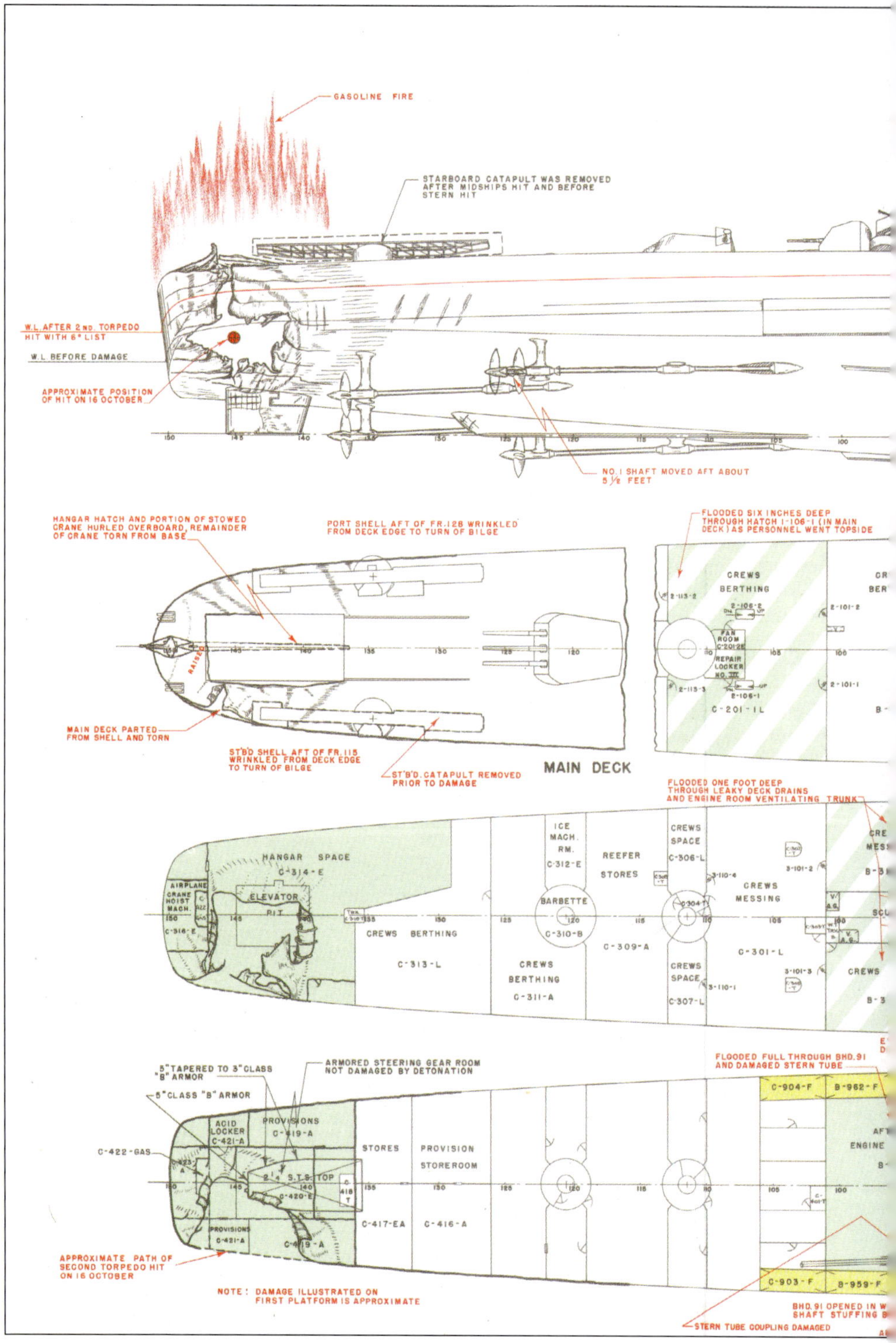

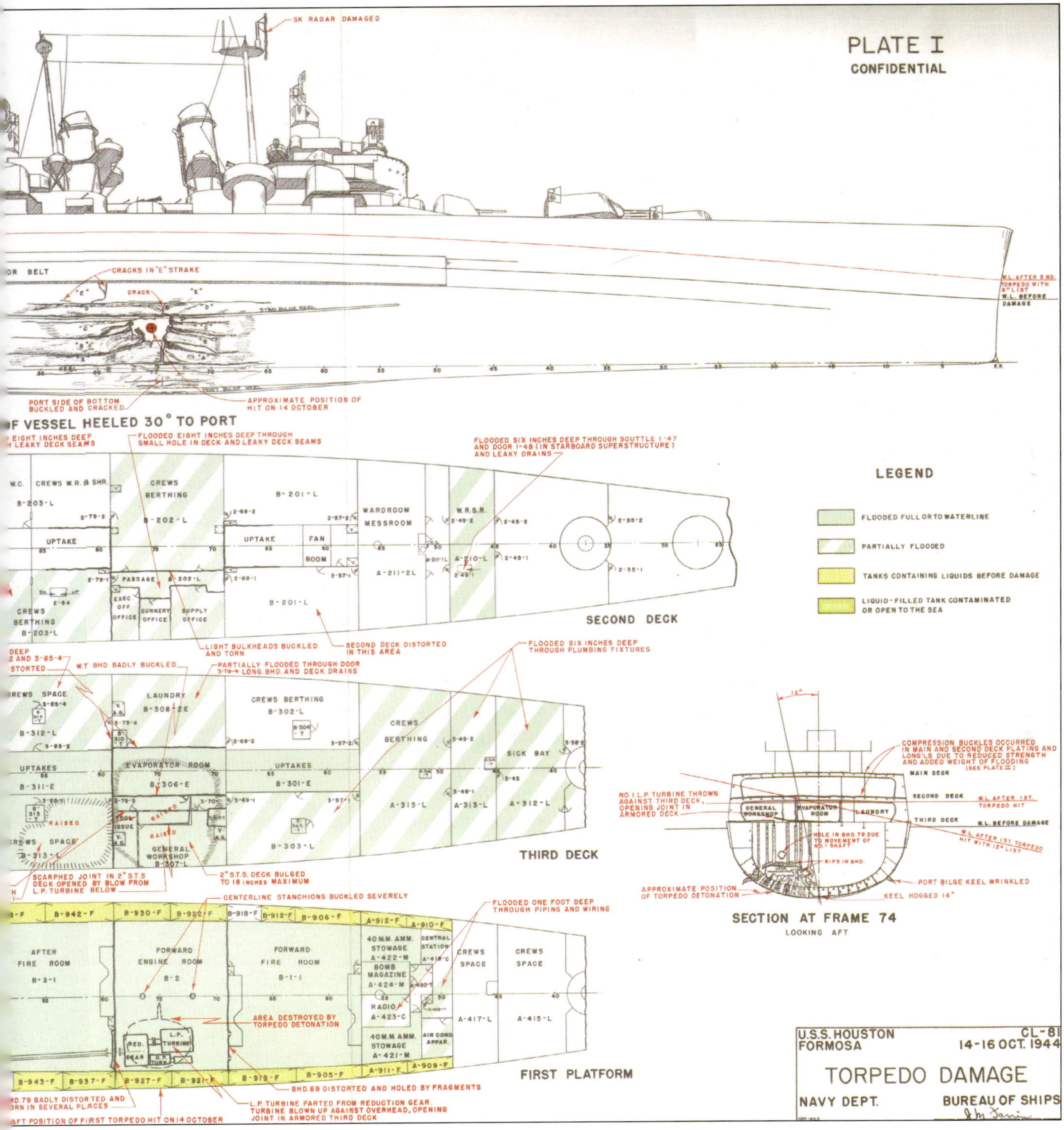

PLATE I
CONFIDENTIAL
SK RADAR DAMAGED
CRACKS IN "E" STRAKE
CRACK
PORT SIDE OF BOTTOM BUCKLED AND CRACKED
APPROXIMATE POSITION OF HIT ON 14 OCTOBER
W.L. AFTER 2 ND. TORPEDO WITH 6° LIST
W.L. BEFORE DAMAGE
F VESSEL HEELED 30° TO PORT
FLOODED EIGHT INCHES DEEP THROUGH SMALL HOLE IN DECK AND LEAKY DECK SEAMS
FLOODED SIX INCHES DEEP THROUGH SCUTTLE 1-47 AND DOOR 1-48 (IN STARBOARD SUPERSTRUCTURE) AND LEAKY DRAINS
LEGEND
FLOODED FULL OR TO WATERLINE
PARTIALLY FLOODED
TANKS CONTAINING LIQUIDS BEFORE DAMAGE
LIQUID-FILLED TANK CONTAMINATED OR OPEN TO THE SEA
CREWS BERTHING
WARDROOM MESSROOM
UPTAKE
FAN ROOM
PASSAGE
EXEC OFF. OFFICE
GUNNERY OFFICE
SUPPLY OFFICE
SECOND DECK
LIGHT BULKHEADS BUCKLED AND TORN
SECOND DECK DISTORTED IN THIS AREA
FLOODED SIX INCHES DEEP THROUGH PLUMBING FIXTURES
W.T. BHD BADLY BUCKLED
PARTIALLY FLOODED THROUGH DOOR 3-79-4 LONG. BHD. AND DECK DRAINS
LAUNDRY
CREWS SPACE
EVAPORATOR ROOM
UPTAKES
SICK BAY
RAISED
ISSUE
GENERAL WORKSHOP
THIRD DECK
SCARPHED JOINT IN 2" S.T.S. DECK OPENED BY BLOW FROM L.P. TURBINE BELOW
2" S.T.S. DECK BULGED TO 18 INCHES MAXIMUM
CENTERLINE STANCHIONS BUCKLED SEVERELY
FLOODED ONE FOOT DEEP THROUGH PIPING AND WIRING
AFTER FIRE ROOM
FORWARD ENGINE ROOM
FORWARD FIRE ROOM
40 MM. AMM. STOWAGE
CENTRAL STATION
BOMB MAGAZINE
RADIO
AIR COND. APPAR.
AREA DESTROYED BY TORPEDO DETONATION
RED. GEAR
L.P. TURBINE
FIRST PLATFORM
BHD. 69 DISTORTED AND HOLED BY FRAGMENTS
L.P. TURBINE PARTED FROM REDUCTION GEAR. TURBINE BLOWN UP AGAINST OVERHEAD, OPENING JOINT IN ARMORED THIRD DECK
AFT POSITION OF FIRST TORPEDO HIT ON 14 OCTOBER
COMPRESSION BUCKLES OCCURRED IN MAIN AND SECOND DECK PLATING AND LONG'LS DUE TO REDUCED STRENGTH AND ADDED WEIGHT OF FLOODING
MAIN DECK
SECOND DECK
THIRD DECK
W.L. AFTER 1ST. TORPEDO HIT
W.L. BEFORE DAMAGE
NO. 1 L.P. TURBINE THROWN AGAINST THIRD DECK, OPENING JOINT IN ARMORED DECK
PORT BILGE KEEL WRINKLED
KEEL HOGGED 14"
APPROXIMATE POSITION OF TORPEDO DETONATION
SECTION AT FRAME 74
LOOKING AFT
U.S.S. HOUSTON CL-81
FORMOSA 14-16 OCT. 1944
TORPEDO DAMAGE
NAVY DEPT.
BUREAU OF SHIPS

USS *South Dakota* Damage

"During the action off Guadalcanal on the night of 14–15 November 1942, *South Dakota* was hit by at least 26 projectiles. The most serious material damage was that sustained by electrical wiring circuits. Many interior communication and fire control circuits were severed, particularly in the superstructure where the damage was most extensive. In spite of numerous hits, *South Dakota* received only superficial damage. Neither the strength, buoyancy nor stability were measurably impaired."
USS South Dakota *Gunfire Damage Report*

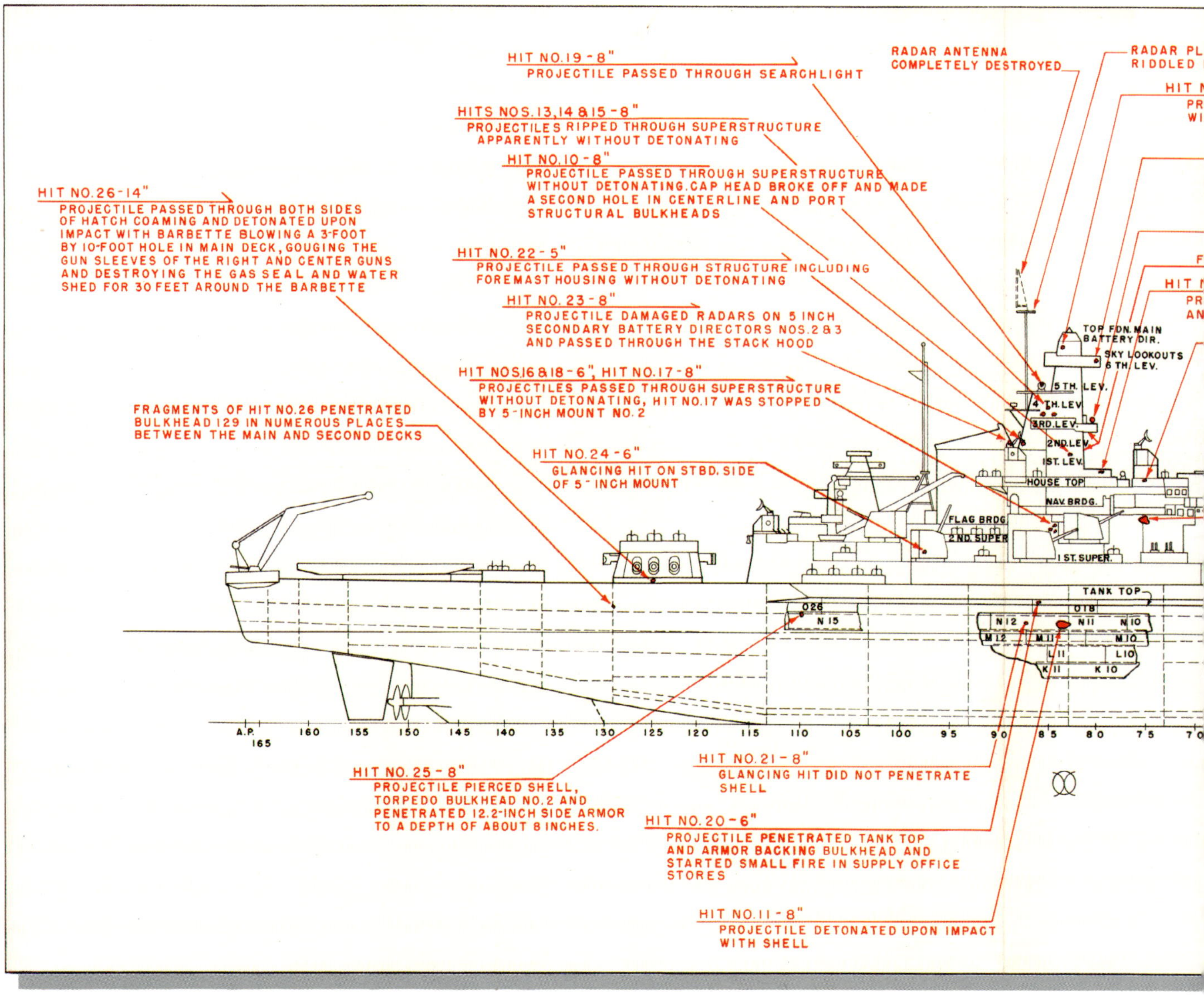

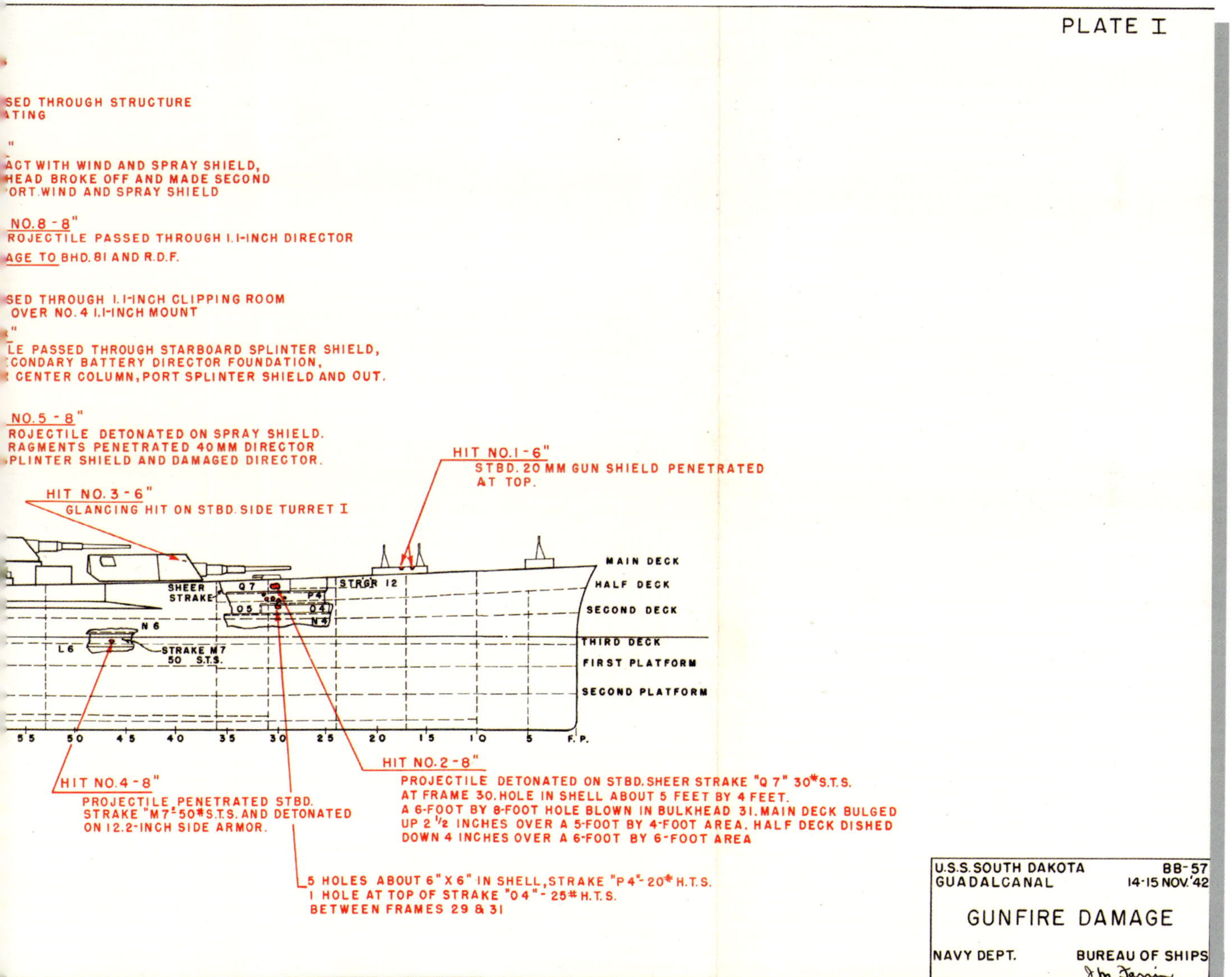
PLATE I
SED THROUGH STRUCTURE
ATING
ACT WITH WIND AND SPRAY SHIELD,
HEAD BROKE OFF AND MADE SECOND
ORT. WIND AND SPRAY SHIELD
NO. 8 - 8"
ROJECTILE PASSED THROUGH 1.1-INCH DIRECTOR
AGE TO BHD. 81 AND R.D.F.
SED THROUGH 1.1-INCH CLIPPING ROOM
OVER NO. 4 1.1-INCH MOUNT
LE PASSED THROUGH STARBOARD SPLINTER SHIELD,
CONDARY BATTERY DIRECTOR FOUNDATION,
CENTER COLUMN, PORT SPLINTER SHIELD AND OUT.
NO. 5 - 8"
ROJECTILE DETONATED ON SPRAY SHIELD.
RAGMENTS PENETRATED 40 MM DIRECTOR
PLINTER SHIELD AND DAMAGED DIRECTOR.
HIT NO. 1 - 6"
STBD. 20 MM GUN SHIELD PENETRATED AT TOP.
HIT NO. 3 - 6"
GLANCING HIT ON STBD. SIDE TURRET I
MAIN DECK
HALF DECK
SECOND DECK
THIRD DECK
FIRST PLATFORM
SECOND PLATFORM
SHEER STRAKE
Q 7
STRGR 12
O 5
P 4
O 4
N 4
N 6
L 6
STRAKE M 7 50 S.T.S.
55 50 45 40 35 30 25 20 15 10 5 F.P.
HIT NO. 2 - 8"
PROJECTILE DETONATED ON STBD. SHEER STRAKE "Q 7" 30# S.T.S.
AT FRAME 30. HOLE IN SHELL ABOUT 5 FEET BY 4 FEET.
A 6-FOOT BY 8-FOOT HOLE BLOWN IN BULKHEAD 31. MAIN DECK BULGED
UP 2 1/2 INCHES OVER A 5-FOOT BY 4-FOOT AREA. HALF DECK DISHED
DOWN 4 INCHES OVER A 6-FOOT BY 6-FOOT AREA
HIT NO. 4 - 8"
PROJECTILE PENETRATED STBD.
STRAKE "M7" 50# S.T.S. AND DETONATED
ON 12.2-INCH SIDE ARMOR.
5 HOLES ABOUT 6" X 6" IN SHELL, STRAKE "P4" - 20# H.T.S.
1 HOLE AT TOP OF STRAKE "O4" - 25# H.T.S.
BETWEEN FRAMES 29 & 31
U.S.S. SOUTH DAKOTA BB-57
GUADALCANAL 14-15 NOV. '42
GUNFIRE DAMAGE
NAVY DEPT. BUREAU OF SHIPS

USS *Enterprise* Damage

The *Enterprise* was the most decorated warship of World War II, earning 20 battle stars. She and the USS *Saratoga* were the only U.S. carriers to survive the entire war. "During the period of the war she was damaged by the enemy on six separate occasions by 13 hits or near-misses from bombs or suicide planes. In addition, she was damaged by a fire caused by the detonation of a 'friendly' 5-inch anti-aircraft shell. In all cases but one, her excellent damage control organization prevented serious consequences and enabled *Enterprise* to continue in action. Damage to her flight deck, which resulted from the suicide plane crash of 14 May 1945, so impaired her operating efficiency that she was forced to retire the following day."

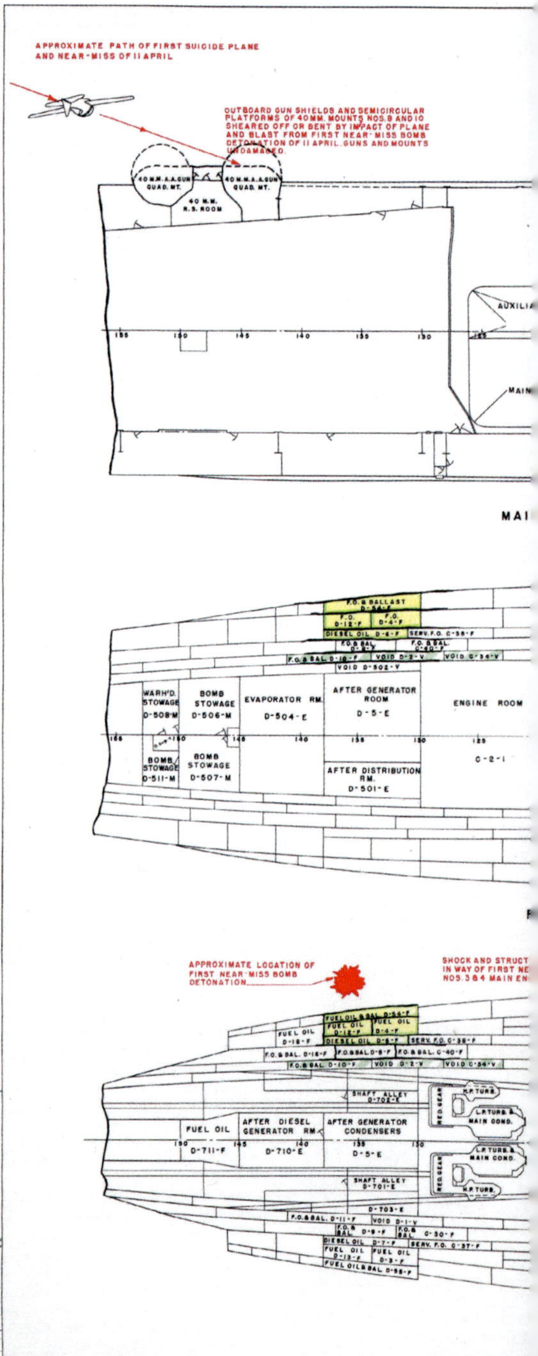

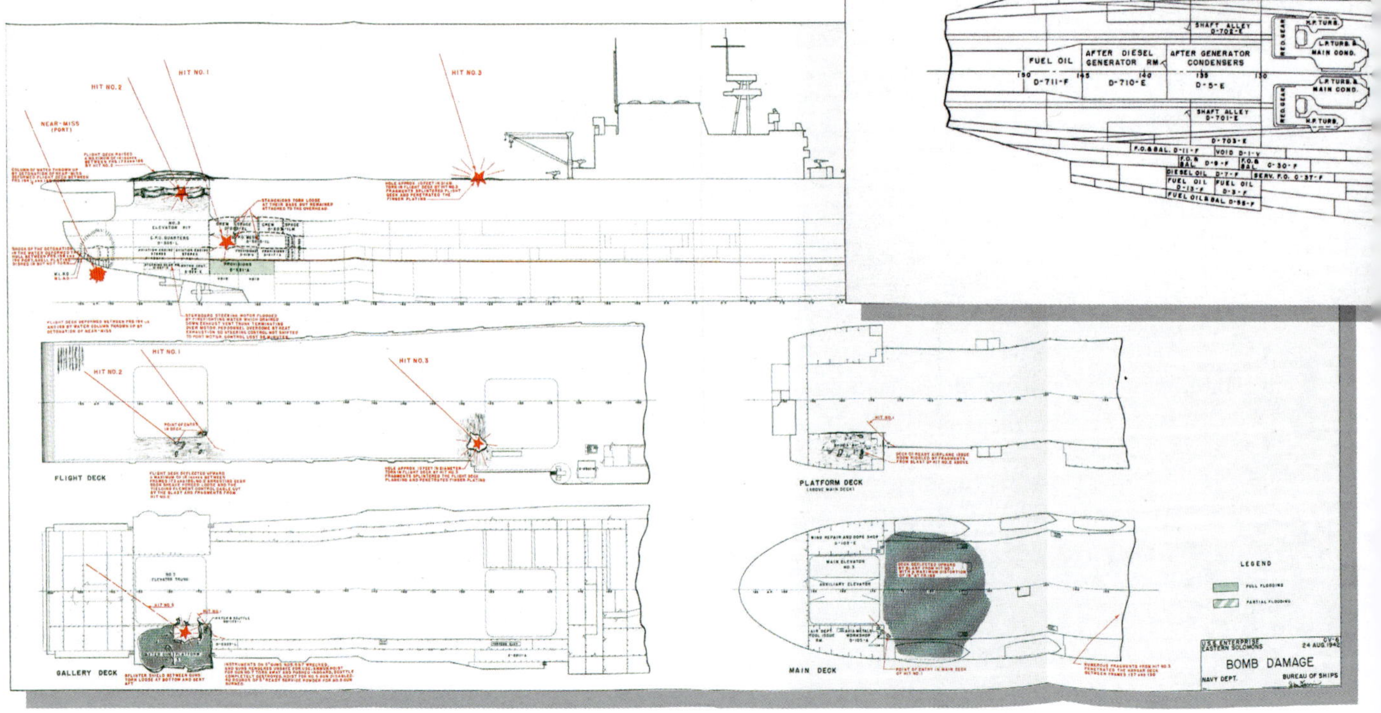

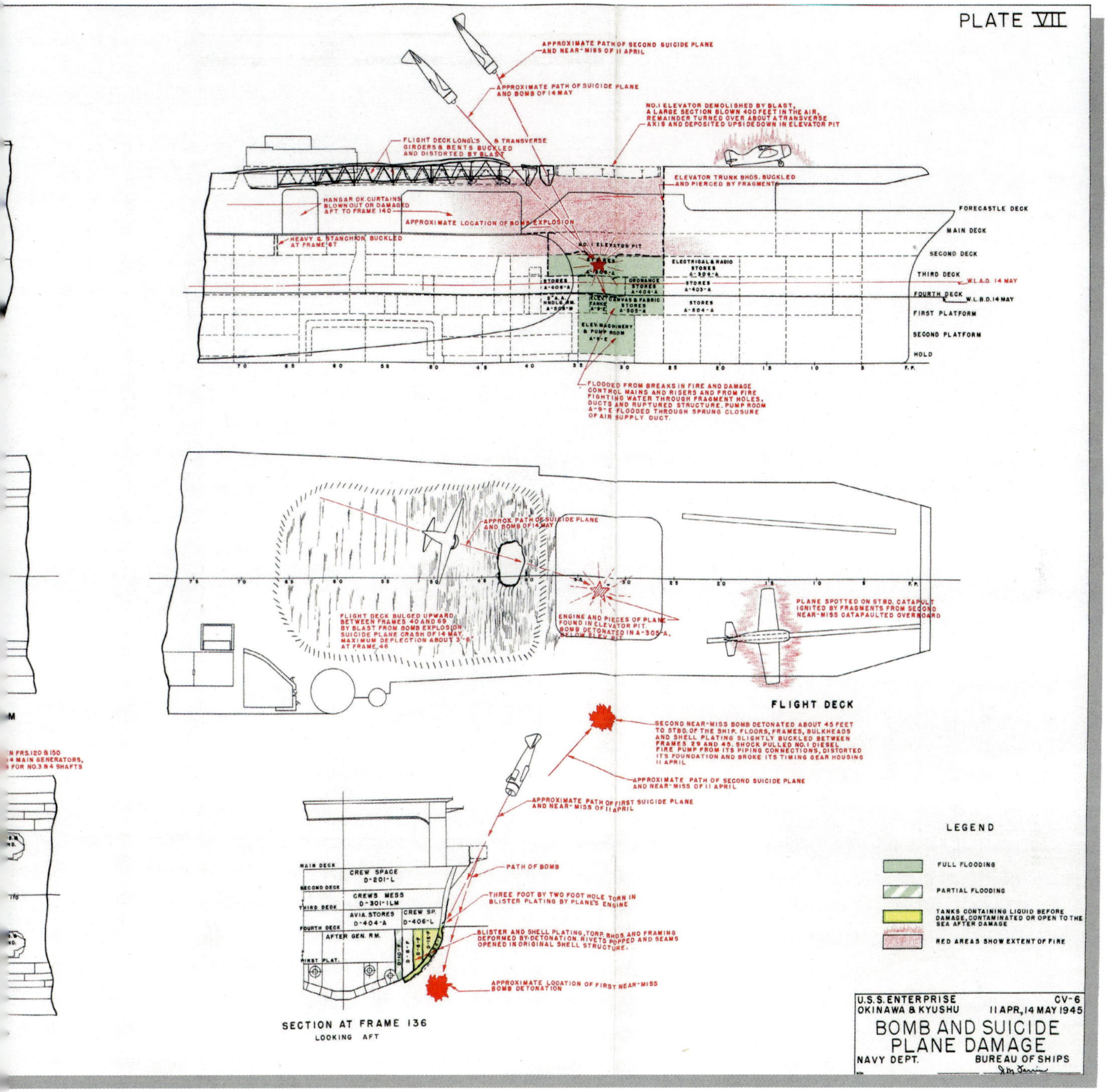
PLATE VII
APPROXIMATE PATH OF SECOND SUICIDE PLANE AND NEAR-MISS OF 11 APRIL
APPROXIMATE PATH OF SUICIDE PLANE AND BOMB OF 14 MAY
NO. 1 ELEVATOR DEMOLISHED BY BLAST, A LARGE SECTION BLOWN 400 FEET IN THE AIR, REMAINDER TURNED OVER ABOUT A TRANSVERSE AXIS AND DEPOSITED UPSIDE DOWN IN ELEVATOR PIT
FLIGHT DECK LONGL'S & TRANSVERSE GIRDERS & BENTS BUCKLED AND DISTORTED BY BLAST
ELEVATOR TRUNK BHDS. BUCKLED AND PIERCED BY FRAGMENTS
HANGAR DK. CURTAINS BLOWN OUT OR DAMAGED AFT TO FRAME 140
APPROXIMATE LOCATION OF BOMB EXPLOSION
HEAVY & STANCHION BUCKLED AT FRAME 67
NO. 1 ELEVATOR PIT
STORES A-406-A
5" A.A. HNDLG. RM. A-505-M
ELEV. TANKS A-9-E
CANVAS & FABRIC STORES A-505-A
ORDNANCE STORES A-404-A
ELEV. MACHINERY & PUMP ROOM A-9-E
ELECTRICAL & RADIO STORES A-504-A
STORES A-403-A
STORES A-504-A
FORECASTLE DECK
MAIN DECK
SECOND DECK
THIRD DECK
W.L.A.D. 14 MAY
FOURTH DECK
W.L.B.D. 14 MAY
FIRST PLATFORM
SECOND PLATFORM
HOLD
FLOODED FROM BREAKS IN FIRE AND DAMAGE CONTROL MAINS AND RISERS AND FROM FIRE FIGHTING WATER THROUGH FRAGMENT HOLES, DUCTS AND RUPTURED STRUCTURE. PUMP ROOM A-9-E FLOODED THROUGH SPRUNG CLOSURE OF AIR SUPPLY DUCT.
APPROX. PATH OF SUICIDE PLANE AND BOMB OF 14 MAY
FLIGHT DECK BULGED UPWARD BETWEEN FRAMES 40 AND 69 BY BLAST FROM BOMB EXPLOSION SUICIDE PLANE CRASH OF 14 MAY. MAXIMUM DEFLECTION ABOUT 3'-6" AT FRAME 46
ENGINE AND PIECES OF PLANE FOUND IN ELEVATOR PIT. BOMB DETONATED IN A-305-A, BELOW ELEV. PIT
PLANE SPOTTED ON STBD. CATAPULT IGNITED BY FRAGMENTS FROM SECOND NEAR-MISS CATAPAULTED OVERBOARD
FLIGHT DECK
SECOND NEAR-MISS BOMB DETONATED ABOUT 45 FEET TO STBD. OF THE SHIP. FLOORS, FRAMES, BULKHEADS AND SHELL PLATING SLIGHTLY BUCKLED BETWEEN FRAMES 29 AND 45. SHOCK PULLED NO. 1 DIESEL FIRE PUMP FROM ITS PIPING CONNECTIONS, DISTORTED ITS FOUNDATION AND BROKE ITS TIMING GEAR HOUSING 11 APRIL
APPROXIMATE PATH OF SECOND SUICIDE PLANE AND NEAR-MISS OF 11 APRIL
APPROXIMATE PATH OF FIRST SUICIDE PLANE AND NEAR-MISS OF 11 APRIL
MAIN DECK
CREW SPACE D-201-L
SECOND DECK
CREWS MESS D-301-ILM
THIRD DECK
AVIA. STORES D-404-A
CREW SP. D-406-L
FOURTH DECK
AFTER GEN. RM.
FIRST PLAT.
PATH OF BOMB
THREE FOOT BY TWO FOOT HOLE TORN IN BLISTER PLATING BY PLANE'S ENGINE
BLISTER AND SHELL PLATING, TORP. BHDS. AND FRAMING DEFORMED BY DETONATION. RIVETS POPPED AND SEAMS OPENED IN ORIGINAL SHELL STRUCTURE.
APPROXIMATE LOCATION OF FIRST NEAR-MISS BOMB DETONATION
SECTION AT FRAME 136
LOOKING AFT
LEGEND
FULL FLOODING
PARTIAL FLOODING
TANKS CONTAINING LIQUID BEFORE DAMAGE, CONTAMINATED OR OPEN TO THE SEA AFTER DAMAGE
RED AREAS SHOW EXTENT OF FIRE
U.S.S. ENTERPRISE CV-6
OKINAWA & KYUSHU 11 APR, 14 MAY 1945
BOMB AND SUICIDE PLANE DAMAGE
NAVY DEPT. BUREAU OF SHIPS

USS *Tang* Torpedo Damage

Fifty-two U.S. submarines were lost during the period from December 7, 1941, to August 15, 1945, through enemy action or for reasons unknown. On October 24, 1944, during her fifth war patrol, *Tang* was sunk in Formosa Strait because of the malfunctioning of one of her own torpedoes, which made a circular run and returned to strike the hull abreast the after-torpedo room. The resulting detonation caused the ship to plunge by the stern within a few seconds. There were only a few survivors.

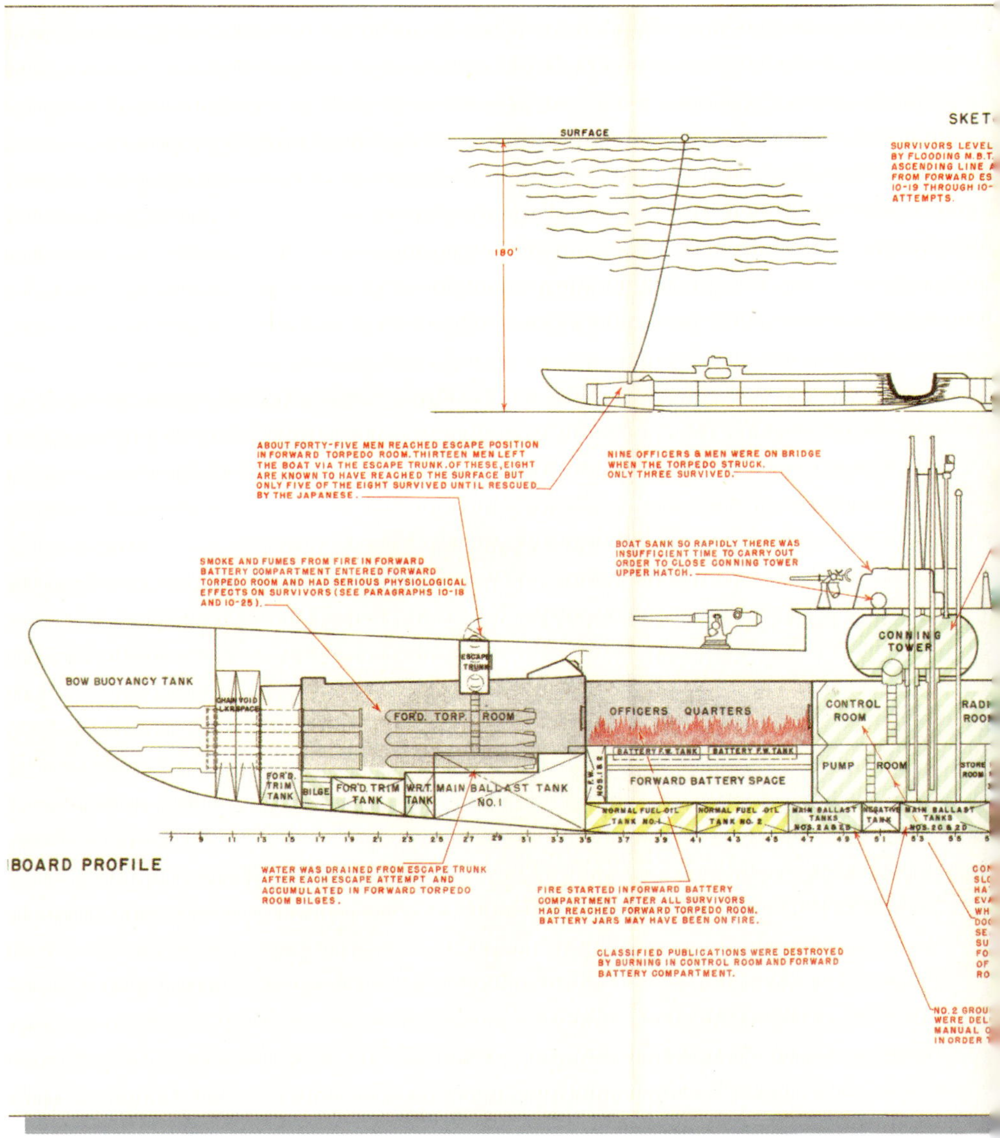

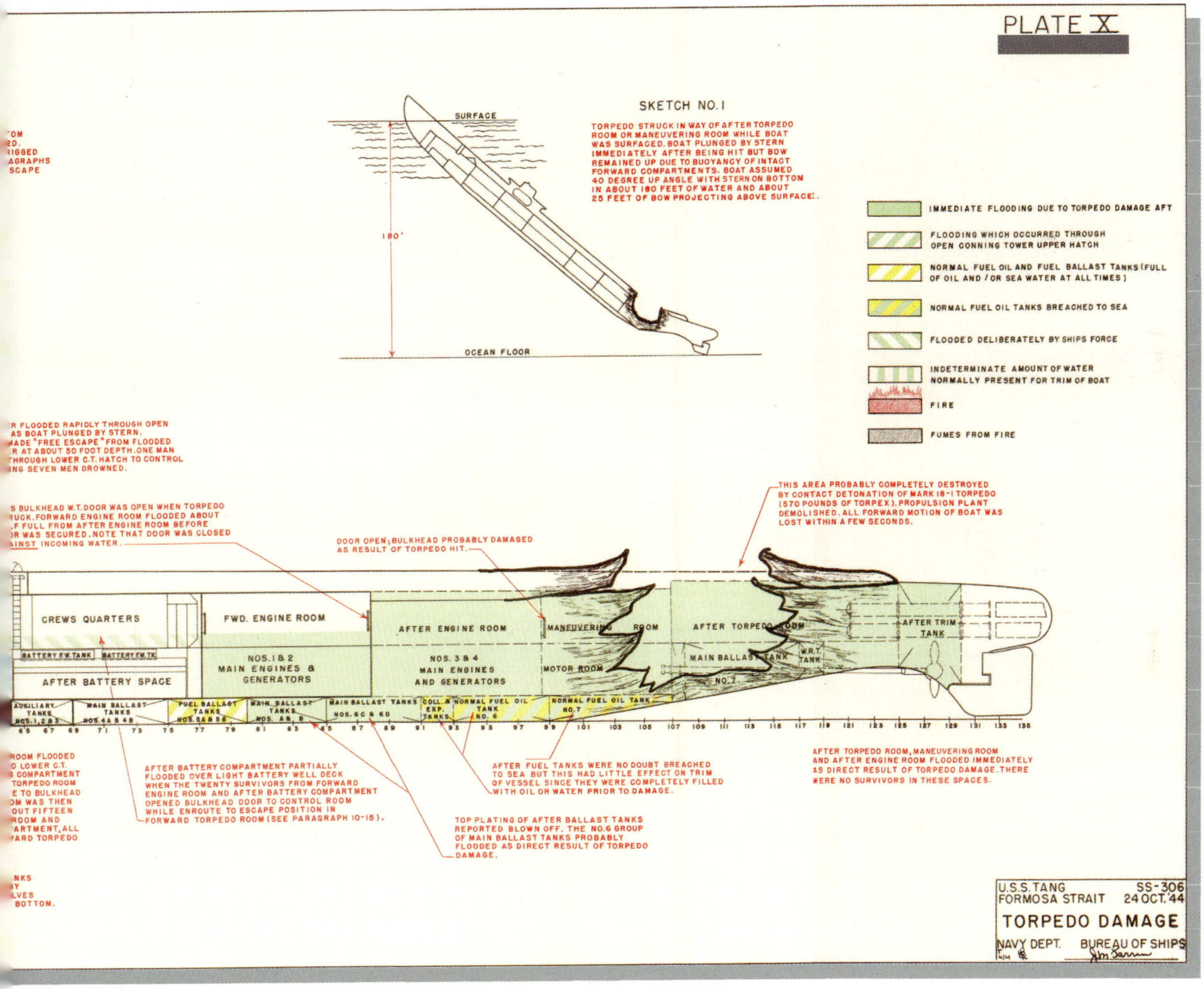
PLATE X
SKETCH NO. I
SURFACE
180'
OCEAN FLOOR
TORPEDO STRUCK IN WAY OF AFTER TORPEDO ROOM OR MANEUVERING ROOM WHILE BOAT WAS SURFACED. BOAT PLUNGED BY STERN IMMEDIATELY AFTER BEING HIT BUT BOW REMAINED UP DUE TO BUOYANCY OF INTACT FORWARD COMPARTMENTS. BOAT ASSUMED 40 DEGREE UP ANGLE WITH STERN ON BOTTOM IN ABOUT 180 FEET OF WATER AND ABOUT 25 FEET OF BOW PROJECTING ABOVE SURFACE.
IMMEDIATE FLOODING DUE TO TORPEDO DAMAGE AFT
FLOODING WHICH OCCURRED THROUGH OPEN CONNING TOWER UPPER HATCH
NORMAL FUEL OIL AND FUEL BALLAST TANKS (FULL OF OIL AND / OR SEA WATER AT ALL TIMES)
NORMAL FUEL OIL TANKS BREACHED TO SEA
FLOODED DELIBERATELY BY SHIPS FORCE
INDETERMINATE AMOUNT OF WATER NORMALLY PRESENT FOR TRIM OF BOAT
FIRE
FUMES FROM FIRE
THIS AREA PROBABLY COMPLETELY DESTROYED BY CONTACT DETONATION OF MARK 18-1 TORPEDO (570 POUNDS OF TORPEX). PROPULSION PLANT DEMOLISHED. ALL FORWARD MOTION OF BOAT WAS LOST WITHIN A FEW SECONDS.
DOOR OPEN; BULKHEAD PROBABLY DAMAGED AS RESULT OF TORPEDO HIT.
CREWS QUARTERS
BATTERY F.W. TANK
BATTERY F.W. TK
AFTER BATTERY SPACE
FWD. ENGINE ROOM
NOS. 1 & 2 MAIN ENGINES & GENERATORS
AFTER ENGINE ROOM
NOS. 3 & 4 MAIN ENGINES AND GENERATORS
MANEUVERING ROOM
MOTOR ROOM
AFTER TORPEDO ROOM
MAIN BALLAST TANK
NO. 7
W.R.T. TANK
AFTER TRIM TANK
AUXILIARY TANKS NOS. 1, 2 & 3
MAIN BALLAST TANKS NOS. 4A & 4B
FUEL BALLAST TANKS NOS. 5A & 5B
MAIN BALLAST TANKS NOS. 6A, B
MAIN BALLAST TANKS NOS. 6C & 6D
COLL. & EXP. TANKS
NORMAL FUEL OIL TANK NO. 6
NORMAL FUEL OIL TANK NO. 7
65 67 69 71 73 75 77 79 81 83 85 87 89 91 93 95 97 99 101 103 105 107 109 111 113 115 117 119 121 123 125 127 129 131 133 135
AFTER BATTERY COMPARTMENT PARTIALLY FLOODED OVER LIGHT BATTERY WELL DECK WHEN THE TWENTY SURVIVORS FROM FORWARD ENGINE ROOM AND AFTER BATTERY COMPARTMENT OPENED BULKHEAD DOOR TO CONTROL ROOM WHILE ENROUTE TO ESCAPE POSITION IN FORWARD TORPEDO ROOM (SEE PARAGRAPH 10-15).
AFTER FUEL TANKS WERE NO DOUBT BREACHED TO SEA BUT THIS HAD LITTLE EFFECT ON TRIM OF VESSEL SINCE THEY WERE COMPLETELY FILLED WITH OIL OR WATER PRIOR TO DAMAGE.
TOP PLATING OF AFTER BALLAST TANKS REPORTED BLOWN OFF. THE NO. 6 GROUP OF MAIN BALLAST TANKS PROBABLY FLOODED AS DIRECT RESULT OF TORPEDO DAMAGE.
AFTER TORPEDO ROOM, MANEUVERING ROOM AND AFTER ENGINE ROOM FLOODED IMMEDIATELY AS DIRECT RESULT OF TORPEDO DAMAGE. THERE WERE NO SURVIVORS IN THESE SPACES.
U.S.S. TANG SS-306
FORMOSA STRAIT 24 OCT. '44
TORPEDO DAMAGE
NAVY DEPT. BUREAU OF SHIPS

USS *San Francisco* Damage

The Naval Battle of Guadalcanal occurred the night of November 12–13, 1942, when the USS *San Francisco*, in company with one heavy cruiser, three light cruisers and eight destroyers, encountered a Japanese force of three battleships, two heavy cruisers, three light cruisers and 11 or 12 destroyers of Guadalcanal. During the battle, *San Francisco* suffered approximately 45 separate hits, plus numerous small machine gun or fragment hits. U.S. losses amounted to two light cruisers and two destroyers. Japanese losses amounted to one battleship and two destroyers.

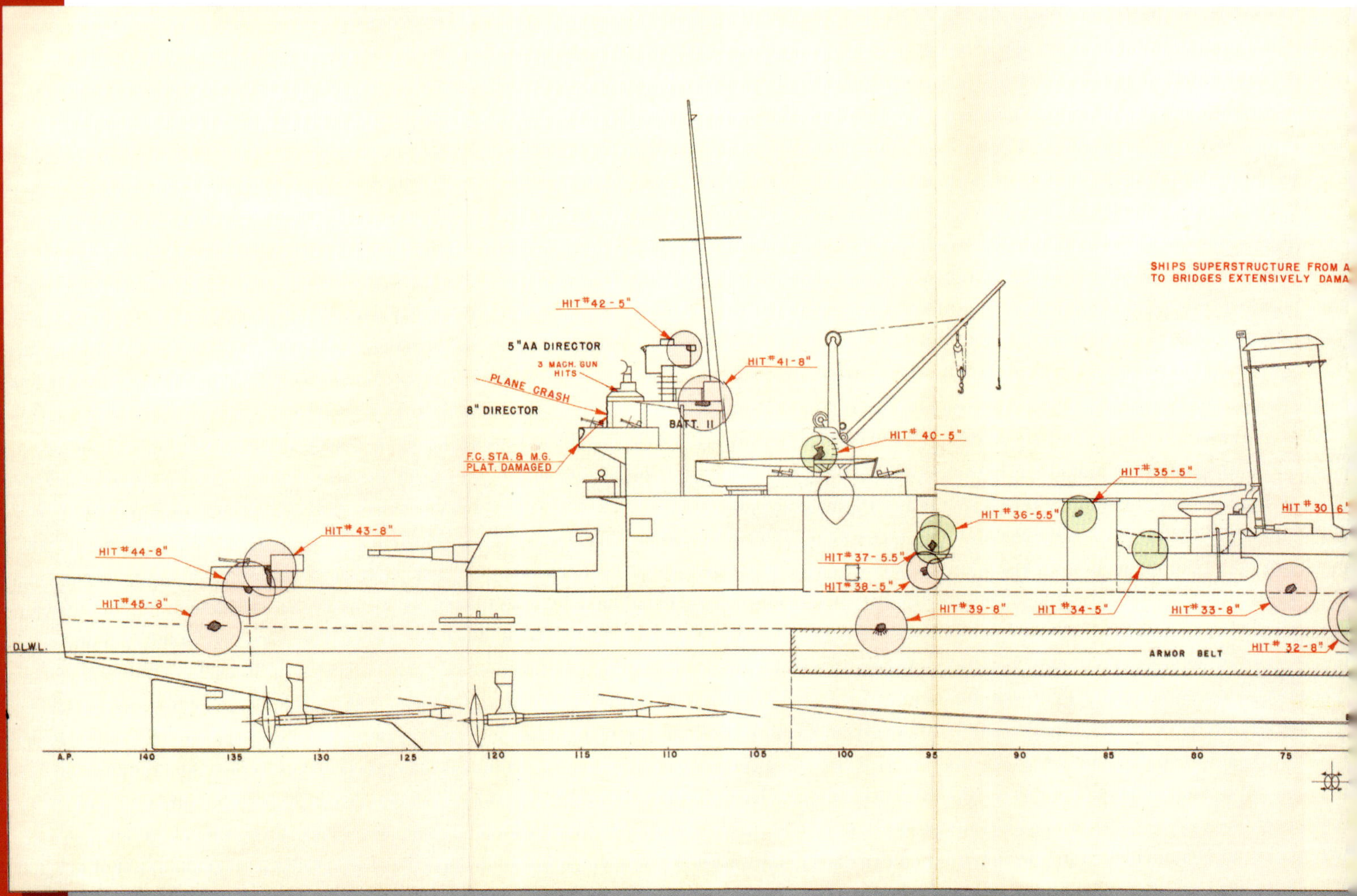

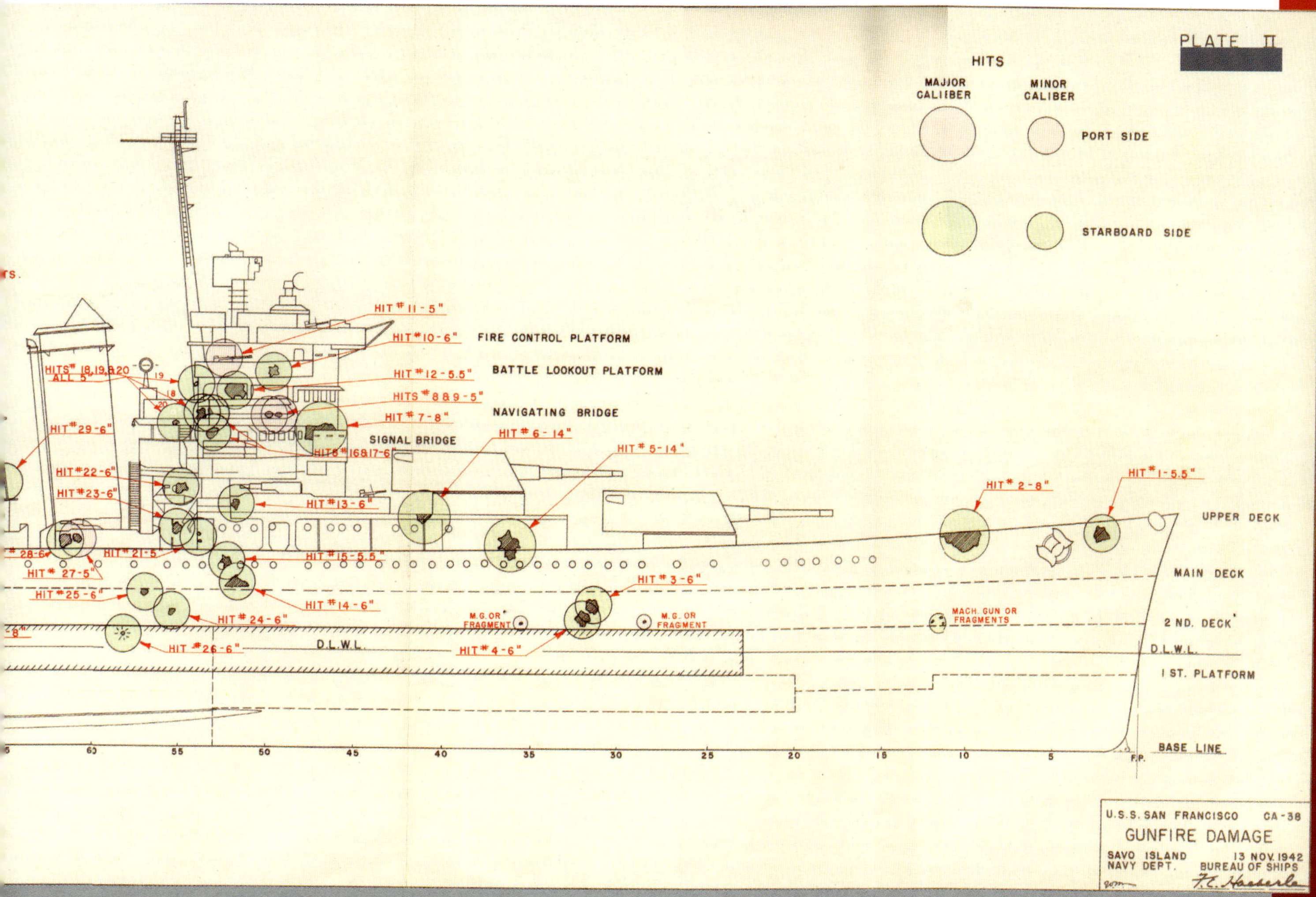
PLATE II
HITS
MAJOR CALIBER
MINOR CALIBER
PORT SIDE
STARBOARD SIDE
HIT # 11 - 5"
HIT # 10 - 6"
FIRE CONTROL PLATFORM
HITS # 18, 19, & 20 ALL 5"
HIT # 12 - 5.5"
BATTLE LOOKOUT PLATFORM
HITS # 8 & 9 - 5"
HIT # 7 - 8"
NAVIGATING BRIDGE
HIT # 29 - 6"
SIGNAL BRIDGE
HITS # 16 & 17 - 6"
HIT # 6 - 14"
HIT # 5 - 14"
HIT # 22 - 6"
HIT # 23 - 6"
HIT # 13 - 6"
HIT # 2 - 8"
HIT # 1 - 5.5"
UPPER DECK
HIT # 21 - 5"
HIT # 15 - 5.5"
HIT # 27 - 5"
HIT # 25 - 6"
HIT # 14 - 6"
HIT # 3 - 6"
MAIN DECK
HIT # 24 - 6"
M.G. OR FRAGMENT
M.G. OR FRAGMENT
MACH. GUN OR FRAGMENTS
2 ND. DECK
HIT # 26 - 6"
D.L.W.L.
HIT # 4 - 6"
D.L.W.L.
1 ST. PLATFORM
60
55
50
45
40
35
30
25
20
15
10
5
F.P.
BASE LINE
U.S.S. SAN FRANCISCO CA - 38
GUNFIRE DAMAGE
SAVO ISLAND 13 NOV. 1942
NAVY DEPT. BUREAU OF SHIPS

USS *Astoria* Damage

The sea battle of Savo Island (August 8–9, 1942) was a disaster for the U.S. Navy. Shortly after the U.S. Marine landings on Guadalcanal, the Japanese responded with a force of five heavy cruisers, one light cruiser and one destroyer. The U.S. met that force with six heavy cruisers, two light cruisers and 15 destroyers. The heavy cruisers *Astoria*, *Quincy*, *Vincennes* and HMAS *Canberra* were sunk.

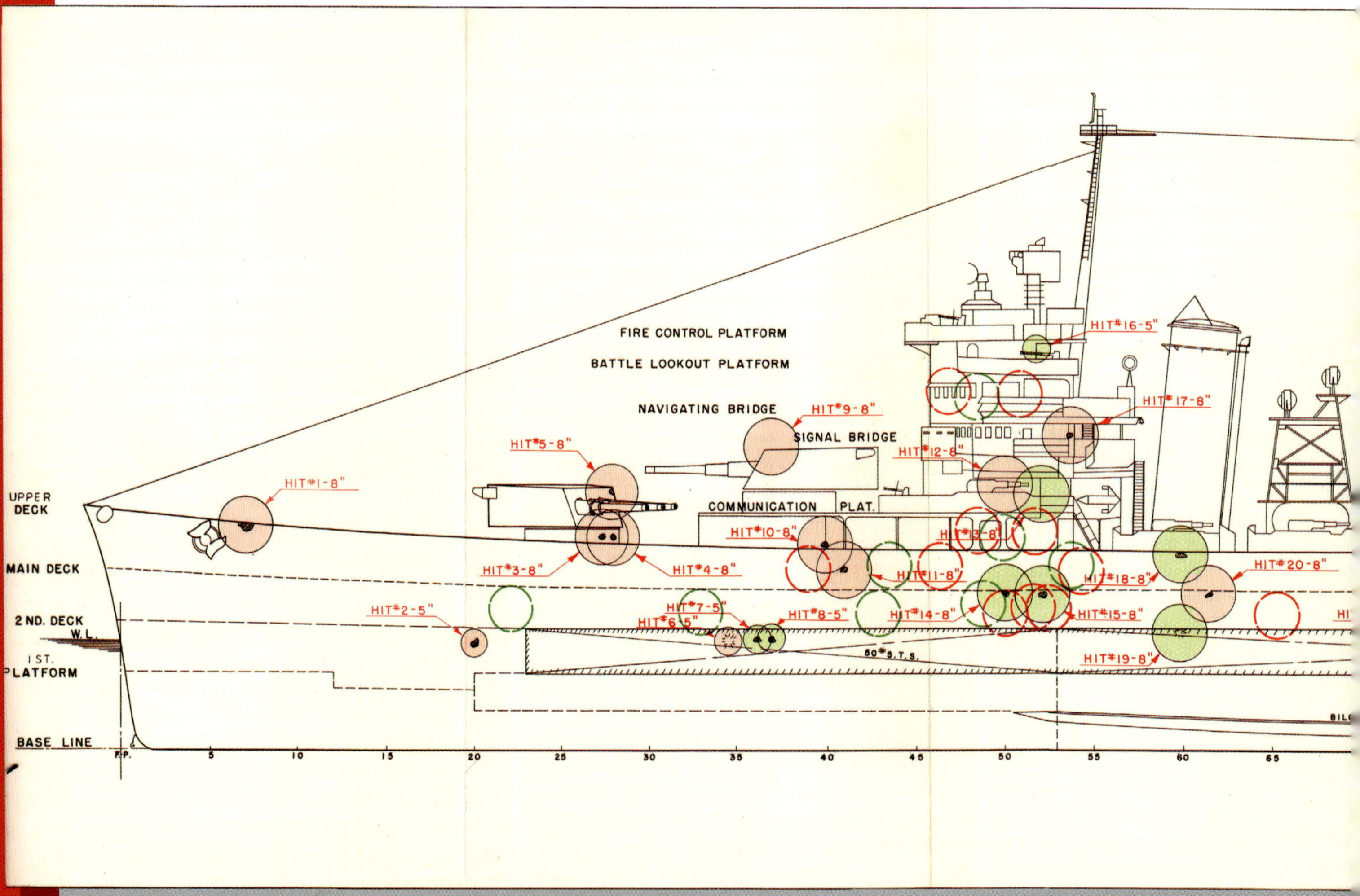

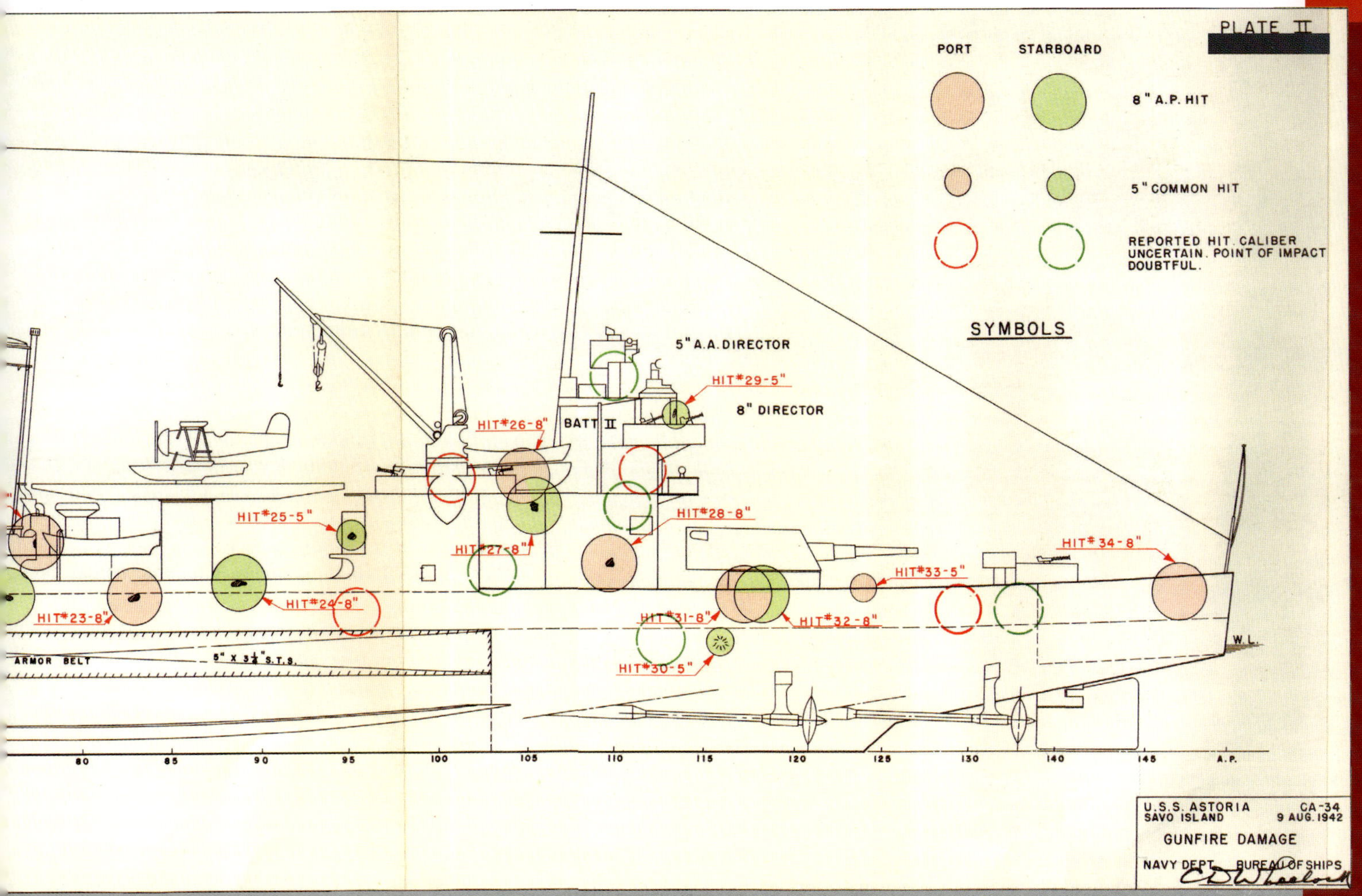
PLATE II
PORT
STARBOARD
8" A.P. HIT
5" COMMON HIT
REPORTED HIT. CALIBER UNCERTAIN. POINT OF IMPACT DOUBTFUL.
SYMBOLS
5" A.A. DIRECTOR
HIT#29-5"
8" DIRECTOR
HIT#26-8"
BATT II
HIT#25-5"
HIT#28-8"
HIT#27-8"
HIT#34-8"
HIT#33-5"
HIT#23-8"
HIT#24-8"
HIT#31-8"
HIT#32-8"
HIT#30-5"
ARMOR BELT
5" X 3½" S.T.S.
W.L.
80
85
90
95
100
105
110
115
120
125
130
140
145
A.P.
U.S.S. ASTORIA CA-34
SAVO ISLAND 9 AUG. 1942
GUNFIRE DAMAGE
NAVY DEPT. BUREAU OF SHIPS

USS *Independence* Damage

On November 20, 1943, the light carrier USS *Independence* (CVL-22) was struck by a Japanese air-dropped torpedo which detonated on impact. A 12 x 6-meter (40 x 20-foot) hole was created. Amazingly, the non-critical damage was a testament to the ability of the ship to absorb damage and withstand flooding.

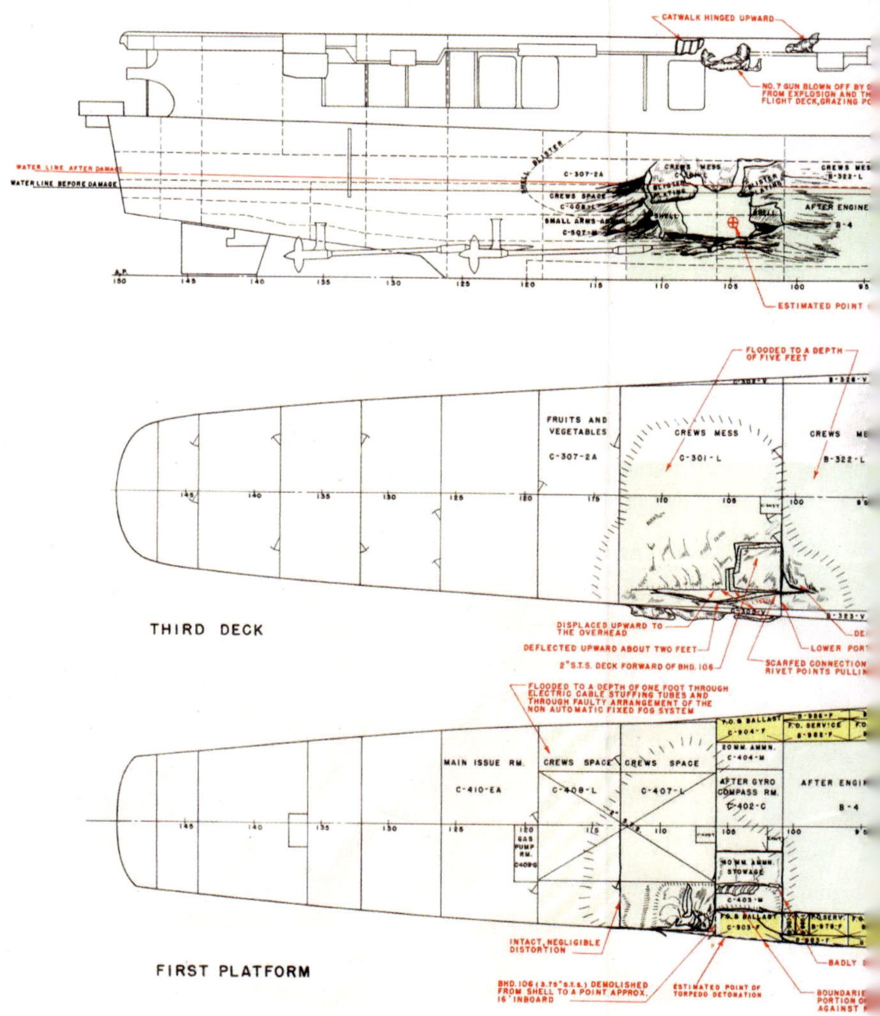

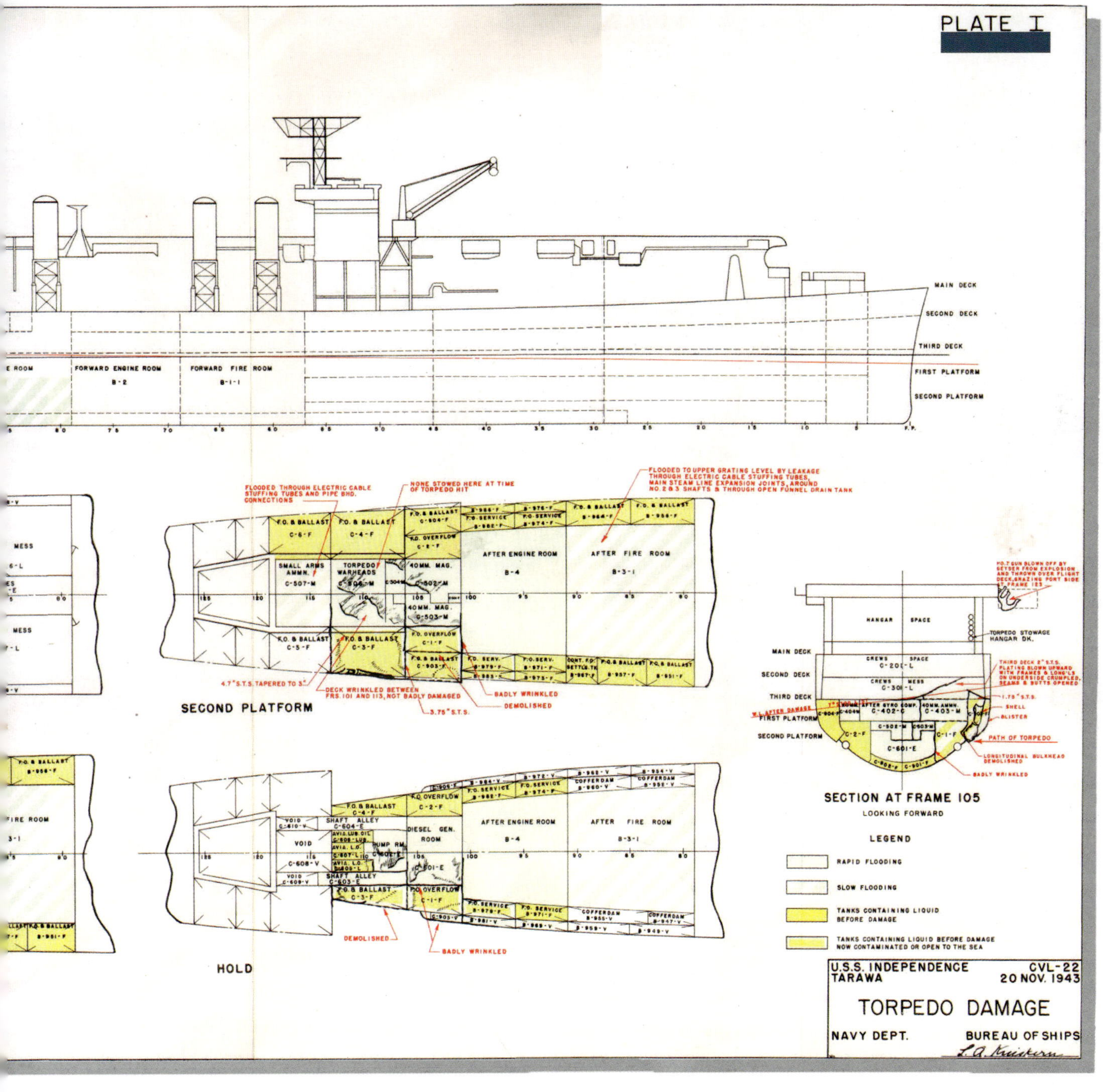
PLATE I
MAIN DECK
SECOND DECK
THIRD DECK
FIRST PLATFORM
SECOND PLATFORM
FORWARD ENGINE ROOM
B-2
FORWARD FIRE ROOM
B-1-1
SECOND PLATFORM
HOLD
AFTER ENGINE ROOM
B-4
AFTER FIRE ROOM
B-3-1
SECTION AT FRAME 105
LOOKING FORWARD
LEGEND
RAPID FLOODING
SLOW FLOODING
TANKS CONTAINING LIQUID BEFORE DAMAGE
TANKS CONTAINING LIQUID BEFORE DAMAGE NOW CONTAMINATED OR OPEN TO THE SEA
U.S.S. INDEPENDENCE CVL-22
TARAWA 20 NOV. 1943
TORPEDO DAMAGE
NAVY DEPT.
BUREAU OF SHIPS

16-inch Breech

All U.S. battleships built after World War I and during World War II were armed with 16-inch guns. It is remarkable that during four years of war in the Pacific, American and Japanese battleships met only twice, with the USN emerging victorious.

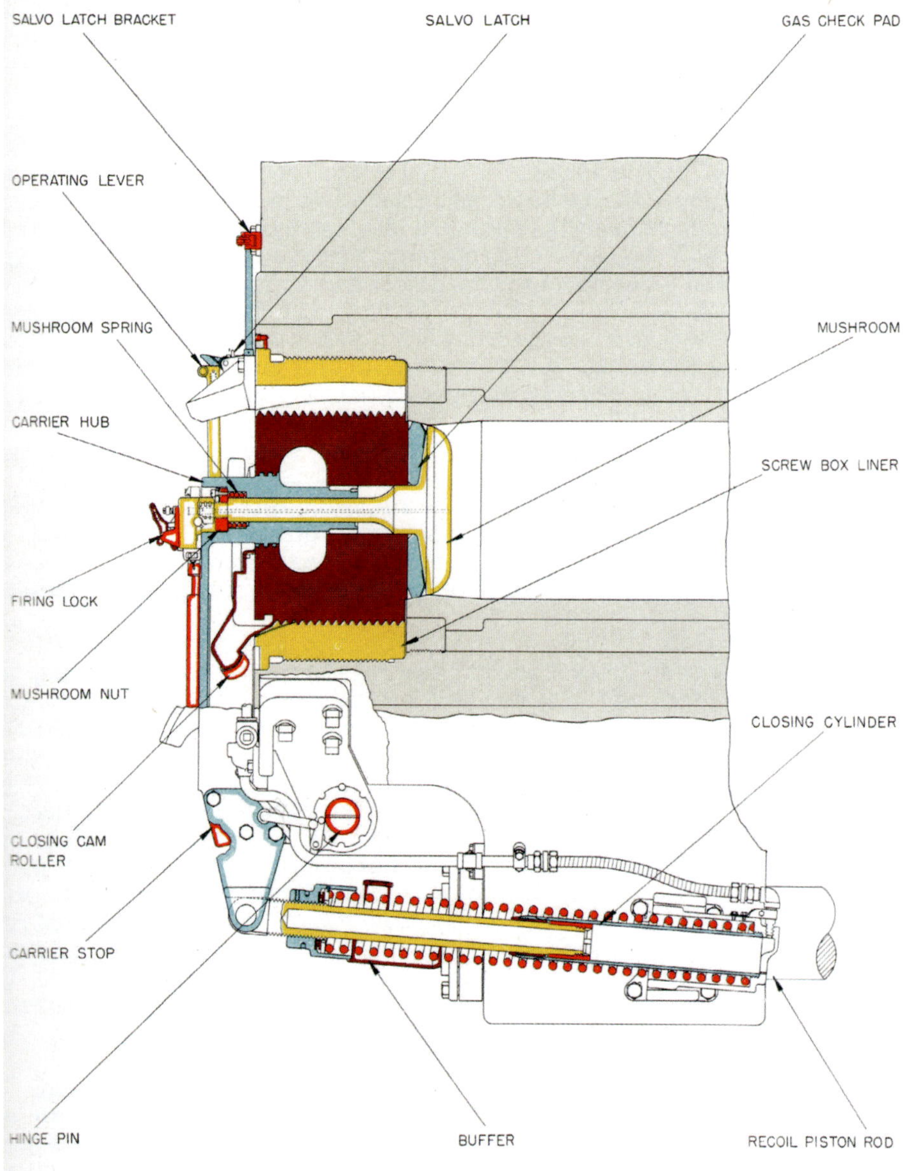

16-INCH BREECH MECHANISM, MARK 4 - SECTIONAL VIEW

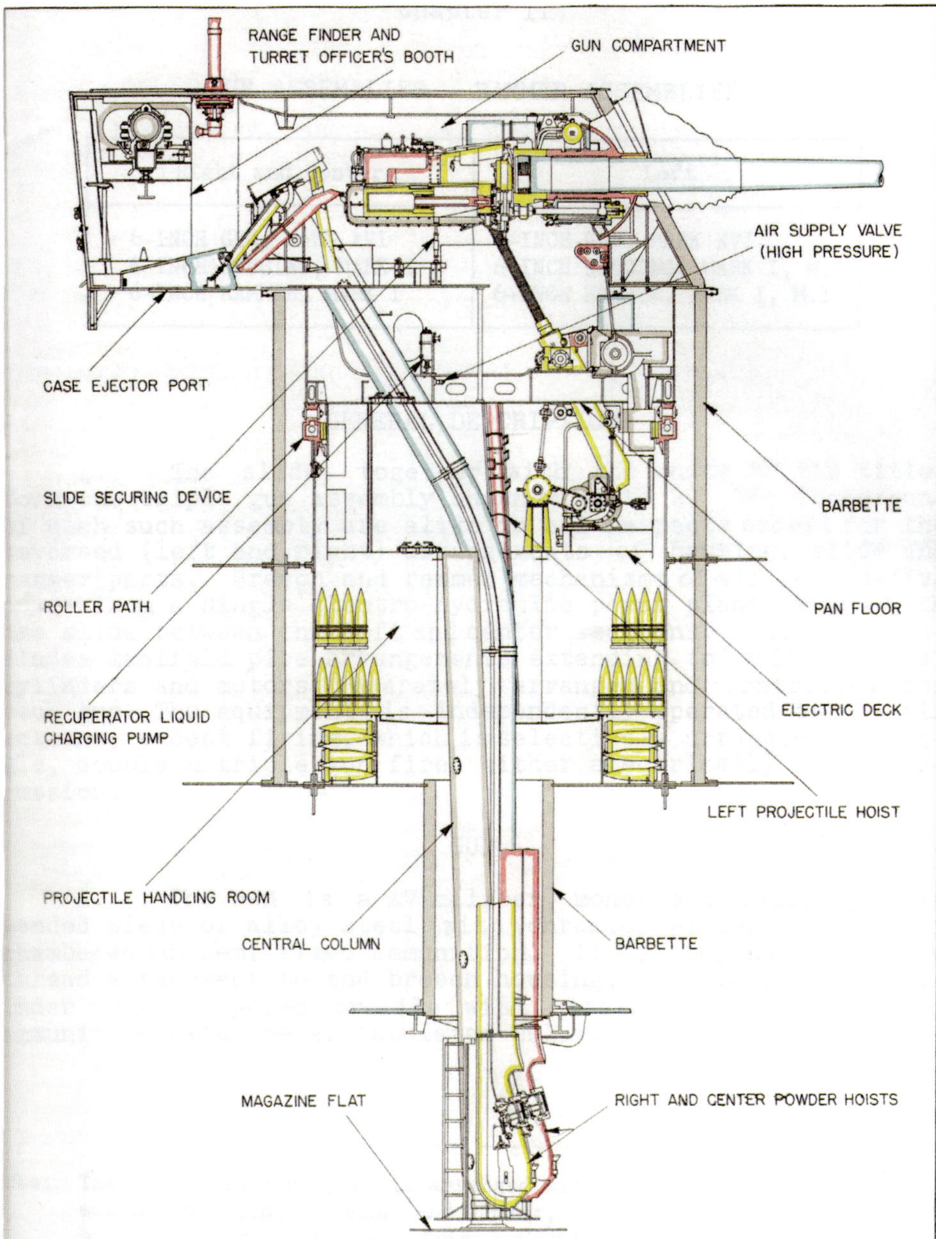

6 - INCH (47 CAL.) TRIPLE TURRET MOUNT - SECTIONAL VIEW

6-inch Triple Turret

These guns were built for the USN *Brooklyn*- and *Cleveland*-class light cruisers. Each turret required three officers and 53 enlisted men to operate. The crew was well protected, being encased in armor plate that measured 16.5 cm (6.5 in) on its face, 3.8 cm (1.25 in) on its sides and at the rear, and 5.1 cm (2 in) on its roof.

6-inch Shell

This drawing shows both armor-piercing and high-explosive 6-inch rounds.

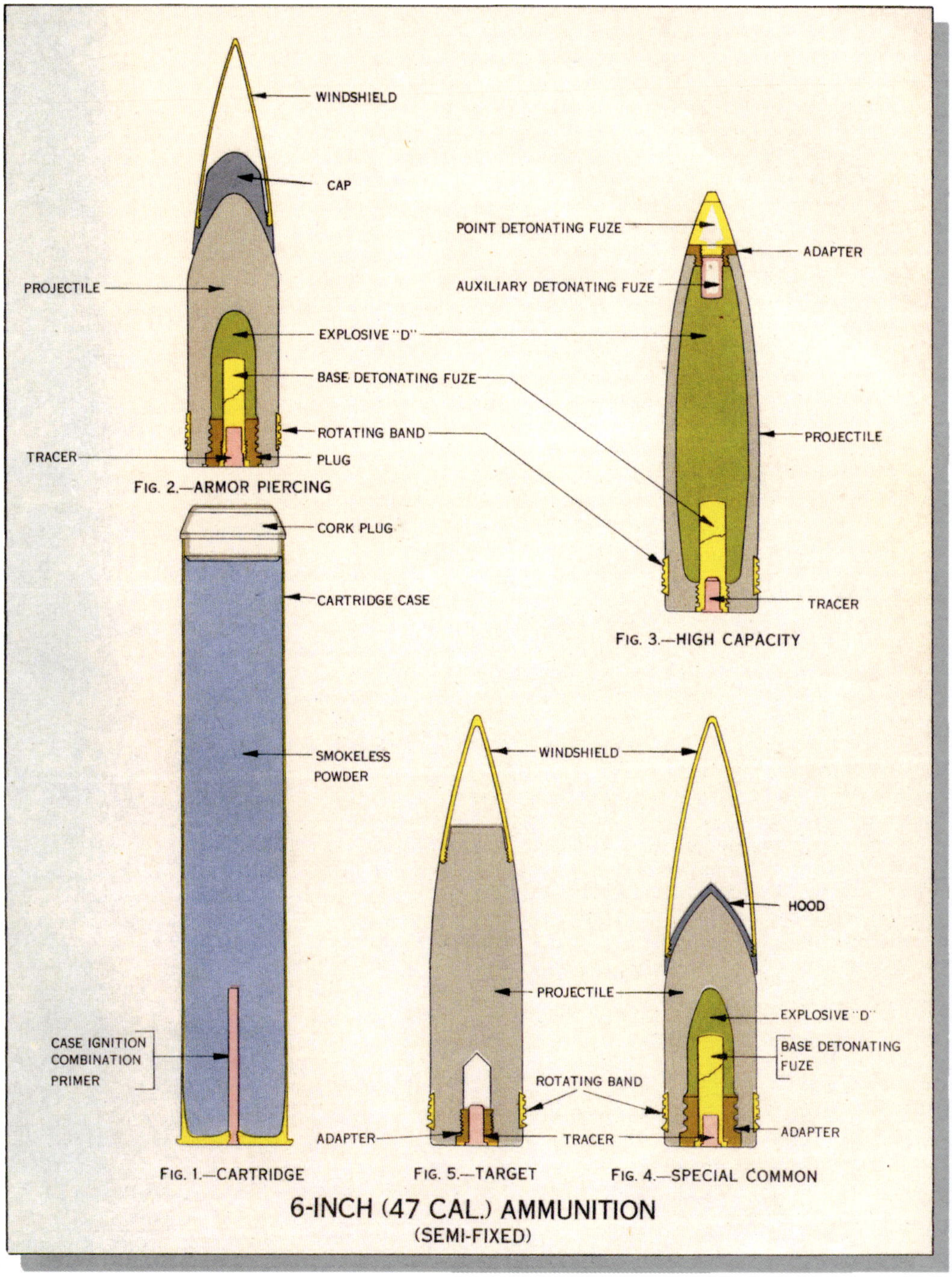

5-inch Twin Mount Installation

The 5-inch/38-caliber twin turret was found on every U.S. battleship, aircraft carrier and cruiser. The guns were handloaded but power-rammed. Its high rate of fire and easy loading at any angle made it an effective AA gun.

5-inch Twin Turret General Arrangement

Over 8,000 5-inch/38-caliber guns were built between 1934 and 1945 with 2,168 in single mounts and 2,714 guns in twin turrets, along with 3,290 more single mounts for auxiliary ships and merchantmen.

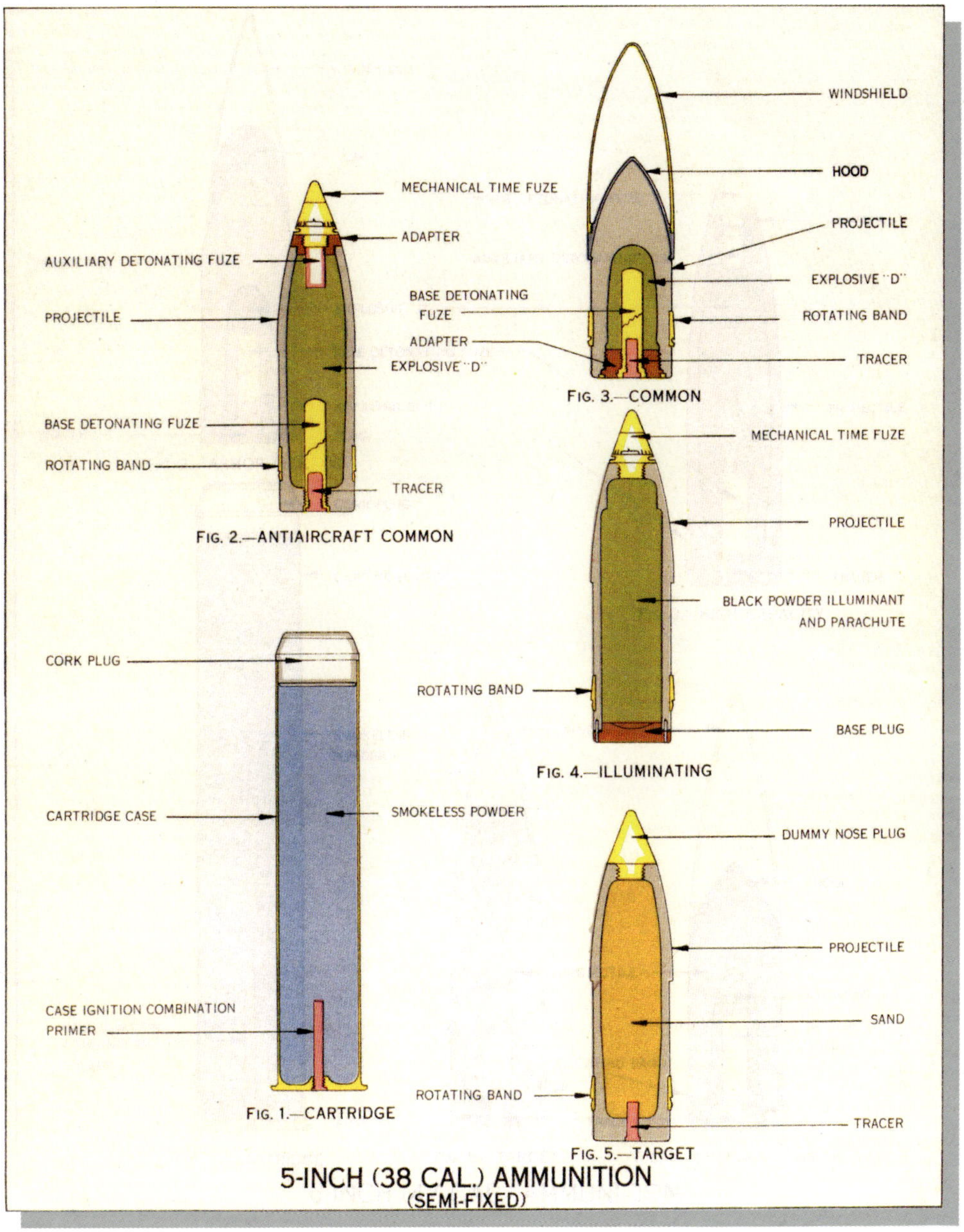

5-inch Shell

Yorktown- and *Essex*-class carriers carried 400 5-inch/38-caliber rounds per barrel for a total of 4,800 rounds. *Iowa*-class battleships carried 9,000 rounds.

UNITED STATES

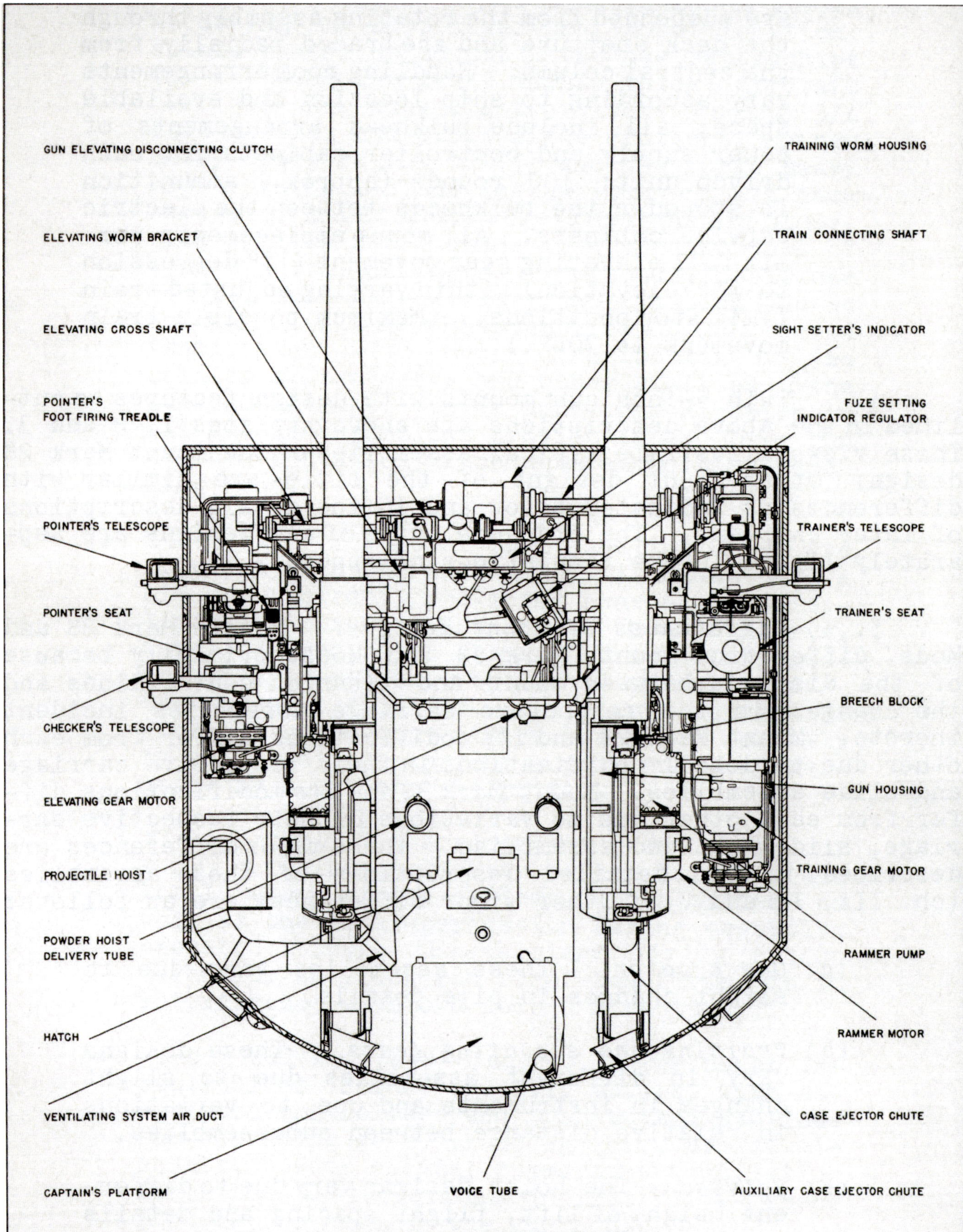

5-INCH (38 CAL.) TWIN MOUNT, MARK 32, MOD. 1
PLAN VIEW

5-inch Twin Mount Line Drawings (Two Drawings)

The 5-inch/38-caliber twin turret had a crew of 14. Manning a turret aboard a rolling and pitching ship was intense and dangerous. It was hot, noisy and filled with the acrid odor of powder fumes that burned the eyes and throat. One misstep or stumble could lead to crushed limbs or sudden death caused by the elevation or the powerful recoil of the gun.

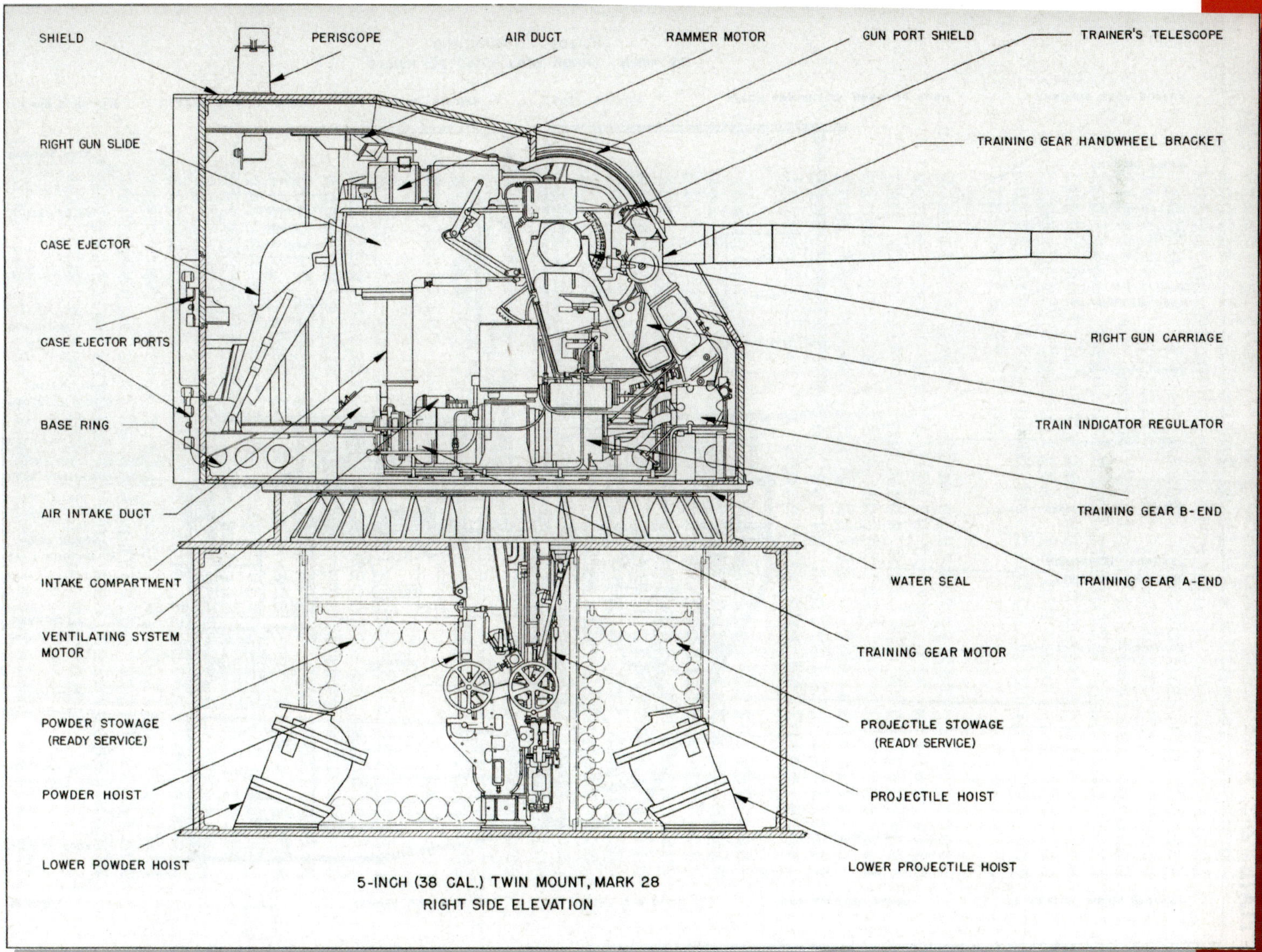

5-INCH (38 CAL.) TWIN MOUNT, MARK 28
RIGHT SIDE ELEVATION

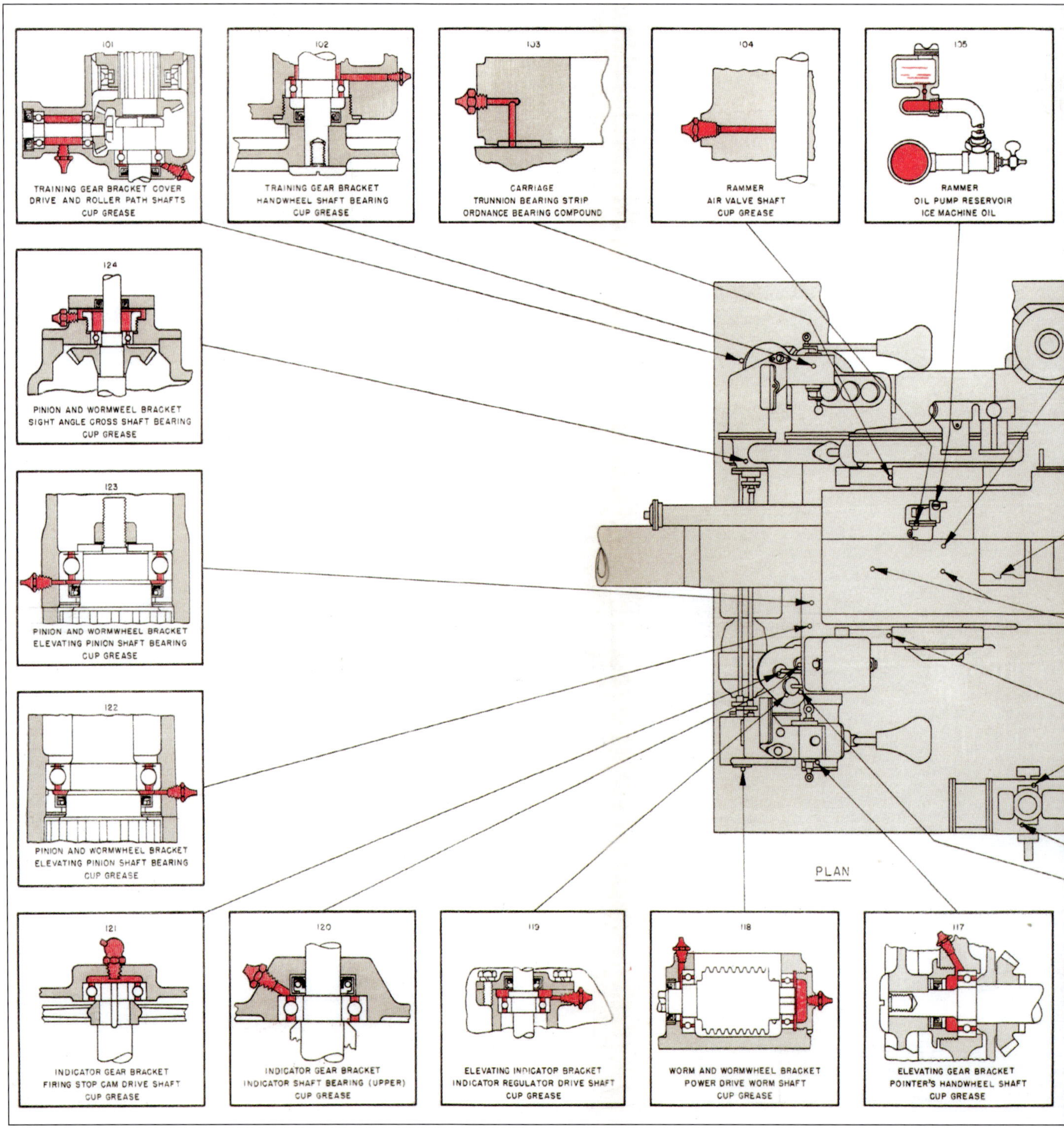
101
TRAINING GEAR BRACKET COVER
DRIVE AND ROLLER PATH SHAFTS
CUP GREASE
102
TRAINING GEAR BRACKET
HANDWHEEL SHAFT BEARING
CUP GREASE
103
CARRIAGE
TRUNNION BEARING STRIP
ORDNANCE BEARING COMPOUND
104
RAMMER
AIR VALVE SHAFT
CUP GREASE
105
RAMMER
OIL PUMP RESERVOIR
ICE MACHINE OIL
124
PINION AND WORMWEEL BRACKET
SIGHT ANGLE CROSS SHAFT BEARING
CUP GREASE
123
PINION AND WORMWHEEL BRACKET
ELEVATING PINION SHAFT BEARING
CUP GREASE
122
PINION AND WORMWHEEL BRACKET
ELEVATING PINION SHAFT BEARING
CUP GREASE
PLAN
121
INDICATOR GEAR BRACKET
FIRING STOP CAM DRIVE SHAFT
CUP GREASE
120
INDICATOR GEAR BRACKET
INDICATOR SHAFT BEARING (UPPER)
CUP GREASE
119
ELEVATING INDICATOR BRACKET
INDICATOR REGULATOR DRIVE SHAFT
CUP GREASE
118
WORM AND WORMWHEEL BRACKET
POWER DRIVE WORM SHAFT
CUP GREASE
117
ELEVATING GEAR BRACKET
POINTER'S HANDWHEEL SHAFT
CUP GREASE

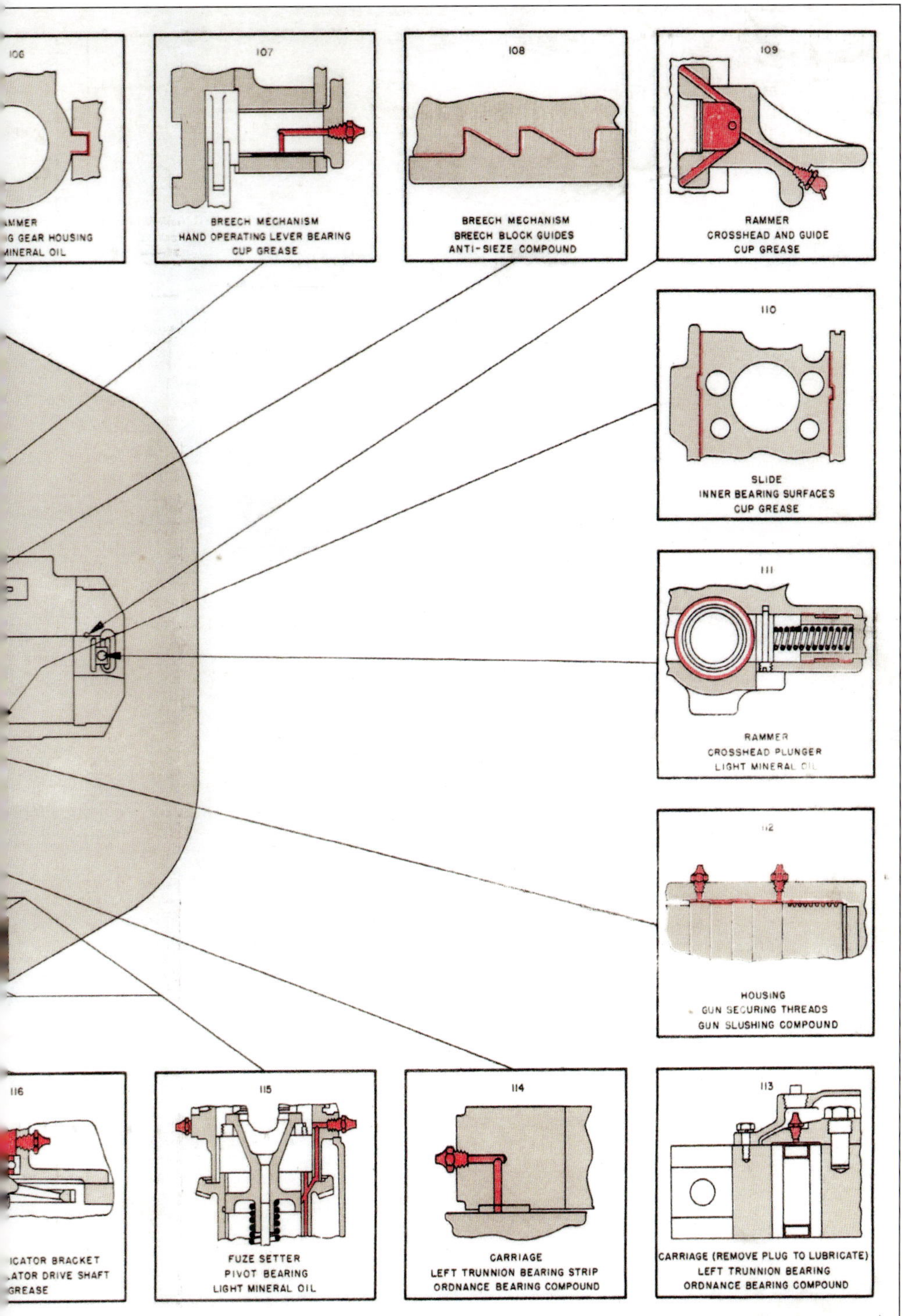

5-inch Gun Single Mount Turret

The primary armament of a U.S. destroyer was the excellent 5-inch/38-caliber dual-purpose gun. Destroyers were armed with this weapon in single mounts. Single turret shields had an all-round armor plate of 3 mm (0.12 in). It was the most effective dual-purpose naval gun of the war.

1.1-inch Quad Mount

To increase the effectiveness of U.S. warship AA defences, the 1.1-inch quad mount was introduced in 1939. During early service, the weapon was found to be unreliable, prone to jamming and ineffective. After the Battle of Midway, it was rapidly replaced by the superior 20 mm Oerlikon and 40 mm Bofors.

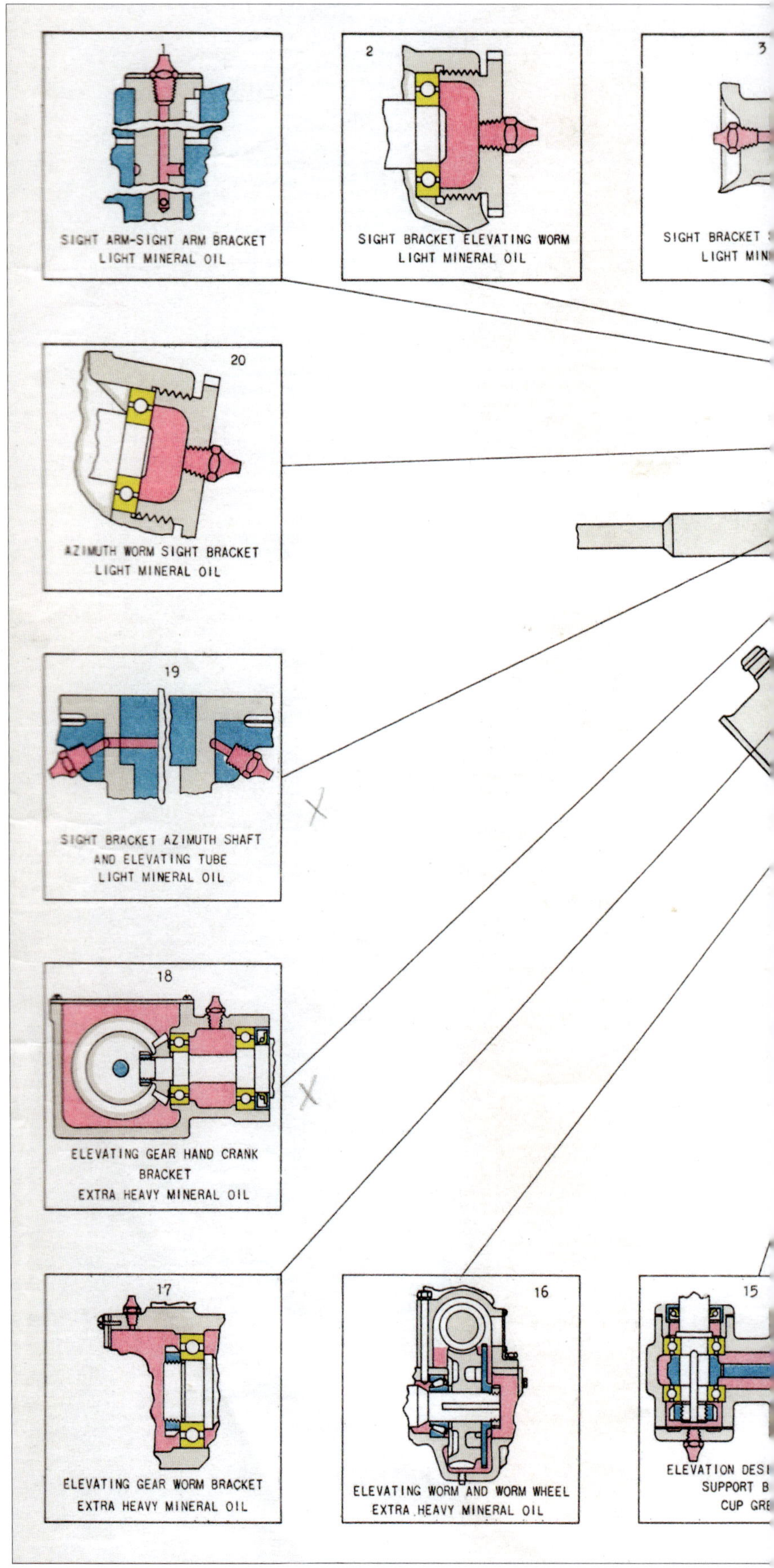

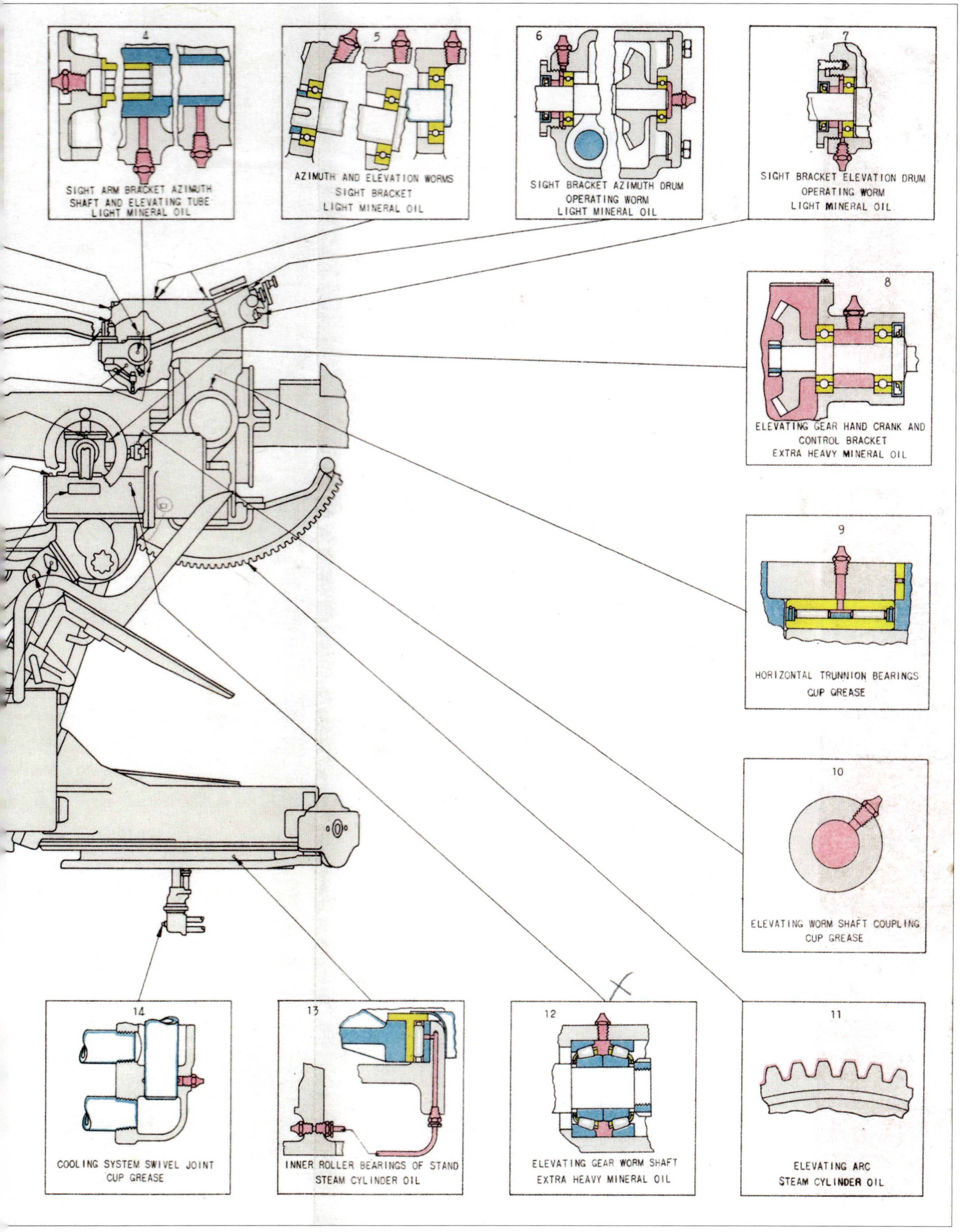
4
SIGHT ARM BRACKET AZIMUTH SHAFT AND ELEVATING TUBE LIGHT MINERAL OIL
5
AZIMUTH AND ELEVATION WORMS SIGHT BRACKET LIGHT MINERAL OIL
6
SIGHT BRACKET AZIMUTH DRUM OPERATING WORM LIGHT MINERAL OIL
7
SIGHT BRACKET ELEVATION DRUM OPERATING WORM LIGHT MINERAL OIL
8
ELEVATING GEAR HAND CRANK AND CONTROL BRACKET EXTRA HEAVY MINERAL OIL
9
HORIZONTAL TRUNNION BEARINGS CUP GREASE
10
ELEVATING WORM SHAFT COUPLING CUP GREASE
11
ELEVATING ARC STEAM CYLINDER OIL
12
ELEVATING GEAR WORM SHAFT EXTRA HEAVY MINERAL OIL
13
INNER ROLLER BEARINGS OF STAND STEAM CYLINDER OIL
14
COOLING SYSTEM SWIVEL JOINT CUP GREASE

1.1-inch Quad Mount Crew Diagram

The 1.1-inch AA gun required a crew of eight men. The gun was disliked by its crews and proved frustrating in combat.

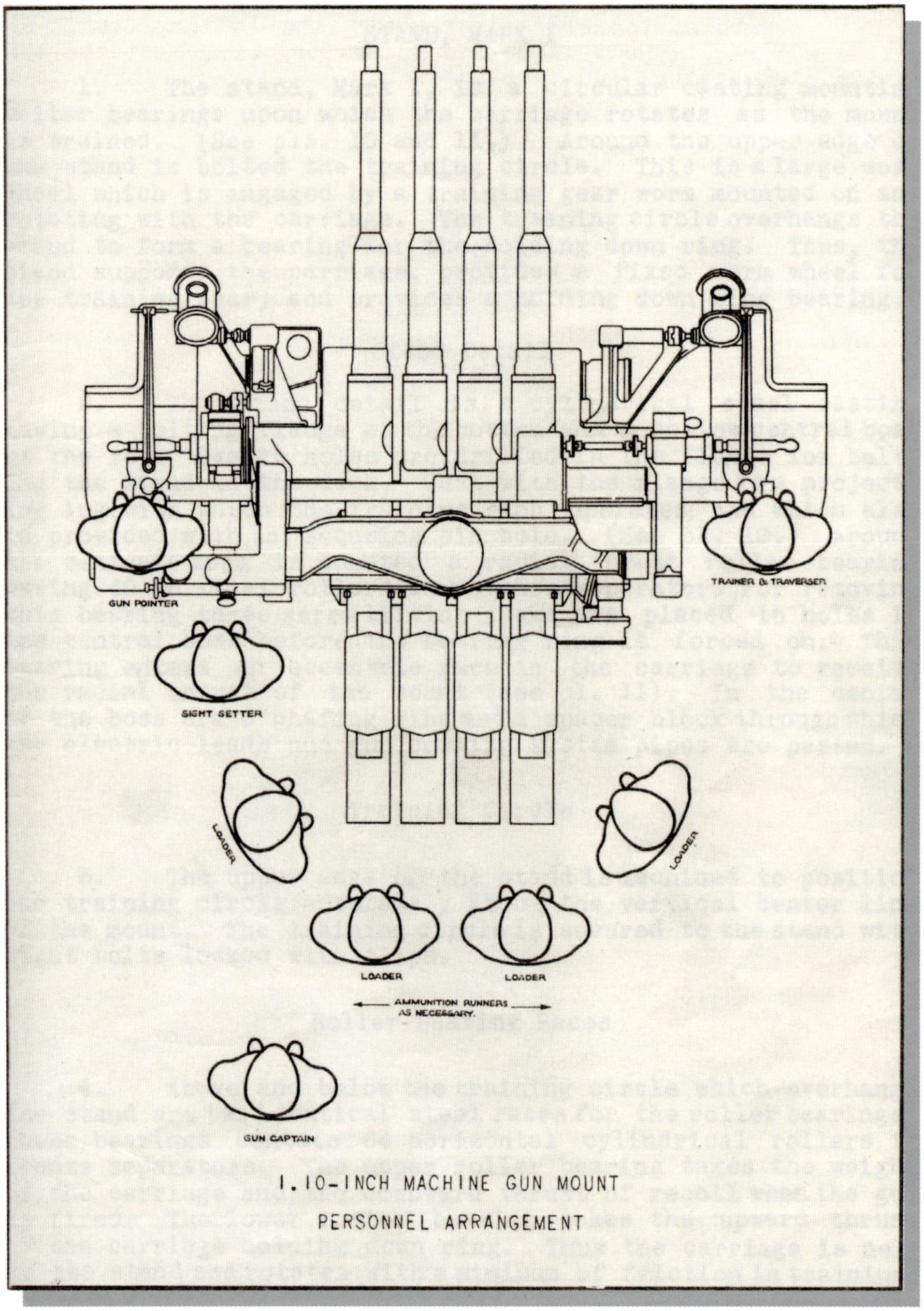

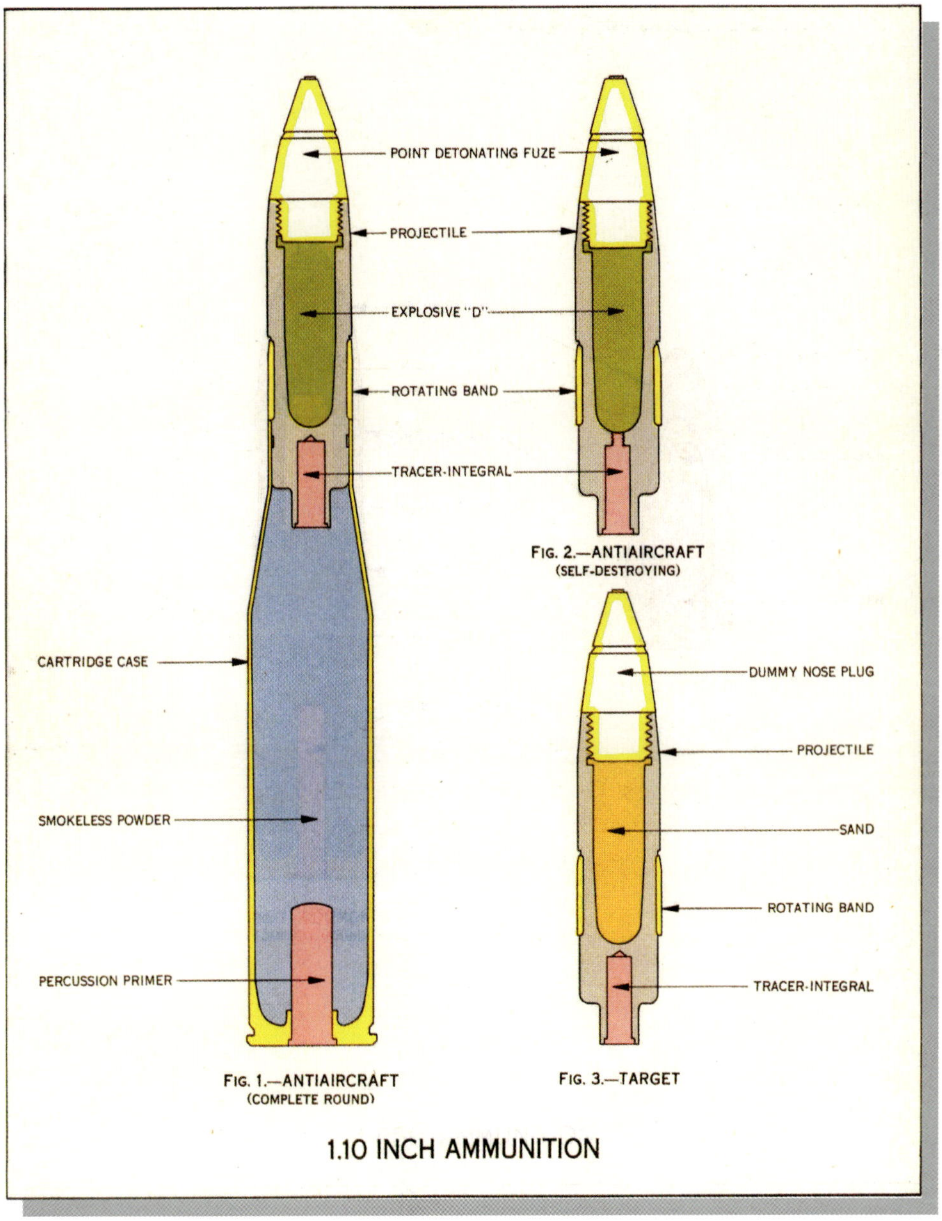

1.1-inch Shell

The shells for the 1.1-inch gun had an explosive filler which was set off by a "super-quick" fuze. After testing, the Navy concluded that a hit by a single 1.1-inch shell anywhere on an aircraft's structure would result in a forced landing.

Depth Charge

The standard depth charges the U.S. Navy used were the Mark 6, 7 and 9. The Mark 6 as shown here weighed 145 kg (320 lbs) with 136 kg (300 lbs) of TNT. The Mark 6 could be set to explode between 15 and 91 meters (50 and 300 feet).

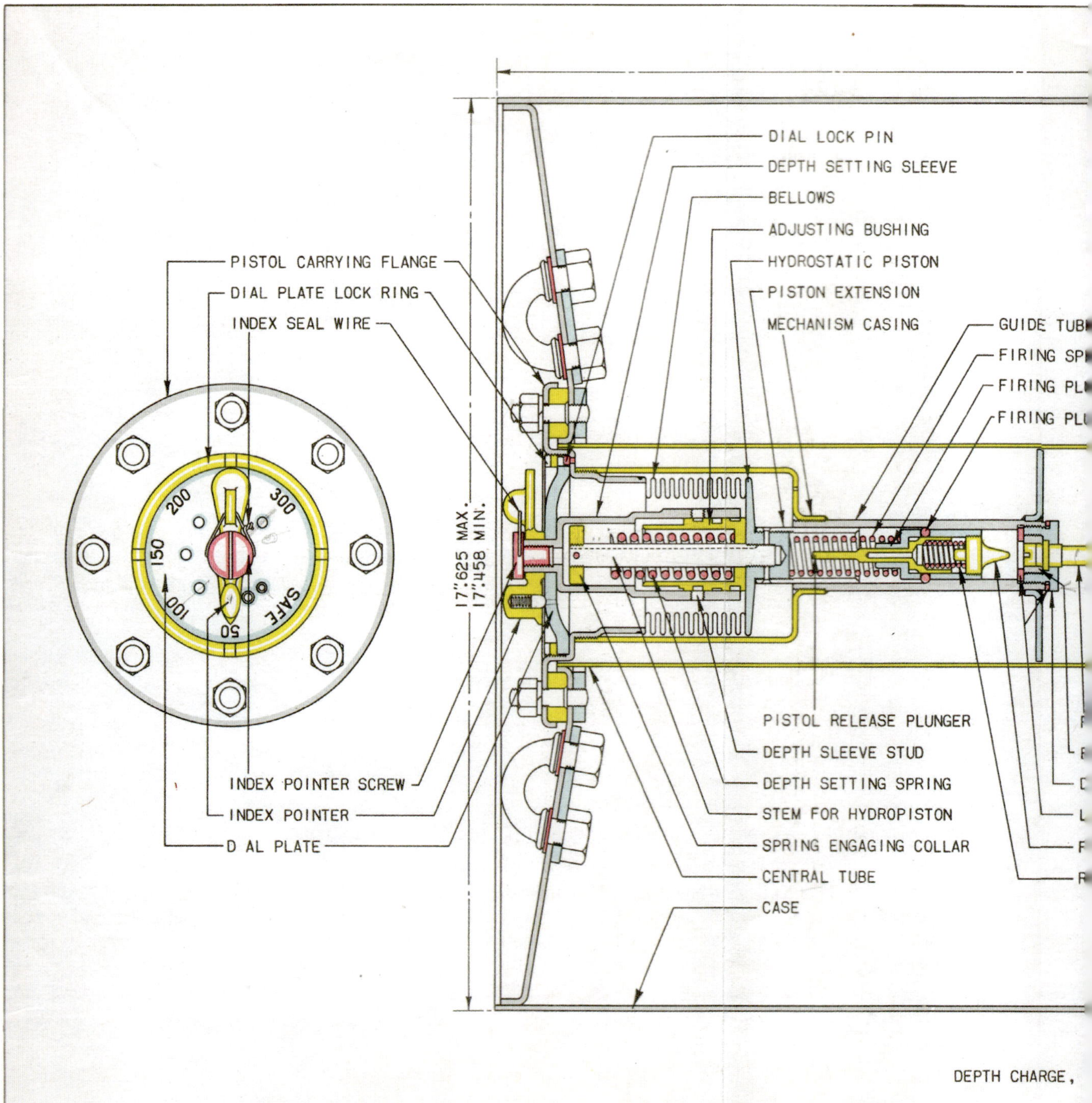

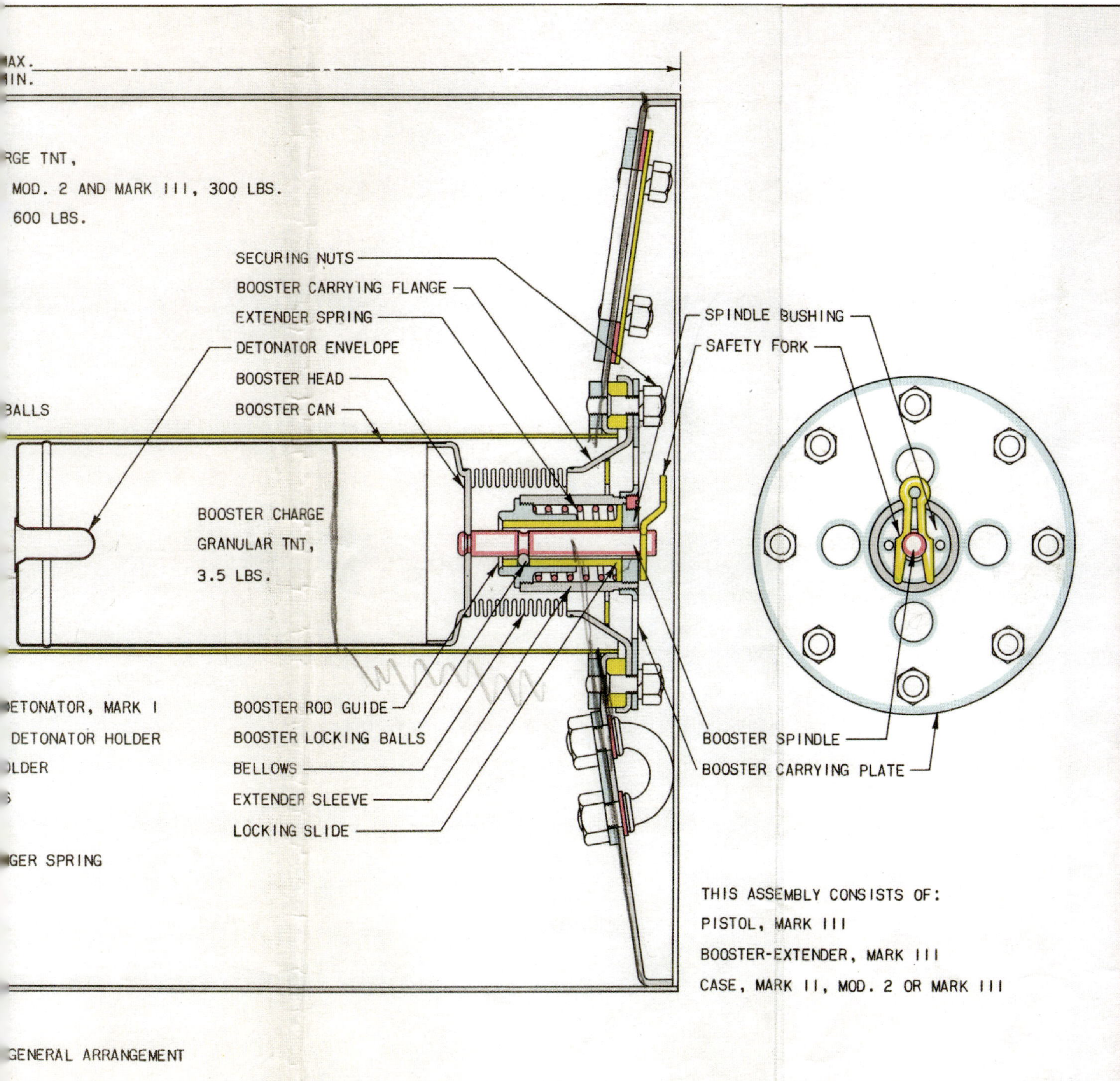
AX.
IN.
RGE TNT,
MOD. 2 AND MARK III, 300 LBS.
600 LBS.
SECURING NUTS
BOOSTER CARRYING FLANGE
EXTENDER SPRING
DETONATOR ENVELOPE
BOOSTER HEAD
BALLS
BOOSTER CAN
SPINDLE BUSHING
SAFETY FORK
BOOSTER CHARGE
GRANULAR TNT,
3.5 LBS.
ETONATOR, MARK I
DETONATOR HOLDER
LDER
GER SPRING
BOOSTER ROD GUIDE
BOOSTER LOCKING BALLS
BELLOWS
EXTENDER SLEEVE
LOCKING SLIDE
BOOSTER SPINDLE
BOOSTER CARRYING PLATE
THIS ASSEMBLY CONSISTS OF:
PISTOL, MARK III
BOOSTER-EXTENDER, MARK III
CASE, MARK II, MOD. 2 OR MARK III
GENERAL ARRANGEMENT

Depth Charge Line Drawing

The Mark 9 depth charge entered service in 1943. Its streamlined teardrop shape with stern-mounted fins gave it a higher sink rate and proved more effective against U-boats.

RESTRICTED—Security Information

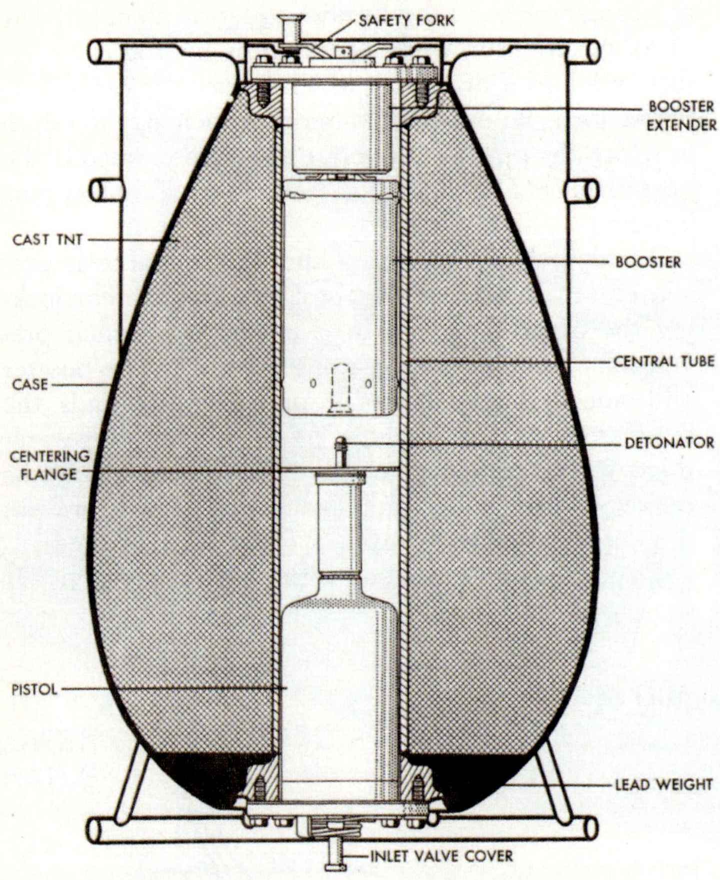

FIGURE 15B4.—Depth charge, sectional view.

Depth Charge

This diagram shows the two methods used by the U.S. Navy to launch depth charges. The exploding depth charge was projected from a K-gun, while the other depth charge was rolled off a depth charge rack.

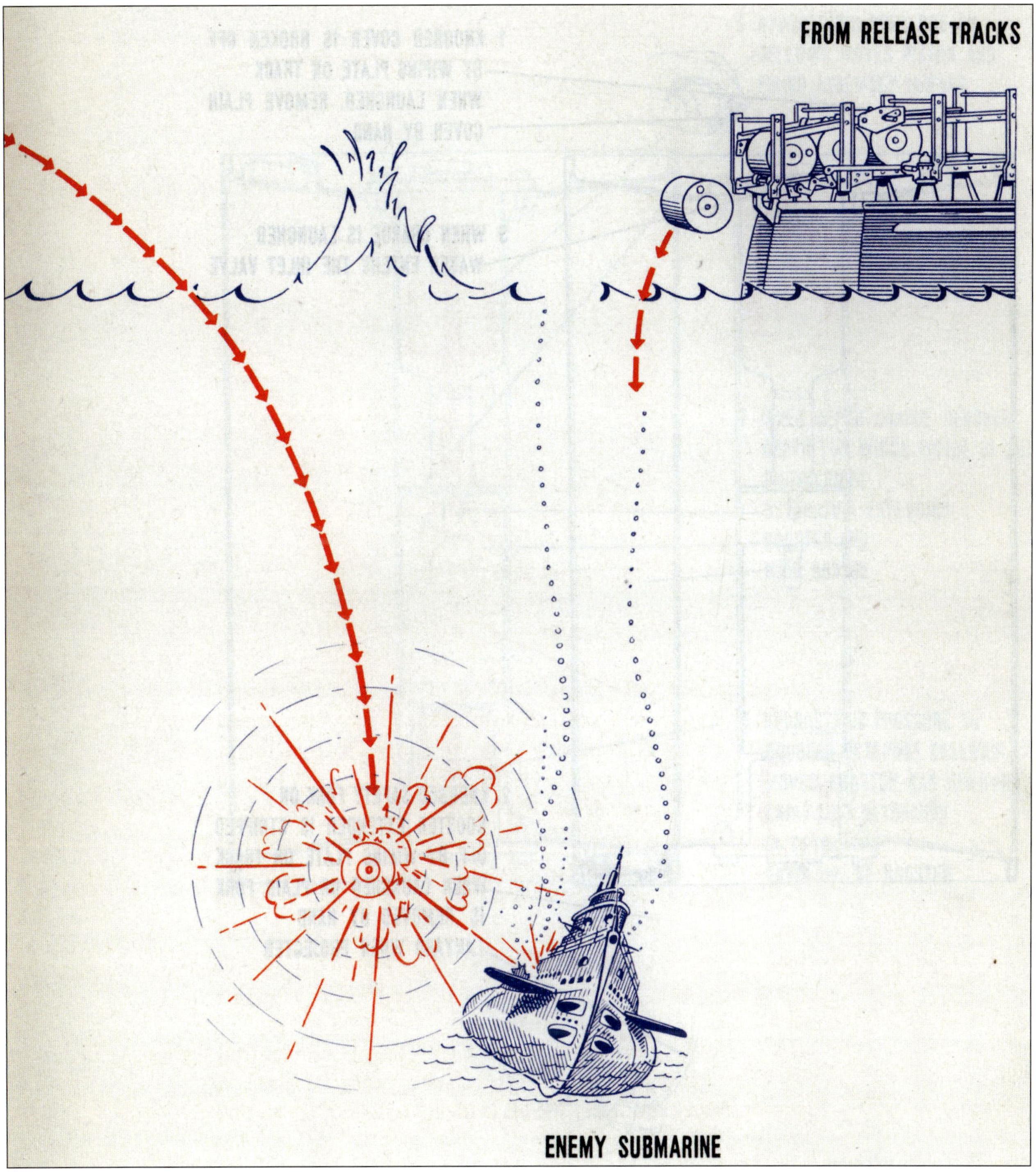

USS *New York* (BB-34) Camouflage Pattern

Camouflage Measure 31a, Design 8B. Drawing prepared by the Bureau of Ships for a camouflage scheme intended for the battleships *New York* (BB-34) and *Texas* (BB-35). This plan, approved by Captain Torvald A. Solberg, USN, is dated October 11, 1944. It shows the ship's starboard side, exposed decks and superstructure ends. *New York* wore this pattern in late 1944 and early 1945.

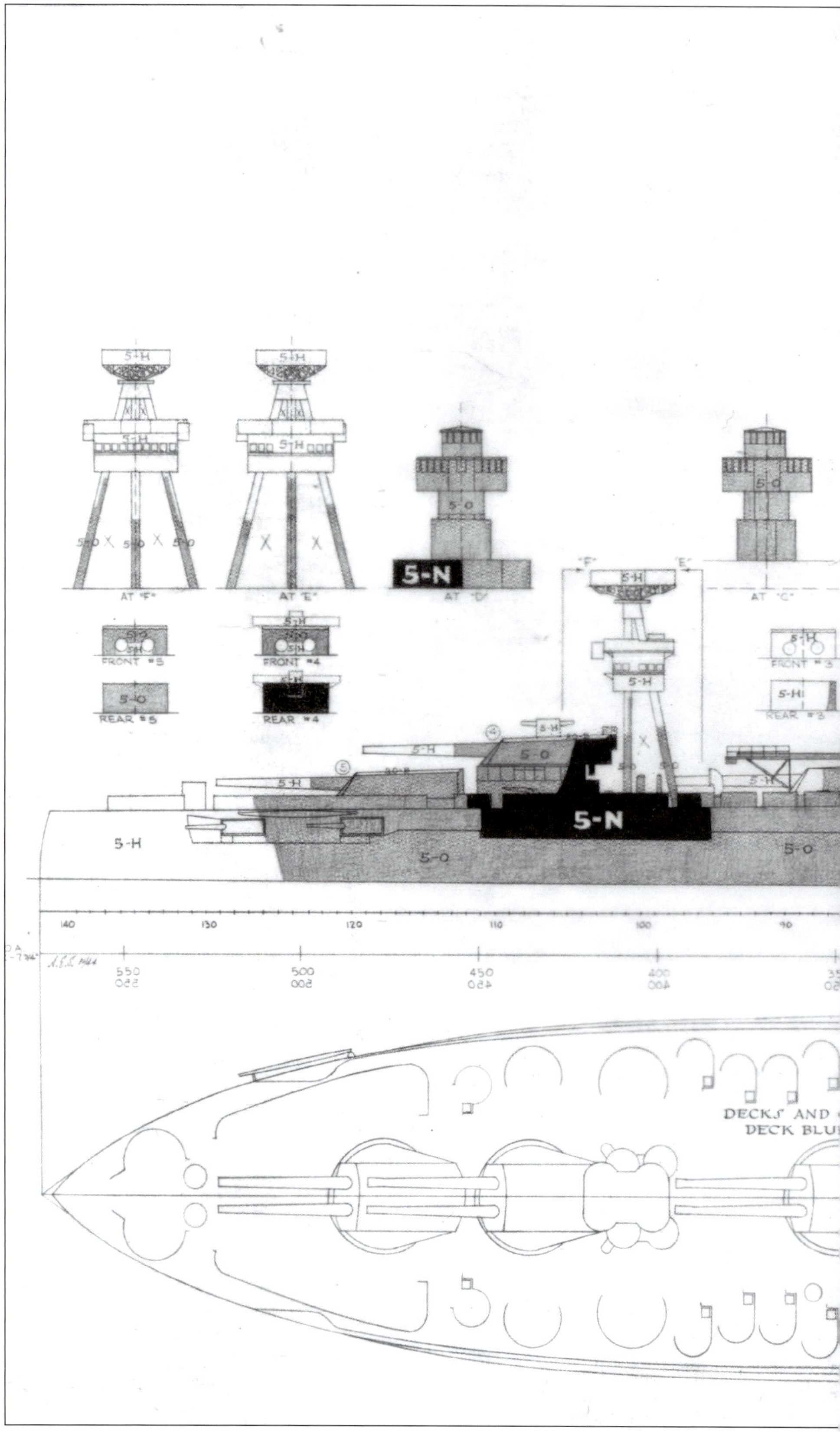

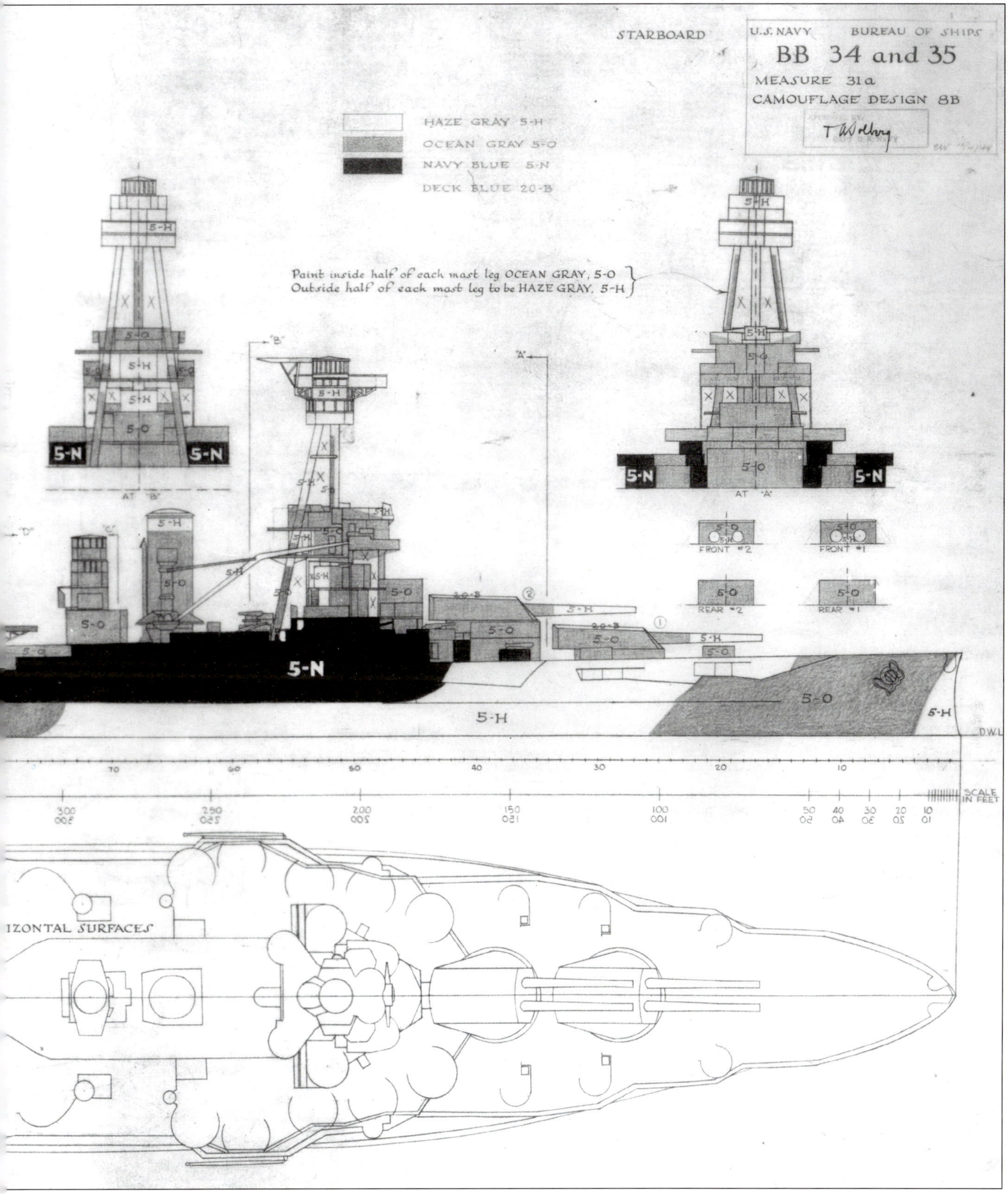
STARBOARD
U.S. NAVY BUREAU OF SHIPS
BB 34 and 35
MEASURE 31a
CAMOUFLAGE DESIGN 8B
HAZE GRAY 5-H
OCEAN GRAY 5-O
NAVY BLUE 5-N
DECK BLUE 20-B
Paint inside half of each mast leg OCEAN GRAY, 5-O
Outside half of each mast leg to be HAZE GRAY, 5-H
AT "B"
AT "A"
FRONT #2
FRONT #1
REAR #2
REAR #1
5-N
5-O
5-H
20-B
D.W.L.
SCALE IN FEET
IZONTAL SURFACES

LST Camouflage Pattern

Camouflage Measure 31, Design 8L. Drawing prepared by the Bureau of Ships for a camouflage scheme intended for Landing Ships, Tank [LST]. This plan, dated December 22, 1943, shows the ship's starboard side, superstructure ends and exposed decks. It was approved by Captain Henry A. Ingram, USN. The camouflage scheme applies to the entire hull, including the portion below the waterline.

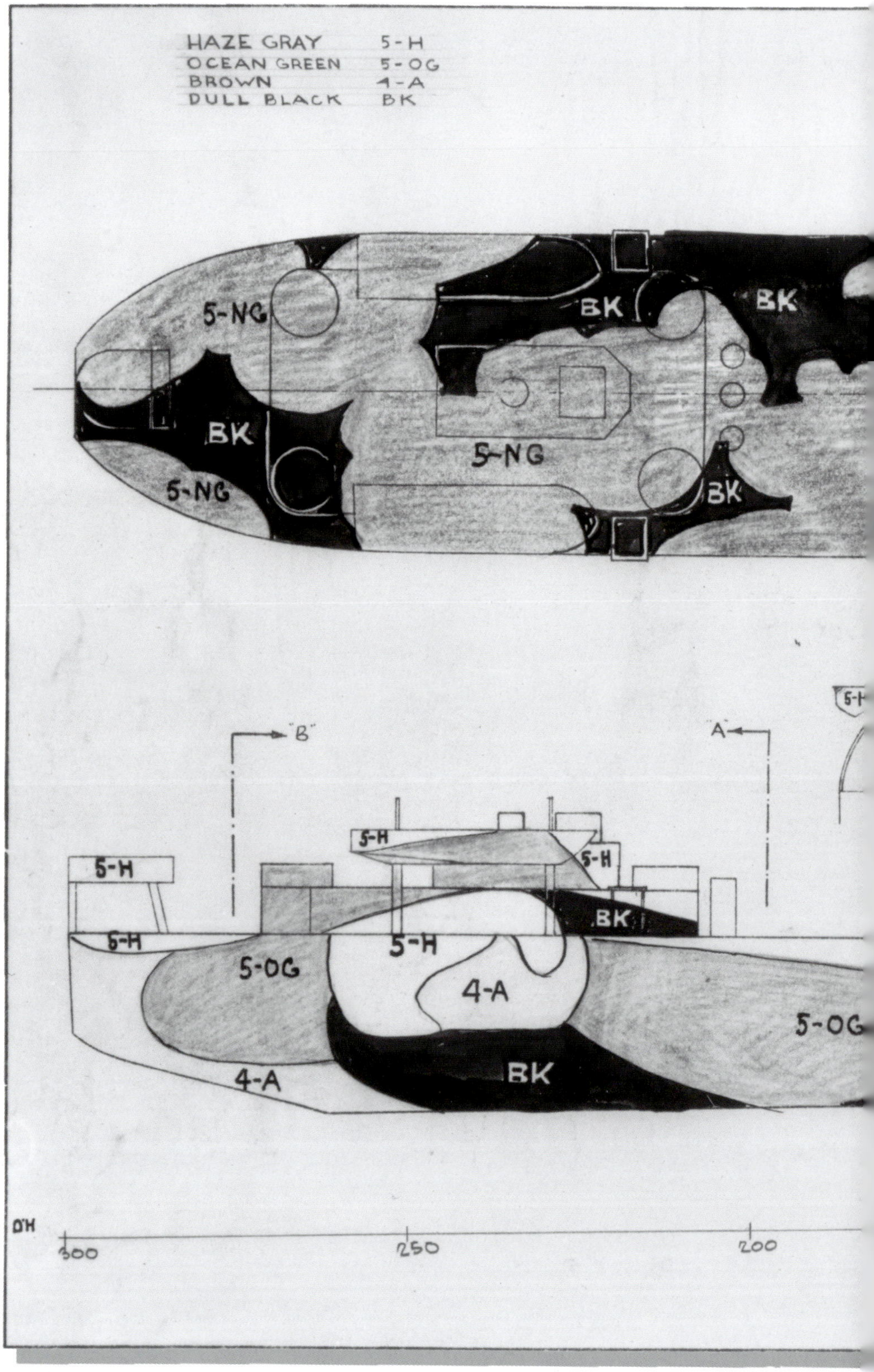

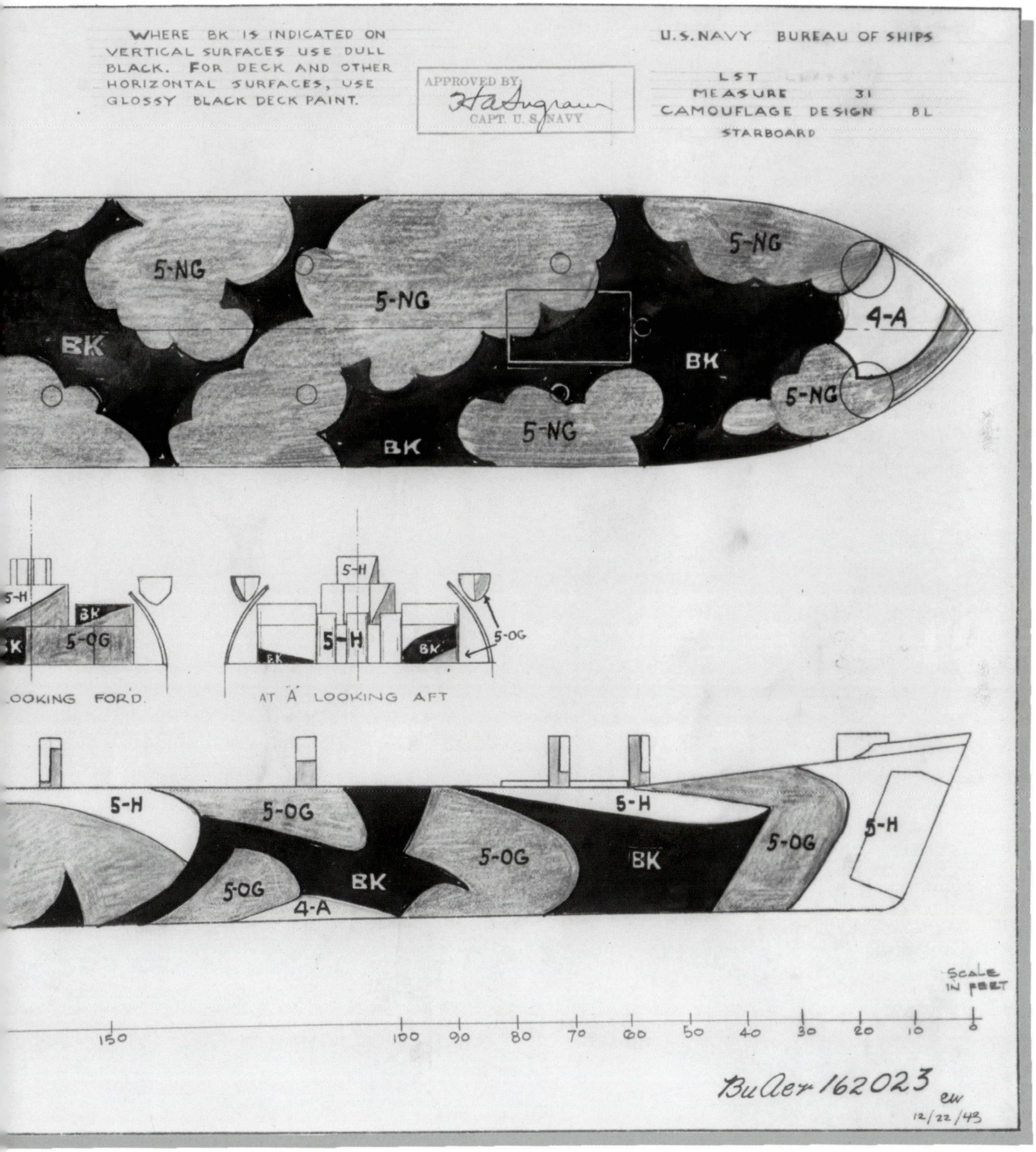

WHERE BK IS INDICATED ON VERTICAL SURFACES USE DULL BLACK. FOR DECK AND OTHER HORIZONTAL SURFACES, USE GLOSSY BLACK DECK PAINT.
APPROVED BY:
CAPT. U. S. NAVY
U.S. NAVY BUREAU OF SHIPS
LST
MEASURE 31
CAMOUFLAGE DESIGN 8L
STARBOARD
5-NG
BK
4-A
5-H
5-OG
LOOKING FORD.
AT A LOOKING AFT
SCALE IN FEET
150
100
90
80
70
60
50
40
30
20
10
0
BuAer 162023
12/22/43

Razzle Dazzle Camouflage

Developed during the First World War, 'razzle dazzle' camouflage was designed to help protect ships from submarines. Various patterns were designed to make it difficult for an observer to judge the correct speed, distance and direction of a ship. Dazzle camouflage was resurrected by the U.S. Navy during World War II. (NARA)

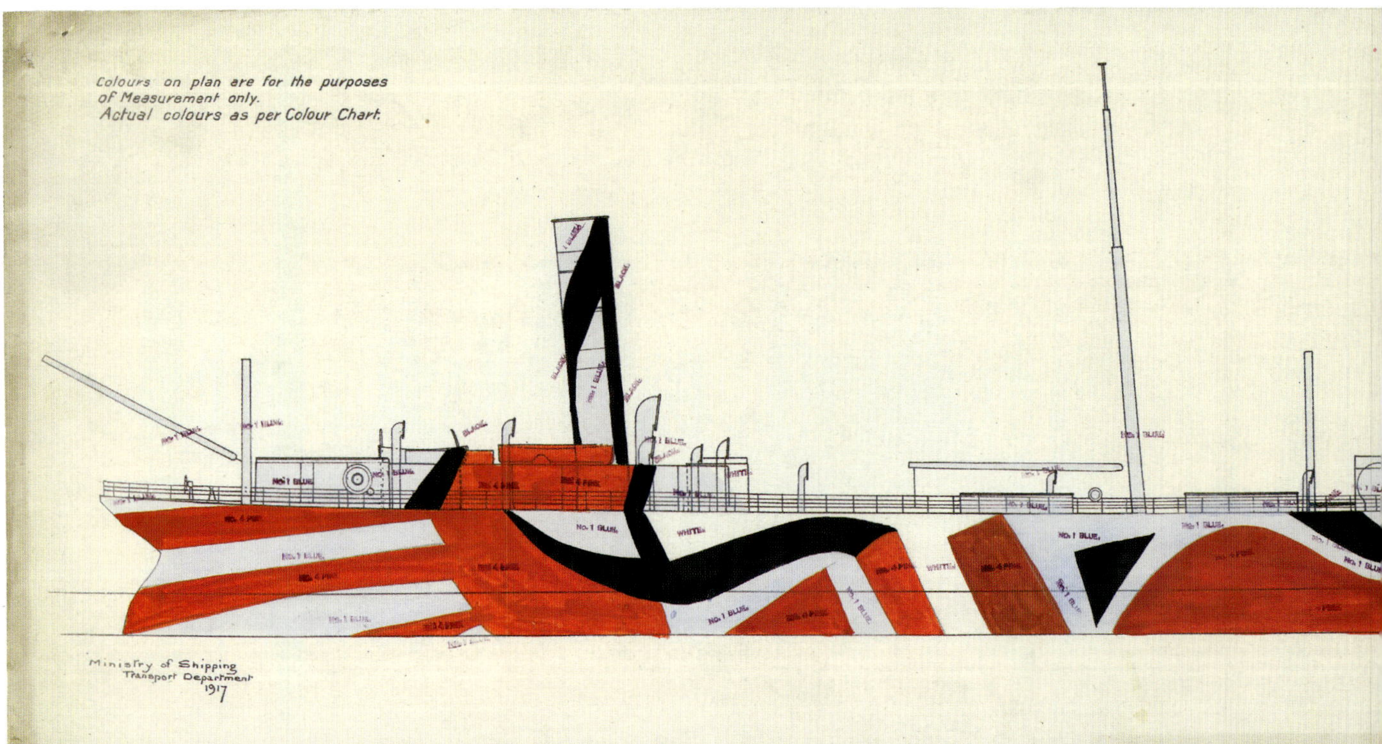

TYPE 10
DESIGN C.
SCALE 1/16" = 1 FOOT
STARBOARD COPY
No. 5
COLOURS.
LOAD DRAFT
LIGHT DRAFT
LENGTH B.P. 500 FEET
Norman Wilkinson
Lieut RNVR

TYPE 11
DESIGN C
STARBOARD COPY
No. 9
COLOURS
LOAD DRAFT
LIGHT DRAFT
Norman Wilkinson
Lieut RNVR

GERMAN NAVY UNIFORM
Bordmütze
Overseas cap
Worn at sea
Knopf
Button
Kriegsmarine
Mütze
Cap
Admiralstlagge
Admiral's Flag
Worn on left arm above all other insignia by subordinate personnel attached to admiral's staff
Hoheitsabzeichen
National Emblem
Brustabzeichen (below)
Device worn on left side of blous below pocket indicating tha wearer has seen action in this wa in the type of service portraye
Dienstgradabzeichen
Rating Stripes
Worn by seamen on upper left sleeve below corps insignia
Matrosengefreiter
Seaman 2nd class
Matrosenobergefreiter
Seaman 1st class
Matrosenhauptgefreiter
Seaman 1st class with 4½ years' seniority
Matrosenobergefreiter mit mehr als 6 Dienstjahren
Seaman 1st class with more than 6 years' seniority
Matrosengefreiter als geprüfter Unteroffizier-anwärter
Seaman 2nd class awaiting promotion to Petty Officer
Dienstgradabzeichen
Insignia of Rating
For 2nd and 3rd class Petty Officers
Worn on upper left sleeve above specialist insignia
Steuermannsmaat
Quartermaster 3rd class
Bootsmannsmaat
Coxwain (Boatswain's mate 3rd class)
Verwaltungsmaat
Storekeeper 3rd class
Obermaschinenmaat
Machinist's mate 2nd class
An anchor is the distinguishing mark of 2nd and 3rd class Petty Officers; for the former with a stripe added to it. The anchor with rope attached is the form used for deck ratings. Boatswains wear crossed anchors. All other corps have their corps insignia incorporated with the anchor in the badge as shown above.
U-Boots-Kriegsabzeichen 1939
Submarine badge, 1939
Zerstörer-Kriegsabzeichen
Destroyer badge
Kriegsabzeichen für Minensuch-, U-Boots Jagd- und Sicherungsverbände
Badge for Minesweepers and Submarine chasers
Kriegsabzeichen für die Marineartillerie
Naval artillery badge
Kriegsabzeichen für Hilfskreuzer
Auxiliary cruiser badge
Laufbahnabzeichen
Corps Insignia
Worn on upper left sleeve above specialist insignia
Bootsmanns-Laufbahn (Matrose)
Boatswain (seaman)
Signal-
Signal
Fernschreib-
Telegrapher
Zimmermanns-
Carpenter
Artillerie-Mechaniker-
Ordnance engineer
Torpedo-Mechaniker
Torpedo engineer
Schreibers-
Yeoman
Sanitäts-
Pharmacist
Musik
Musician
Maschinen
Machinist's mate
Funk
Radioman
Marine-Artillerie-
Naval artillery
Abzeichen für Sonderausbildung
Insignia for Specialist Branches
Worn on left arm beneath rating badge and corp insignia
Fla-Maschinenwaffenschütze
Antiaircraft machine gunner
Fla-Maschinenwaffenführer
Antiaircraft machine gun crew leader
Geschützführer, Flak
(Chief) Gun captain, antiaircraft
Geschützführer E.
Chief gun captain (two chevrons after 3 years' experience)
Geschützführer T.
Chief turret captain (three chevrons after 6 years' experience)
Geschützführer E.
Chief gun captain (six years' experience)
Flak-Waffenleitvormann
Gun captain, antiaircraft
Waffenleitvormann-Küste
Gun captain, coast artillery
Torpedo-Waffenleitvormann
Torpedoman (launching tube operating crew) 3rd class
Ausbildung am Motor oder Kraftfahrzeug
Training with motor vessels (Motor course III)
Entfernungsmesser
Fire controlman (range-finder operator)
Flak-Entfernungsmesser
Anti-aircraft fire controlman (antiaircraft range-finder operator)
Sperrvormann
Mine captain
Spielmann
Bandsman
Vermessungsdienst
Survey service
Schiffstaucher
Ship's diver
Torpedotaucher
Torpedo diver
Unterwasserhorcher
Hydrophone operator
E-Maschinen Ausbildung (E III Lehrgang)
Electric motor training (E III course)
Sportlehrer
Athletic instructor
Geschützführer (R)
Reserve gun captain
Sperrvormann (R)
Reserve minelayer
NARVIK
1940
Narvikschild
Shield commemorating Narvik action
Worn on left upper sleeve above all other insignia
1941 1942
KRIM
Krimschild
Shield commemorating campaign in Crimea
Matrosen-Gefreiter, Dienstanzug
2nd class Seaman—Summer White Uniform
Has served on a destroyer and in the Narvik campaign
Obermaschinenmaat, Dienstanzug
Machinist's mate, 2nd class,
1st class specialist in motor engineering, service dress
The gold braid on cuffs of jacket is not worn by seamen.
GERMAN PRONUNCIATION CHART
MATROSE (mah-troh-zuh) = apprentice seaman
MATROSENGEFREITER (mah-trohz'n-guh-fryt'r) = S 2/c
MATROSENOBERGEFREITER (mah-trohz'n-ohb'r-guh-fryt'r) = S1/c
BOOTSMANNSMAAT (bohts-mahns-maht) = coxswain
OBERBOOTSMANNSMAAT (ohb'r-bohts-mahns-maht) = boatswain's mate 2/c
BOOTSMANN (bohts-mahn) = boatswain's mate 1/c
STEUERMANNSMAAT (shtoy'r-mahns-maht) = quartermaster 3/c
OBERSTEUERMANNSMAAT (ohb'r-shtoy'r-mahns-maht) = quartermaster 2/c
STEUERMANN (shtoy'r-mahn) = quartermaster 1/c
STABSSTEUERMANN (shtahps-shtoy'r-mahn) = chief quartermaster
OBERSTEUERMANN (ohb'r-shtoy'r-mahn) = quartermaster, warrant
STABSOBERSTEUERMANN (shtahps-ohb'r-shtoy'r-mahn) = quartermaster, chief warrant
EQUIVALENT RATINGS IN U. S. AND GERMAN NAVIES
Matrose = Apprentice Seaman
Matrosengefreiter = Seaman 2nd class
Matrosenobergefreiter = Seaman 1st class
Matrosenhauptgefreiter = Seaman 1st class
Matrosenstabsgefreiter = Seaman 1st class
Maat = Petty Officer 3rd class
Obermaat = Petty Officer 2nd class
Distributed by
ARMY ORIENTATION COURSE, Special Service Division SOS, WAR DEPARTMENT,
Navy Distribution through EDUCATIONAL SERVICES, BuPers, NAVY DEPT.

German Naval Uniforms

This Newsmap image appeared on Monday March 8, 1943, the 182nd week of the war and the 64th week of U.S. participation. To identify additional qualifications, the Kriegsmarine issued 'trade badges.' These were worn as red on blue patches beneath the seaman's rank chevron or petty officer's badge.

Italian Navy Uniforms

During the war, propaganda created by the Royal Navy depicted the Regia Marina as incompetent, cowardly and technically improficient. In fact, the quality of the Regia Marina's personnel and ships was high compared to Italy's other two armed forces. In June 1940, the Regia Marina numbered 168,800 men.

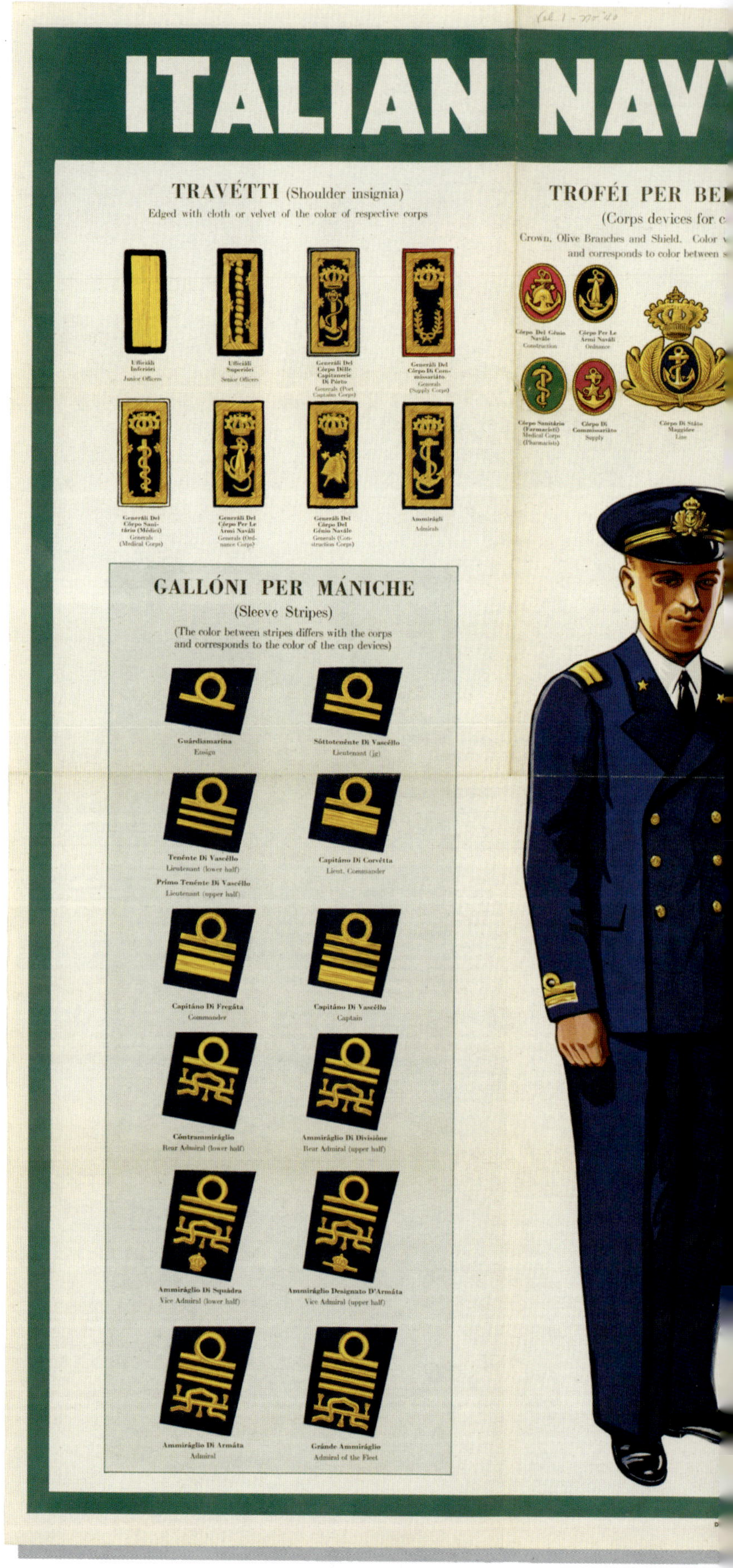

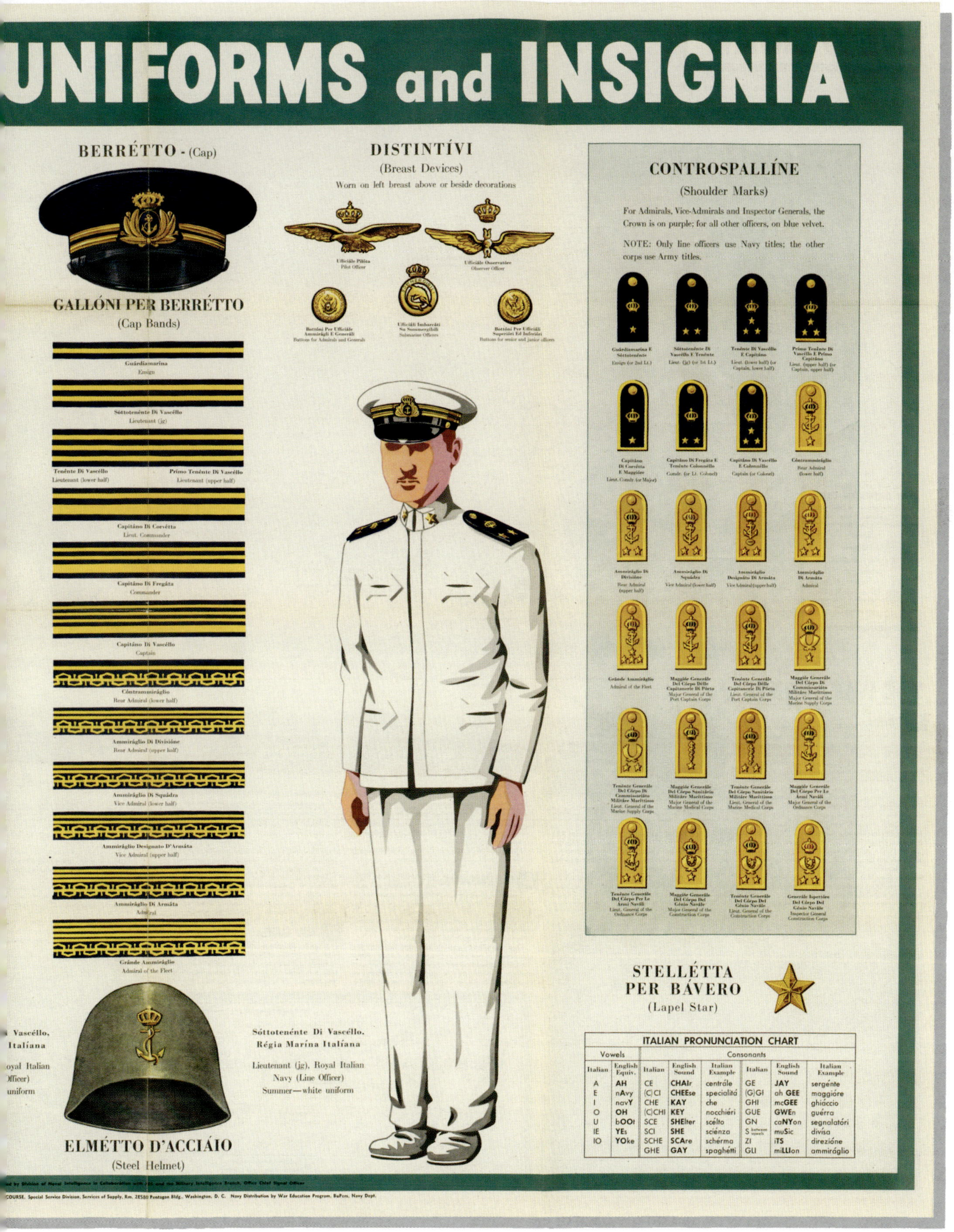

ITALIAN PRONUNCIATION CHART							
Vowels		Consonants					
Italian	English Equiv.	Italian	English Sound	Italian Example	Italian	English Sound	Italian Example
A	AH	CE	CHAIr	centrále	GE	JAY	sergénte
E	nAvy	(C)CI	CHEEse	specialitá	(G)GI	ah GEE	maggióre
I	navY	CHE	KAY	che	GHI	mcGEE	ghiáccio
O	OH	(C)CHI	KEY	nocchiéri	GUE	GWEn	guérra
U	bOOt	SCE	SHElter	scélto	GN	caNYon	segnalatóri
IE	YEs	SCI	SHE	sciénza	S between vowels	muSic	divísa
IO	YOke	SCHE	SCAre	schérma	ZI	iTS	direzióne
		GHE	GAY	spaghétti	GLI	miLLIon	ammiráglio

Aircraft Recognition Pamphlets

Aircraft Recognition Pamphlets were issued monthly to keep sailors up to date with the latest enemy and Allied aircraft entering service. Crews were encouraged to test their recall skills with answers provided on the back of each issue.

IT'S A TRAP! SPOT THE JAP!
LIFT FLAP FOR ANSWER

40 mm Bofors

The 40 mm Bofors anti-aircraft gun was the most successful of the war. The British were one of the first to adopt the 40 mm for ship AA defence. The U.S. followed suit, with production beginning in 1941. During 1944, American industry churned out 6,644 single mounts, approximately 3,650 twin mounts and 750 quad mounts.

FEEDING THE ROUND

Figure 34

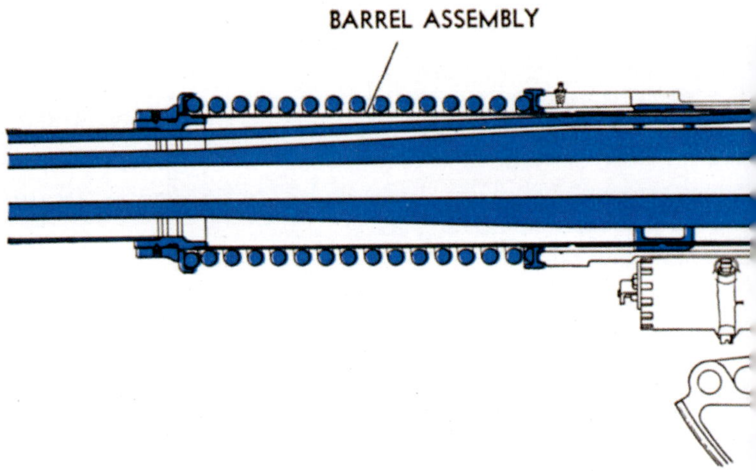

COCKING THE RAMMER

Figure 35

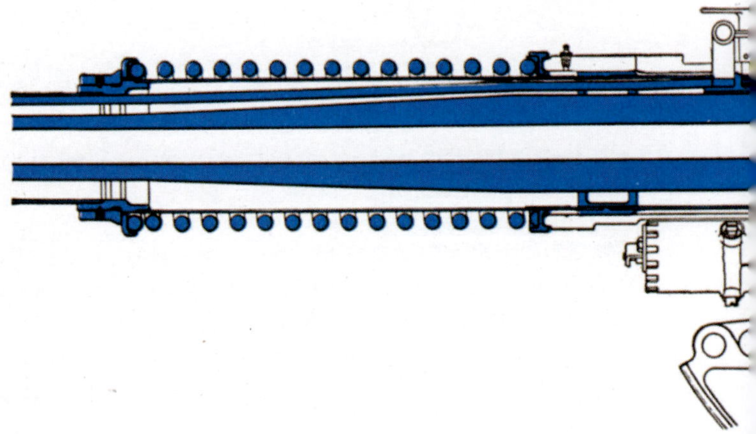

P. 820

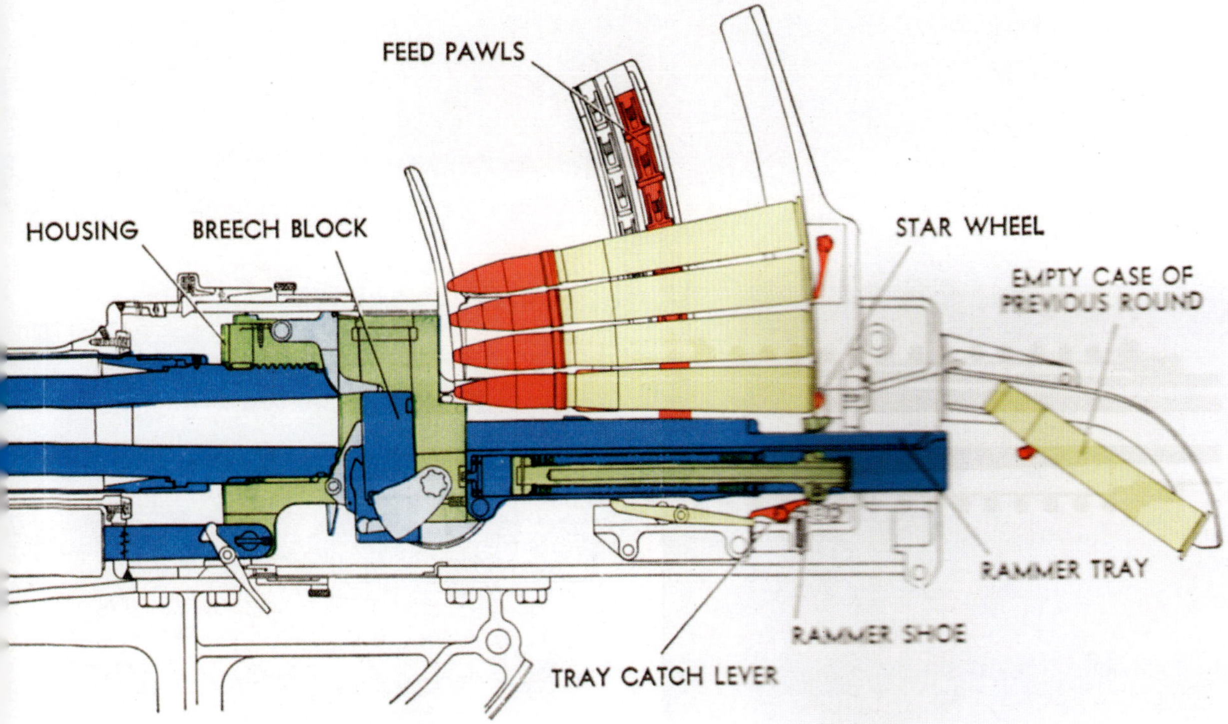
FEED PAWLS
HOUSING
BREECH BLOCK
STAR WHEEL
EMPTY CASE OF PREVIOUS ROUND
RAMMER TRAY
RAMMER SHOE
TRAY CATCH LEVER

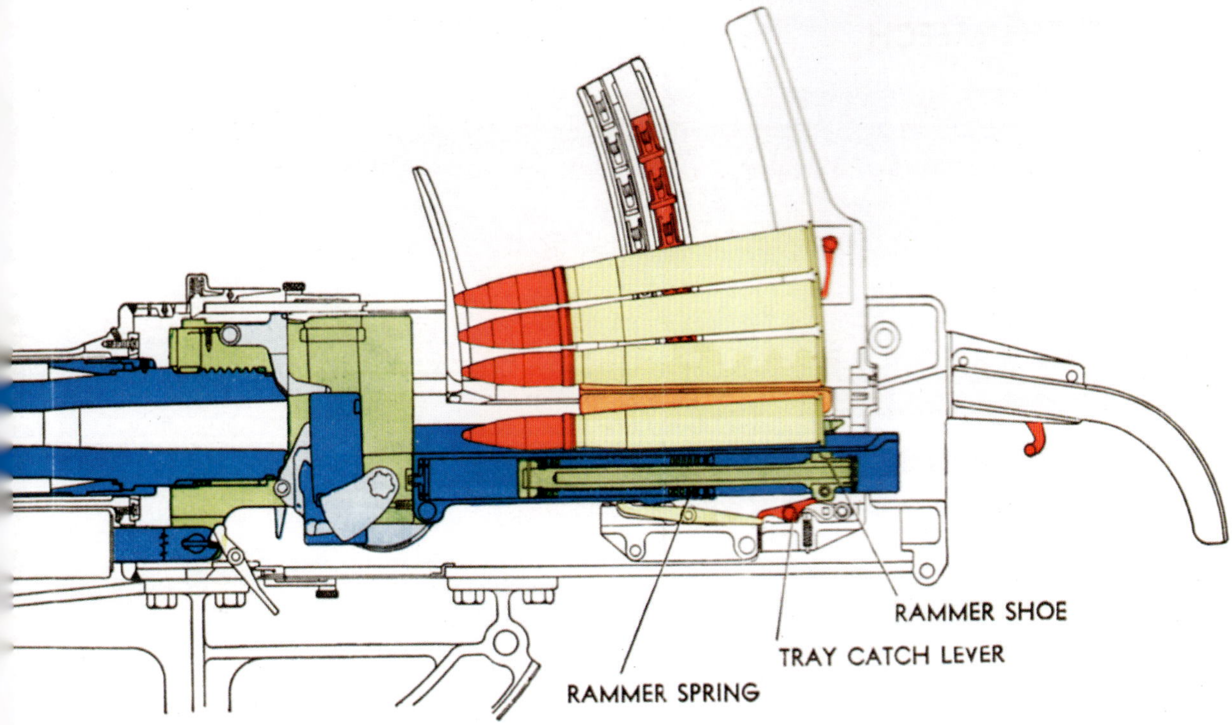
RAMMER SHOE
TRAY CATCH LEVER
RAMMER SPRING

Page 59

20 mm Magazine

The detachable magazine for the 20 mm gun carried an assortment of 60 high-explosive, armor-piercing, incendiary and tracer rounds.

OPERATING FEATURES

Figure 7—Magazine

PAGE 20 CHAPTER 2

SIGHT

Chapter 7

DESCRIPTION OF SIGHTS

There are five types of sights in use: 20 mm. Sights Mark 2, Mark 4, Mark 4 Mod. 1, and Mark 5 and Gun Sight Mark 14 Mod. 2.

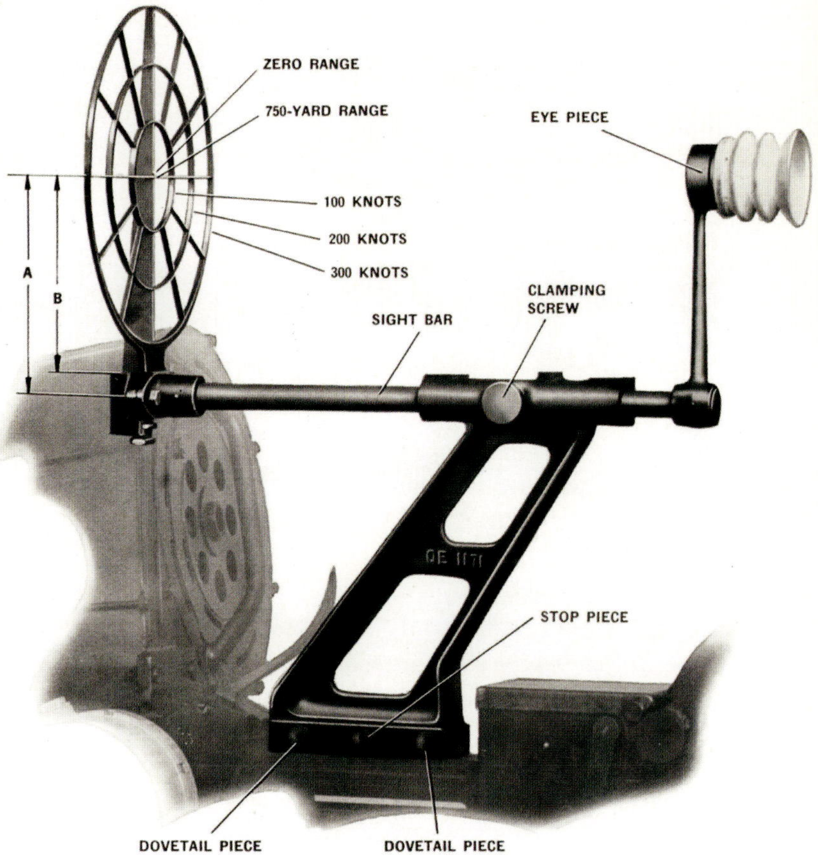

Figure 68—Sight Arrangement—Mark 4

Mark 4 and Mark 4 Mod. 1 sights can be easily distinguished by their name plates. Mark 4 sight is illustrated in Figure 68. The bracket on Mark 4 Mod. 1 is one inch lower than the one on Mark 4, and has less backward slope. This brings the line of sight one inch closer to the gun. Changes in the sight bar maintain the eye piece in the same fore and aft location.

PAGE 82 CHAPTER 7

20 mm Open Sight

Pointing and sighting were performed by the gunner using handlebars and shoulder rests. Originally, gunners used an open sight, with every fifth round fired being a tracer to aid in spotting. By 1944, the Mark 14 gyro-stabilized gun sight had replaced the open model, giving the 20 mm gun far greater accuracy.

20 mm Ammunition

By V-J Day, U.S. industry had produced over a billion rounds of ammunition at a cost of $786,791,000. The 20 mm round of just 0.12 kg (0.27 lbs) of explosive proved ineffective against Japanese kamikaze aircraft attacks in 1944–45. Wherever possible, the 20 mm was replaced by 40 mm guns starting in 1944.

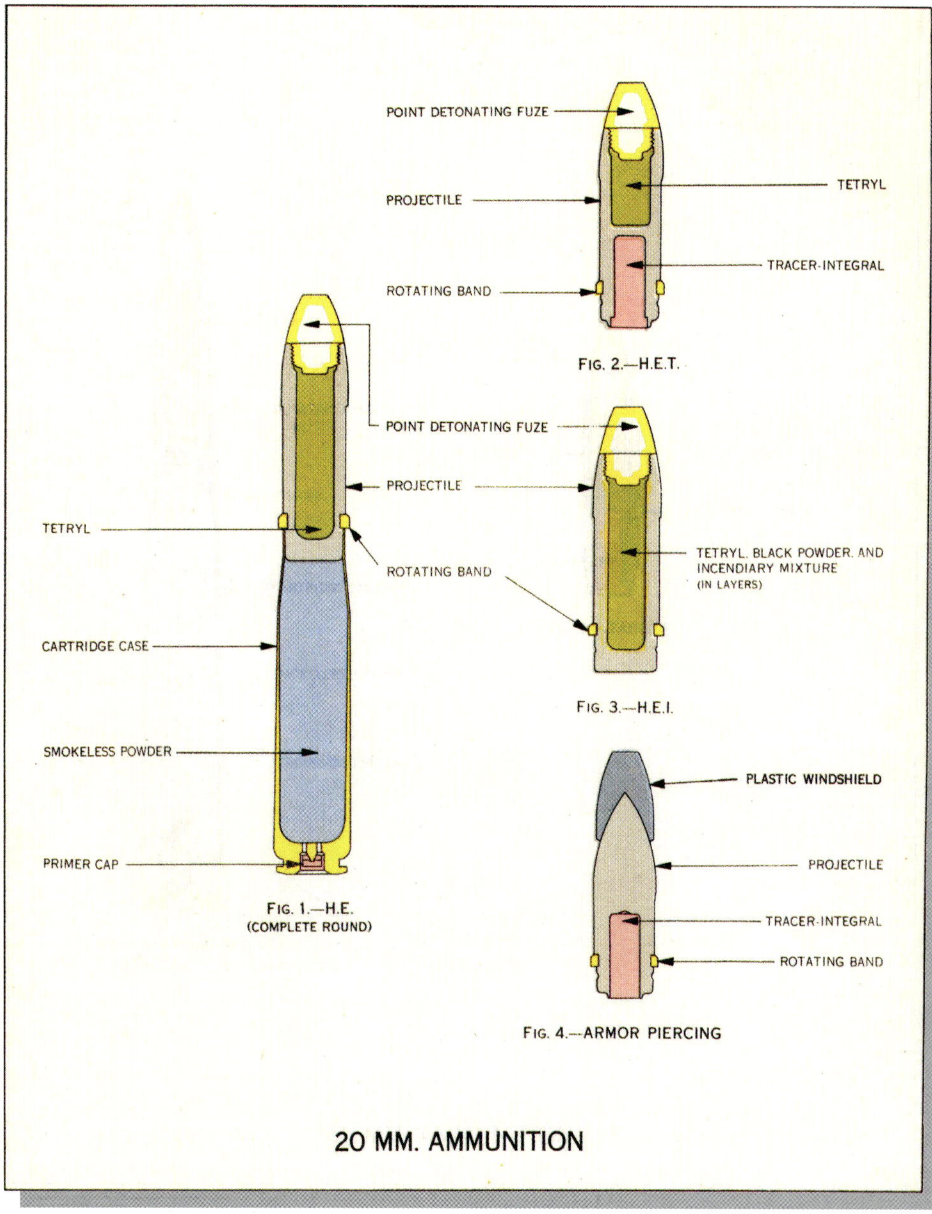

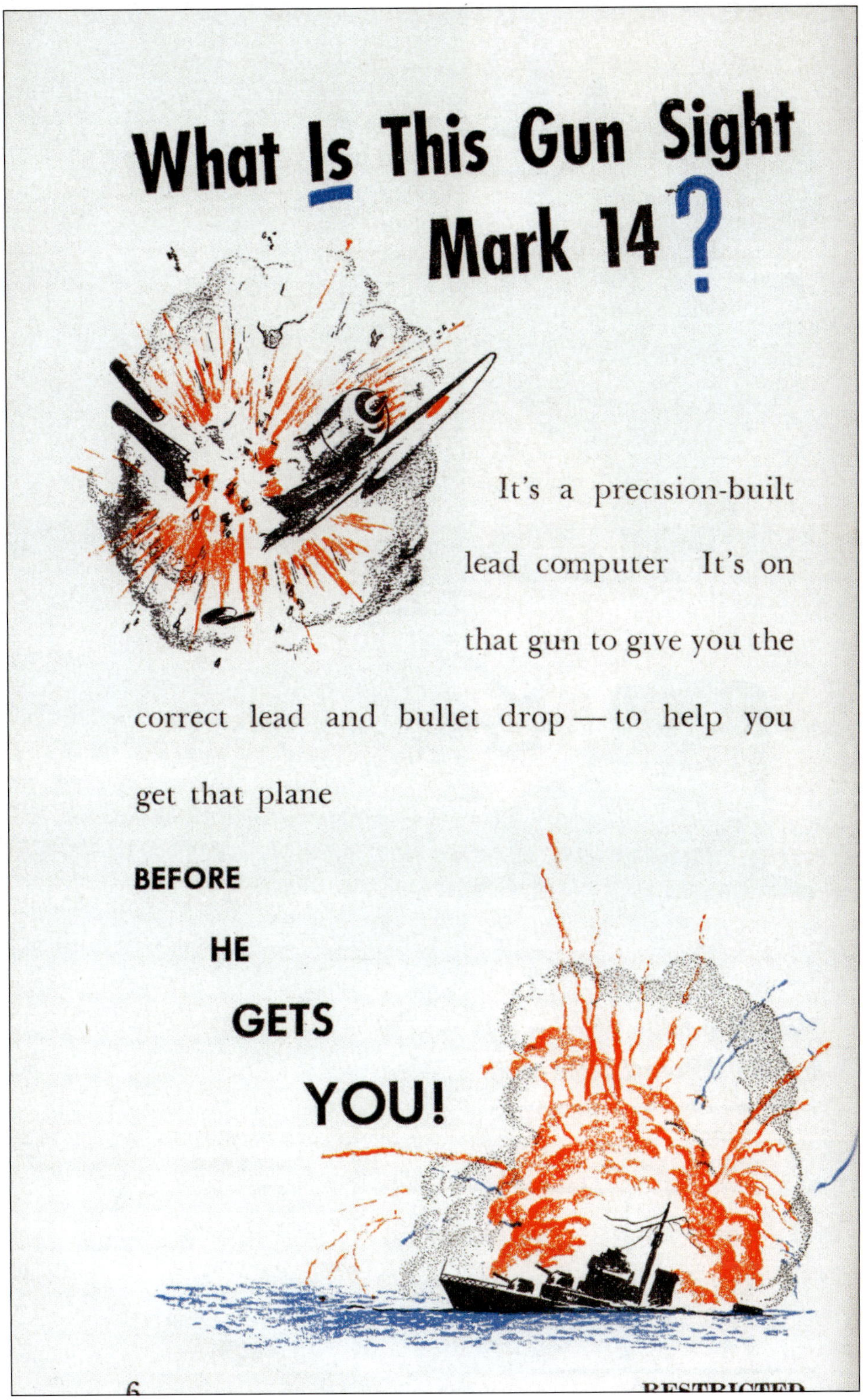

What is this Gun Sight Mark 14

The introduction of the Mark 14 gyro gun sight made the 20 mm cannon up to 50 percent more effective compared to the open sight. It was designed to handle a 200-knot target, but it proved reasonably accurate against aircraft flying at 500 knots.

these mirrors in such a way that as you track a target and keep the reticle centered on it, you move the gun *ahead* by the correct lead to hit that target.

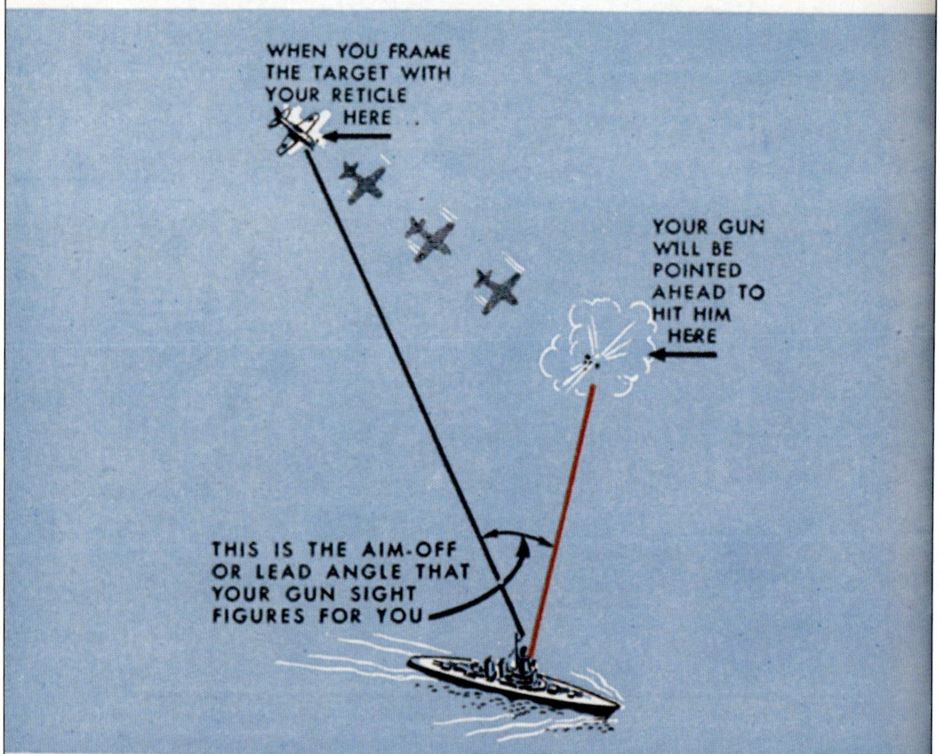

DO THE GYROS MOVE THE GUN?

No, *you* move the gun. Its movement makes the gyros tilt, their tilting moves the mirrors and the reticle image moves away from the barrel of the

Do the Gyros Move the Gun?

As Japanese kamikaze attacks increased in frequency and intensity, so too did the need for more accurate AA fire. The only way to deal with the threat was to destroy the aircraft outright, well before it hit a ship. USN naval gunners were well trained and equipped and proved an effective deterrent against the kamikaze.

When to Open Fire

Trigger discipline was critical for effective AA fire. Firing too soon wasted vast amounts of ammunition and was ineffective. This diagram clearly instructs the AA gunner when to open fire.

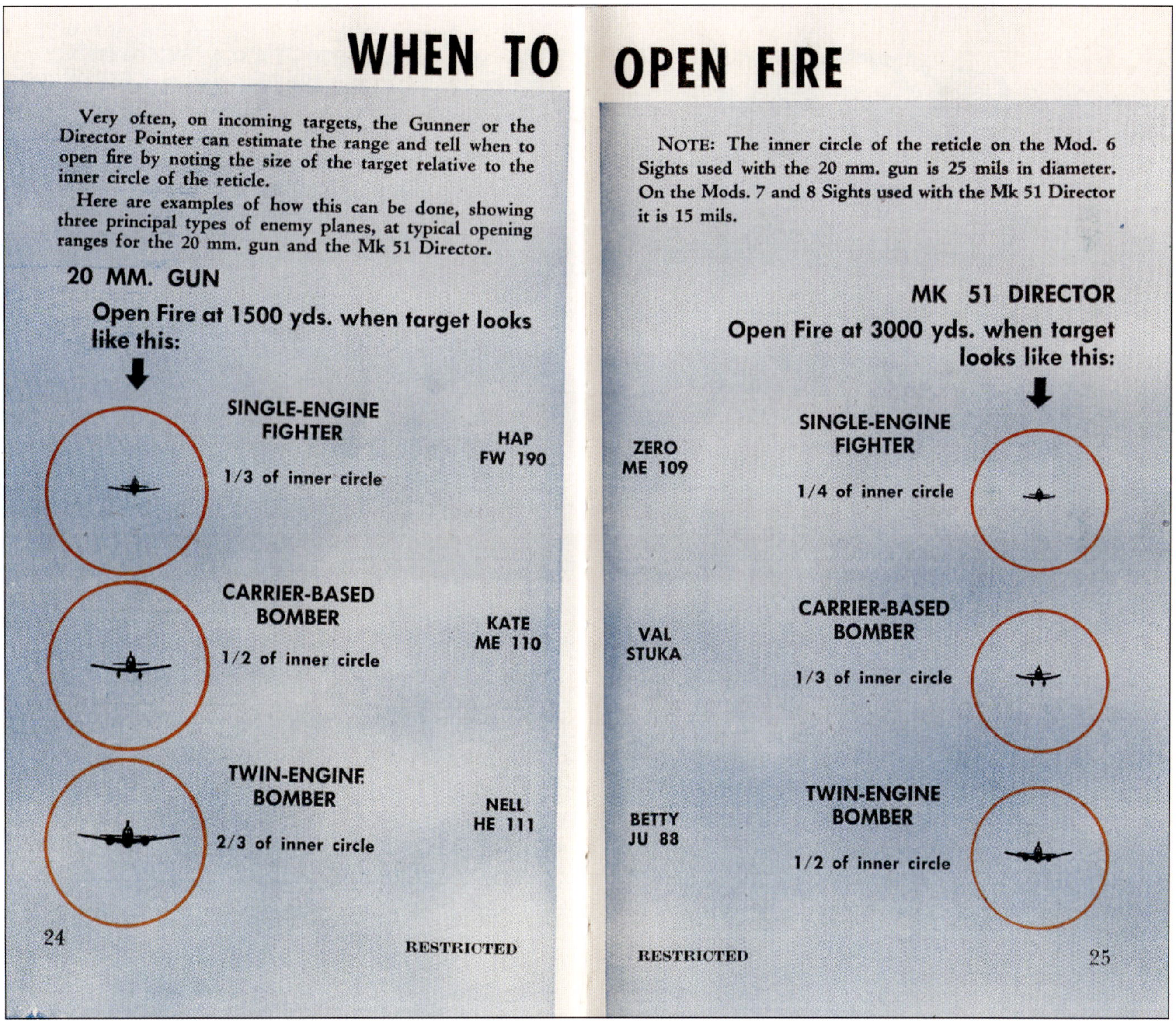

WHEN TO OPEN FIRE

Very often, on incoming targets, the Gunner or the Director Pointer can estimate the range and tell when to open fire by noting the size of the target relative to the inner circle of the reticle.

Here are examples of how this can be done, showing three principal types of enemy planes, at typical opening ranges for the 20 mm. gun and the Mk 51 Director.

20 MM. GUN

Open Fire at 1500 yds. when target looks like this:

SINGLE-ENGINE FIGHTER — 1/3 of inner circle — HAP, FW 190

CARRIER-BASED BOMBER — 1/2 of inner circle — KATE, ME 110

TWIN-ENGINE BOMBER — 2/3 of inner circle — NELL, HE 111

24 RESTRICTED

NOTE: The inner circle of the reticle on the Mod. 6 Sights used with the 20 mm. gun is 25 mils in diameter. On the Mods. 7 and 8 Sights used with the Mk 51 Director it is 15 mils.

MK 51 DIRECTOR

Open Fire at 3000 yds. when target looks like this:

ZERO, ME 109 — SINGLE-ENGINE FIGHTER — 1/4 of inner circle

VAL, STUKA — CARRIER-BASED BOMBER — 1/3 of inner circle

BETTY, JU 88 — TWIN-ENGINE BOMBER — 1/2 of inner circle

RESTRICTED 25

'Betty' Arcs of Fire

The Mitsubishi G4M 'Betty' was the IJNAF's principal bomber. Relatively fast, with a top speed of 231 knots at 4,206 meters (13,800 feet), it could carry torpedoes to attack ships or bombs to attack either land or sea targets. It was armed with four machine guns and a gun in the tail for self-protection.

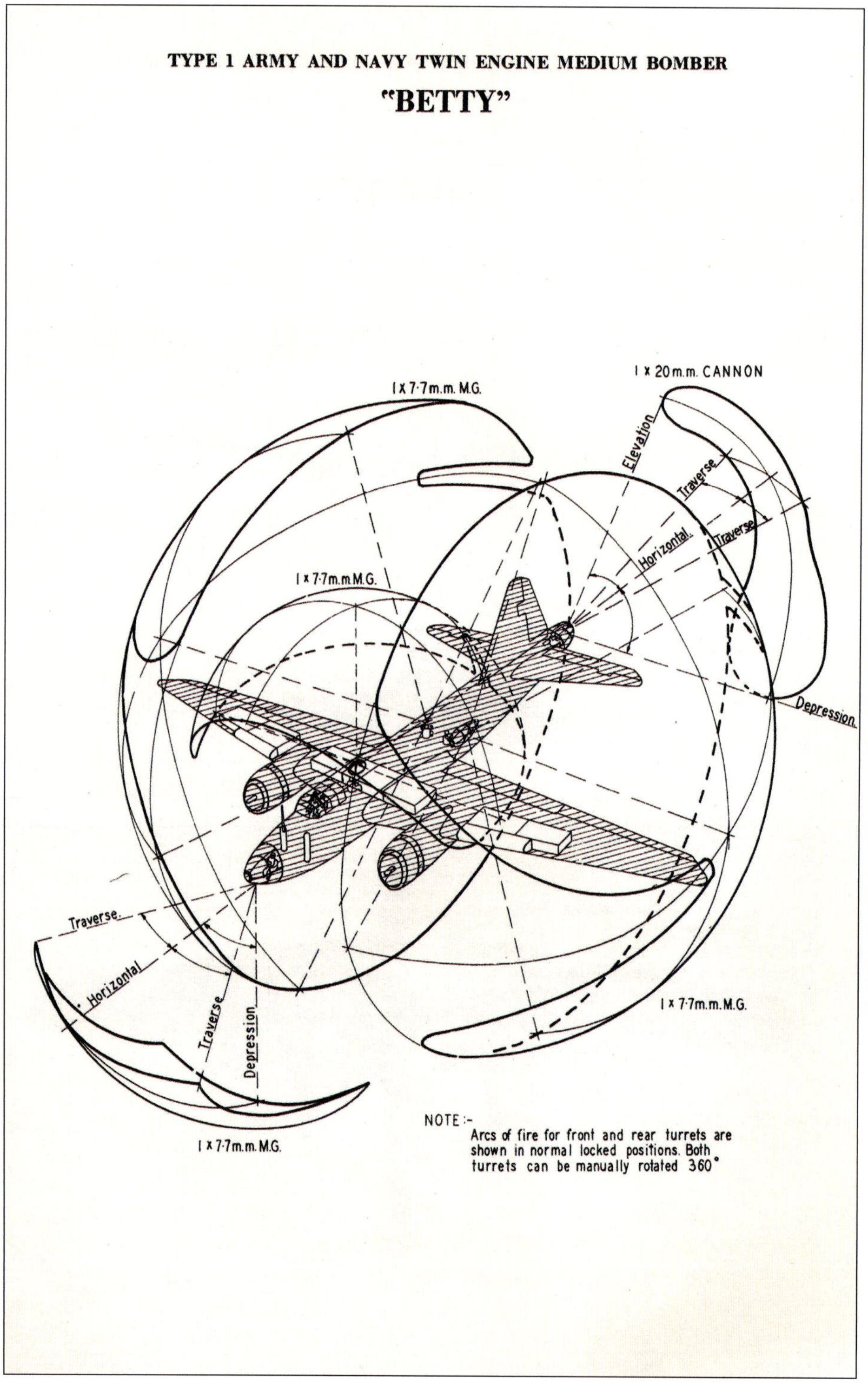

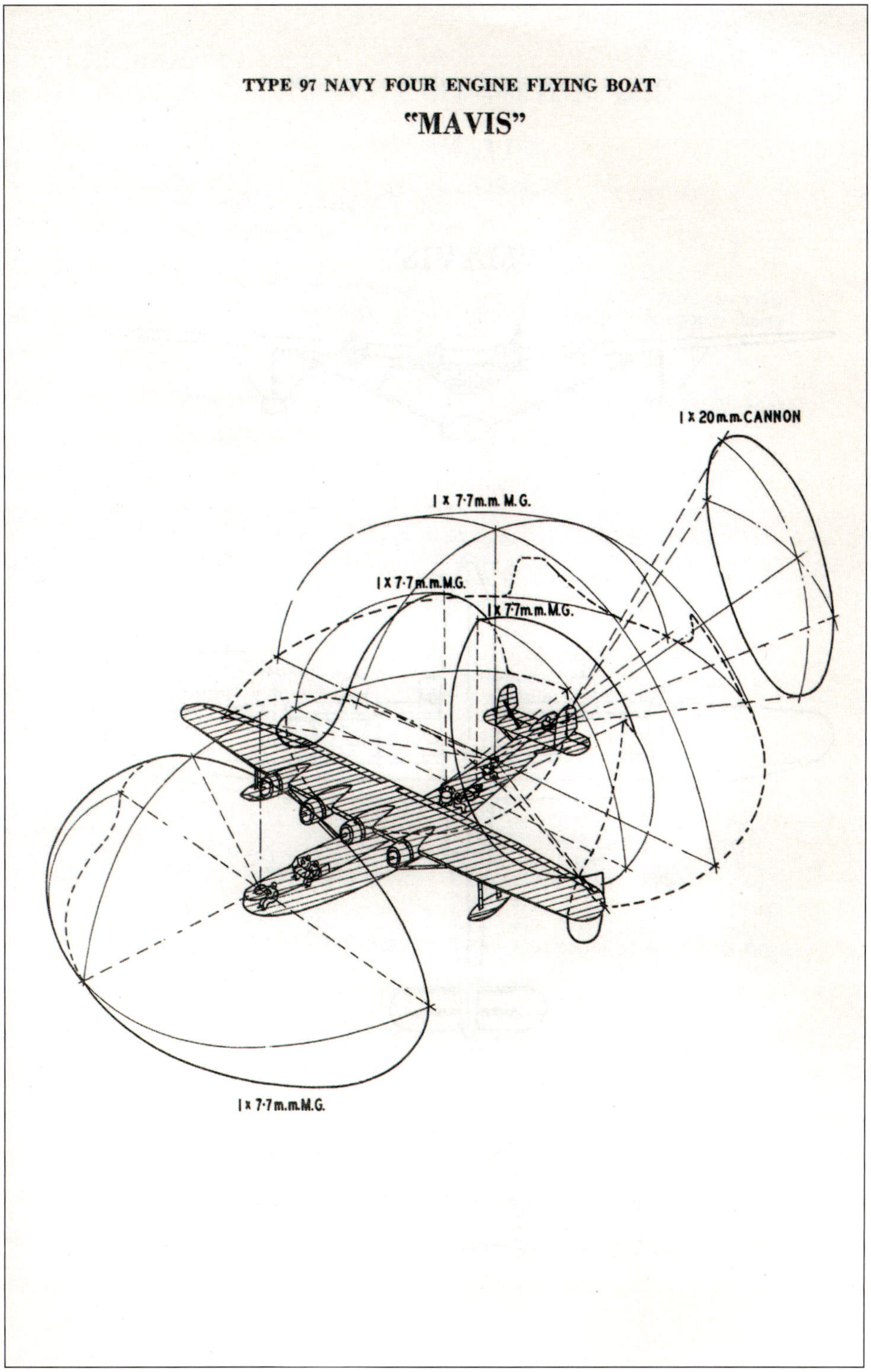

'Mavis' Arcs of Fire

The Kawanishi H6K 'Mavis' was a four-engine flying boat used for long-range reconnaissance by the IJN. It carried single 7.7 mm machine guns in open bow and dorsal mounts and beam blisters, and a 20 mm cannon in a tail turret. It could carry two 800 kg (1,760 lb) aerial torpedoes, or up to 1,000 kg (2,205 lbs) in bombs.

454 kg (1,000 lb) Armor-piercing Bomb

On April 3, 1944, aircraft of the British Fleet Air Arm attacked the German battleship *Tirpitz* while in the Kaafjord, Norway. The Barracuda dive bombers used in the raid were armed with 726 kg (1,600 lbs) of U.S.-made, armor-piercing bombs. Four of these bombs found their mark, but their effectiveness was limited. Due to defects during production, only half of the requisite amount of explosives had been filled into each bomb.

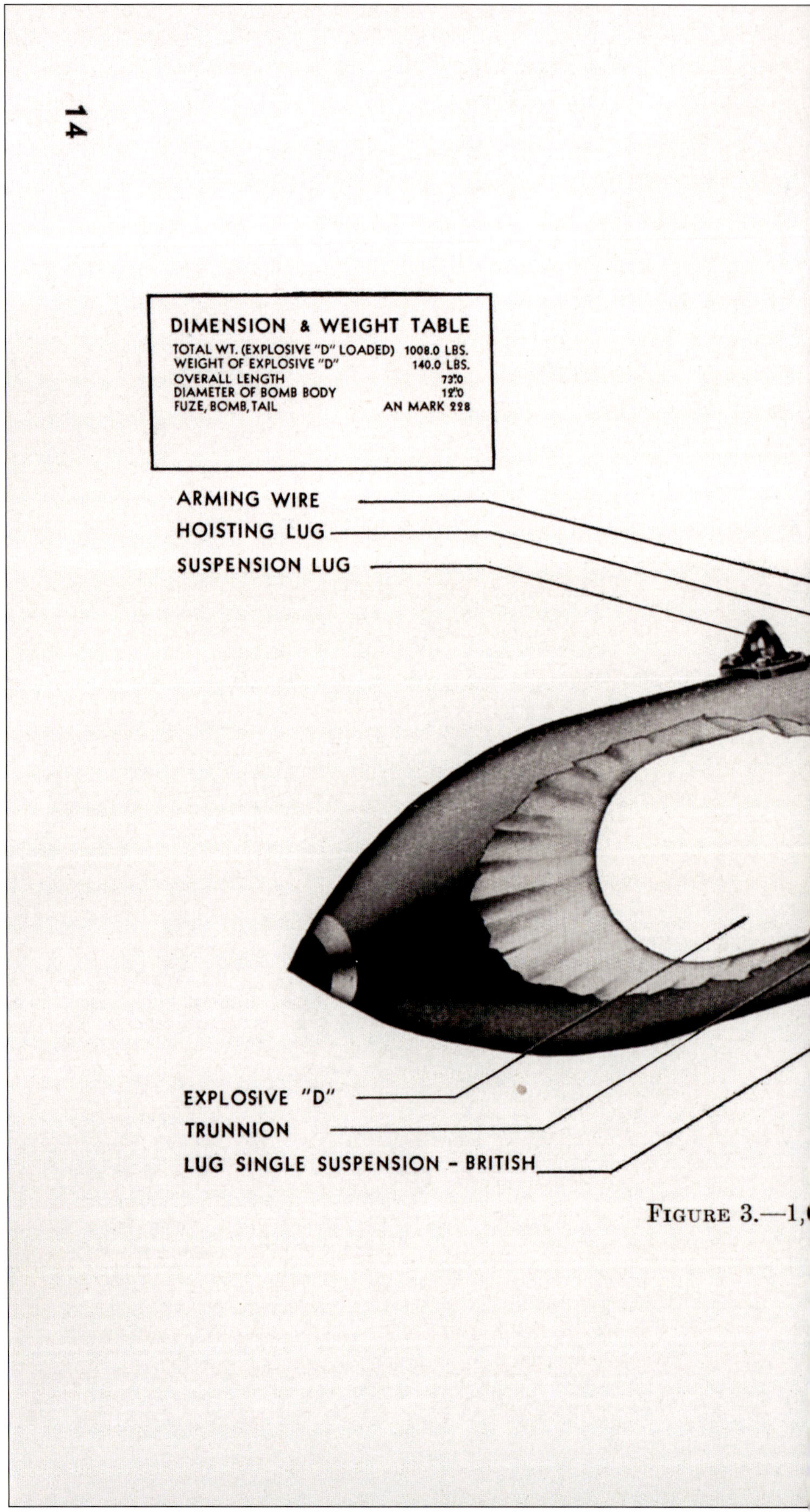

FIGURE 3.—1,

ARMOR-PIERCING BOMBS

O. P. 1019

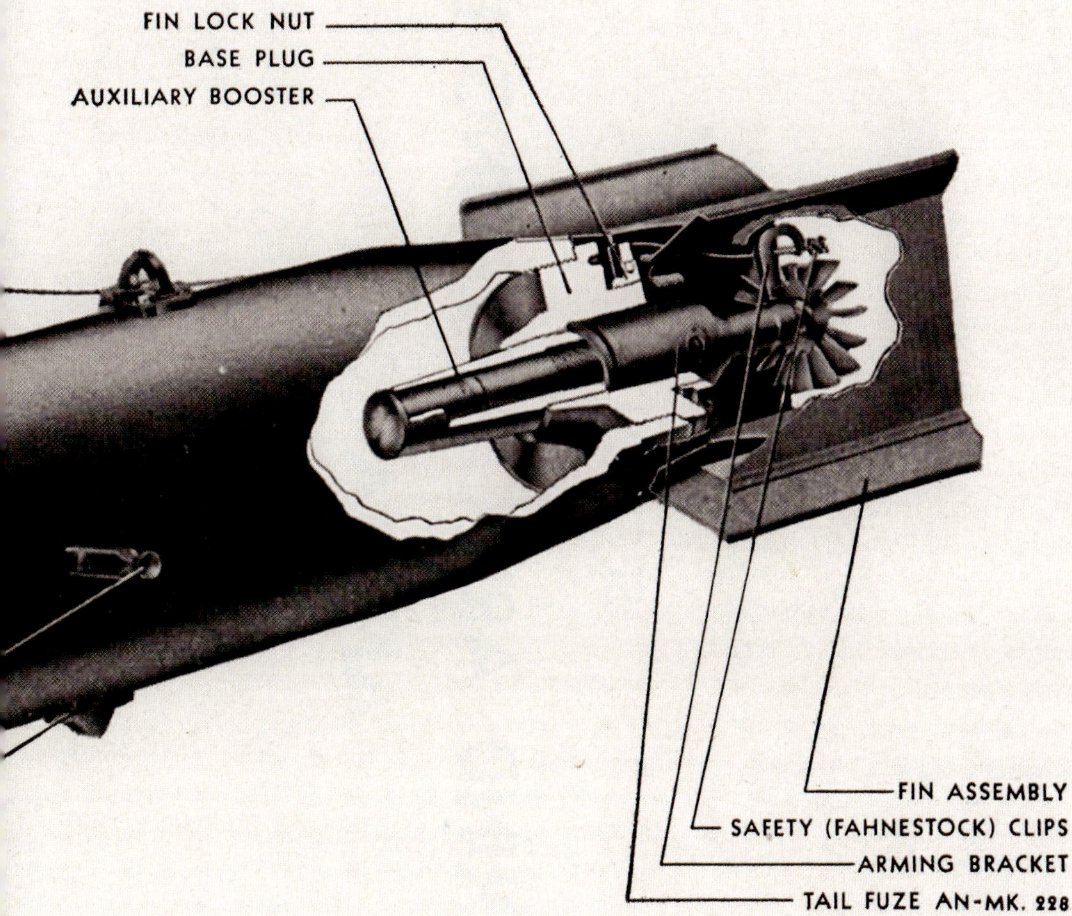

ND A. P BOMB, AN–MARK 33.

Japanese Navy Bomb 1/3

This Japanese Navy cluster munition was used against airfields and parked aircraft. It was carried in clusters of 30 or 76 in a black container. After release, the container burst in mid-air, scattering its bombs.

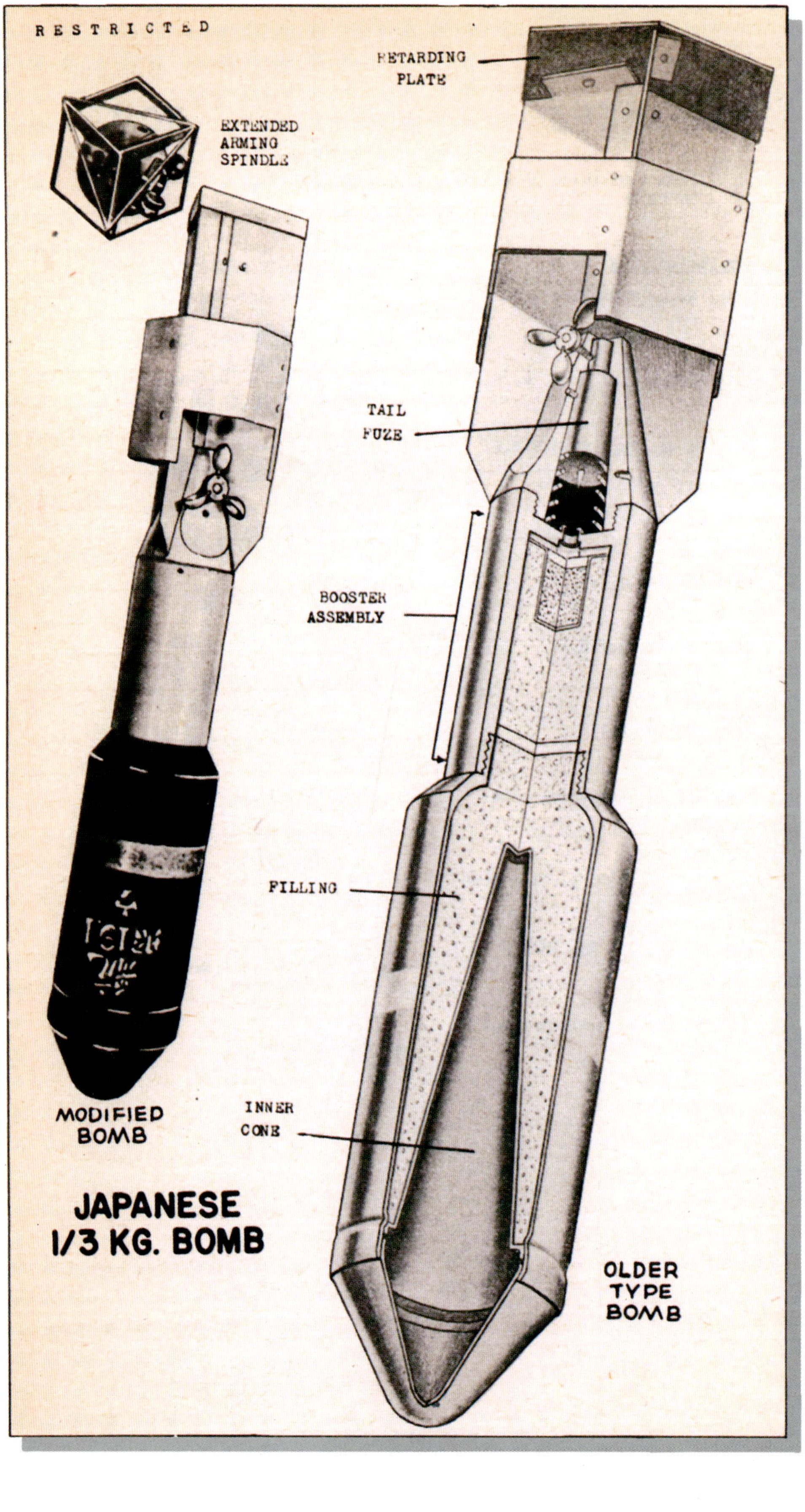

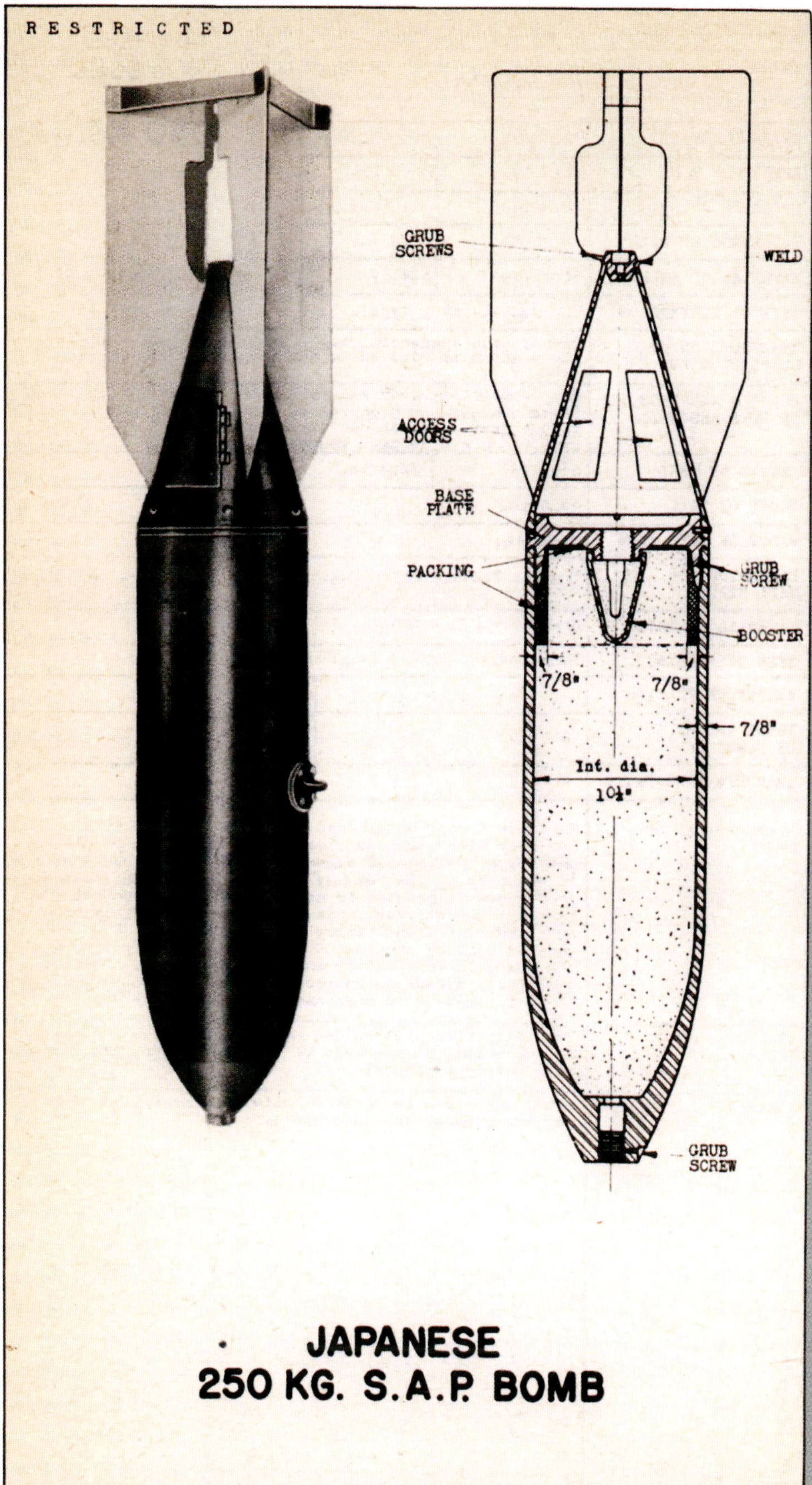

Japanese Navy 250 kg (540 lb) Semi-armor-piercing Bomb

Because of its small explosive content, just 60 kg (133 lbs), this bomb was only effective against cruisers and destroyers. During the carrier Battle of Santa Cruz in October 1942, the USS *Hornet* was hit by five Japanese bombs and three torpedoes, only to be sunk by Japanese destroyer torpedoes.

Combat Air Patrol Cover

This cover of the combat air patrol training manual clearly illustrates the anti-Japanese sentiment that fueled Allied propaganda. Japanese characters were often portrayed in a racist and dehumanizing form in order to fuel a continued hatred of the enemy.

Fighter Escort Cover

The chief lesson learned during the 1942 naval campaign was the need for more naval fighters. As USN training ramped up, so too did the production of training manuals, visual aids and instructional films. By 1944, new pilot cadets would receive the best training in the world.

Know Your PT Boat

During the war, the U.S. Navy established 43 PT (Patrol, Torpedo) squadrons, each with 12 boats. These small, fast boats were used for short-range reconnaissance, and for cutting supply lines and harassing enemy forces.

All Tense but the Magazine

USN PT boats suffered heavy casualties during the war. Weapons had to be constantly maintained and ready for action. This illustration emphasizes the need to keep proper tension on the the 20 mm gun magazine in order to prevent jamming.

ALL TENSE BUT THE MAGAZINE

4. Be sure that prior to any imminent action all magazines are *on full tension at 60 pounds*. If your magazines have been in use a long time, it is wise to pull out a few rounds before loading, but be sure you still have on the full tension. This precaution will give the last few rounds in your magazine an extra push and will prevent jamming.

5. Practice all operations, especially cocking and loading, in the dark or with your eyes closed This type of practice, "blind cocking and blind loading" is invaluable. A PT operates chiefly at night and any kind of illumination of deck is taboo. Get the feel of the gun, the magazine, their every part and get the rhythm in cocking, loading, and firing.

30-Cal. Cockpit Gun.—The "pea shooter" is a very light gun carrying a great amount of tracer ammunition. This gun may be operated by an officer or gunner on the bridge. It is very much like a 50-cal. gun in looks and operation. It can have single or double barrels operation.

21

Broadcast Receivers

Any time a ship used a communication device that generated an electromagnetic wave, it could be detected, and its position fixed. As the Allied merchant marine rapidly expanded, the period of training for new radio operators was cut short, leading to careless mistakes which benefitted the prowling German U-boats.

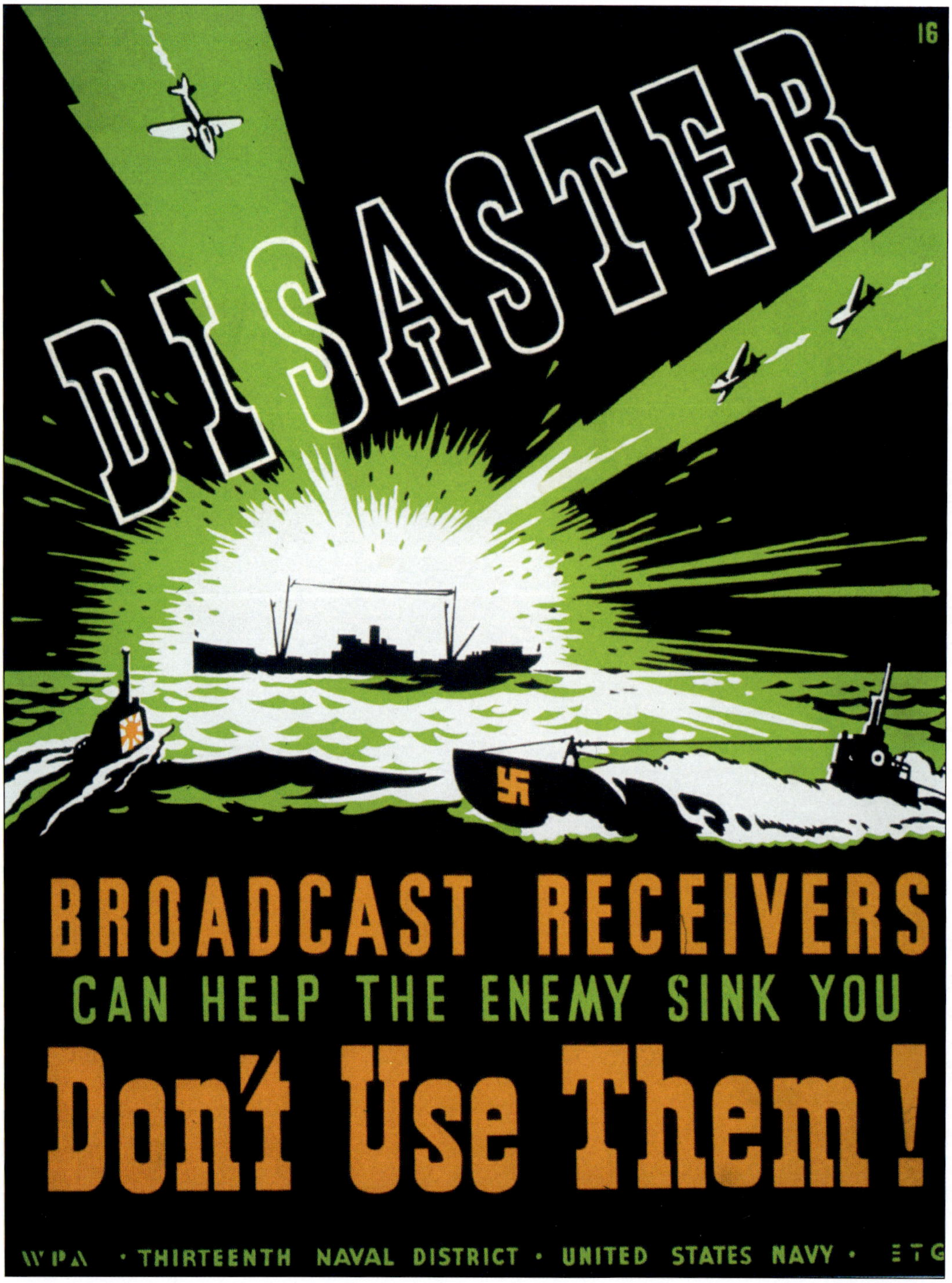

Smoking Stacks Attract Attacks

The distance someone could spot a ship from a typical World War II submarine conning tower was approximately 8.9 kilometers (5.5 miles). Excessive smoke from the stacks made detection easier for a surfaced submarine crew.

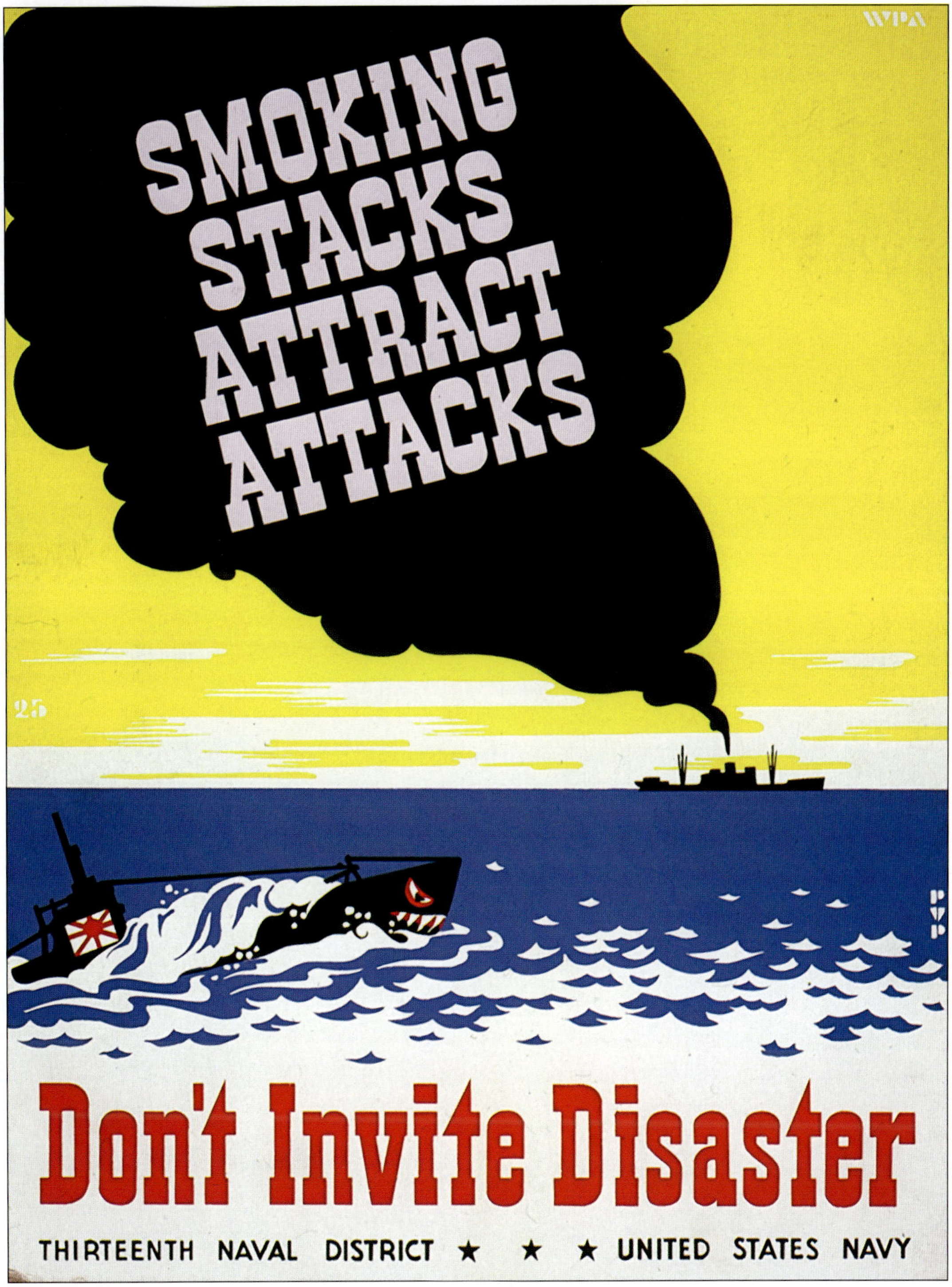

YOUR SUBMARINE

NOTE: *Conning towers have been altered for security reasons.*

"When our surface forces retired to the south from the Philippine Islands . . . As the Japanese advanced through the Netherlands East Indies and into the Solomons, submarines continued to interrupt enemy lines of communications, and since that time have continued their attacks on enemy men-of-war and merchantmen with telling effect. [Of the total Japanese merchant vessel tonnage sunk in this war, 77 per cent is attributed to our Submarine Service—an enviable record.]

"Without adequate shipping, Japan can not hold out, much less support her forces in the islands of the Pacific. Furthermore, the Japanese shipyards have limited capacity. Her shipping, therefore, was a natural target for our submarines, and they have taken a tremendous toll.

". . . Submarine commanding officers are skillful, daring and resourceful. Their crews are well trained and efficient. Their morale is high, and in direct ratio to the success of submarine operations. Materially our submarines are in excellent shape, and we have kept up to the minute in all features of design and scientific development and research.

"The versatility of our submarines has been so repeatedly demonstrated throughout the war that the Japanese know only too well that in no part of the Pacific Ocean are they safe from submarine attacks. When the full story can be told, it will constitute one of the most stirring chapters in the annals of naval warfare."

From the Official Report of Admiral Ernest J. King, USN, Commander in Chief U. S. Fleet, and Chief of Naval Operations, to the Secretary of the Navy.

27 March 1944

Submariners aboard a U. S. submarine enjoying some of the best food in the navy

The commandin[...] conning tower [...]

NEWSMAP Prepared and distributed by ARMY INFORMATION BRANCH ARMY SERVICE FORCES 205 E. 42nd Street, NEW YORK 17, N. Y. Navy distribution by EDUCATIONAL SERVICES SECTION BuPers, Navy Dept., Washington, D. C.

Newsmap USN Submarine

The *Gato*-class submarine was the most important and effective USN submarine of the Pacific War. In total, 77 were built and 20 were lost in combat. U.S. submarine warfare greatly impacted Japanese merchant shipping, accounting for 55 percent of Japanese shipping losses. By the end of 1944, the flow of supplies and fuel from Southeast Asia to Japan had virtually ceased.

Trim and Drainage System, *Gato* submarine

A modern submarine is designed to dive and surface in a controlled manner. To do so quickly and efficiently, the submarine must maintain fore and aft balance and athwartship stability. The chief function of the trim and drain system is to maintain this fore and aft balance by controlling the amount and distribution of water in the various tanks used for this purpose.

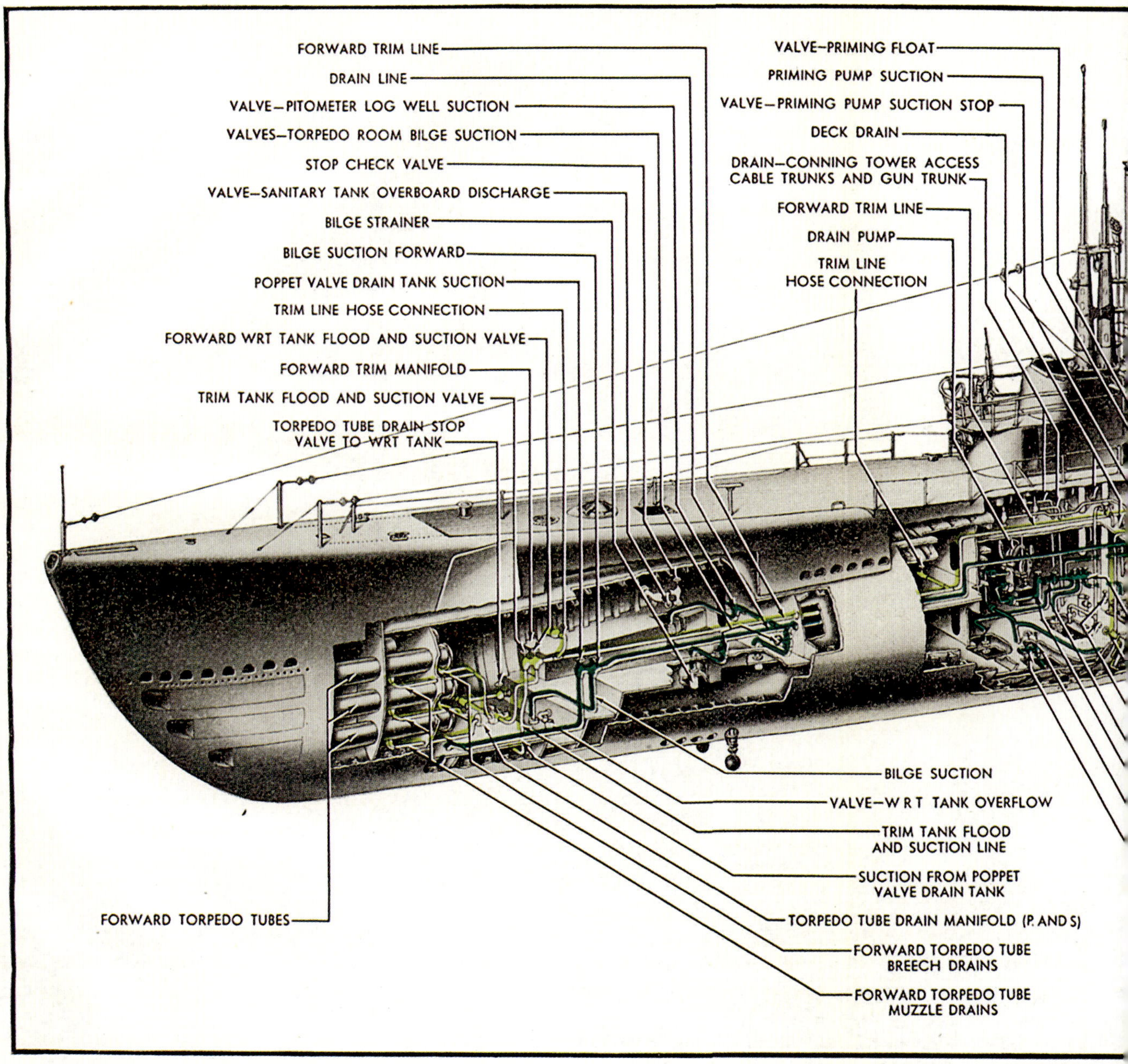

Figure 3-9.

Restricted

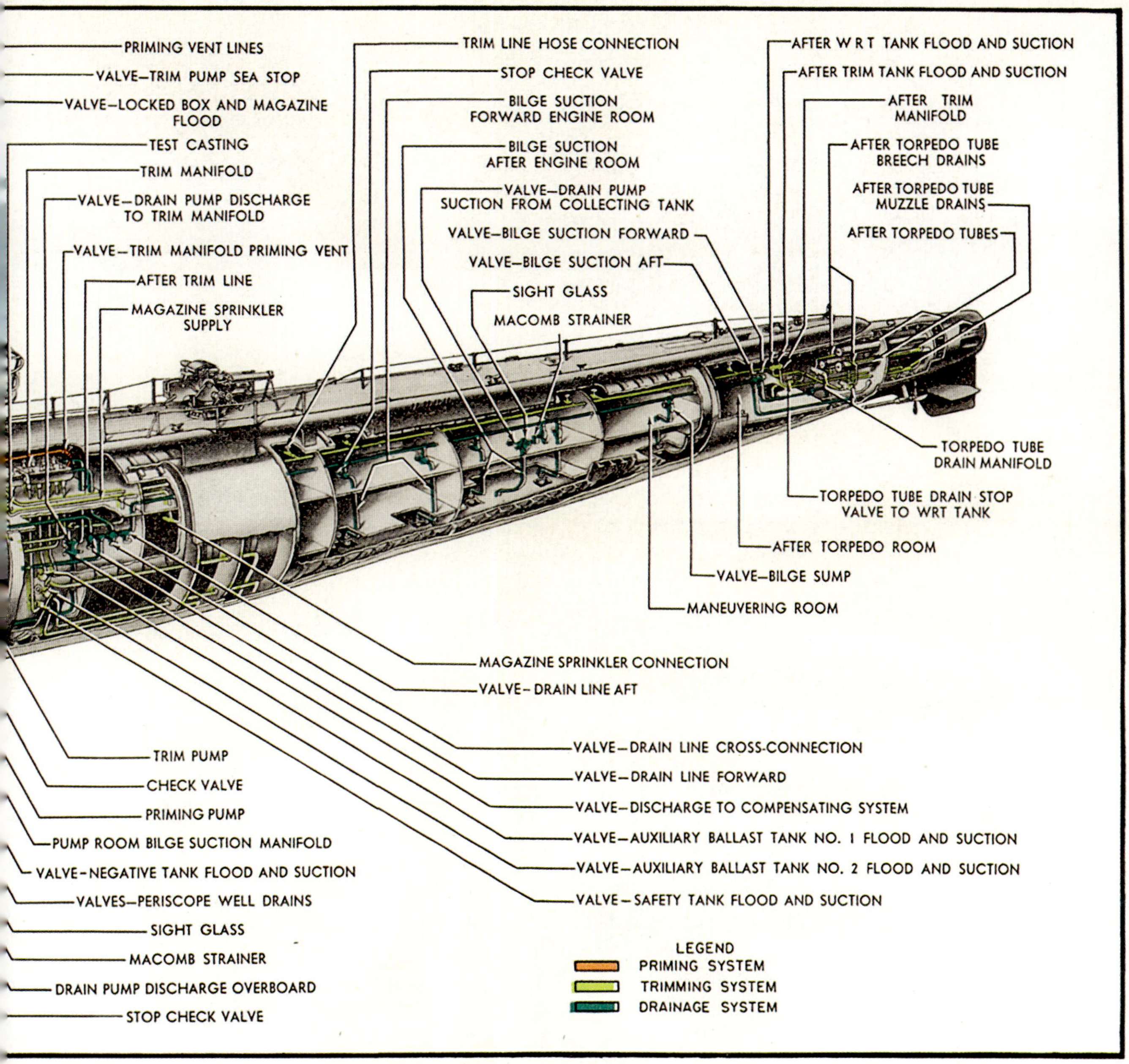

RAIN SYSTEMS.

31

Submarine Periscope

During the last two years of the Pacific War, U.S. Navy submariners had a huge advantage over the Japanese. Using radar, they were able to detect ships, use their speed to get ahead of their targets and make submerged attacks. Using his periscope, the boat's skipper would then estimate the trajectory of the oncoming ship and the direct range. This information was fed into the torpedo data computer that then produced a firing solution.

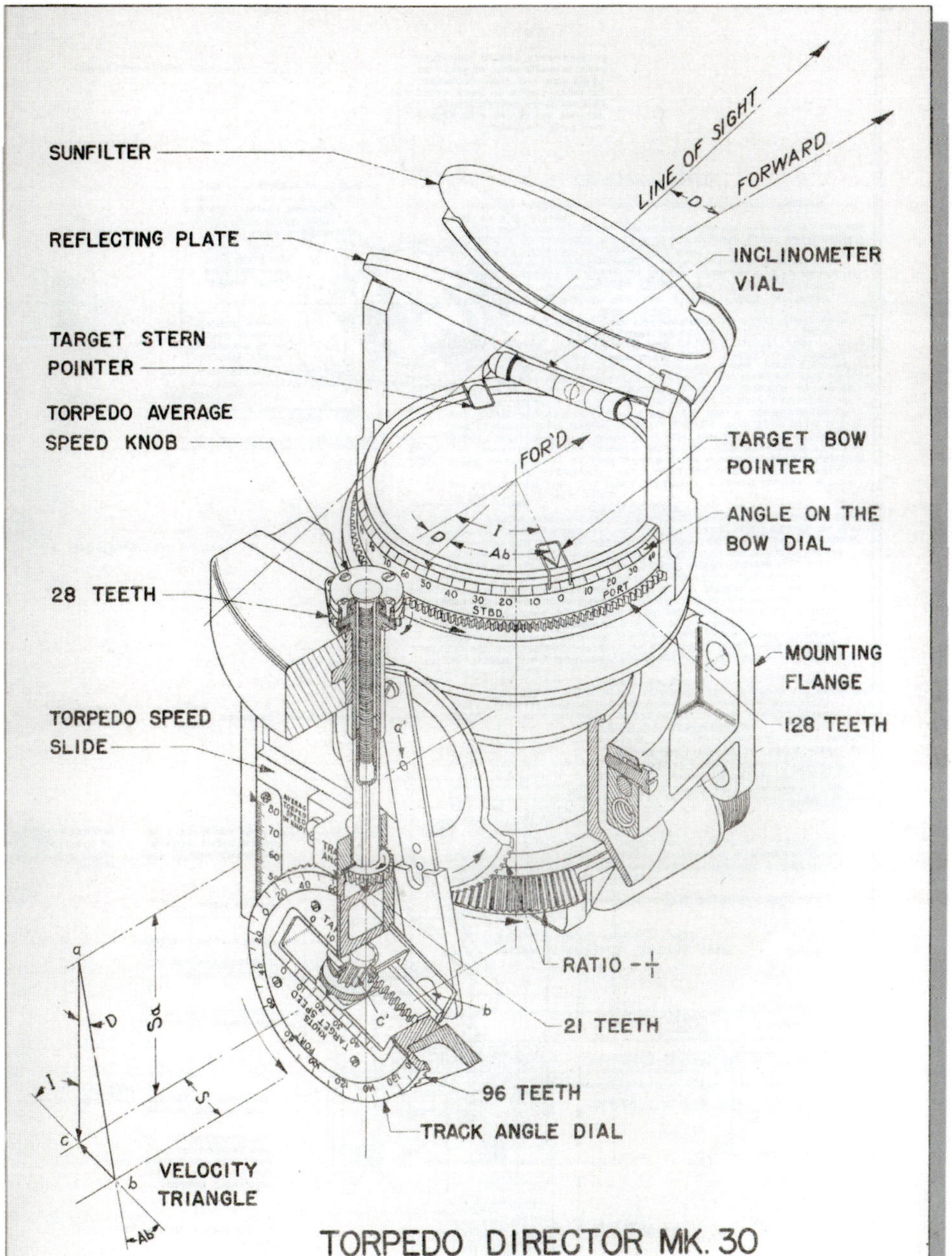

TORPEDO DIRECTOR MK. 30

FIG. 4

Torpedo Director Mk 30

The Grumman TBF/TBM Avenger was equipped with the Torpedo Director Mk 30 sight. Using this sight, the Avenger could drop its weapon while traveling close to the aircraft's top speed of 435 km/h (270 mph) at a maximum altitude of 244 meters (800 feet). On October 24, 1944, the Japanese battleship *Musashi* was attacked by torpedo and dive bombers from U.S. Task Force 38. Between 11 and 15 torpedoes hit the ship, along with 16 bombs, sending the mighty ship to the bottom.

USS *Kingfish* Damage Report

"On 23 March 1943, while on her third war patrol *Kingfish* underwent a severe depth charge attack north of Formosa. A total of over forty depth charges were dropped in the vicinity of *Kingfish* during the 7-1/2 hour period she was under attack. Serious damage was caused by the final pattern of six charges, two of which detonated close over the after portion of the ship while the boat was running at 300-foot depth, forcing her to the bottom in 350 feet of water. Six hours after the termination of the attack, and without undue difficulty, *Kingfish* was able to surface and clear the area at full power." *Submarine Report Depth Charge, Bomb, Mine, Torpedo and Gunfire Damage – December 7, 1941 to August 15, 1945*

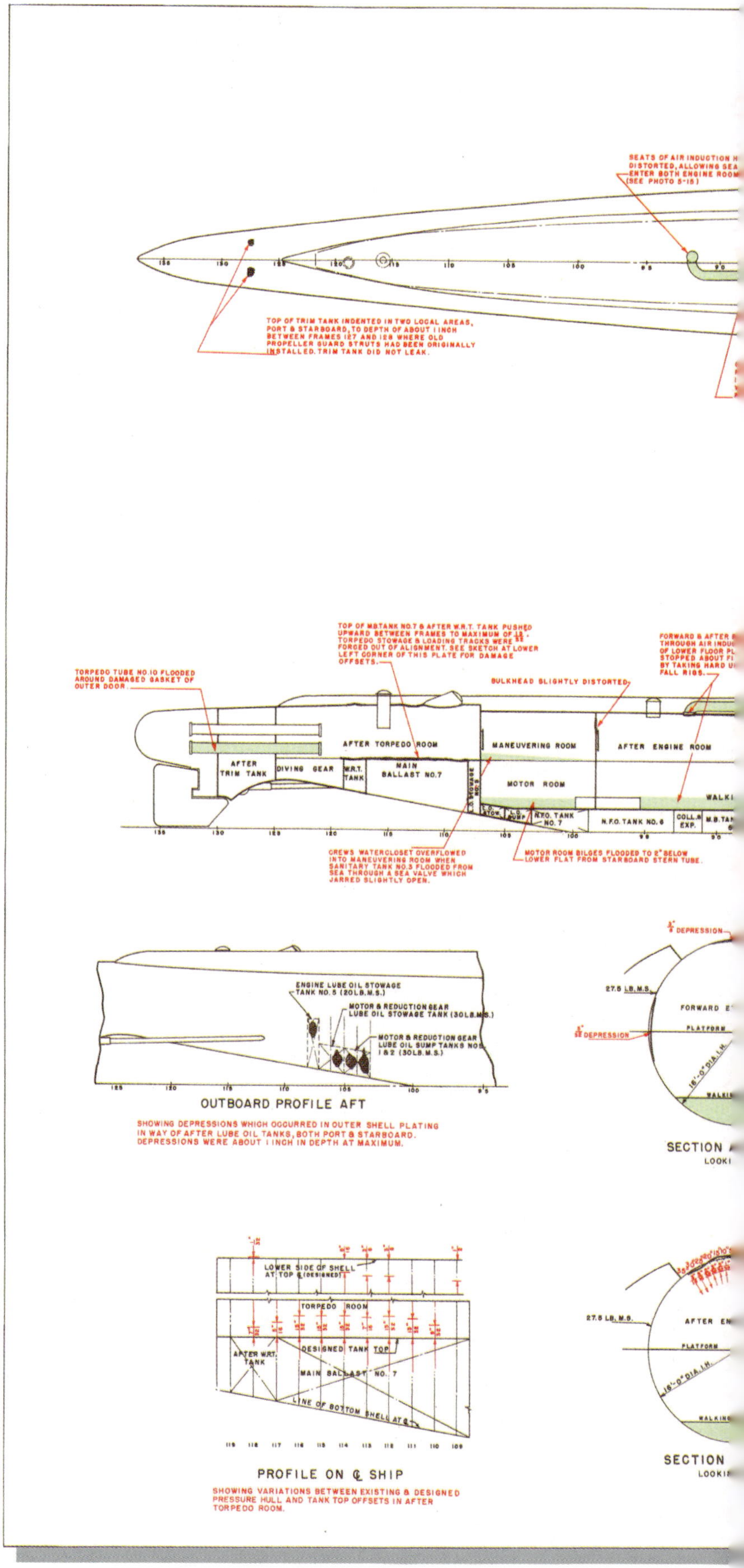

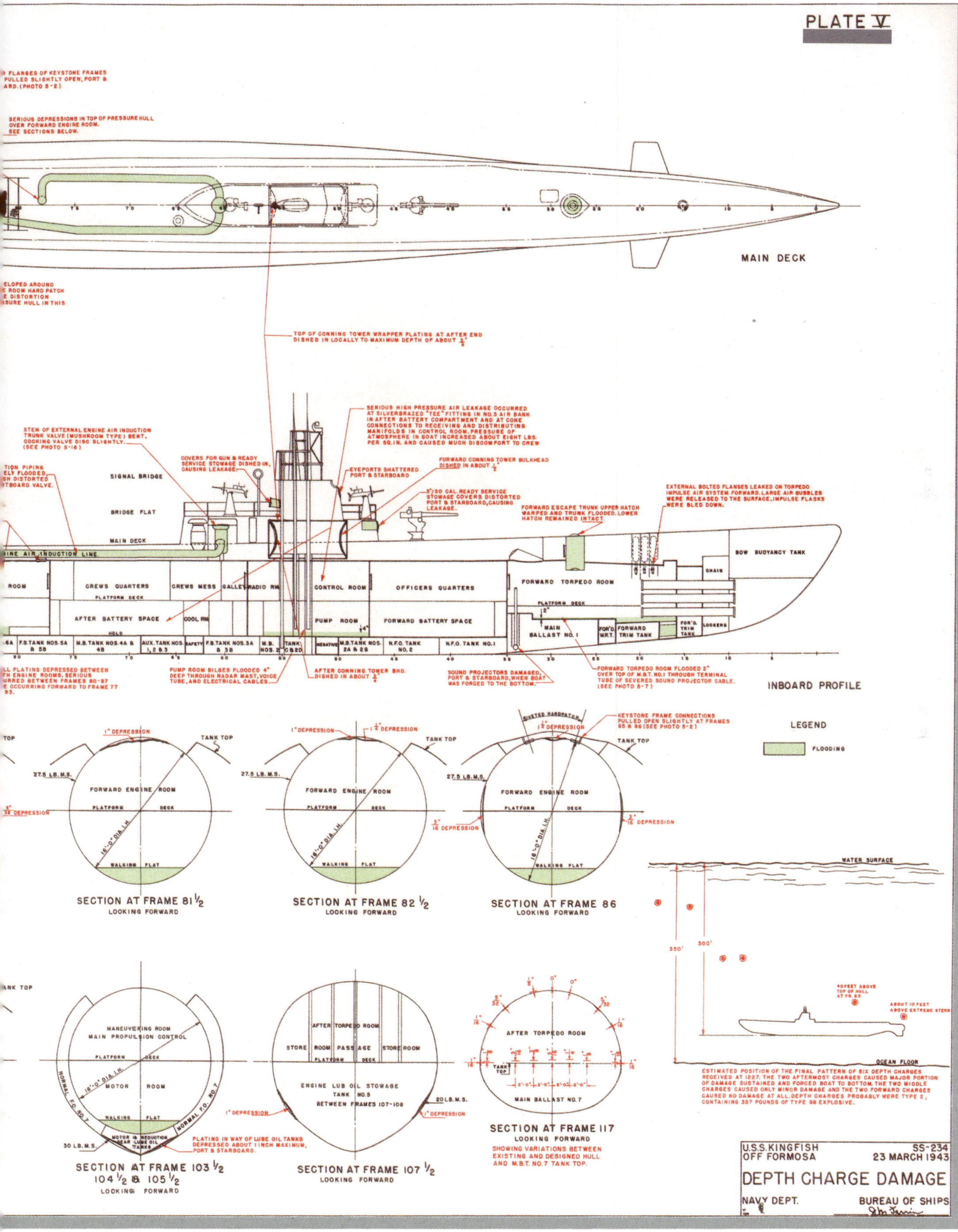
PLATE V
MAIN DECK
INBOARD PROFILE
SIGNAL BRIDGE
BRIDGE FLAT
MAIN DECK
CREWS QUARTERS
CREWS MESS
GALLEY
RADIO RM
CONTROL ROOM
OFFICERS QUARTERS
FORWARD TORPEDO ROOM
BOW BUOYANCY TANK
AFTER BATTERY SPACE
PUMP ROOM
FORWARD BATTERY SPACE
LEGEND
FLOODING
SECTION AT FRAME 81 1/2
LOOKING FORWARD
SECTION AT FRAME 82 1/2
LOOKING FORWARD
SECTION AT FRAME 86
LOOKING FORWARD
SECTION AT FRAME 103 1/2
104 1/2 & 105 1/2
LOOKING FORWARD
SECTION AT FRAME 107 1/2
LOOKING FORWARD
SECTION AT FRAME 117
LOOKING FORWARD
SHOWING VARIATIONS BETWEEN EXISTING AND DESIGNED HULL AND M.B.T. NO.7 TANK TOP.
WATER SURFACE
OCEAN FLOOR
U.S.S. KINGFISH
OFF FORMOSA
SS-234
23 MARCH 1943
DEPTH CHARGE DAMAGE
NAVY DEPT.
BUREAU OF SHIPS

The Fairbanks-Morse Model 38 Diesel Engine

Fairbanks-Morse and General Motors engines powered the U.S. *Gato*-class submarine. Each sub was equipped with four engines, which provided power for surface travel and to recharge the batteries for the electrical motors while submerged.

Inner Workings of the Fairbanks-Morse Diesel Engine

Before World War II, these engines were used almost exclusively on submarines. With the expansion of the Navy, however, these engines were also used on destroyer escorts, amphibious craft, escort-type patrol vessels and various auxiliary craft.

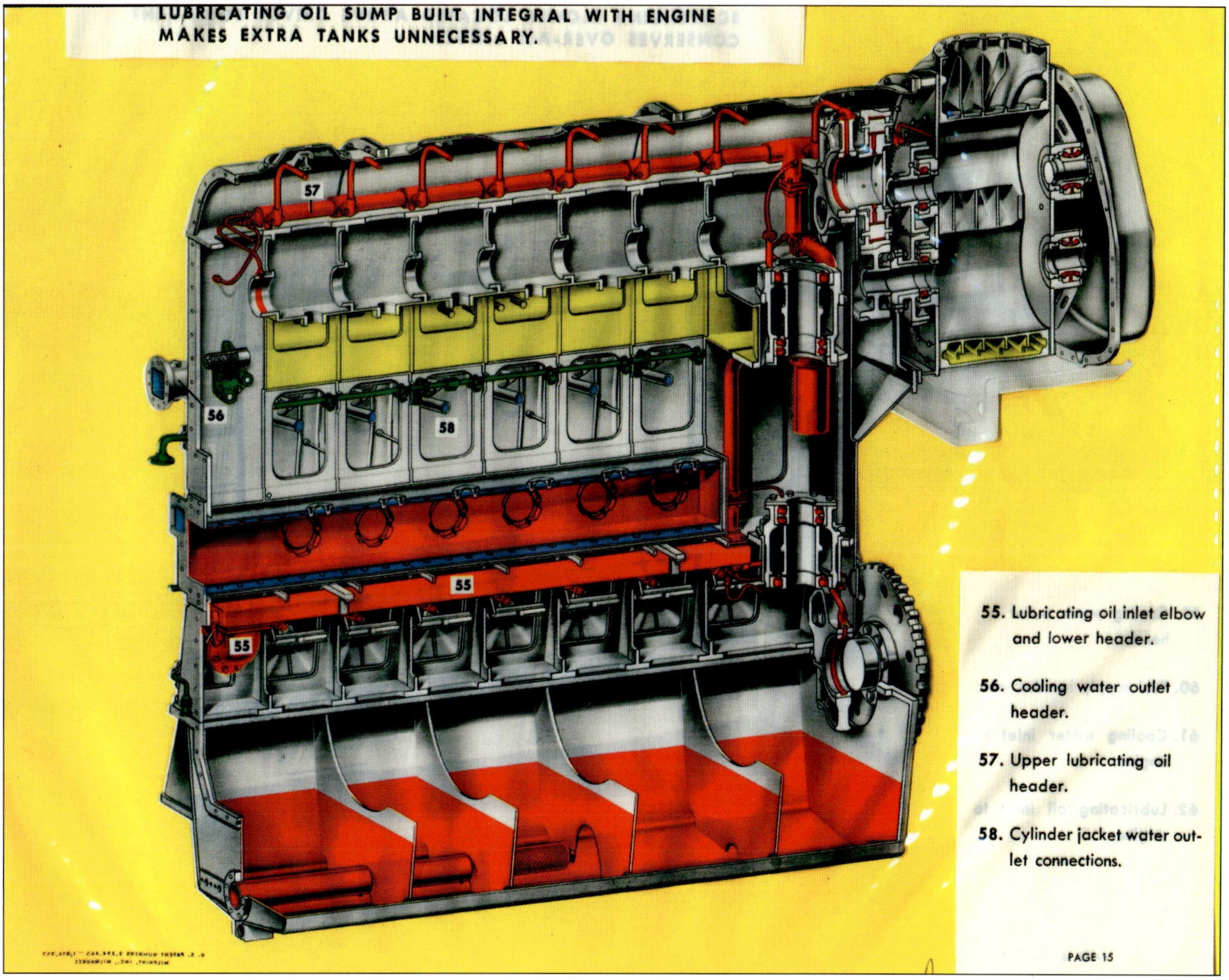

UNITED STATES

Merchant Ships Wartime Functions

The rapidly changing sea war led to the development of many specialized ships. Many older freighters and other ships were converted to perform as anti-aircraft ships and blockade runners.

ONI 223–M

WARTIME FUNCTIONS

CARGO TYPES

ENGINE-AFT TYPES

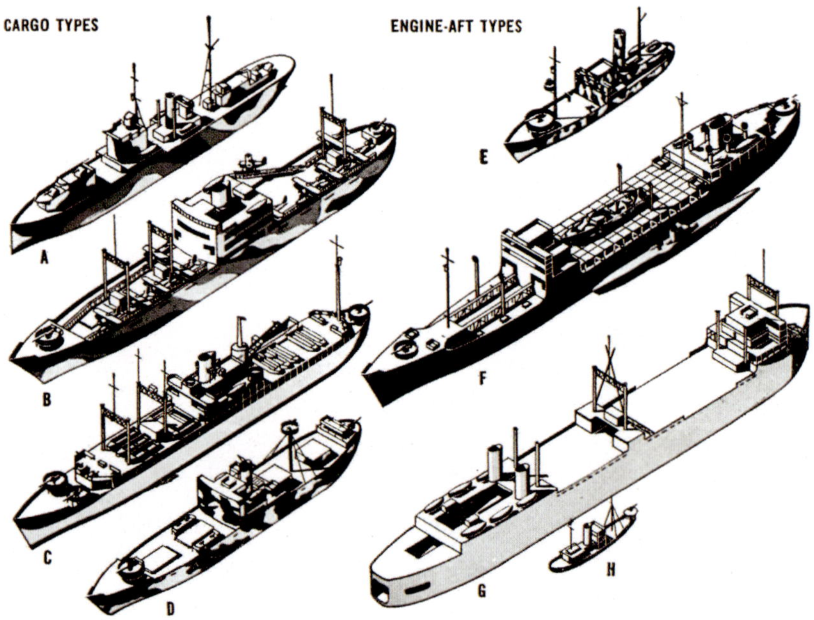

A *Anti-Aircraft Ship (Old Freighter).*
B *Attack Cargo Ship (Modern Cargo Type) or Aircraft Transport.*
C *Tenders and Repair Ship (Modern Cargo Type).*
D *"Sperrbrecher," Blockade Runner and Raider (Fruit Ship).*
E *Patrol and Escort Craft (Trawler).*
F *Supply Ship and Tender (Tanker).*
G *Supply Ship and Tender (Whale Factory).*
H *Patrol Craft (Whale Killer).*

OLD FREIGHTERS—Unsuited to most other naval uses older freighters have been successfully used as coastal mine layers, AA ships, and as hospital ships (by the Japanese). Conversions to aircraft transports and seaplane tenders have also been frequent in the Japanese merchant marine.

MODERN FREIGHTERS—To keep pace with naval expansion and extended operations, many larger cargo ships have been converted to tenders and supply vessels for destroyers, submarines, PT boats, and patrol planes.

FRUIT SHIPS—These German freighter conversions, called Sperrbrechers, are combination escort, mine sweeping and AA ships. The Japanese have converted fruit ships to similar purposes or used them as raiders.

TANKERS—These vessels, when they can be spared, have occasionally been employed as tenders for submarines, PT boats, and patrol aircraft. An additional temporary deck is often built over the wells, making them useful carriers of heavy deck cargo.

WHALE FACTORIES—Easily altered to serve as tankers and bulk carriers, these huge vessels are also believed to be used by the Japanese as tenders for PT boats, midget subs, and landing craft, as well as aircraft transports and tenders.

FISHING CRAFT Trawlers, drifters, whalers, and other fishing craft are being used as coastal escorts, patrol craft, mine sweepers, AA ships, plane rescue craft, or coastal transports.

Many smaller modern merchantmen have been equipped for convoy-escort, patrol and mine-sweeping detail, or to serve as mother ships to fleets of small mine sweepers.

13

Miscellaneous Craft

Until specialized vessels were built and put into service, the Royal and U.S. Navies converted their trawlers, coasters and yachts into emergency naval ships. These ships engaged in coast-watching and near-sea trade.

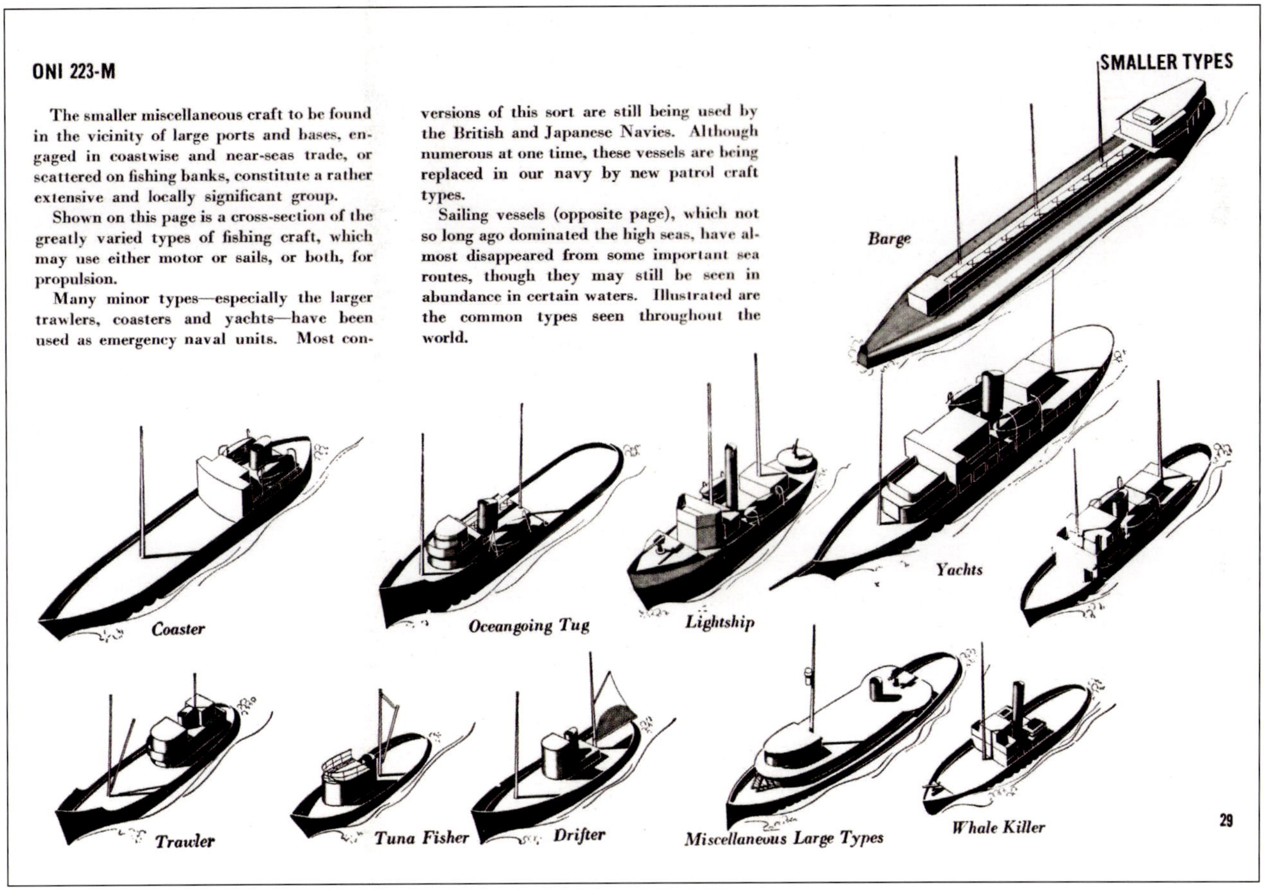

ONI 223-M

SMALLER TYPES

The smaller miscellaneous craft to be found in the vicinity of large ports and bases, engaged in coastwise and near-seas trade, or scattered on fishing banks, constitute a rather extensive and locally significant group.

Shown on this page is a cross-section of the greatly varied types of fishing craft, which may use either motor or sails, or both, for propulsion.

Many minor types—especially the larger trawlers, coasters and yachts—have been used as emergency naval units. Most conversions of this sort are still being used by the British and Japanese Navies. Although numerous at one time, these vessels are being replaced in our navy by new patrol craft types.

Sailing vessels (opposite page), which not so long ago dominated the high seas, have almost disappeared from some important sea routes, though they may still be seen in abundance in certain waters. Illustrated are the common types seen throughout the world.

29

Destroyer Escort Cutaway (above)

The Destroyer Escort (DE) was a ship the U.S. Navy did not want. Designed for convoy escort, they were slower than a standard destroyer (21 knots compared to a destroyer's 35) and not suited for fleet service. During the war, 503 were built.

***Tirpitz* BB 4** (right)

Like the *Bismarck*, the German battleship *Tirpitz* garnered a fearsome reputation for a ship that never fired her guns at an enemy vessel. While only a single vessel, the *Tirpitz* managed to tie up vital Royal Navy and RAF resources in case she put to sea.

RESTRICTED
TYPICAL DESTROYER ESCORT
SHIP SECTION 6

Admiral Scheer

An early ship identification silhouette of the German 'pocket battleship' *Admiral Scheer.* Armed with six 11-inch guns, eight 5.9-inch guns and six twin 4.1-inch AA gun turrets, she also carried two Arado Ar 196 floatplanes.

300'
400'
500'
596'-2"
ADMIRAL SCHEER
Germany - CA
(DEUTSCHLAND Class)
(1941)

517-ton Type U-boat

This U.S. Navy drawing shows the inner workings of the Type VII U-boat. Her crew consisted of four officers and 40 to 52 men. Her surface range was 13,679 kilometers (8,500 miles) at 18 knots.

STRUCTURE

517-TON TYPE. While this type has a single hull with l
withstand pressures and explosive charges almost as we
protected boats. Plating amidships is 18.6 mm. (about ³/

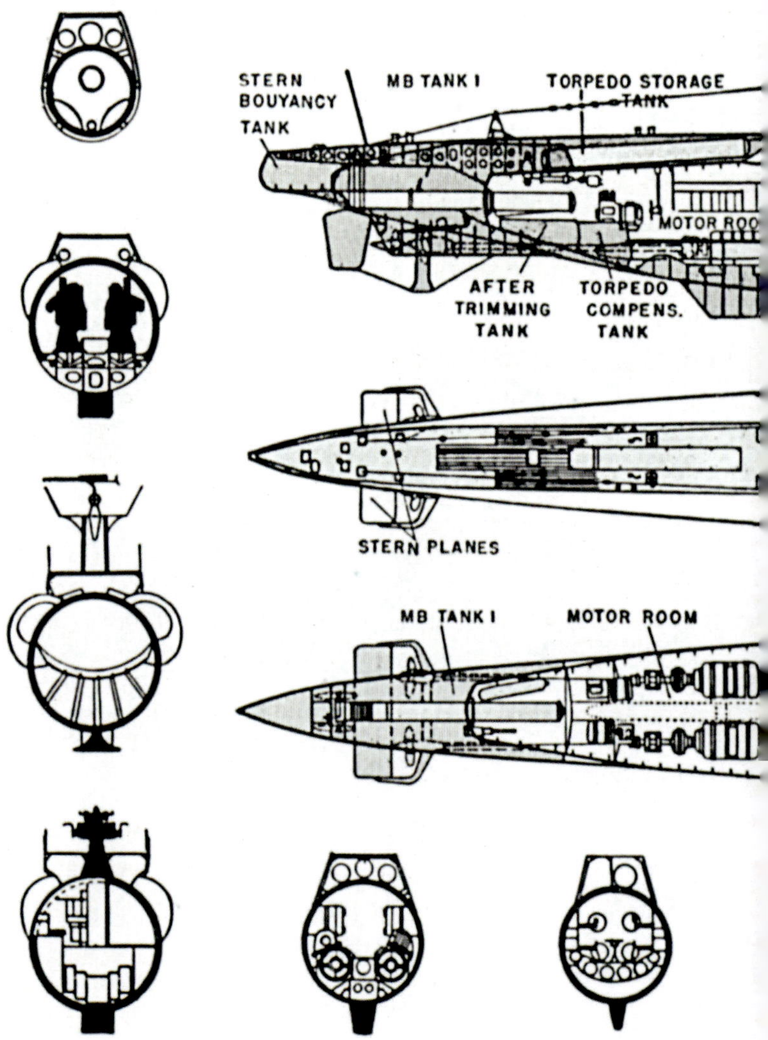

6

lle tanks, it can
ger and better
ad tapers to 16

mm. at the pressure hull extremities. Pressure hull and bu khead is 35 mm. and conning tower plating 32 mm thick. Photo of the grounded 517-ton submarine shows an additional saddle tank for fuel stowage fitted over the original tanks.

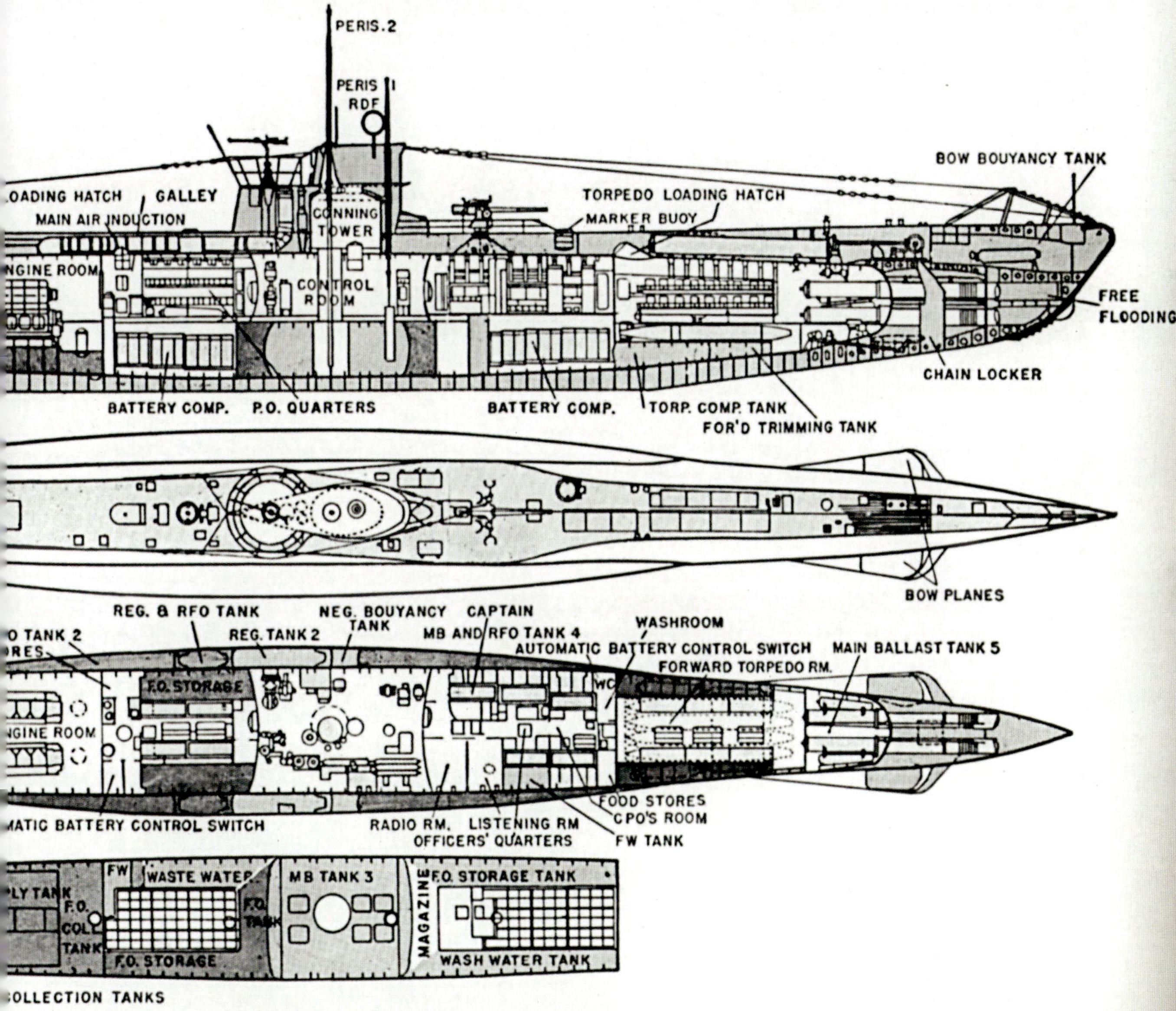

Submarine Crash Dive Diagram

German U-boats spent most of their time on the surface. When submerged, they were slower, and time below the surface was measured in hours. When faced with an imminent attack, most U-boats opted to dive to their maximum depth, changing direction in the process.

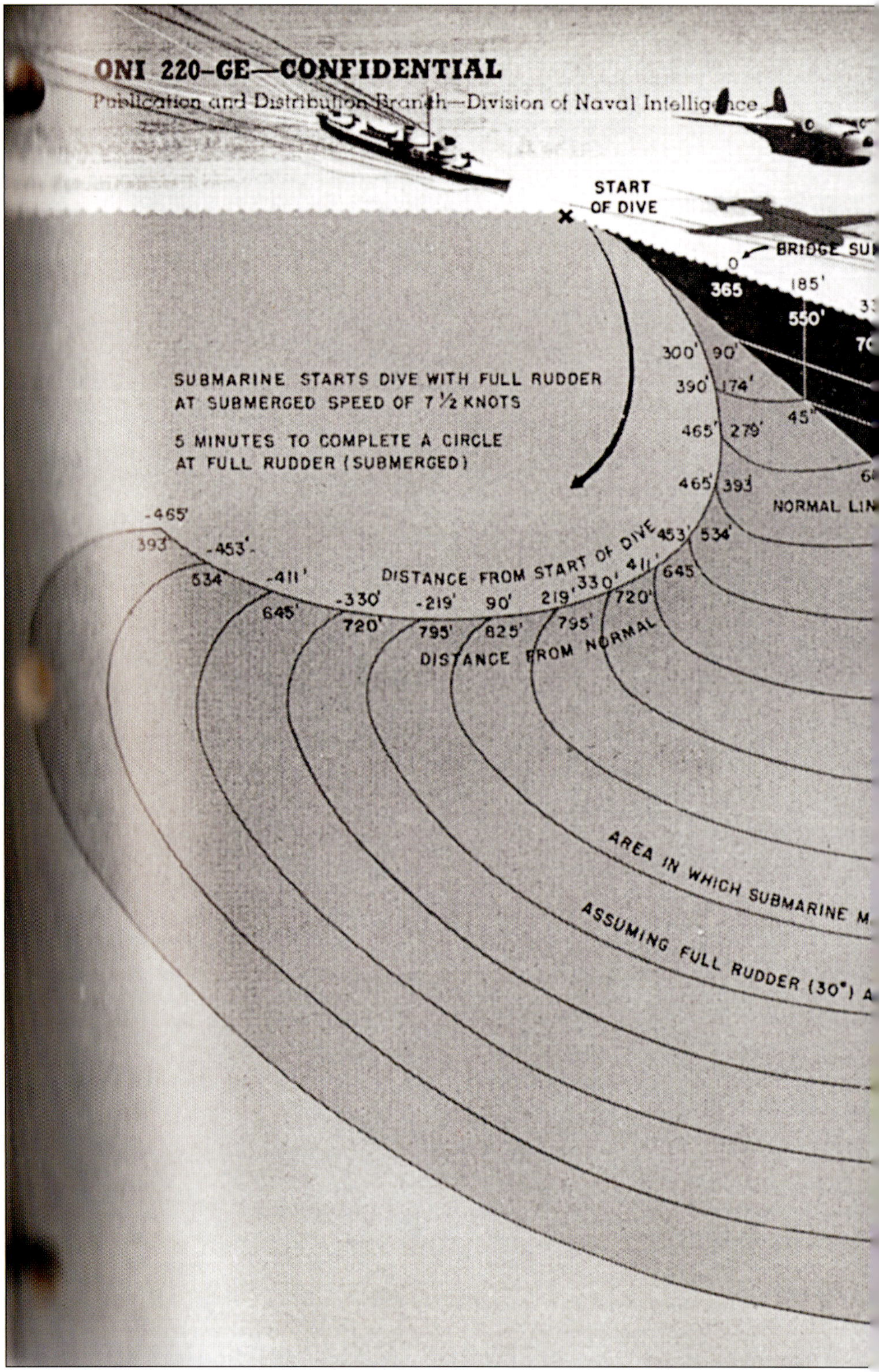

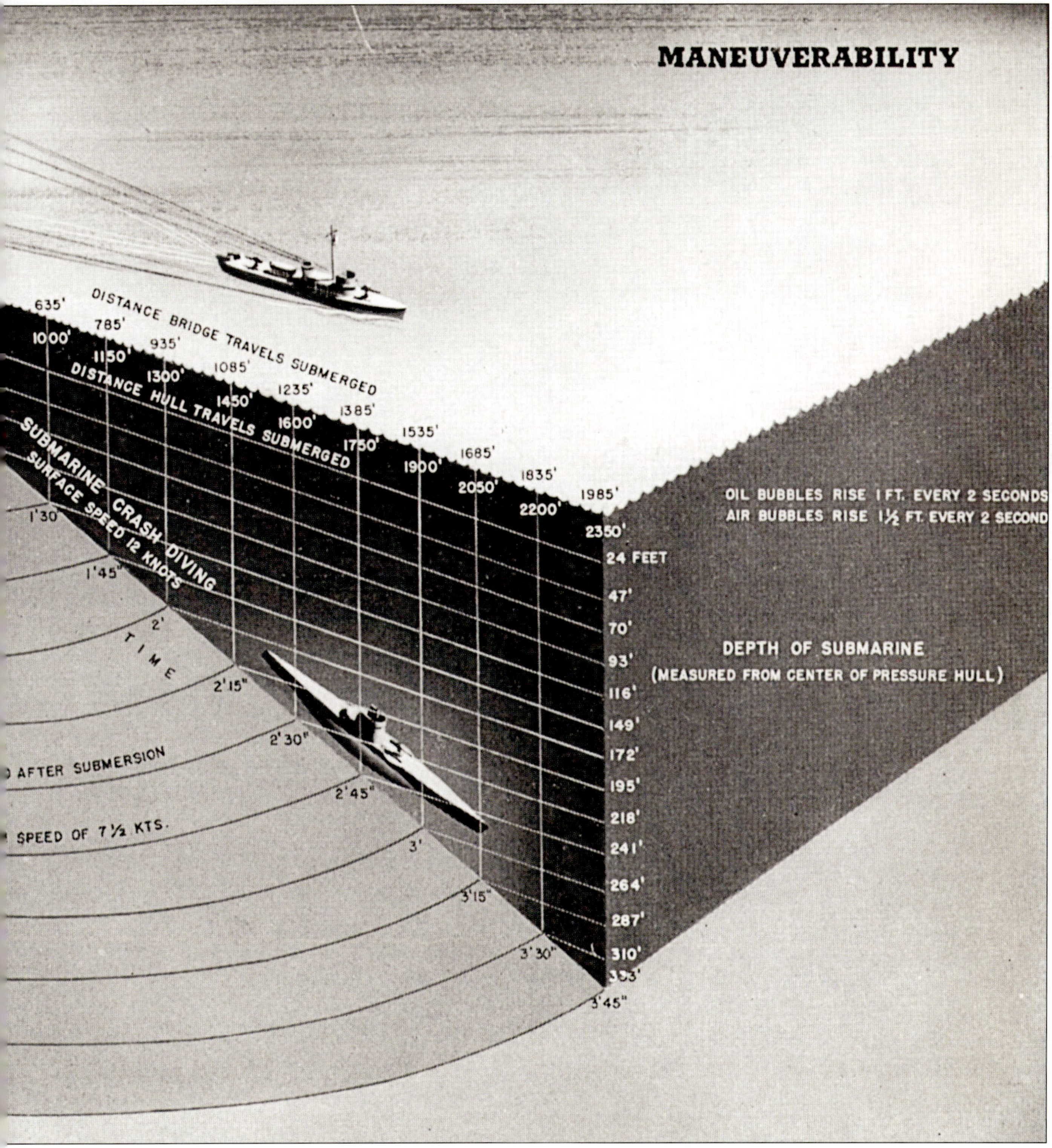
MANEUVERABILITY
DISTANCE BRIDGE TRAVELS SUBMERGED
635'
785'
935'
1085'
1235'
1385'
1535'
1685'
1835'
1985'
DISTANCE HULL TRAVELS SUBMERGED
1000'
1150'
1300'
1450'
1600'
1750'
1900'
2050'
2200'
2350'
SUBMARINE CRASH DIVING
SURFACE SPEED 12 KNOTS
TIME
1'30"
1'45"
2'
2'15"
2'30"
2'45"
3'
3'15"
3'30"
3'45"
AFTER SUBMERSION
SPEED OF 7½ KTS.
OIL BUBBLES RISE 1 FT. EVERY 2 SECONDS
AIR BUBBLES RISE 1½ FT. EVERY 2 SECOND
24 FEET
47'
70'
93'
116'
149'
172'
195'
218'
241'
264'
287'
310'
333'
DEPTH OF SUBMARINE
(MEASURED FROM CENTER OF PRESSURE HULL)

Type XXI U-boat

An early intelligence sketch of the new German Type XXI U-boat. Had the German Type XXI entered service in 1942, the Battle of the Atlantic would have been far different. The XXI was faster with improved underwater range, giving it greater protection against air attack.

U-boat AA Guns

By 1942, Allied aircraft equipped with radar were capable of hunting U-boats both day and night. By 1943, daylight surface runs by U-boat crews were suicidal. In response, more anti-aircraft guns were added to offer more protection. The additional guns were not enough, and when faced with determined air attacks by multiple aircraft, U-boats were forced to dive and hope for the best.

517-TON TYPE

Illustration above shows current Armament of two 20 mm singles and a 37 mm. single mount This is reported being changed by installation of a 37 mm gun on lower platform, and quadruple mount 20 mm. on upper platform. Other photos on this page show earlier and intermediate stages in armament arrangement of this type

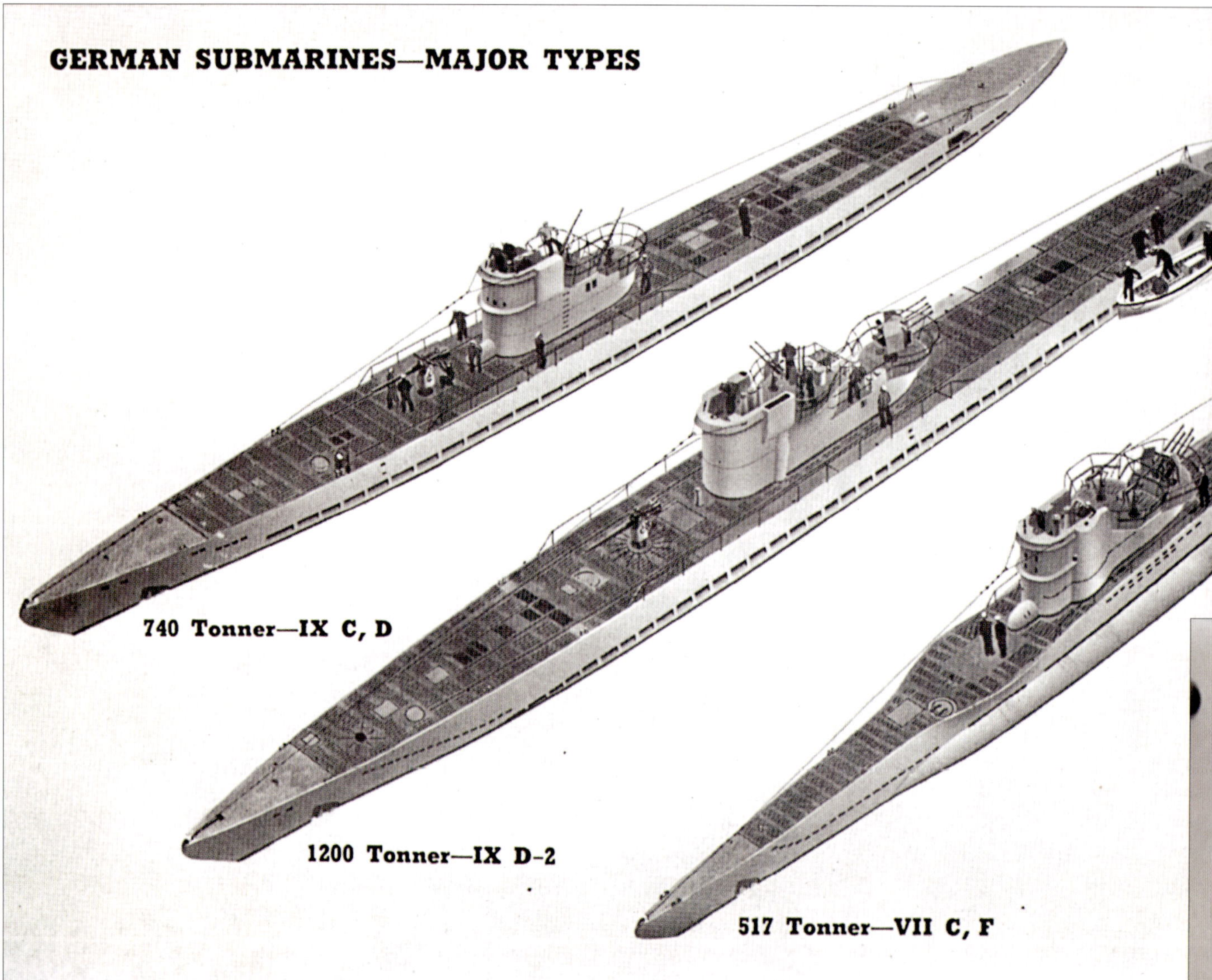

German Submarines, Major and Minor Types

When Germany discarded the Treaty of Versailles limitations in 1936, it already had the three basic U-boat designs ready for service in World War II. The Type II U-boats were the smallest of the three designs and practical for coastal patrols. By August 1939, they were being retired to training. The Type VII and IX U-boats were the open ocean hunter-killers. Both boats had test depths of 229 meters (750 feet) and could reach speeds of 17 to 18 knots on the surface and 7.6 knots submerged. The Type IX U-boats had incredible range, with the Type IXD capable of traveling from Germany to Japan. The other two types were the Type X minelayer U-boat and the Type XIV supply U-Boat. The Type XIV were called 'Milch Cows' and used for mid-ocean supply of Type VII and IX boats.

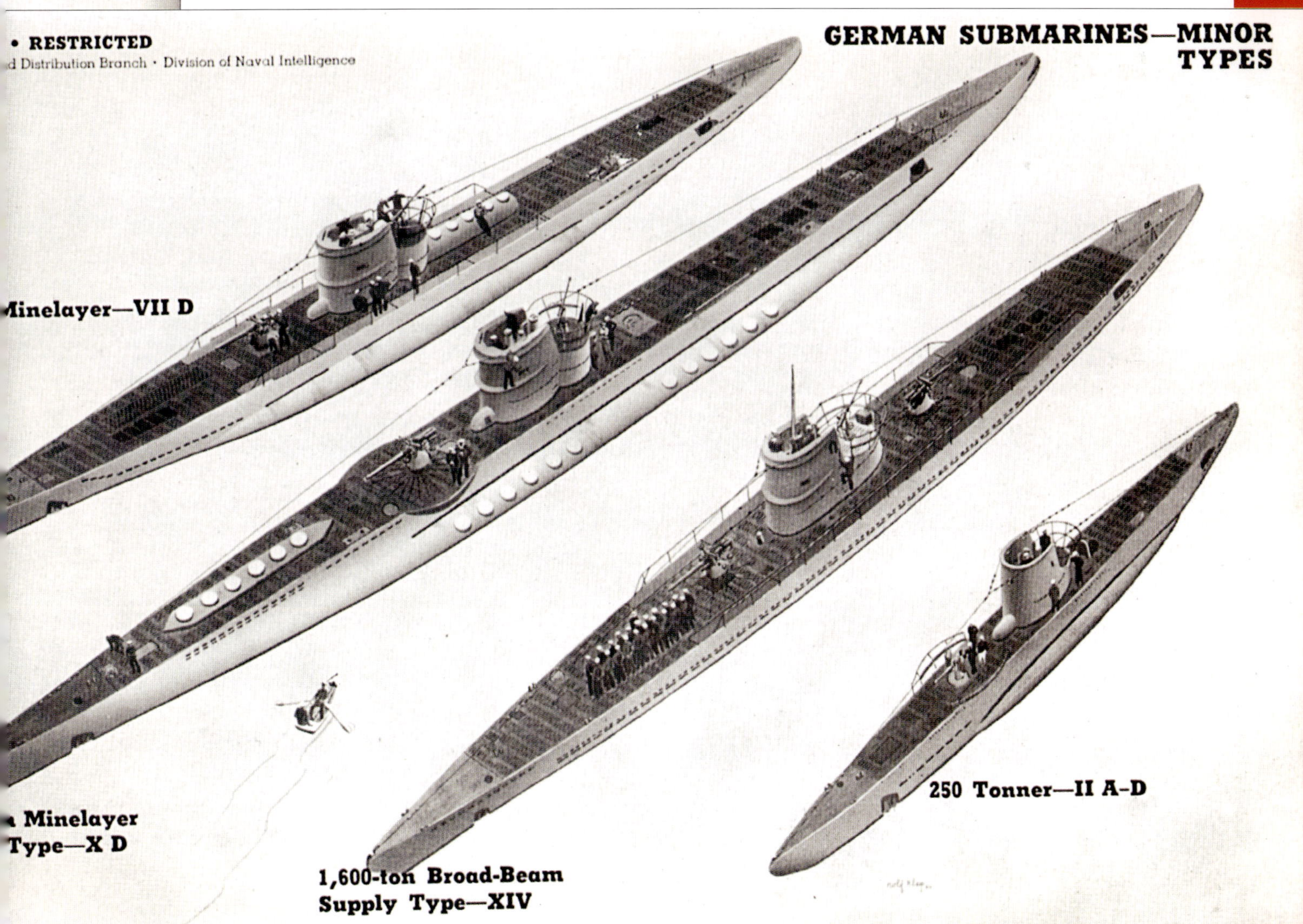
• RESTRICTED
d Distribution Branch • Division of Naval Intelligence
GERMAN SUBMARINES—MINOR TYPES
linelayer—VII D
Minelayer Type—X D
1,600-ton Broad-Beam Supply Type—XIV
250 Tonner—II A-D

Aircraft Engines

U.S. carrier aircraft were powered by air-cooled radial engines. These engines were less complicated and easier to maintain compared to their liquid-cooled cousins. The F6F Hellcat and F4U Corsair were both equipped with the Pratt & Whitney R-2800 Double Wasp, one of the best engines of World War II.

Fire in the Air

During intermediate flight training, new trainees would be introduced to the larger, more powerful (600 hp) aircraft like the SNV Valiant and the famous North American SNJ Texan. These aircraft were heavier, and when in-flight emergencies occurred, immediate action was required to prevent a crash or death.

Navy Flight Training 'Roar'

Accidents were all too common during flight training. Of the 65,000 naval aviators trained between 1941 and 1945, close to 5,000 were killed during the training process.

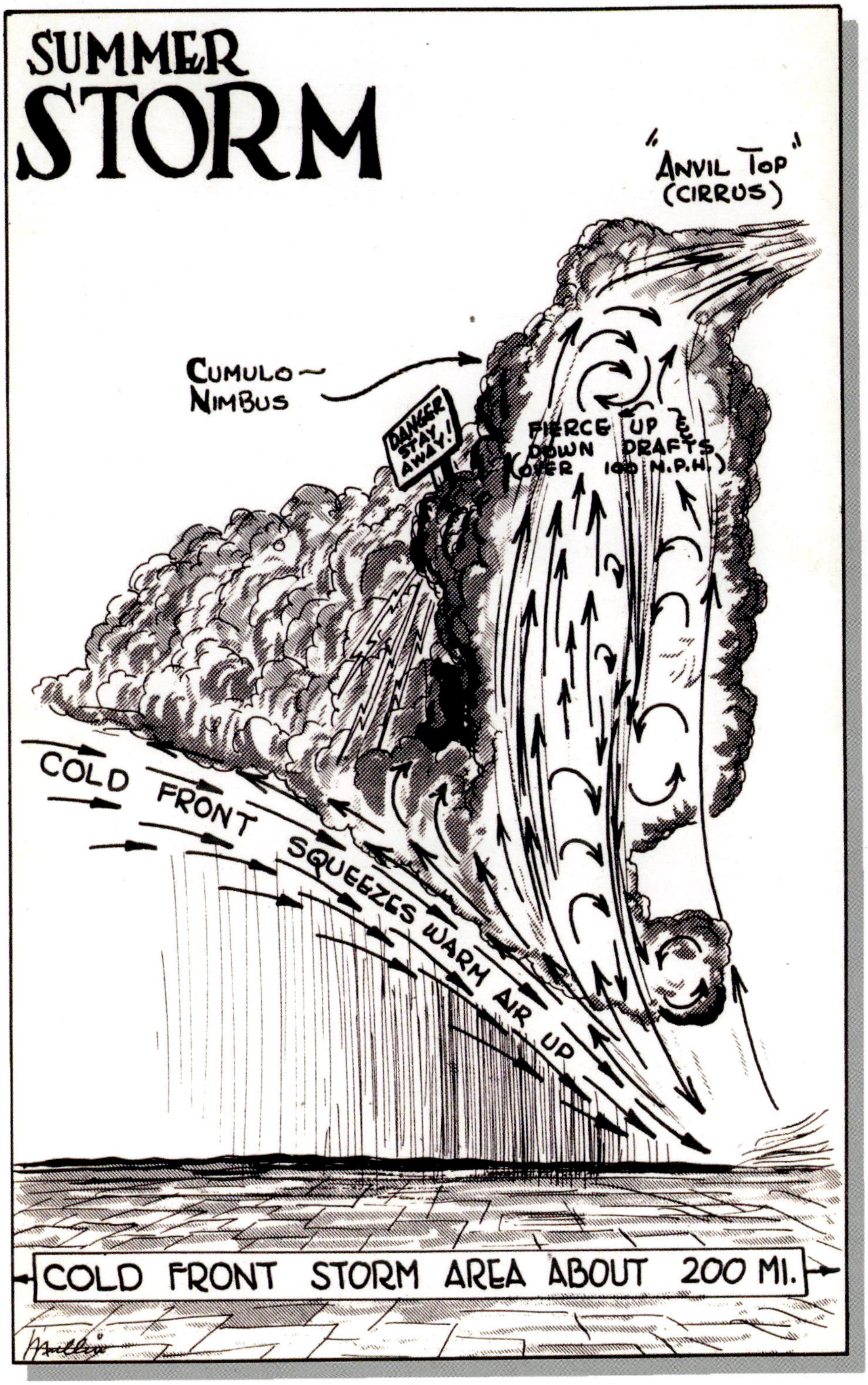

Summer Storm

Weather was a constant threat to both new trainees and combat-experienced pilots. Thunderstorms formed quickly and were extremely dangerous. The odds of flying through a thunderstorm and coming out alive were extremely slim.

flight
FLIGHT THRU IN

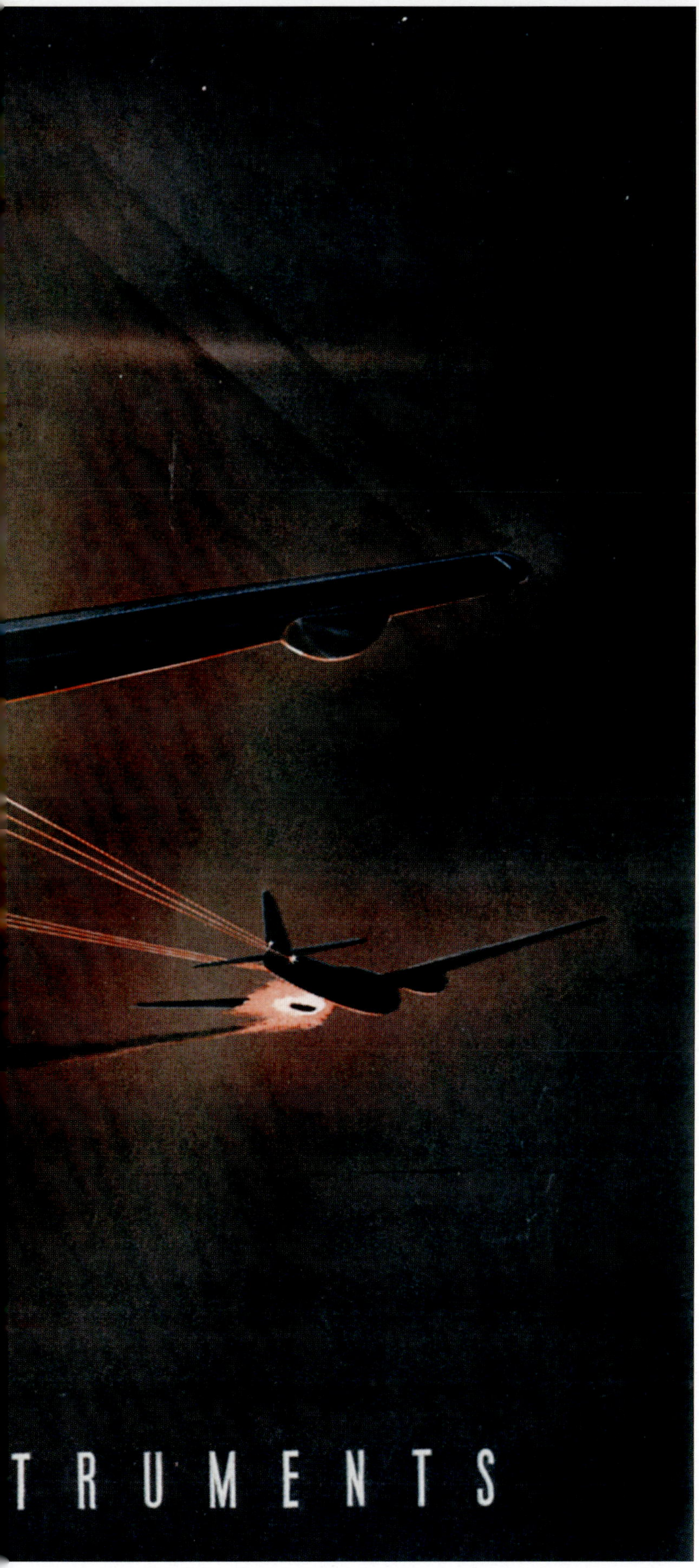

Flight/Fight Thru Instruments

By 1943, the IJNAF changed their tactics and began to mount more night torpedo-bombing attacks. In response, U.S. fast carriers developed a minimum night fighter capability by first using the F4U Corsair modified with an airborne radar. By December 1944, the F6F-5N Hellcat had replaced the F4U Corsair as the standard night fighter. F6F-5Ns were equipped with radio altimeters and the APS-6 airborne radar.

Changes in Load of Flight Conditions

Combat aircraft, when fully loaded, carried tons of fuel and ordnance. As fuel was burned and tanks were switched, the center of gravity shifted, causing unbalanced flight. The sudden release of bombs, rockets or torpedoes also caused a sudden change in the center of gravity. Pilots had to anticipate these changes and adjust quickly to the changing flight conditions.

CHANGES IN LOAD OR FLIGHT CONDITI

In flight, fuel is consumed and bomb loads
naturally affect the total weight of the airp
the distribution of that weight on the wing.
of weight on the wing means shifting the

pped. These factors
·y also usually affect
e in the distribution
's center of gravity.

The result of a shift in the center of gravity during flight is unbalance. Change in the air surrounding your airplane, occasioned by a gust of wind or turbulence of any kind, will likewise disturb the equilibrium of forces which produce balanced flight.

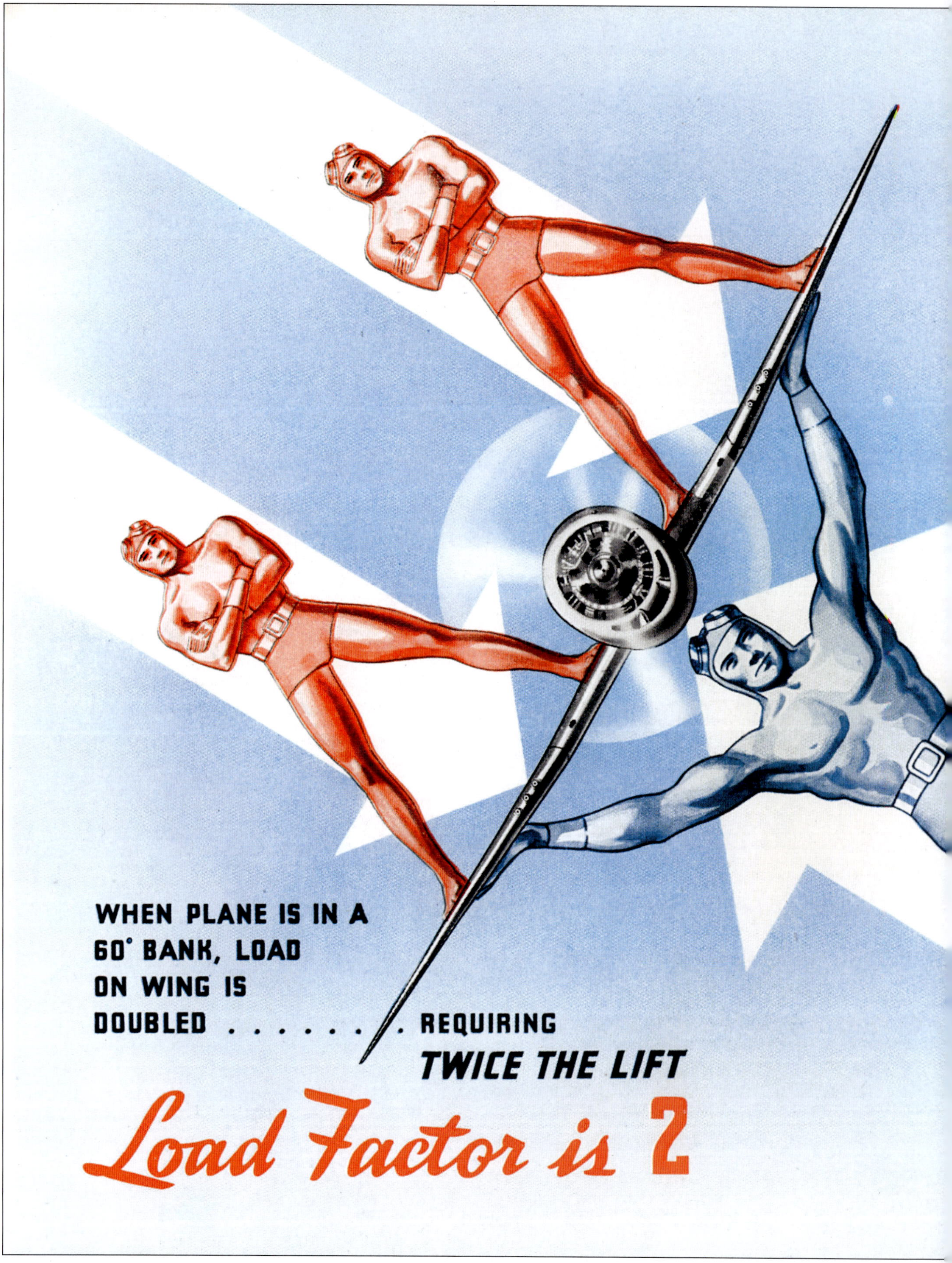
WHEN PLANE IS IN A
60° BANK, LOAD
ON WING IS
DOUBLED . . . . REQUIRING
TWICE THE LIFT
Load Factor is 2

henever the wings have more work to do
an that of holding up the weight of the air-
ane, we say the load factor is greater than 1.
follows that any time the flight path of the
rplane is curved, the load factor is greater
less than 1. In other words, a load factor
greater or less than 1 indicates curved flight
vithin ordinary flight limits).
a 60° bank, the lift necessary to support
airplane is twice as much as is needed to
pport the same airplane in straight flight.
ıerefore, the load factor is 2. You get the
cessary support from an increase of pitch.
his increases the angle of attack, which in turn
creases the lift. Increased load factor means
o things to you—and both are important!

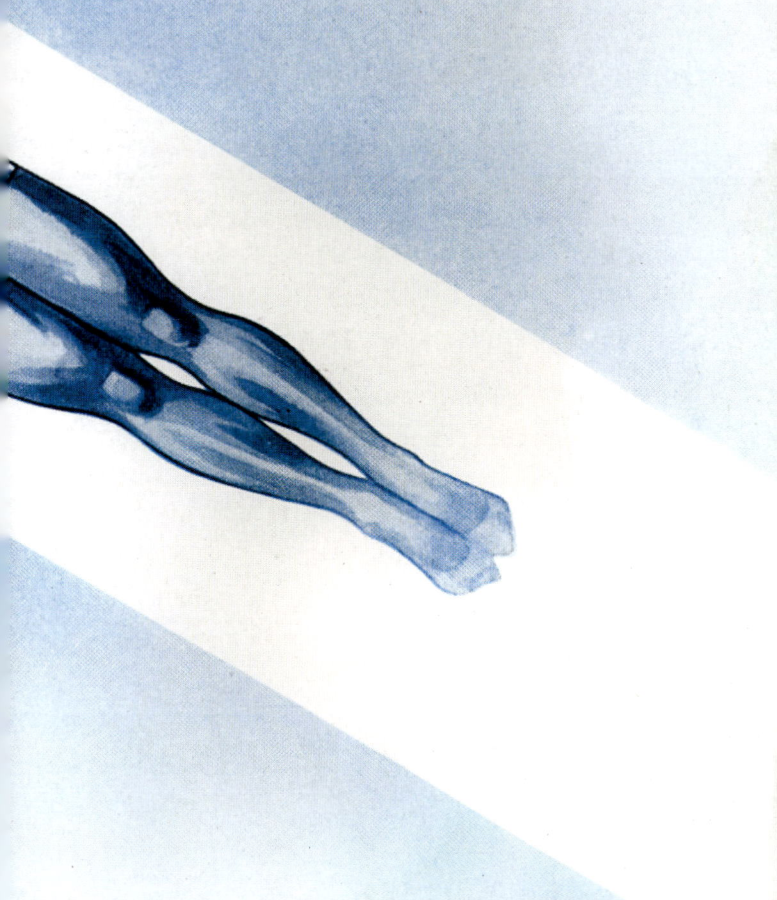

Load Factor is 2

A turning aircraft, if not supplied with enough thrust, will lose height. Turning was essentially a defensive maneuver. Fighter pilots quickly learned that during combat, speed was essential and that vertical maneuvers were superior to horizontal maneuvers. Diving attacks quickly became the established method of attack.

SUMMARY

ATTITUDE + POWER → PERFORMANCE

First, you have this basic formula, which means that a specific power applied to a specific attitude results in a specific performance. Keep this formula in mind always. In all flight you have attitude, and you can "see" it either visually or visualized through instruments. You apply power to attitude and the result is *flight performance.*

A change in performance is accomplished by changing power or attitude or both. If, with an attitude-power combination, you combine directional balance, the result is more than mere performance—it is efficient performance. The basic formula may be restated as follows:

Power, Attitude, Performance

Navy operational training ensured the neophyte pilot learned to fly a high-performance airplane with confidence. Here, young pilots practiced basic maneuvers until they became second nature.

Visualized Horizon

In sharp contrast to the IJNAF's training programs, the U.S. Navy's training programs benefited from an adequate number of experienced instructors, unlimited fuel for flying and a steady supply of training airplanes, plus an abundance of visual aids and instructional films.

VISUALIZED-HORIZON

You must be attitude-conscious at all times. You visualize attitude in two ways: (1) directly, through the attitude-indicating gyro-horizon and (2) indirectly, through the performance-indicating instruments. Since performance is the result of a combination of attitude and power, if you hold *power* constant, the performance instruments indicate indirectly the adjustment to attitude necessary to produce desired performance.

Nose Position

The U.S. Navy pilot training program was wide ranging, covering flying skills, combat tactics, gunnery and instrument flying. If caught in bad weather or at night, pilots had to trust their instruments in order to stay alive.

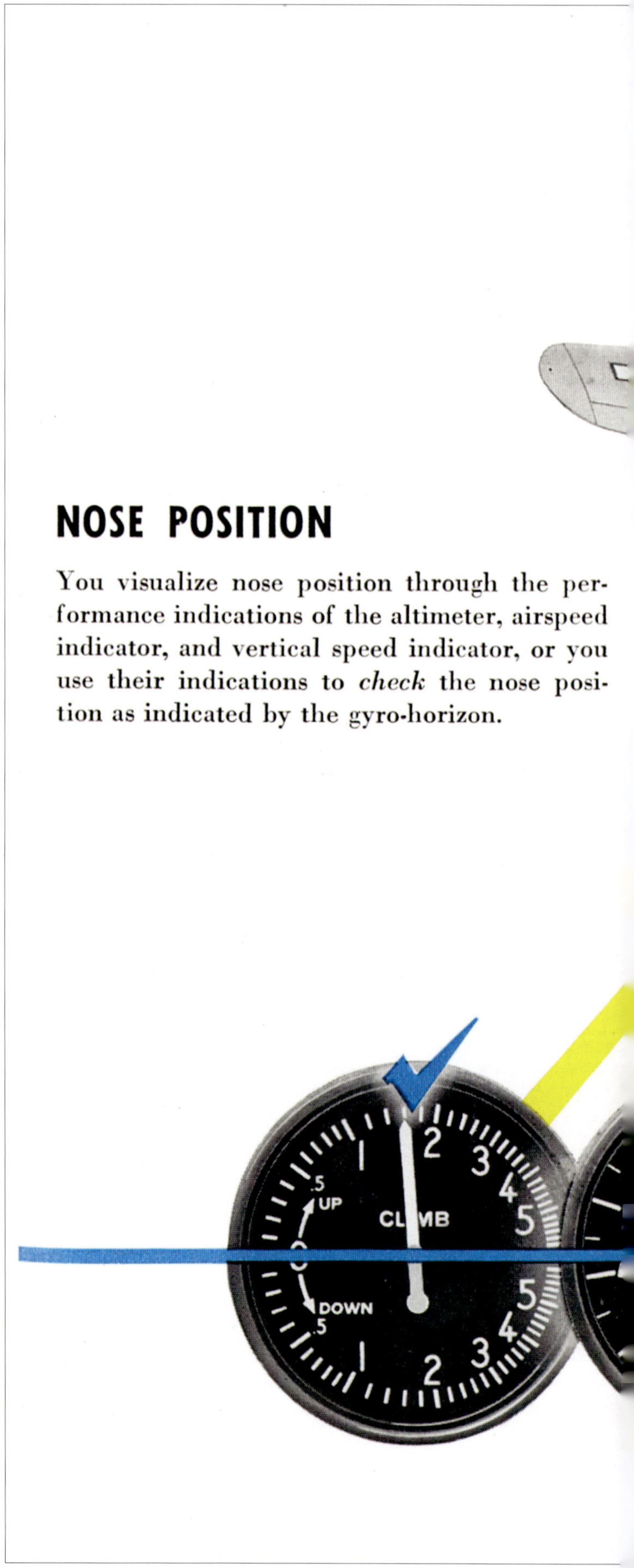

NOSE POSITION

You visualize nose position through the performance indications of the altimeter, airspeed indicator, and vertical speed indicator, or you use their indications to *check* the nose position as indicated by the gyro-horizon.

0
50
100
150
.P.H.
200
1
2
3
4
5
6
7
8
9
29.8
13

is the fact that lift also varies as the *square of the airspeed.*

AIRSPEED-LIFT RATIO

Airspeed	Square of the airspeed	Ratio of new lift to lift at 100
100	10,000	1
200	40,000	4
300	90,000	9

Note that when you double the airspeed, four times as much lift is produced; when you triple the airspeed, the lift is increased nine times. It is obvious, therefore, that (1) the faster the airplane travels, the greater the change in lift which results from a given change in airspeed and (2) the greater the airspeed, the less change you need to make in the angle of attack (pitch) to produce the necessary change in lift required for a desired change in altitude performance.

ıaintain level flight, lift (differential pres-
) must remain very nearly constant. At
er speeds you get this constant lift with a
ler angle of attack. If the airspeed is high
gh, it may even require a negative angle
tack to maintain level flight.
gets you around the corners, pushes you
or lets you down. Lift and thrust are the
forces in flight that you can control. How-
there is another factor which influences
the effects of power and the response of
airplane to changes in attitude—inertia.

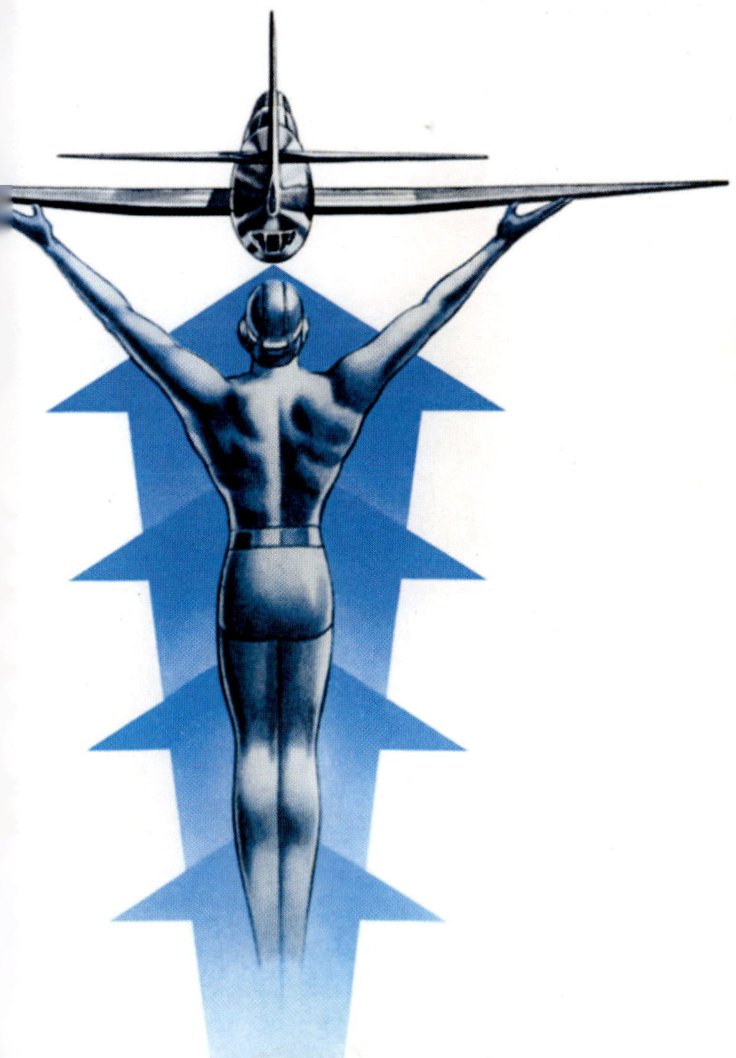

Flight Path Angle of Attack

By 1944 the U.S. Navy's training system was operating at the peak of its efficiency. Manuals were plentiful, well-illustrated and written, and covered every aspect of flight.

Radio Discipline Sense

Radio communication was vital for efficient fleet defence, interception and reconnaissance. Excited, stressed pilots often overloaded the frequencies with long or useless messages. Pilots were drilled to use short, accurate messages using code words that could be easily and quickly understood.

HELLO BLUE BASE THIS IS TACKY TWO. NEGATIVE ! SEND HELLDIVERS WITH SUGAR ABLE PETER FUZES ONE TENTH DELAY. OUT
Provided by CDR. William L. Smith, 519968

Mark 14 Torpedo

The Mark 14 was the U.S. Navy's standard submarine-launched torpedo. Like the Mark 13 aerial torpedo, the Mark 14 proved unreliable and suffered from technical problems that took two years to fix. This drawing shows the various mechanisms powered by compressed air that were vital for the smooth running of the torpedo.

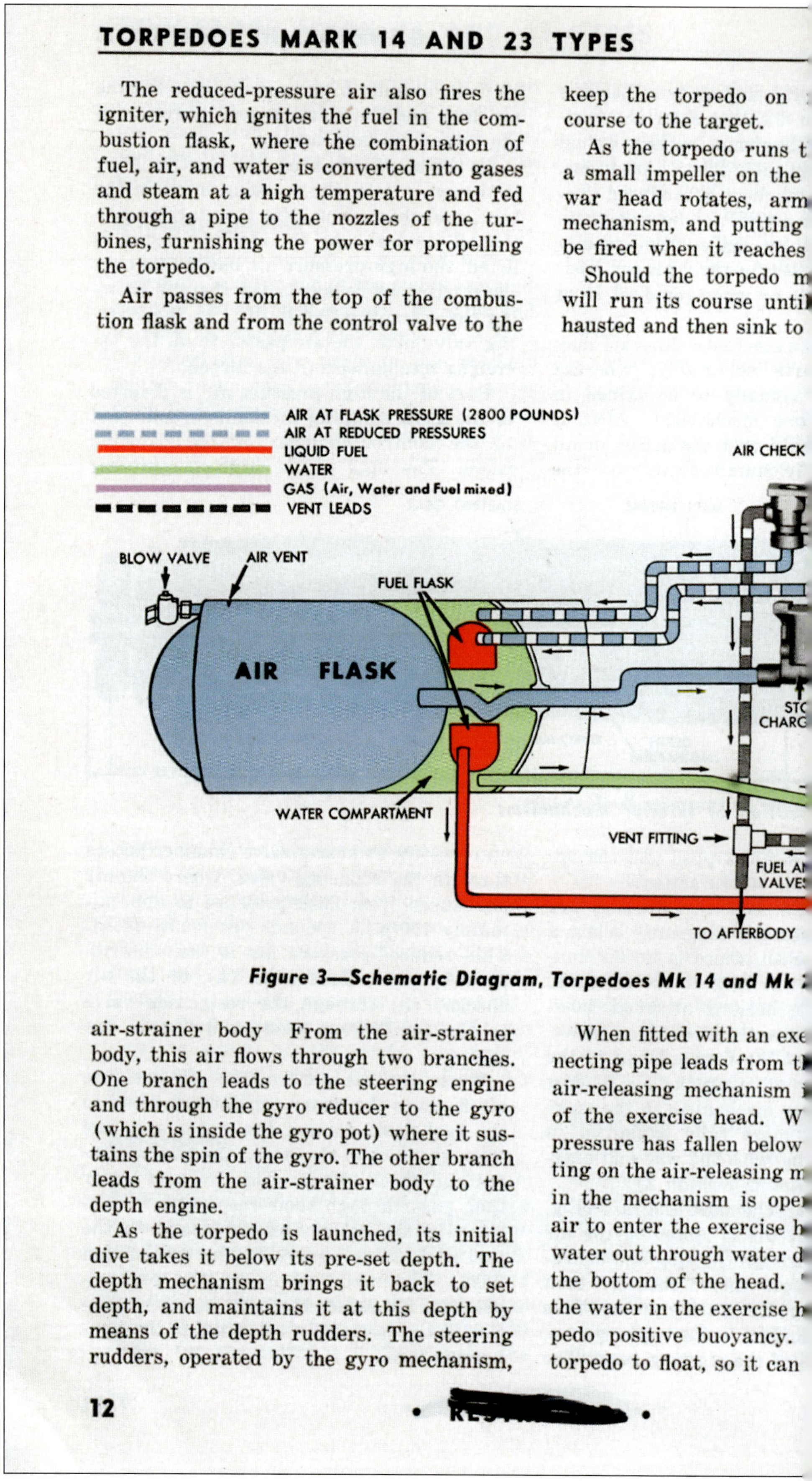
TORPEDOES MARK 14 AND 23 TYPES

The reduced-pressure air also fires the igniter, which ignites the fuel in the combustion flask, where the combination of fuel, air, and water is converted into gases and steam at a high temperature and fed through a pipe to the nozzles of the turbines, furnishing the power for propelling the torpedo.

Air passes from the top of the combustion flask and from the control valve to the

keep the torpedo on
course to the target.

As the torpedo runs t
a small impeller on the
war head rotates, arm
mechanism, and putting
be fired when it reaches

Should the torpedo m
will run its course until
hausted and then sink to

Figure 3—Schematic Diagram, Torpedoes Mk 14 and Mk

air-strainer body From the air-strainer body, this air flows through two branches. One branch leads to the steering engine and through the gyro reducer to the gyro (which is inside the gyro pot) where it sustains the spin of the gyro. The other branch leads from the air-strainer body to the depth engine.

As the torpedo is launched, its initial dive takes it below its pre-set depth. The depth mechanism brings it back to set depth, and maintains it at this depth by means of the depth rudders. The steering rudders, operated by the gyro mechanism,

When fitted with an exe
necting pipe leads from t
air-releasing mechanism
of the exercise head. W
pressure has fallen below
ting on the air-releasing m
in the mechanism is ope
air to enter the exercise h
water out through water d
the bottom of the head.
the water in the exercise h
pedo positive buoyancy.
torpedo to float, so it can

12 • RESTRICTED •

Buoyancy

A torpedo is said to have **positive buoyancy** when it has a tendency to rise to the surface, it is said to have **negative buoyancy** when it has a tendency to sink. The buoyancy of a torpedo in water depends upon the ratio of its weight per unit volume as compared to the weight per unit volume of water

The three factors which affect the buoyancy of a torpedo are (a) the displacement (volume); (b) the fixed (not expendable) weight; and (c) the expendable weight. The air, the water in the water compartment, and the fuel are expended in proportion to the length of the run. The water ballast in the exercise head is expended at the end of the run. If a sufficient amount of weight is expended, the torpedo will obtain **positive buoyancy** and will finish its run on the surface. The buoyancy of the torpedo will, of course, be adversely changed by salt water leakage into the afterbody and the exercise head. A table of approximate buoyancy factors will be found in the appendix at the back of this pamphlet.

Marks and Modifications

The designations Mk 14 Mod 3A, or Mk 14-3A, Mk 23, etc., apply only to the complete torpedoes, including the afterbody and the tail. Each type of war or exercise head, also the gyroscope and the exploder mechanism, are given individual designations, as will be described in the chapters referring to those parts. Usually, when changes or improvements are made in any part of a torpedo, the changed torpedo is given either a modification number or a change in Mark.

For example, the depth mechanism of the Torpedo Mk 14-3 was improved, and the torpedo was designated the Torpedo Mk 14-3A. The Torpedo Mk 14-3A was then changed to a single high-speed torpedo, and it was given the designation Mk 23.

The Torpedoes Mks 14, 14-1, 14-2, and 14-3 are out of service. The Torpedo Mk 14-1A is a two-speed torpedo, with speeds

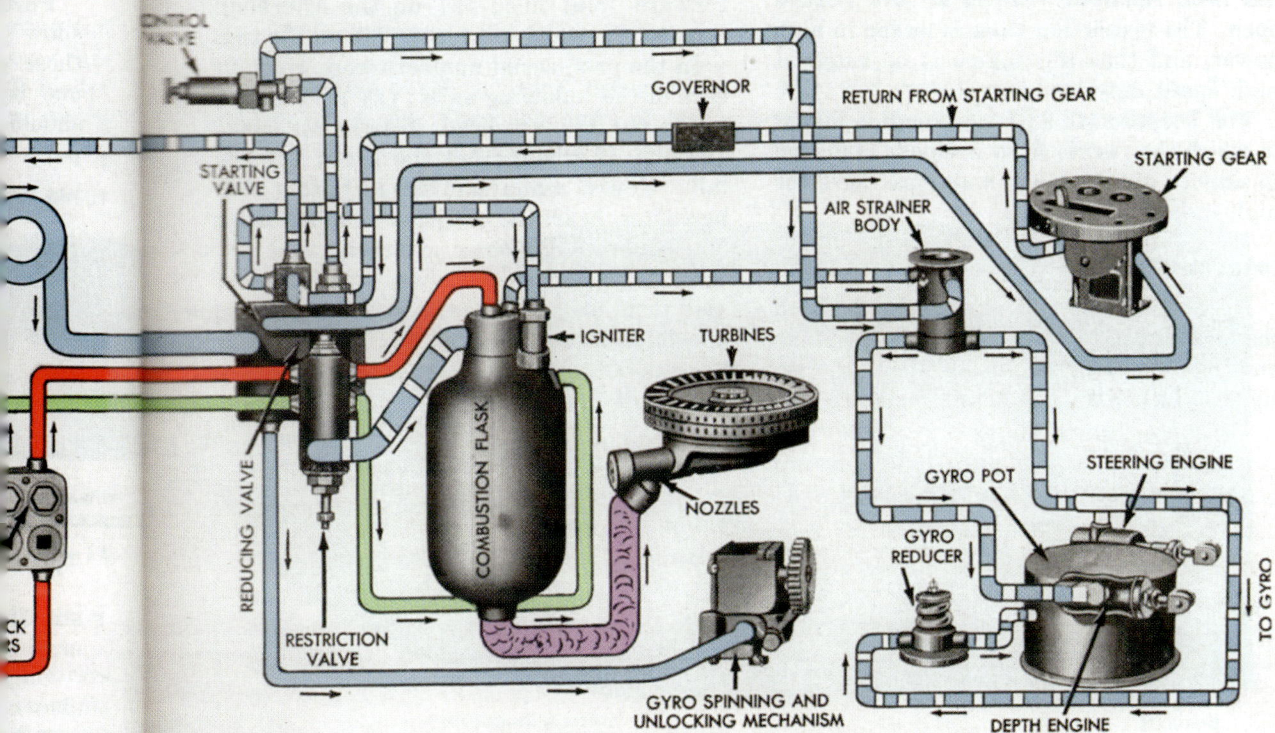

flow of air to operating mechanisms (see explanation in descriptive text)

'Canny Comments Concerning Camouflage'

U.S. Navy 'Seabees' (construction battalions) played a crucial role during the battle for the Pacific. Shore bases had to be built in order to bring in supplies of men and material and to repair damaged ships. "Seabees were responsible for the rapid construction of runways, harbours, warehouses, shelters, hospitals and more. Bases within reach of the Japanese had to be well versed in the art of camouflage."

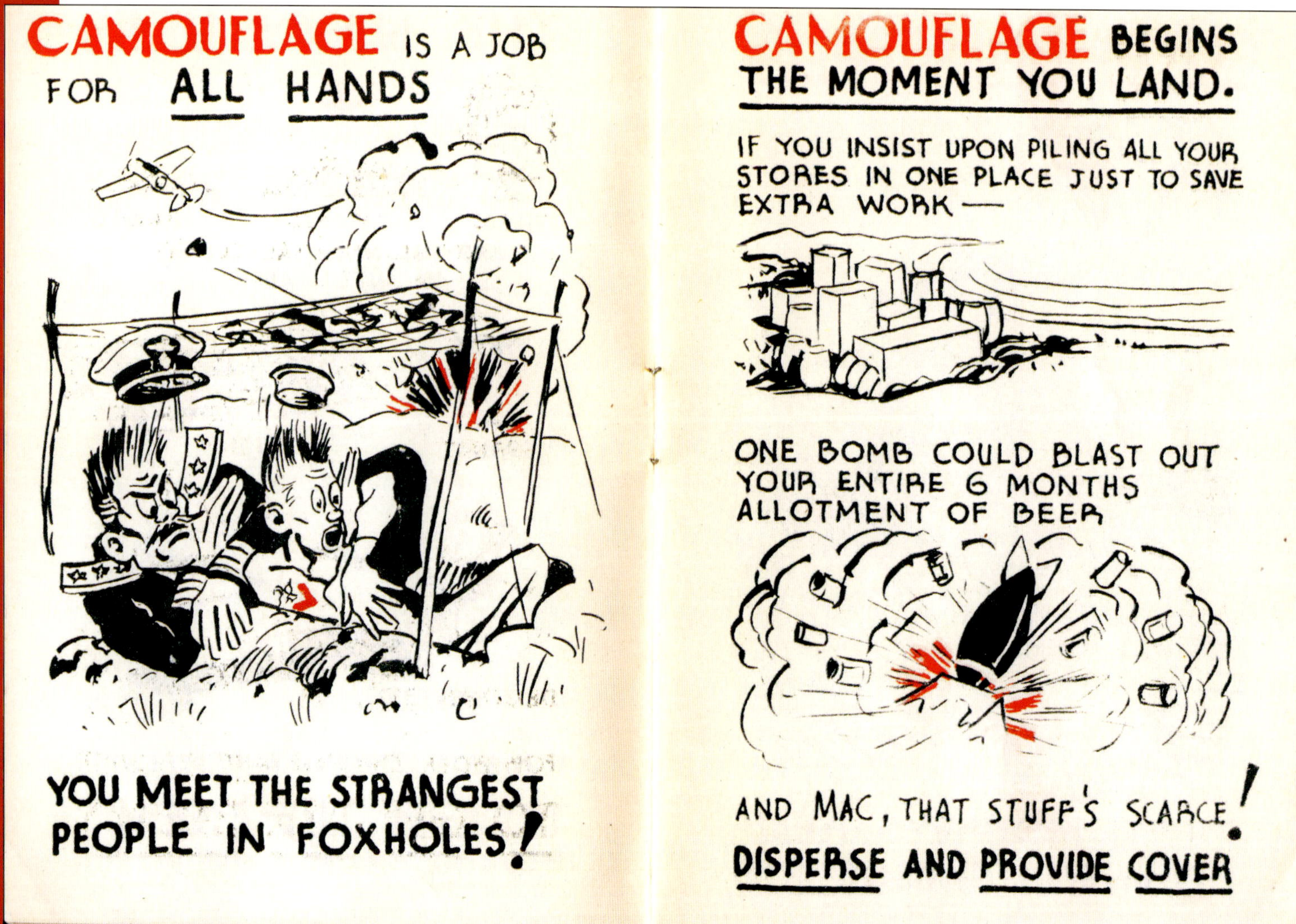

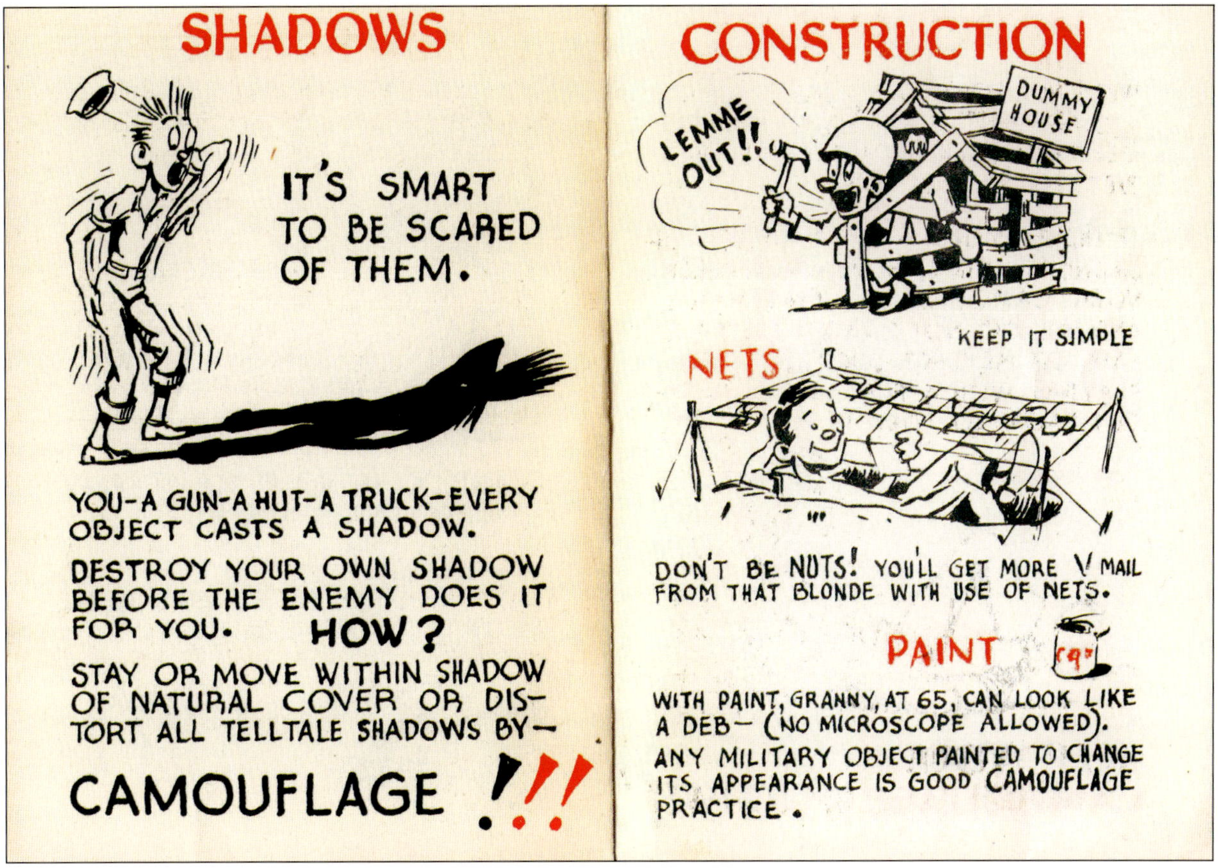

SHADOWS

IT'S SMART TO BE SCARED OF THEM.

YOU–A GUN–A HUT–A TRUCK–EVERY OBJECT CASTS A SHADOW.

DESTROY YOUR OWN SHADOW BEFORE THE ENEMY DOES IT FOR YOU. HOW?

STAY OR MOVE WITHIN SHADOW OF NATURAL COVER OR DISTORT ALL TELLTALE SHADOWS BY–

CAMOUFLAGE !!!

CONSTRUCTION

LEMME OUT!!

DUMMY HOUSE

KEEP IT SIMPLE

NETS

DON'T BE NUTS! YOU'LL GET MORE V MAIL FROM THAT BLONDE WITH USE OF NETS.

PAINT

WITH PAINT, GRANNY, AT 65, CAN LOOK LIKE A DEB– (NO MICROSCOPE ALLOWED).

ANY MILITARY OBJECT PAINTED TO CHANGE ITS APPEARANCE IS GOOD CAMOUFLAGE PRACTICE.

TRUCKS

WATCH YOUR PARKING

BAD — ON FLAT GROUND

FAIR — AMONG ROCKS AND BUSHES

GOOD — UNDER NATURAL GROWTH

THAT EQUIPMENT COST DOUGH; IT TOOK UP VITAL SHIPPING SPACE. HOW YOU PROTECT IT WILL DETERMINE THE LENGTH OF ITS LIFE — AND YOURS.

YOU GUYS HAVE DOUBLE-PARKED ON THOITY THOID STREET BUT HERE YOU GET A ONE-WAY TICKET TO HELL OR HEAVEN FOR THAT MISTAKE. DISPERSE AND CAMOUFLAGE! GET WISE! OTHERWISE —

FUEL TANKS

TYPICAL VIEW OF AN ISLAND BASE WITH UNPROTECTED FUEL STORAGE TANKS.

NETS

FLAT GROUND HARD TO CONCEAL

HILLSIDE EASY TO CONCEAL

WHEN TANKS ARE DESTROYED, NAVAL AND MILITARY OPERATIONS ARE SLOWED UP. OCTANE GAS AND FUEL OIL HAS TO BE SHIPPED THOUSANDS OF MILES FOR REPLACEMENT.

FOIL THE ENEMY AND BOIL HIM IN OIL!

SAVE YOUR GAS TO BOMB HIS–

WHAM!

CAMOUFLAGE!

ANALYSIS OF FIRE CONTROL PROBLEM

A submarine is equipped with torpedo tubes fwd and aft which are parallel to the longitudinal axis of the ship. When a torpedo is fired it travels in a straight line for a certain distance called the Reach. After it has reached the end of this period of straight line travel, it may be caused to start on a circular course of a definite radius. The length of the circular path is determined by the setting of the gyro in the torpedo and the characteristics of the type of torpedo being used. After travelling in the circular path for a prescribed distance, the torpedo once more assumes a straight path and travels thus until it reaches the target.

The method for controlling the torpedo is by setting the Gyro Angle. It is the function of the Computer to take all of the variable factors into account and determine the value of the Gyro Angle for both fwd and aft torpedoes. The Gyro Angle is continuously generated by the Computer to keep up with the change in the problem due to relative motion of Own Ship and Target.

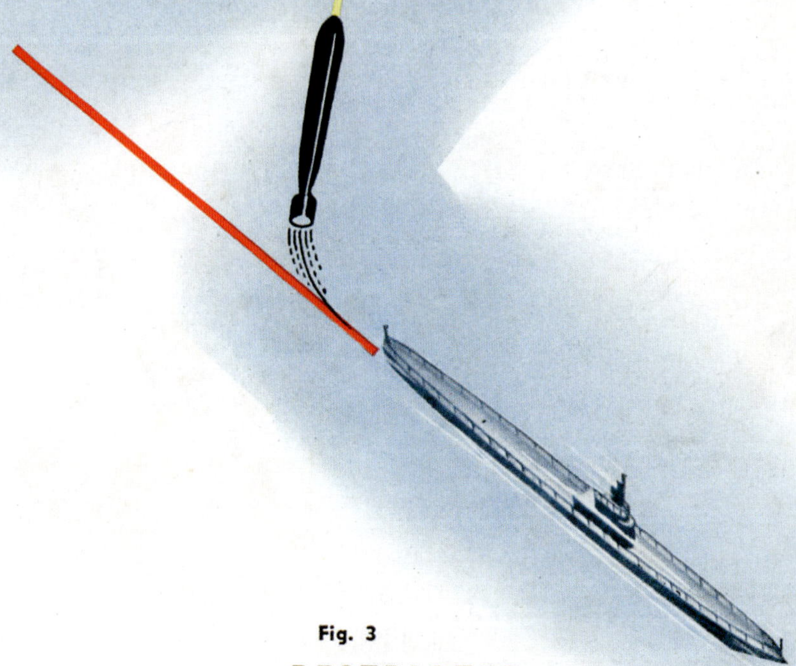

SECTION 1

Fig. 3

RESTRICTED **11**

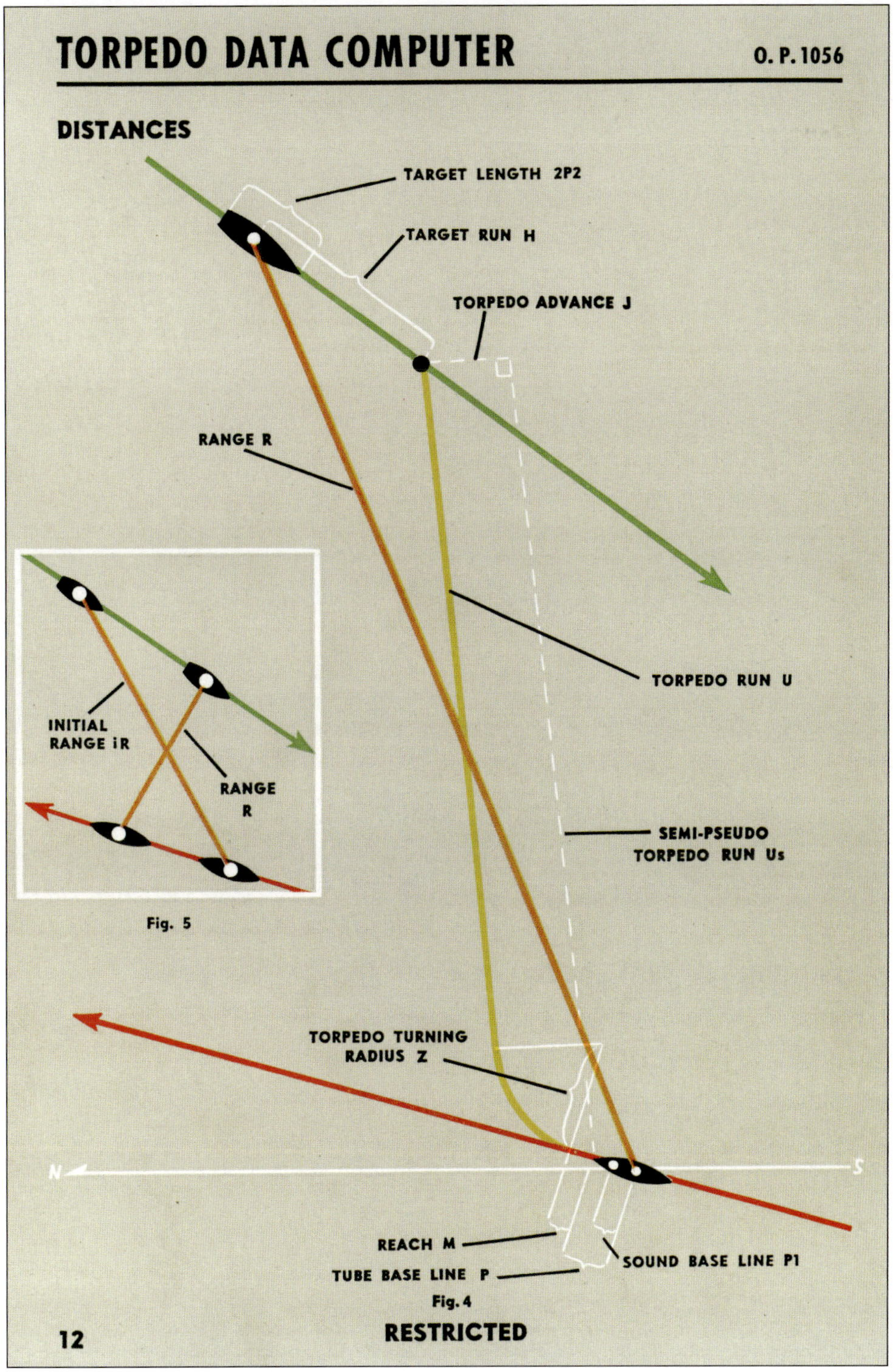

Torpedo Data Computer Mk 3

These two illustrations come from the Torpedo Data Computer Mk 3 manual. Considered a masterpiece of mechanical computing design, the Mk 3 was World War II's most successful torpedo fire control computer. The best torpedo attack profile was to place the target at a right angle to the beam of the submarine. From there, the submarine's captain would estimate the angle on the bow and the range of the oncoming ship. This information was then fed into the torpedo data computer, which generated a firing solution.

GERMANY

The German War Fleet — Die Deutsche Kriegsflotte I and II

These two posters, titled The German War Fleet I and II, are dated to 1941. They depict the major and minor combatants then in Kriegsmarine service. These posters show the battleship *Scharnhorst* and the 'pocket' battleship *Lützow*, along with the heavy cruiser *Admiral Hipper* and all the smaller types then in service. Also included is the aircraft carrier *Graf Zeppelin*, which was never completed. By 1941, the Kriegsmarine had just six battleships in service — *Bismarck*, *Tirpitz*, *Gneisenau*, *Scharnhorst*, *Admiral Scheer* and *Lützow*.

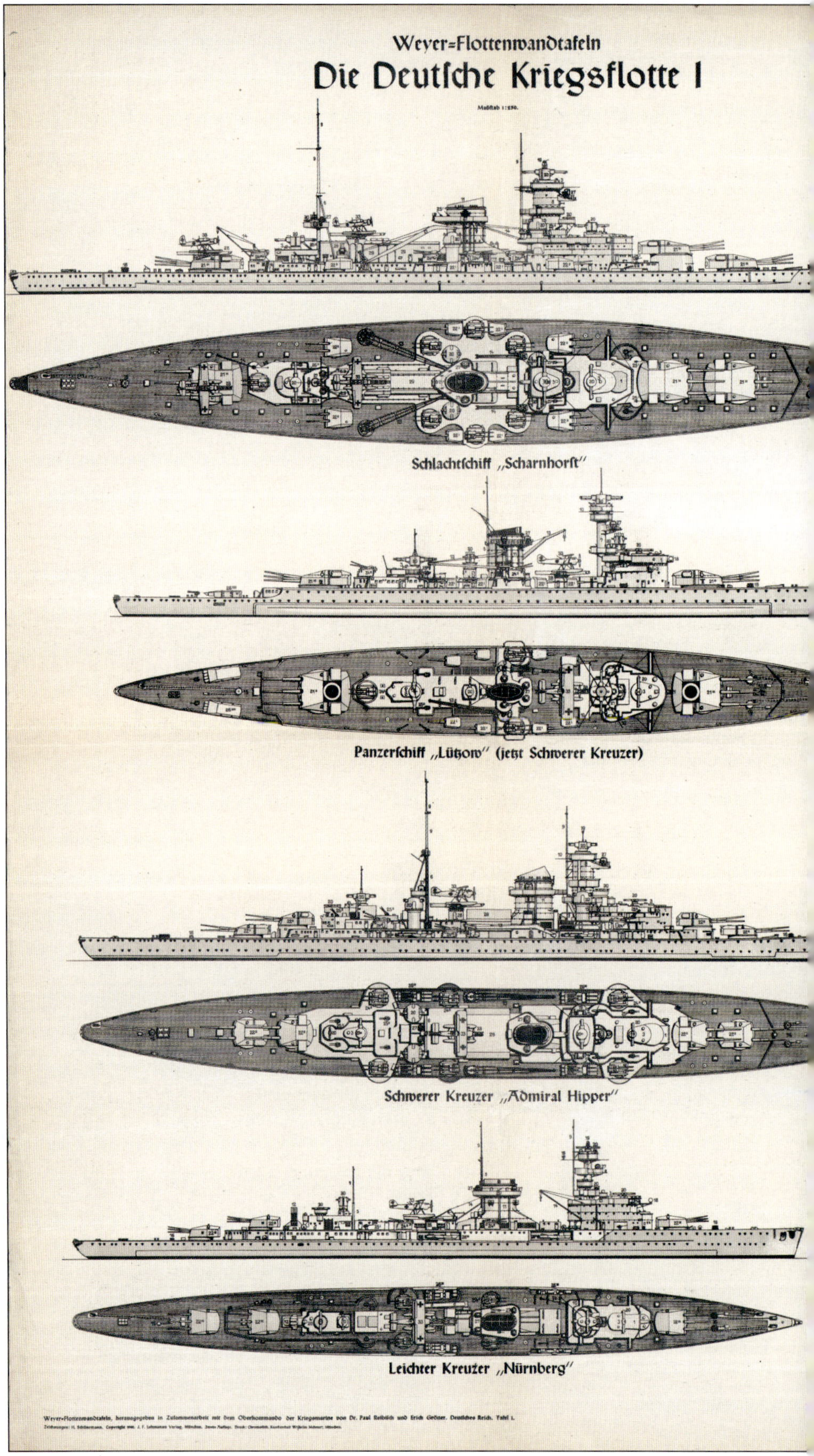

Tafel 1

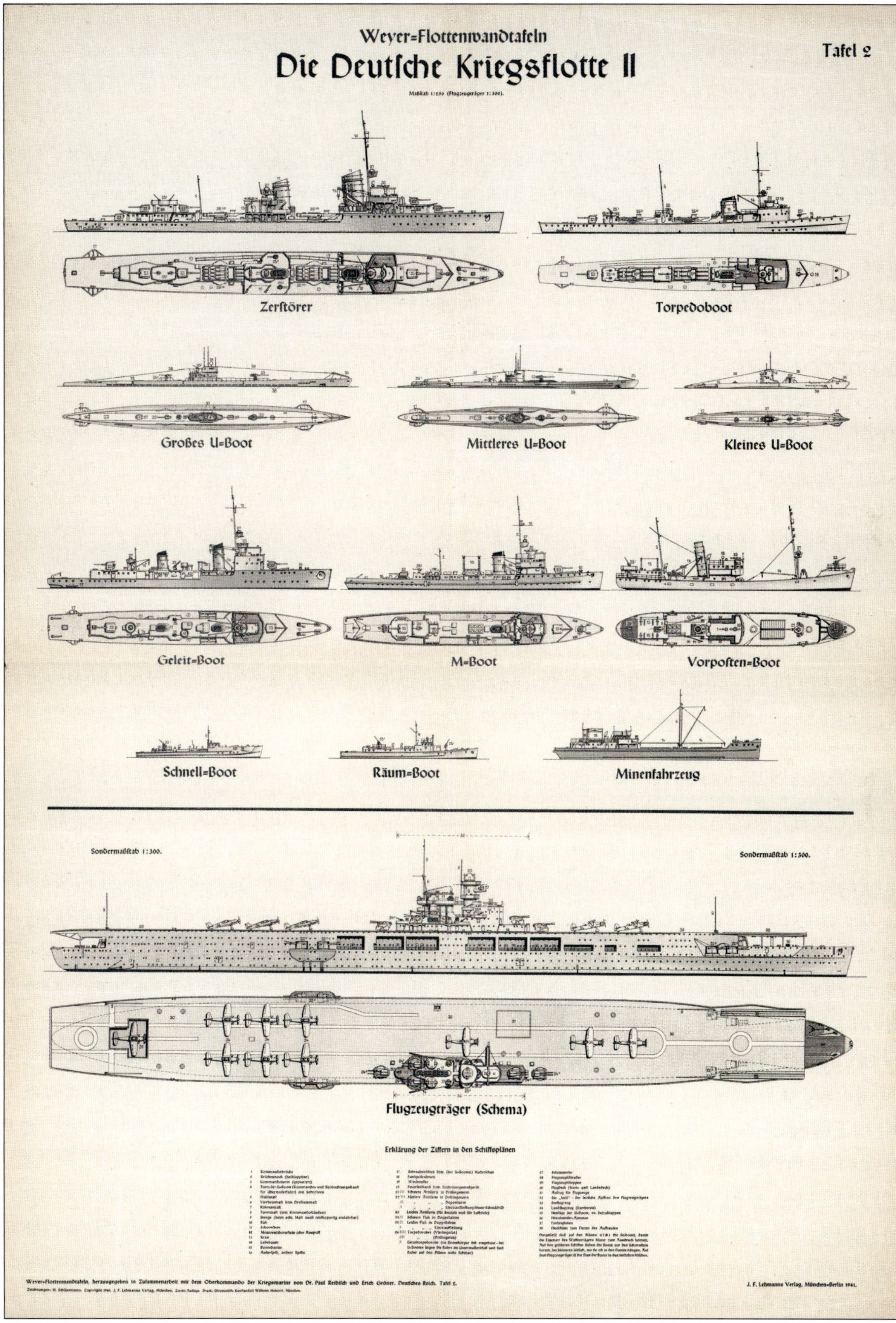
Weyer=Flottenwandtafeln
Die Deutsche Kriegsflotte II
Tafel 2
Zerstörer
Torpedoboot
Großes U=Boot
Mittleres U=Boot
Kleines U=Boot
Geleit=Boot
M=Boot
Vorposten=Boot
Schnell=Boot
Räum=Boot
Minenfahrzeug
Sondermaßstab 1:500.
Sondermaßstab 1:500.
Flugzeugträger (Schema)
Erklärung der Ziffern in den Schiffsplänen
Weyer=Flottenwandtafeln, herausgegeben in Zusammenarbeit mit dem Oberkommando der Kriegsmarine von Dr. Paul Reibisch und Erich Gröner. Deutsches Reich. Tafel 2.
J. F. Lehmanns Verlag, München=Berlin 1941.

Bismarck — Battleship Ventilation System, 1938

This blueprint drawing shows the *Bismarck*'s ventilation system. As one of the Second World War's most famous battleships, the *Bismarck* has often been described, at the time, as the most powerful vessel afloat. While an impressive ship, the *Bismarck* had its strengths and weaknesses and was no better when compared to contemporary British, French, American, Japanese, and Italian battleships.

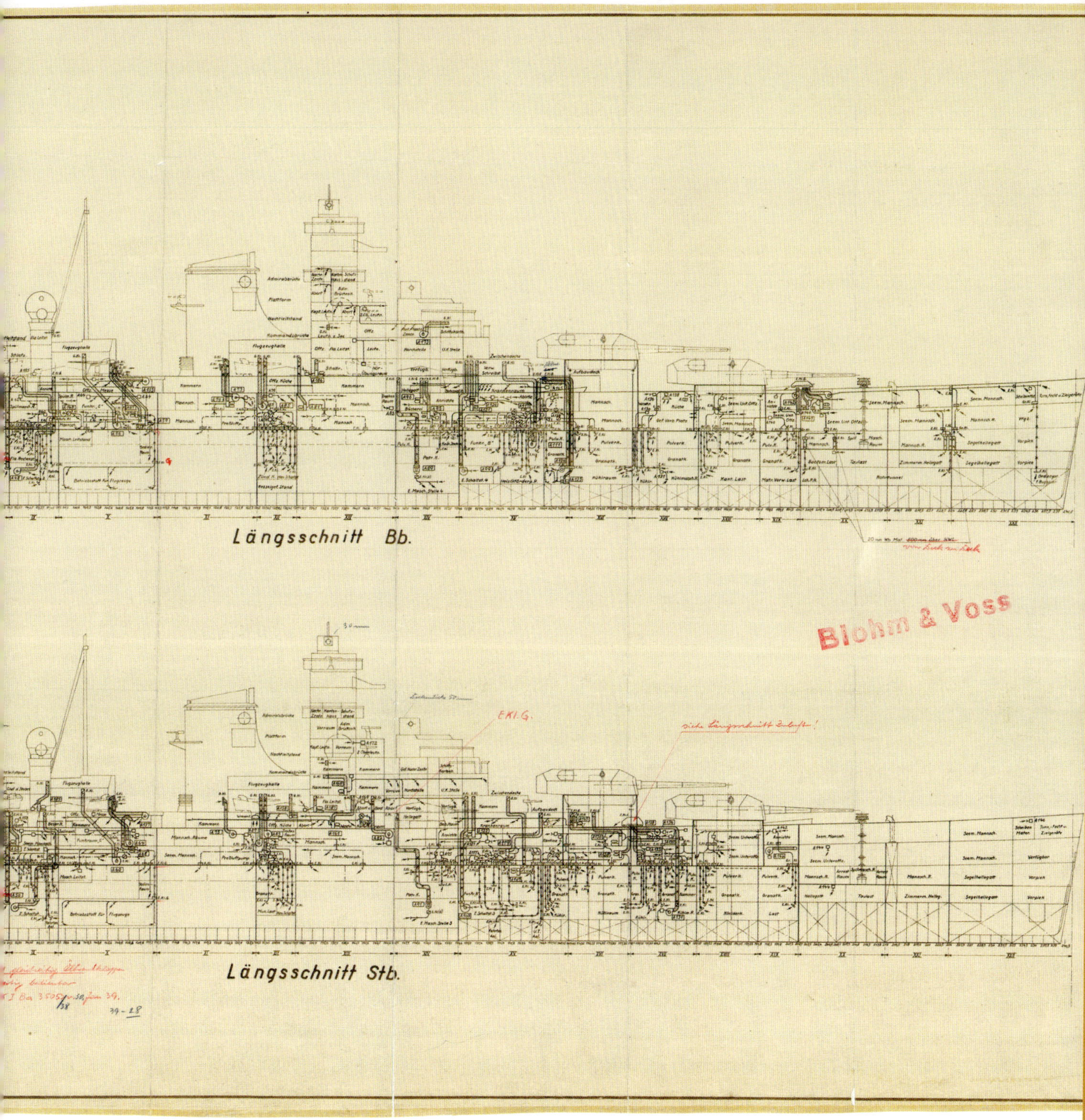
Längsschnitt Bb.
Blohm & Voss
Längsschnitt Stb.

Tirpitz — Battleship Ventilation System, 1942

The *Tirpitz* and *Bismarck* were considered the most modern capital ships afloat in 1941. After the *Bismarck* was sunk in May 1941, the *Tirpitz* rarely put to sea and never fired her main guns at an enemy vessel. Assigned to Norway in January 1942, the *Tirpitz*'s presence was a direct threat to northern-bound convoys to Russia. The British Royal Navy and RAF expended a great deal of resources to damage and eventually sink the ship. After a midget submarine attack, numerous bombing attacks by the RAF and Russian aircraft and several strikes by the Fleet Air Arm in 1944, the *Tirpitz* was finally sunk by 'Tallboy' bombs dropped by RAF Lancasters of 617 Squadron in November 1944.

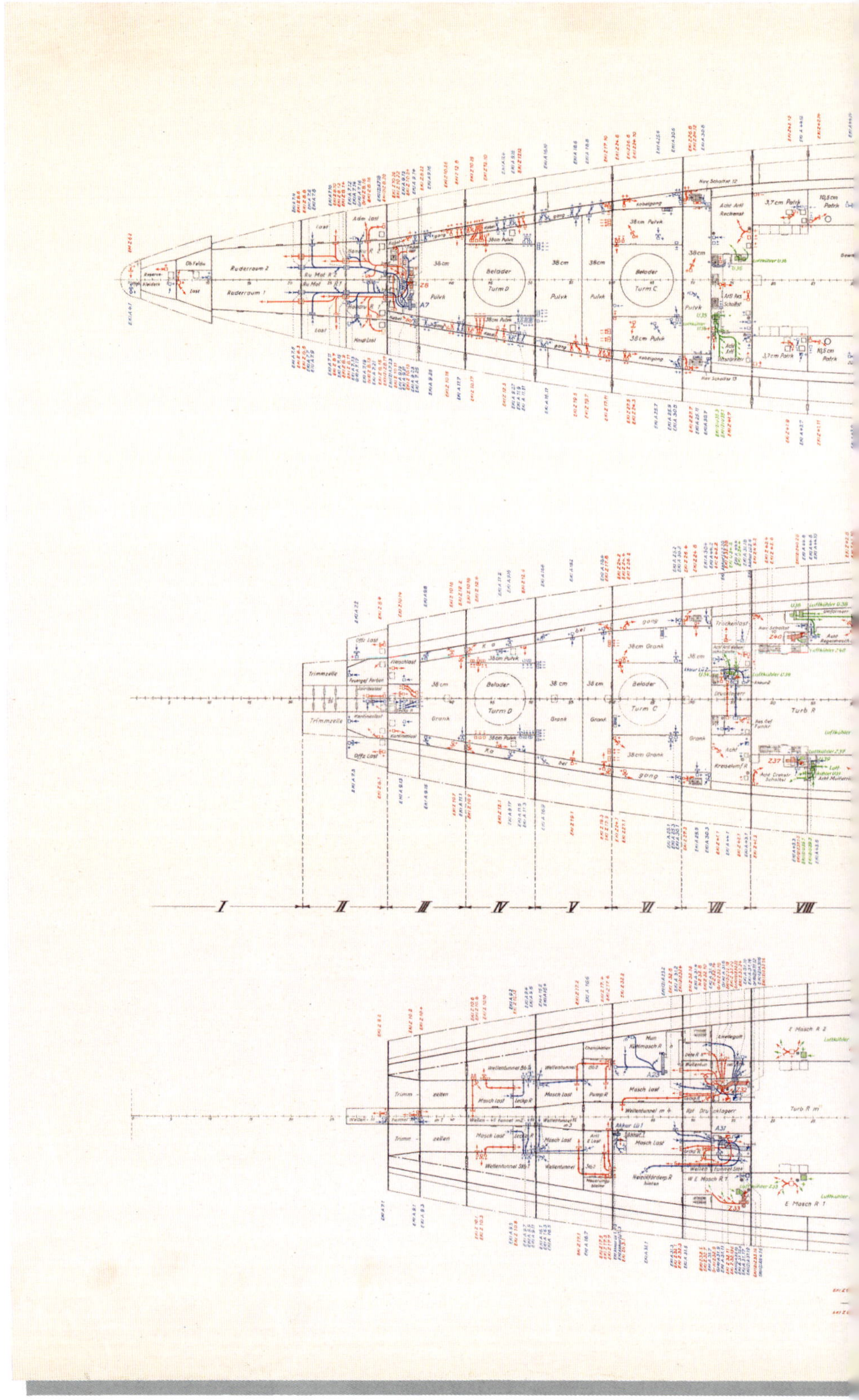

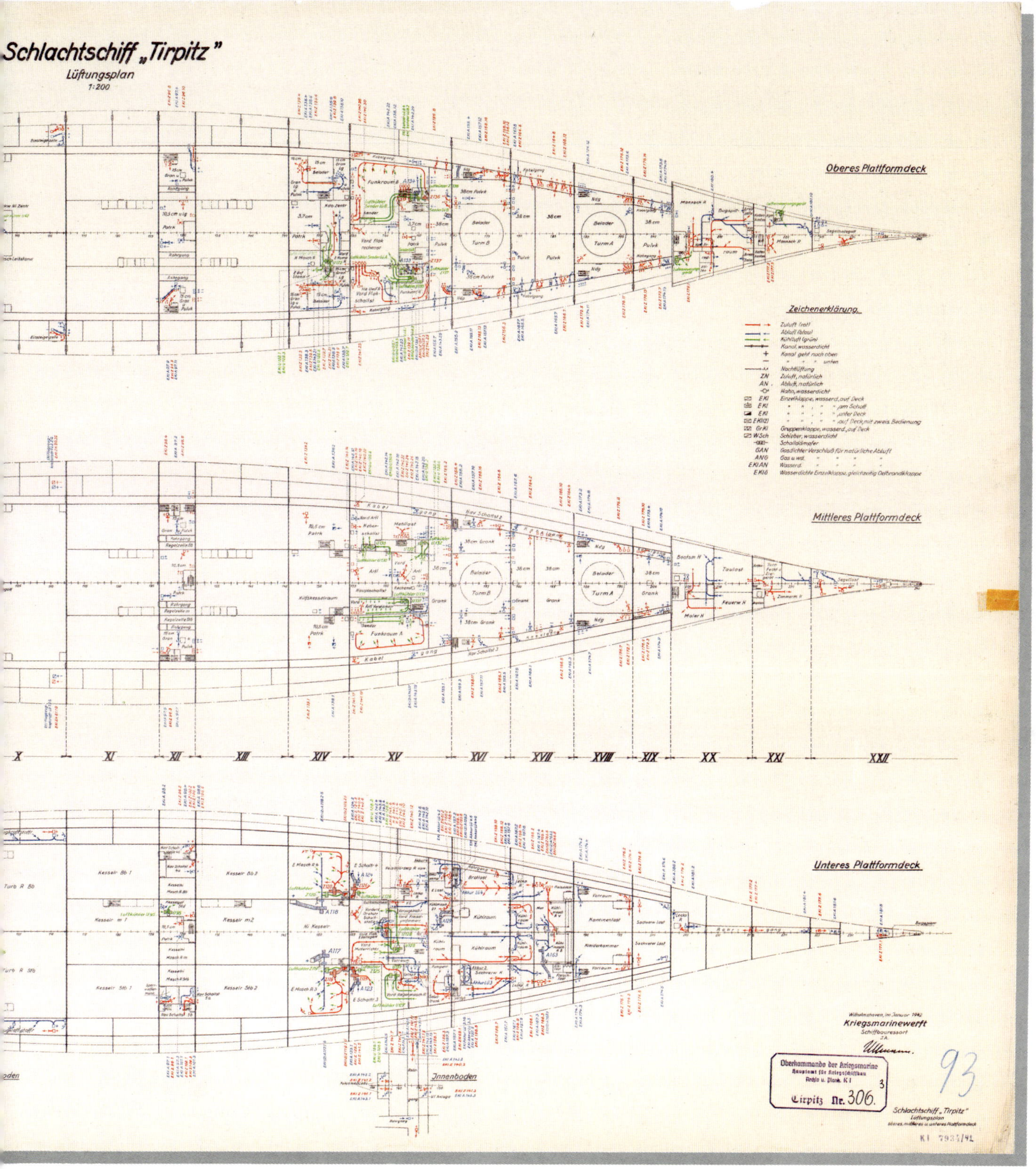
Schlachtschiff „Tirpitz"
Lüftungsplan
1:200
Oberes Plattformdeck
Zeichenerklärung.
Mittleres Plattformdeck
Unteres Plattformdeck
Innenboden
Kriegsmarinewerft
Oberkommando der Kriegsmarine
Tirpitz Nr. 306.
93

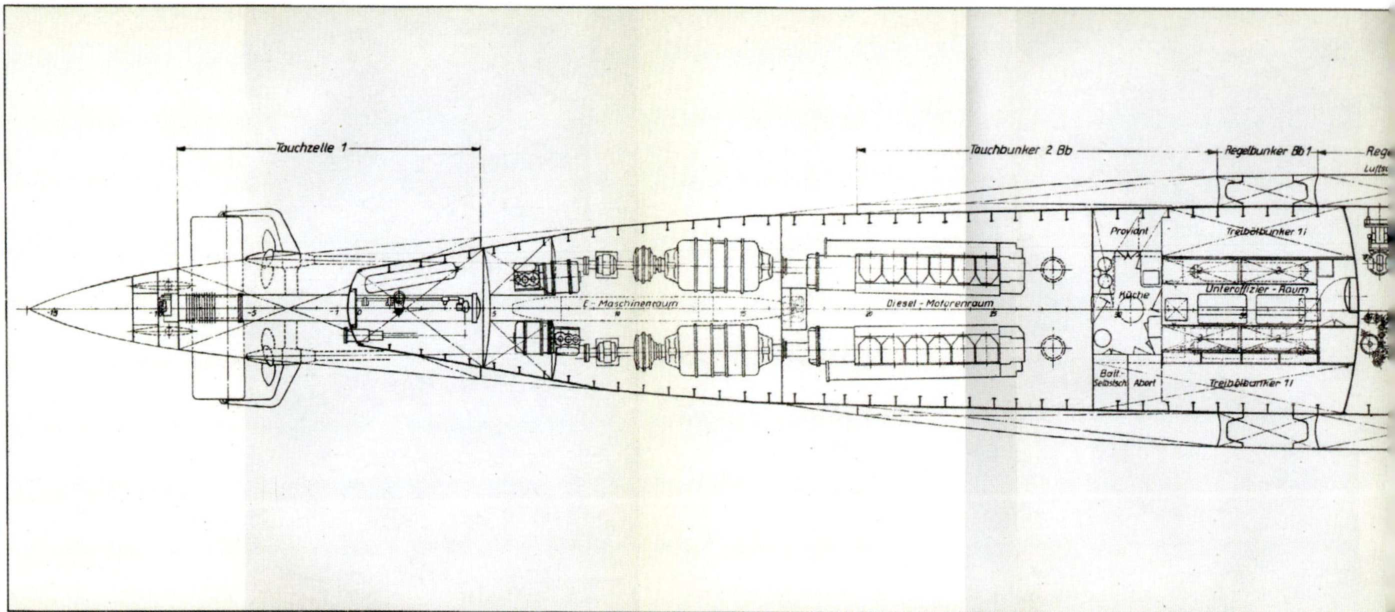

U-Boat Type VIIC (above)

This top-view drawing shows the inner workings of the Type VIIC U-boat. This boat was the most widely produced during the war, with 568 built. With the fall of France, the Kriegsmarine could operate their boats from French ports, which increased the VIIC's range, allowing them to operate as far east as Newfoundland.

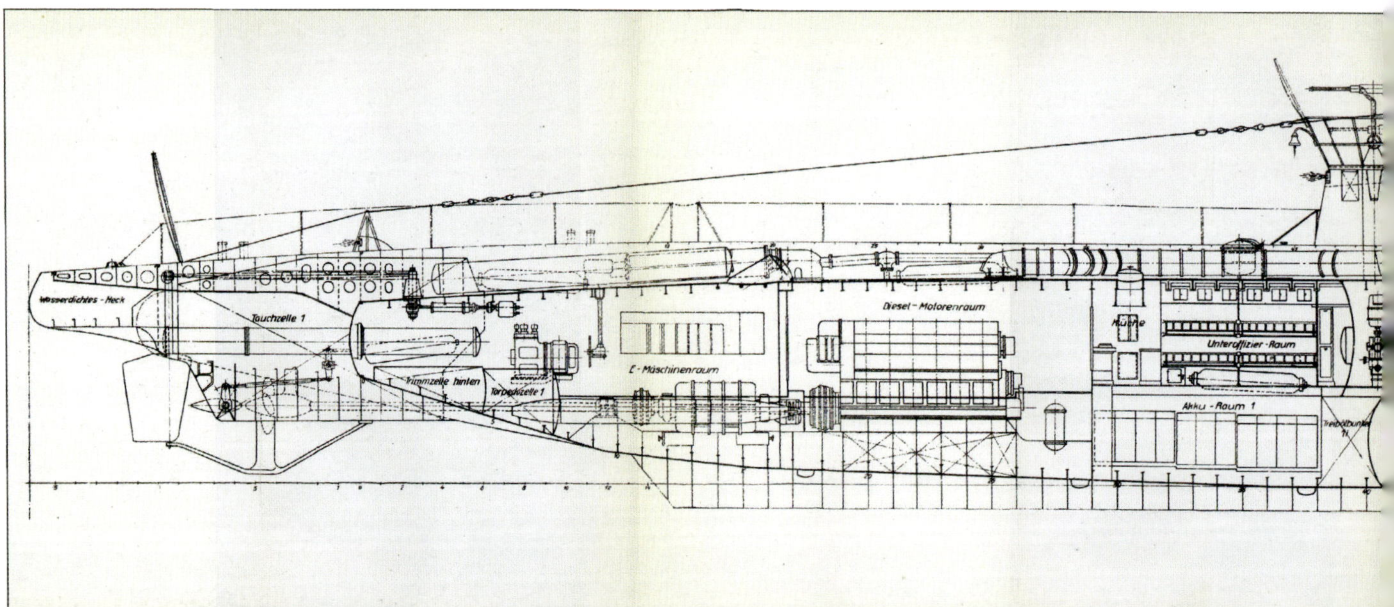

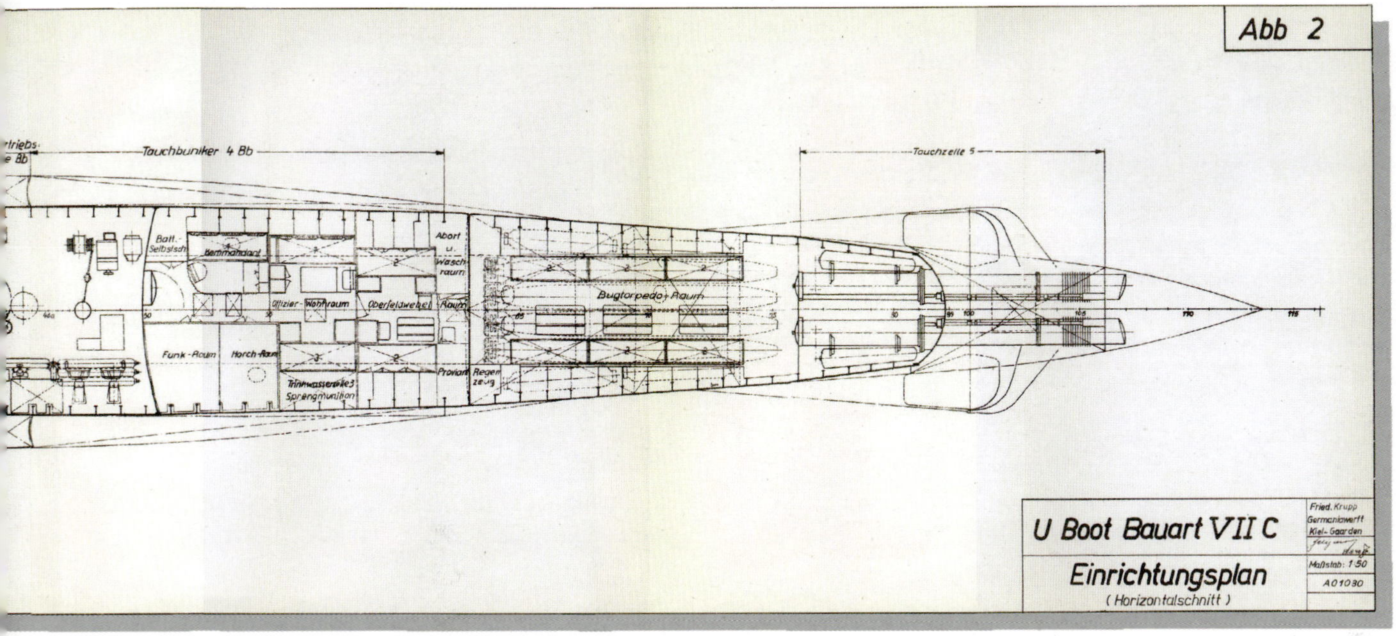

U-Boat Type VIIC (below)

This cross-section 'facility plan' clearly shows the bow and stern torpedo tubes (four in the bow, one in the stern). Each Type VII boat was armed with 14 21-inch torpedoes, one 88 mm/65 deck gun (220 rounds) and one 20 mm AA gun. Her range was 13,679 kilometers (8,500 miles) surfaced at 10 knots.

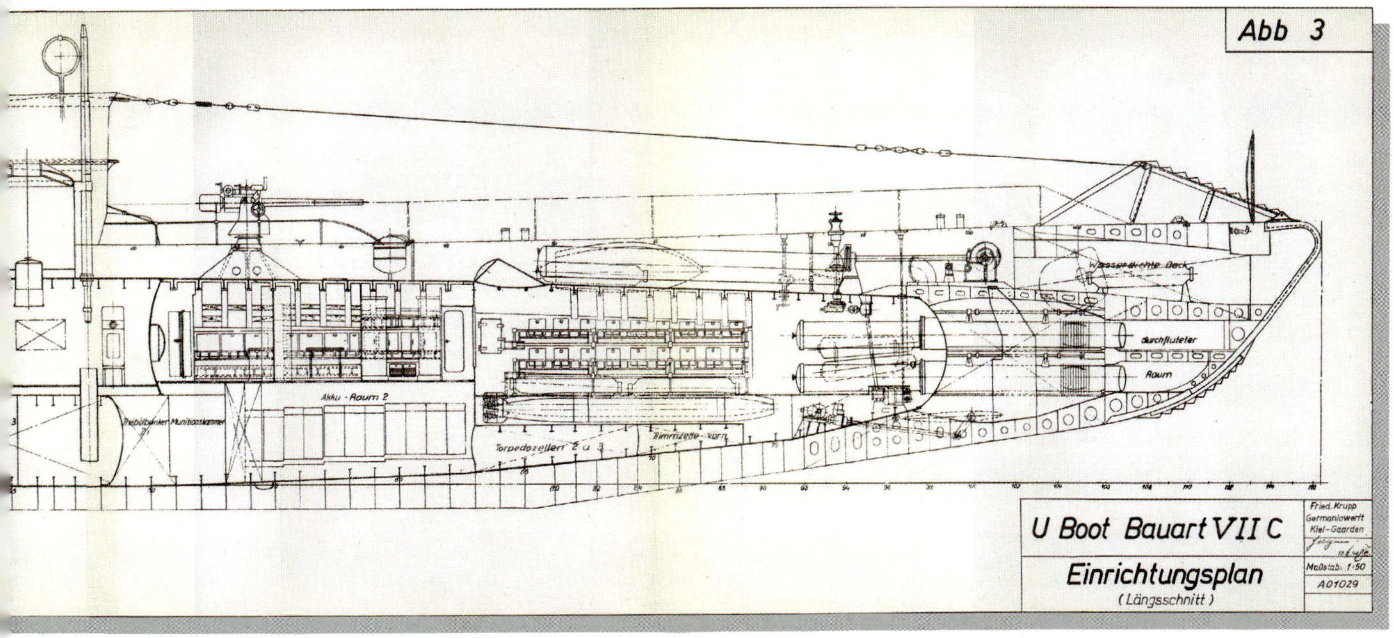

Zellenplan und Trimmtabelle — Cell Plan and Trim Table Type VIIC

All German U-boats used a double-hull design. The inner hull was a pressure hull, as seen here in the darker outline. The crew lived within the pressure hull and conning tower. The pressure hull maintained one atmosphere of pressure. This would be maintained until the boat reached its crush depth. The Type VII could dive to a depth of 230 meters (740 feet), more than British and American submarines. The areas in pink are labelled 'fuel oil bunker,' and those in green are labelled 'diving cell.'

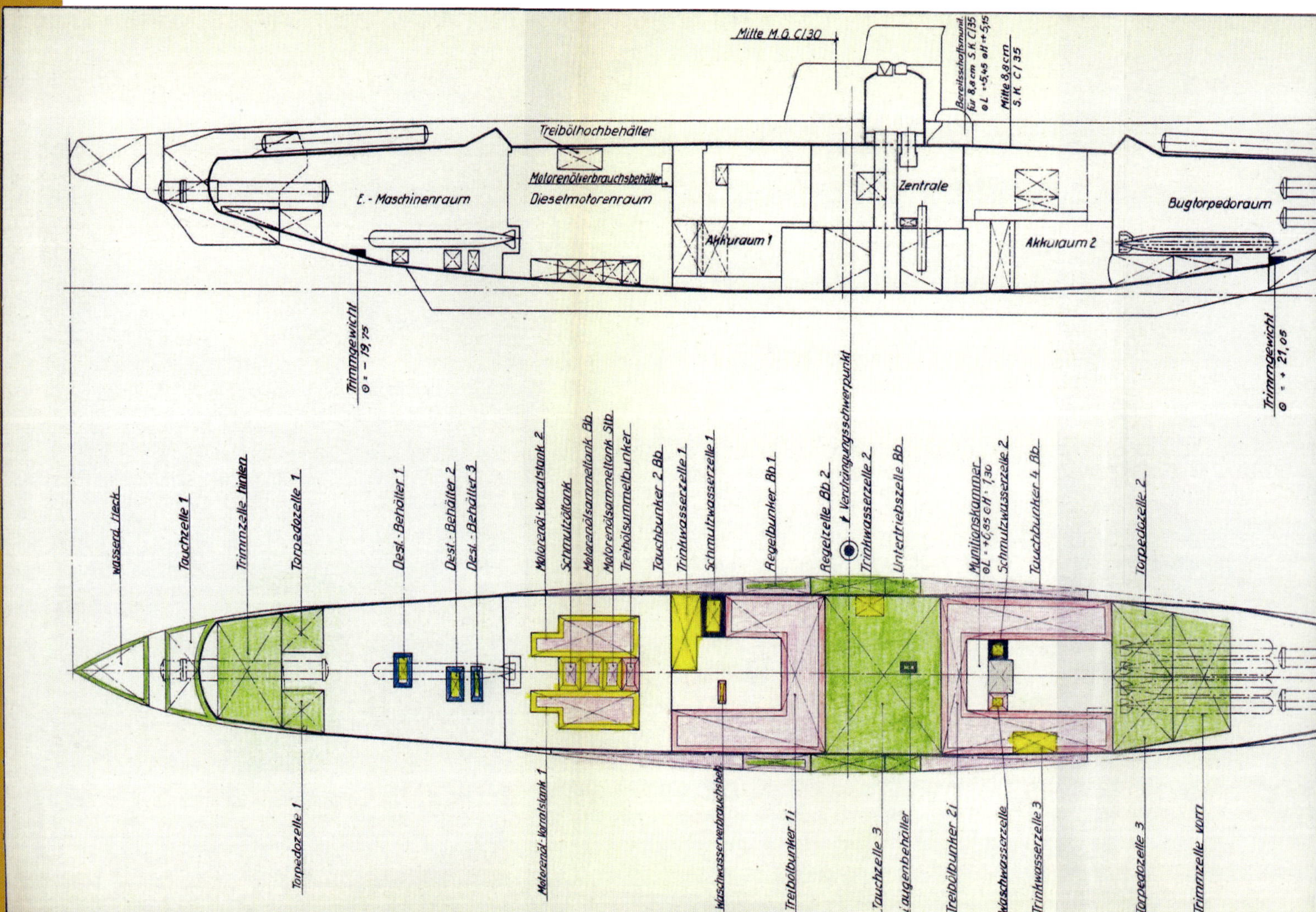

Füllungen bei Vierkantlage und Restauftrieb .... t

Bezeichnung	Gesamtinhalt Liter	Art	Füllung bei Versuch Liter	⊙ vor ± V m ⊙	⊙ über Basis (vall – Th)	Bemerkung
Regelbunker Stb 1	4700	Wasser		-3,25	3,74	
Regelbunker Bb 1	4700	″		-3,25	3,74	
Regelzelle Stb 2	7850	″		-0,10	3,75	
Regelzelle Bb 2	7850	″		-0,10	3,75	
Trimmzelle hinten	3550	″		-23,05	2,36	
Trimmzelle vorn	3600	″		+18,55	1,22	
Untertriebzelle Stb	2150	″		+2,45	3,75	
Untertriebzelle Bb	2150	″		+2,45	3,75	
Torpedozelle 1	2350	″		-21,15	2,02	
Torpedozelle 2	5750	″		+15,25	1,19	
Torpedozelle 3	5750	″		+15,25	1,19	
Treibölbunker 1i	37900	Treiböl		-3,25	2,12	γ =
Treibölbunker 2i	32800	″		+8,30	1,65	
Regelbunker Stb 1	4700	″		-3,25	3,75	
Regelbunker Bb 1	4700	″		-3,25	3,75	
Tauchbunker 2 Stb	11300	″		-7,95	3,84	
Tauchbunker 2 Bb	11300	″		-7,95	3,84	
Tauchbunker 4 Stb	13300	″		+7,05	3,87	
Tauchbunker 4 Bb	13300	″		+7,05	3,87	
Treibölsammelbunker	425	″		-9,55	0,70	
Treibölhochbehälter	730	″		-11,50	4,37	
Motorenölvorratstank 1	3270	Mot. Öl		-11,45	0,84	γ =
Motorenölvorratstank 2	3230	″		-11,45	0,84	
Motorenölsammeltank Bb	800	″		-11,65	0,67	
Motorensammeltank Stb	800	″		-10,45	0,63	
Motorenölverbrauchsbehälter	26	″		-7,55	3,42	
Schmutzöltank	790	″		-12,85	0,69	
Trinkwasserzelle 1	2625	Wasser		-7,05	1,45	
Trinkwasserzelle 2	465	″		+1,25	3,42	
Trinkwasserzelle 3	785	″		+9,90	3,47	
Waschwasserzelle	485	″		+7,75	1,29	
Waschwasserverbrauchsbeh.	30	″		-5,90	3,95	
Schmutzwasserzelle 1	760	″		-6,05	1,65	
Schmutzwasserzelle 2	485	″		+7,75	1,29	
Destillatbehälter 1	149	″		-18,50	1,09	
Destillatbehälter 2	199	″		-16,70	1,00	
Destillatbehälter 3	153	″		-16,25	0,96	
Torpedorohr I mit/ohne Kolben	1680/1740	″		+25,25/25,10	3,335	
Torpedorohr II ″ ″ ″	″ ″	″		″ ″	″	
Torpedorohr III ″ ″ ″	″ ″	″		″ ″	2,375	
Torpedorohr IV ″ ″ ″	″ ″	″		″ ″	″	
Torpedorohr V ″ ″ ″	″ ″	″		-26,15/26,00	3,17	
Decksbehälter hinten	2500	″		-19,80	4,86	
Decksbehälter vorn	2500	″		+18,75	4,95	
Hintere Batterie		Säure		-4,75		1 % = 11,2 kg
Vordere Batterie		″		+10,75		1 % = 11,2 kg
Laugenbehälter	30	Lauge		+3,05	2,17	
Druckluftgruppe	12 × 325	Luft		+3,70	3,50	Soll 205 at
Sauerstoffgruppe	10 × 50	Sauerstoff		+3,05	2,66	Soll 150 at

Beladung mit T. u. T.M.

Torpedorohr I	
Torpedorohr II	
Torpedorohr III	
Torpedorohr IV	
Torpedorohr V	
Reservelagerung hinten	
Reservelagerung vorn	
Decksbehälter hinten	
Decksbehälter vorn	

Trimm –
± Krängungs – Versuch
± Krängungs –

am .... 19..

Messungen nach dem Versuch

Tiefgang hinten	m
Tiefgang mitte	″
Tiefgang vorn	″
Schlagseite in Graden	Bb
″ ″ ″	Stb

Sonstige Feststellungen

Trimmgewichte	Stck.	kg.	0. Spt.

Spezifisches Gewicht des Seewassers .... γ = ...

Unterdruck im Boot beim Versuch ....

Abb 4

U Boote Bauart VIIC	Fried. Krupp Germaniawerft AG Kiel-Gaarden
Zellenplan und Trimmtabelle	

Tauchzellenflut- und Entlüftungsanl, Abgas-und Notausblaseeinrichtung

Diving Cell Flooding and Ventilation System, Exhaust and Emergency Blow-out Device

In mid-1941, the Royal Navy captured *U-570*, a type VIIC U-boat. The boat was examined, and the intelligence report stated, "great radius of action, high speed on the surface, large torpedo storage, great depth of dive, quickness of dive and reliability."

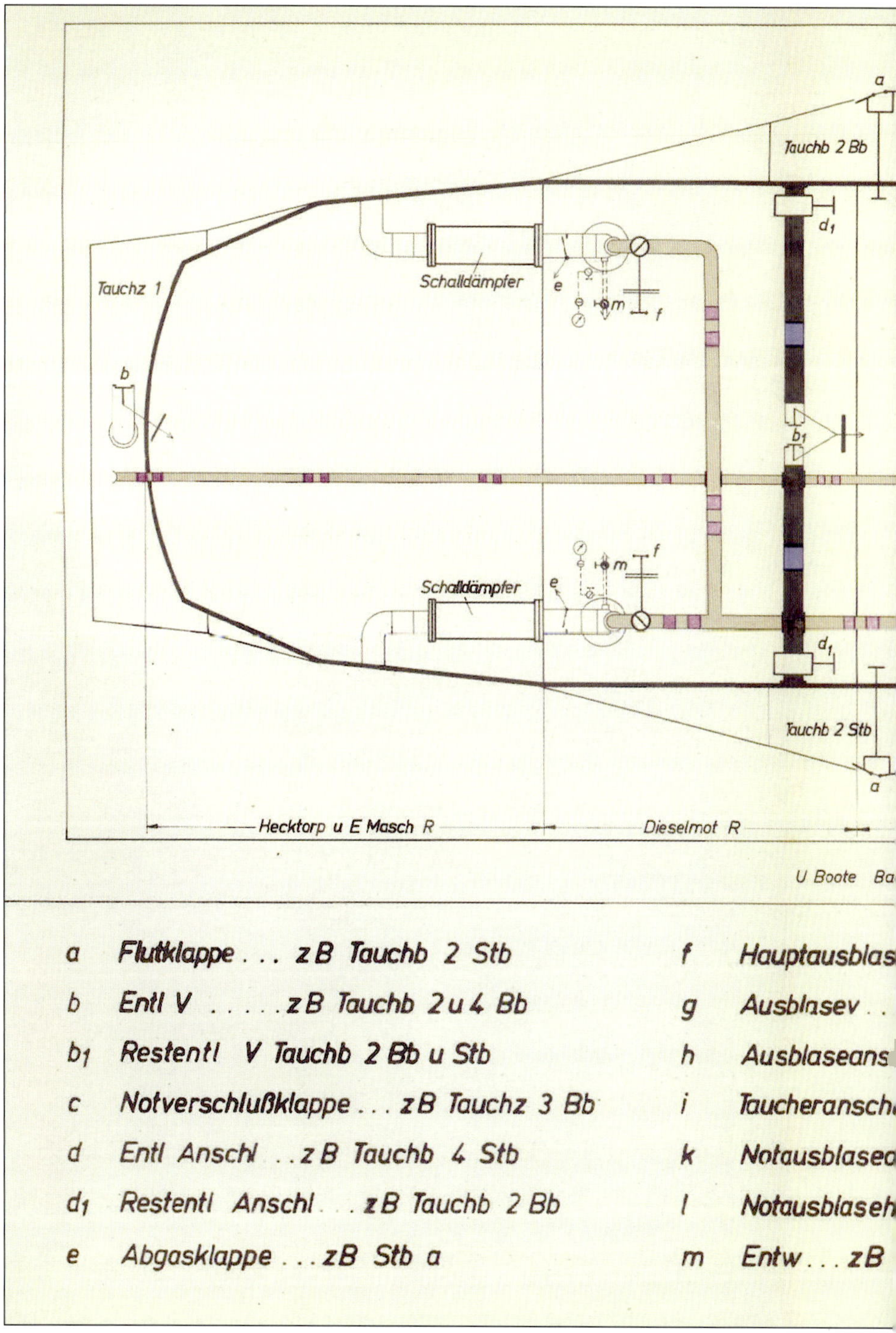

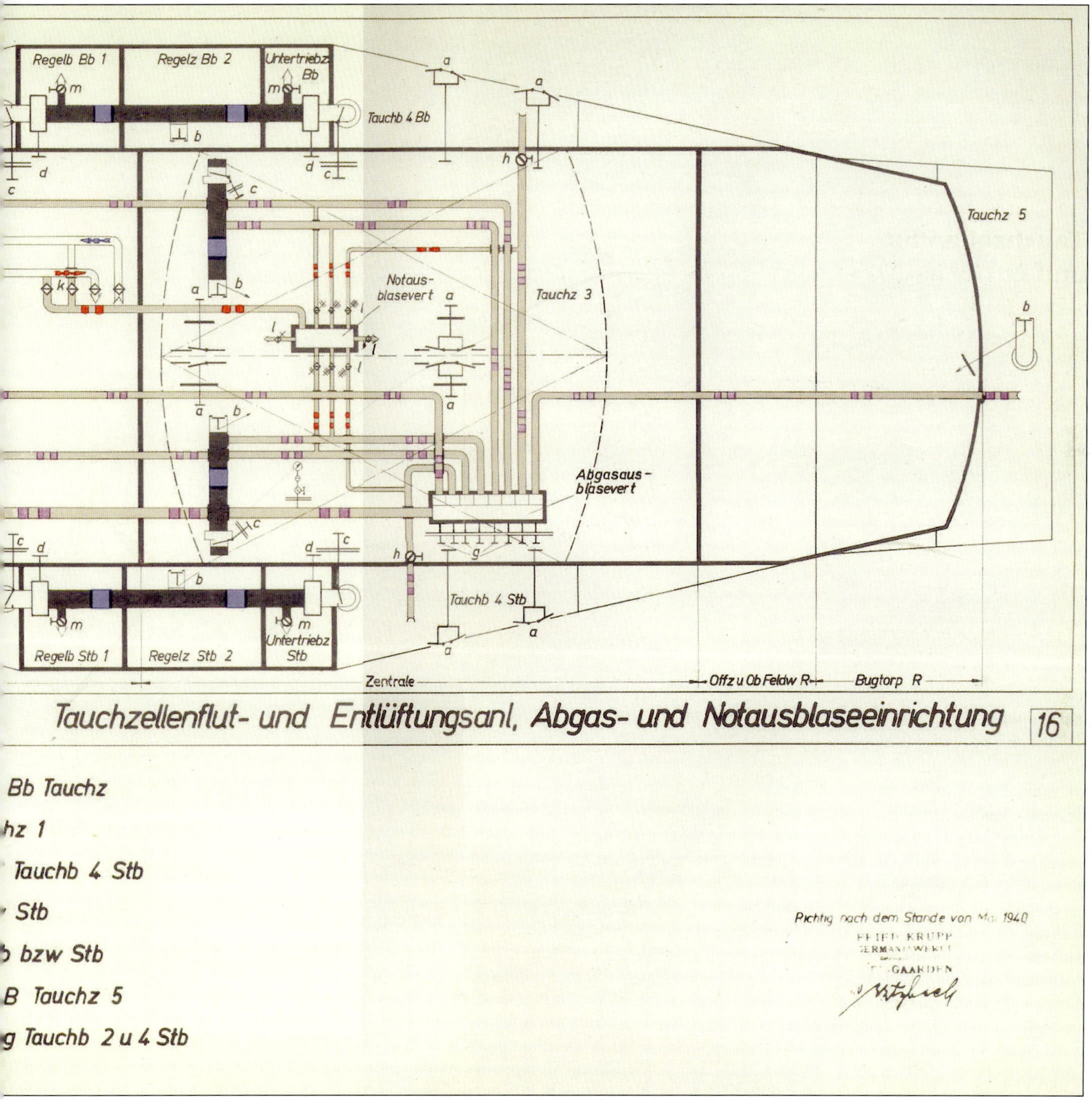
Regelb Bb 1
Regelz Bb 2
Untertriebz Bb
Tauchb 4 Bb
Tauchz 5
Notaus-
blasevert
Tauchz 3
Abgasaus-
blasevert
Tauchb 4 Stb
Regelb Stb 1
Regelz Stb 2
Untertriebz Stb
Zentrale
Offz u Ob Feldw R
Bugtorp R
Tauchzellenflut- und Entlüftungsanl, Abgas- und Notausblaseeinrichtung
16
Bb Tauchz
hz 1
Tauchb 4 Stb
Stb
bzw Stb
B Tauchz 5
g Tauchb 2 u 4 Stb
Richtig nach dem Stande von Mai 1940

Russian Ship Identification Silhouettes

Taken from the Kriegsmarine's *Manual Book for Admiralty Staff Soviet Russia* are two ship identification silhouettes depicting Russian battleships of the *Sevastopol*-class and two heavy cruisers.

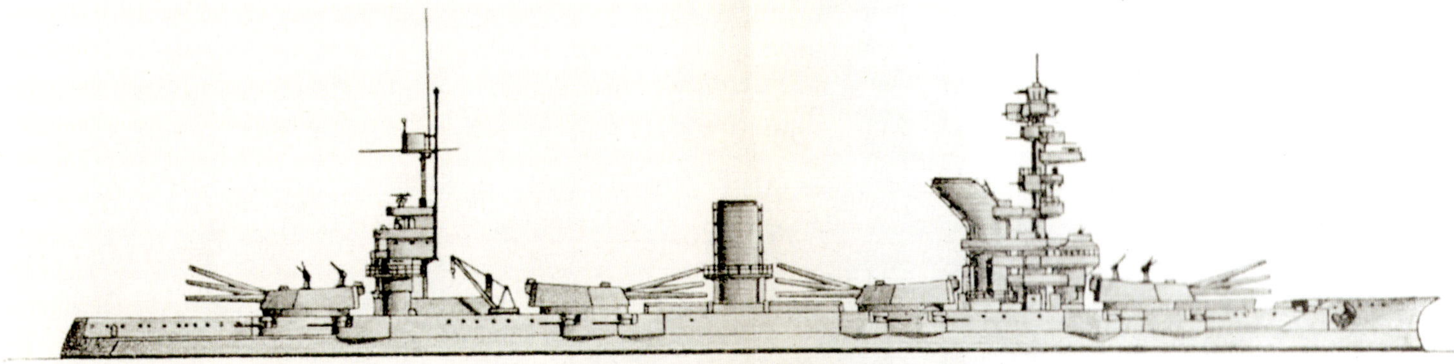

Schl. Sch. »Marat« (Oſtſeeflotte)
Schl. Sch. »Pariſchſkaja Kommuna« (Schwarzmeerflotte)

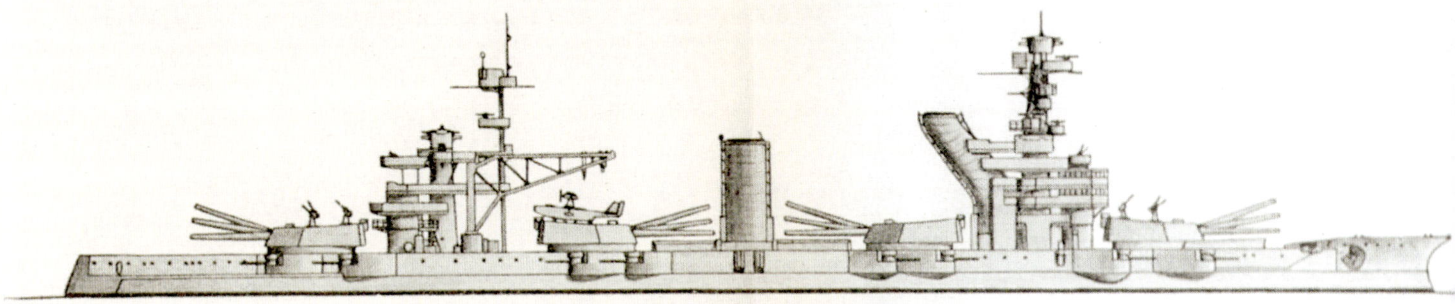

Schl. Sch. »Oktjabrſkaja Revoluzia« (Oſtſeeflotte)

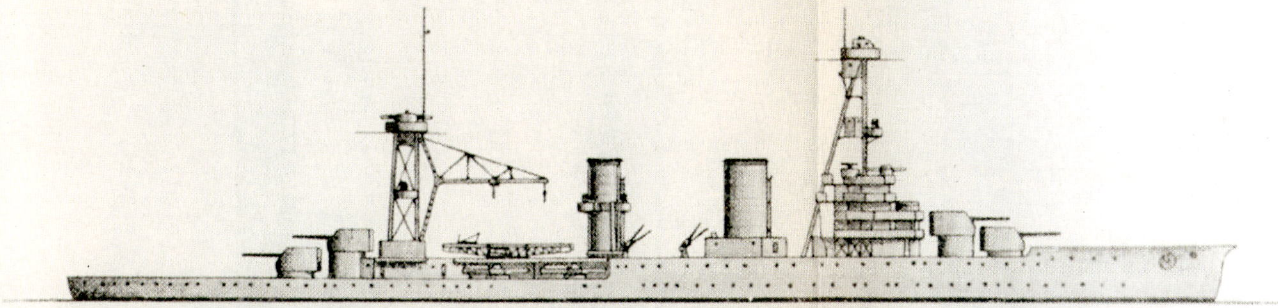

Kreuzer »Krassny Kawkas« (Schwarzmeerflotte)

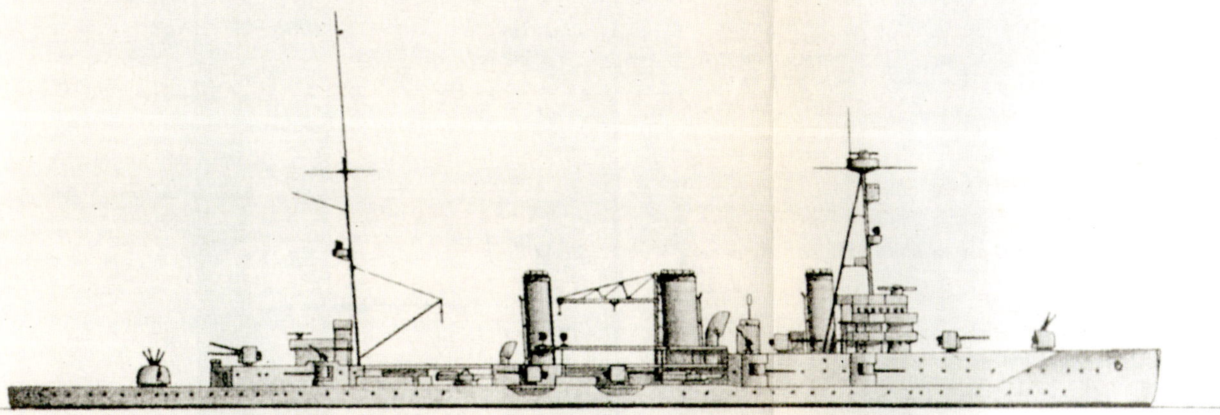

Kreuzer »Profintern« und »Tscherwona Ukraina« (Schwarzmeerflotte)

Northern Artic Sea and Eastern Karelia Map

Two of the most important Allied ports are depicted in this U-Boat map. Both Murmansk and Archangel were vital for the supply of Allied land lease equipment, fuel and food for the Soviet Union, all of which were delivered by sea. During the war, the Allies sent 811 ships in 40 Arctic convoys to the Soviets. Of the cargo, 93 percent arrived safely. Called the 'Suicide Run,' the Allies lost 16 warships and 85 merchantmen during the war. The Kriegsmarine paid a heavy price with the loss of battleships *Tirptiz* and *Scharnhorst*, several destroyers, at least 30 U-boats and over 200 aircraft.

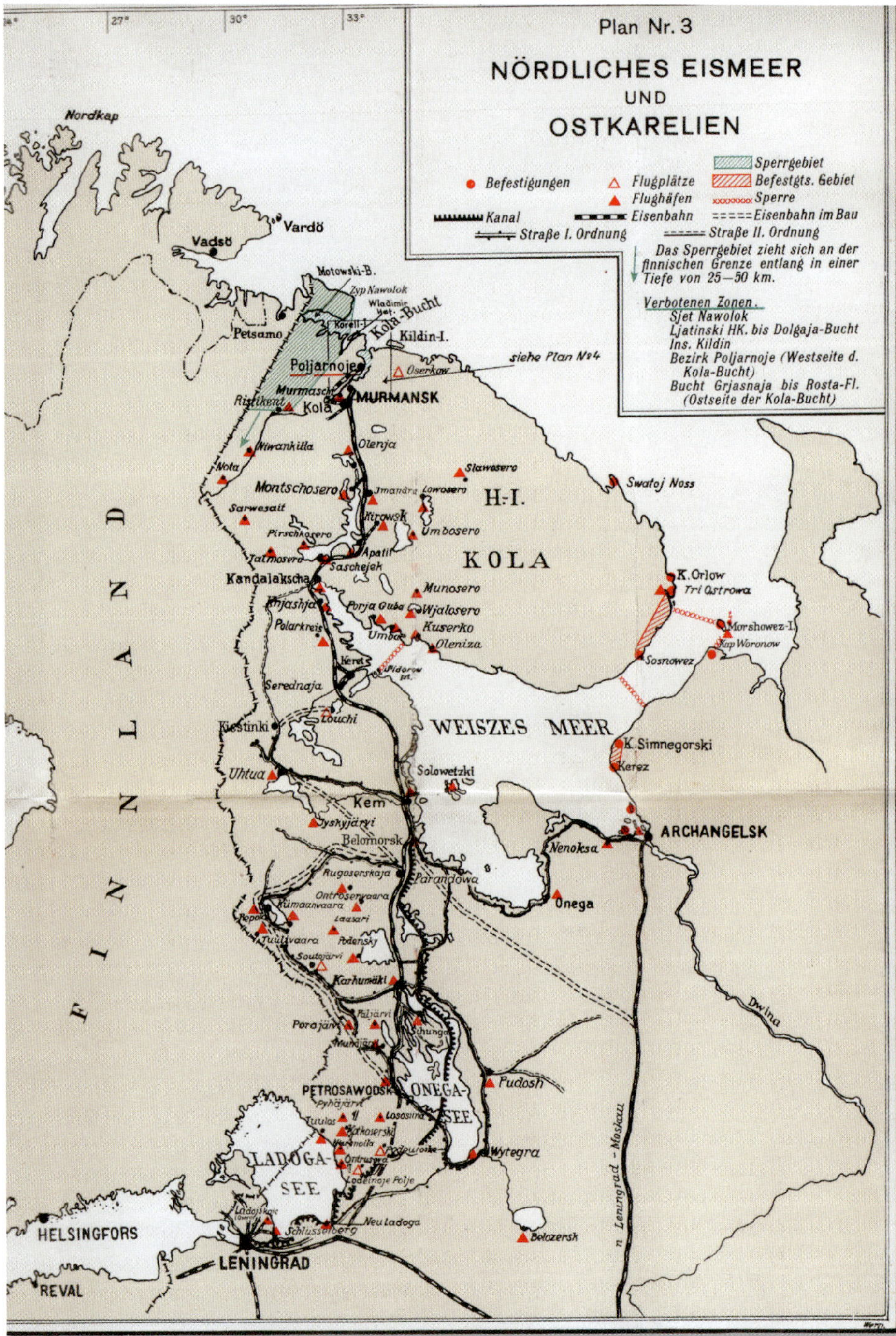

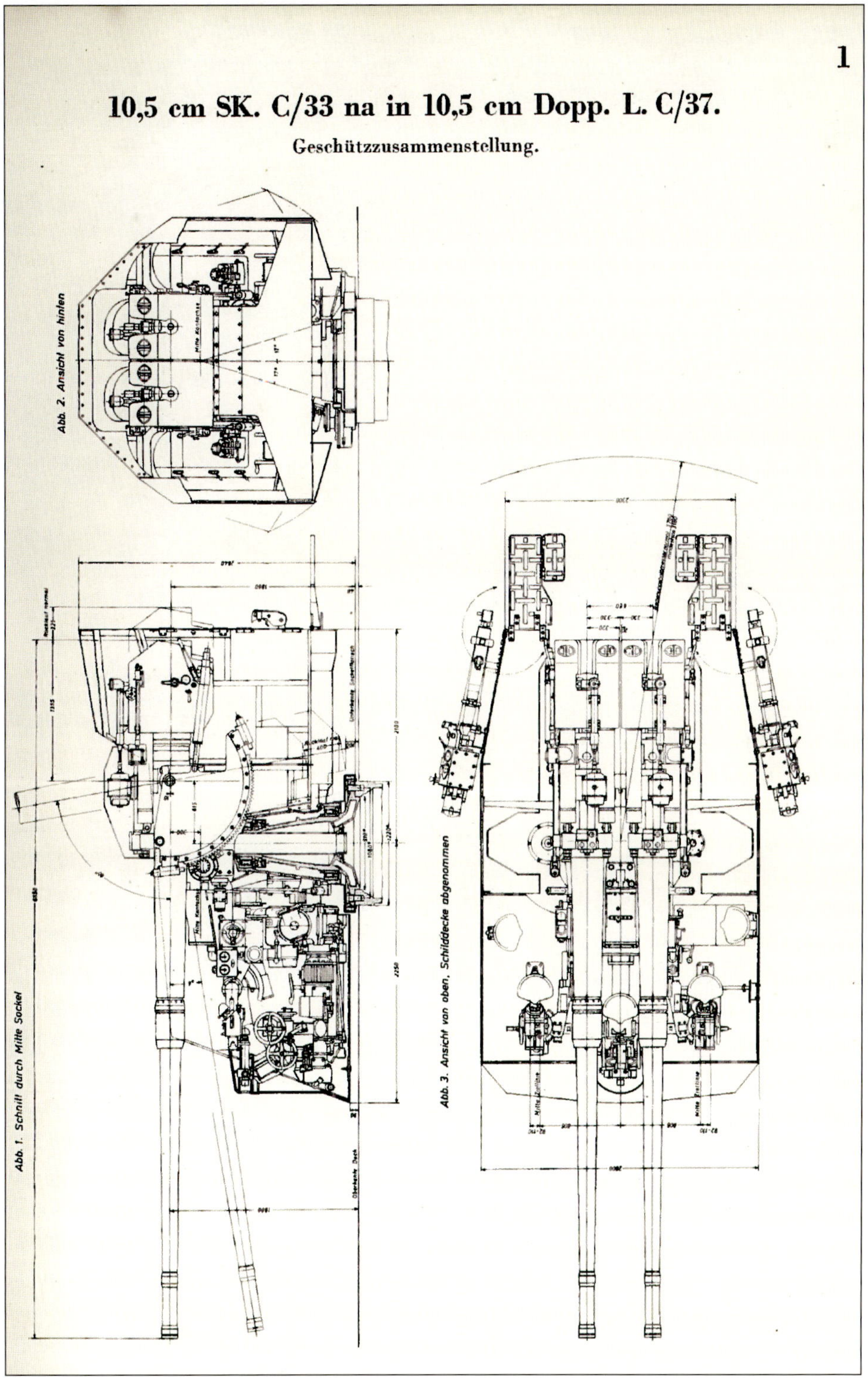

Dimensional Drawing of 10.5 cm/65 SK C/33 Guns

The 10.5 cm was a dual-purpose gun capable of engaging both surface and aircraft. It fired a 15.1 kg (33.3 lb) round and had a maximum rate of fire of 18 rounds per minute. Its maximum surface range was 17.6 kilometers (10.9 miles), with a maximum ceiling of 11,400 meters (37,400 feet). This gun equipped all major Kriegsmarine vessels with the *Bismarck*-class mounting of eight twin mounts. Its job was to lay down a box barrage of heavy flak and to deter enemy torpedo, dive and high-level bombers.

Handbook for Admiral Staff Officers — Kriegsmarine

This Kriegsmarine map clearly identifies the major naval and air bases on the continental United States. Blue areas identify naval bases, blue triangles air bases, green dots naval shipyards, and red boxes private shipyards. German U-boats never attacked U.S. Naval bases directly, but between January and June 1942, U-boats roamed along the eastern seaboard and in the Caribbean, sinking 526 ships.

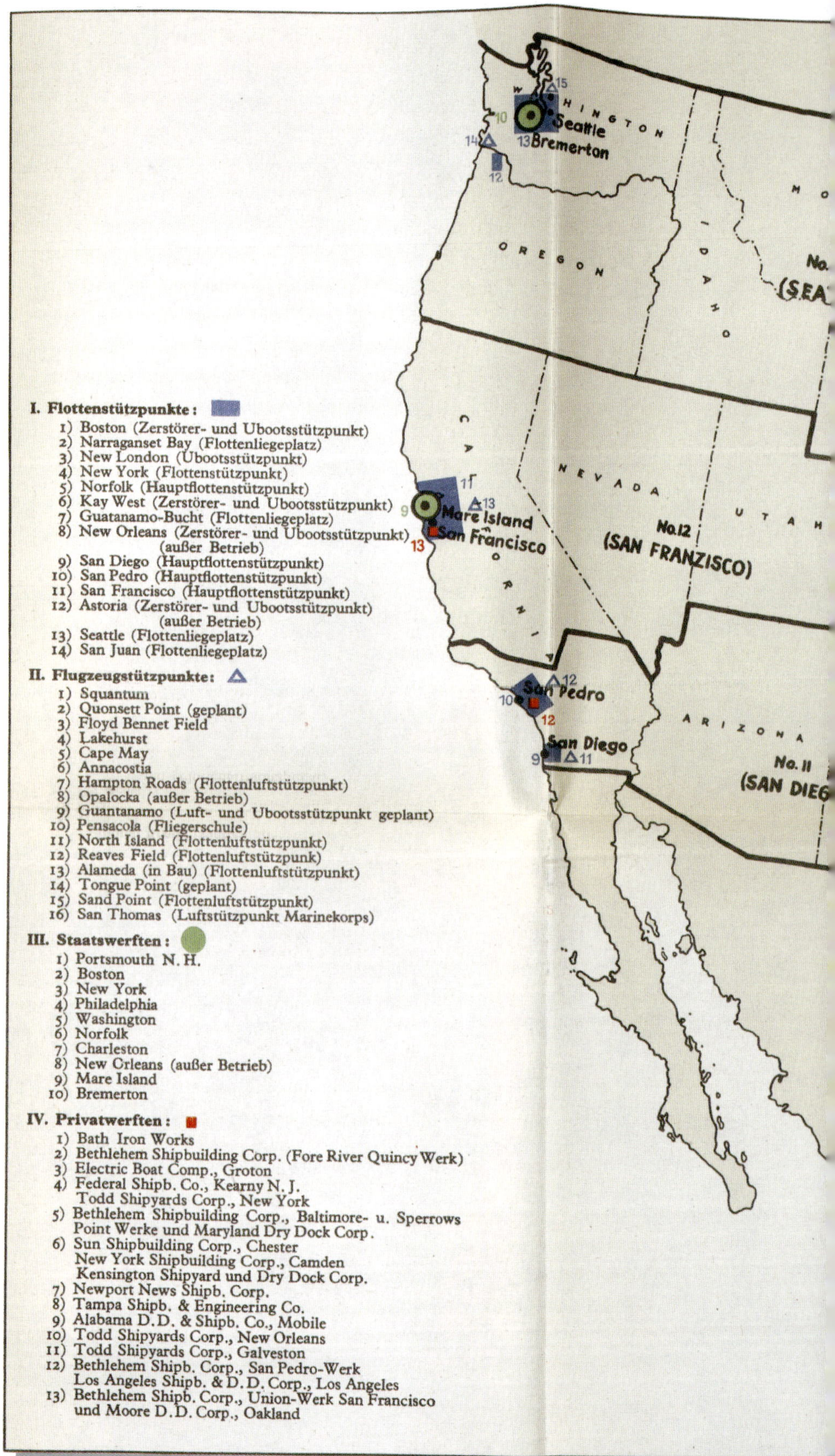

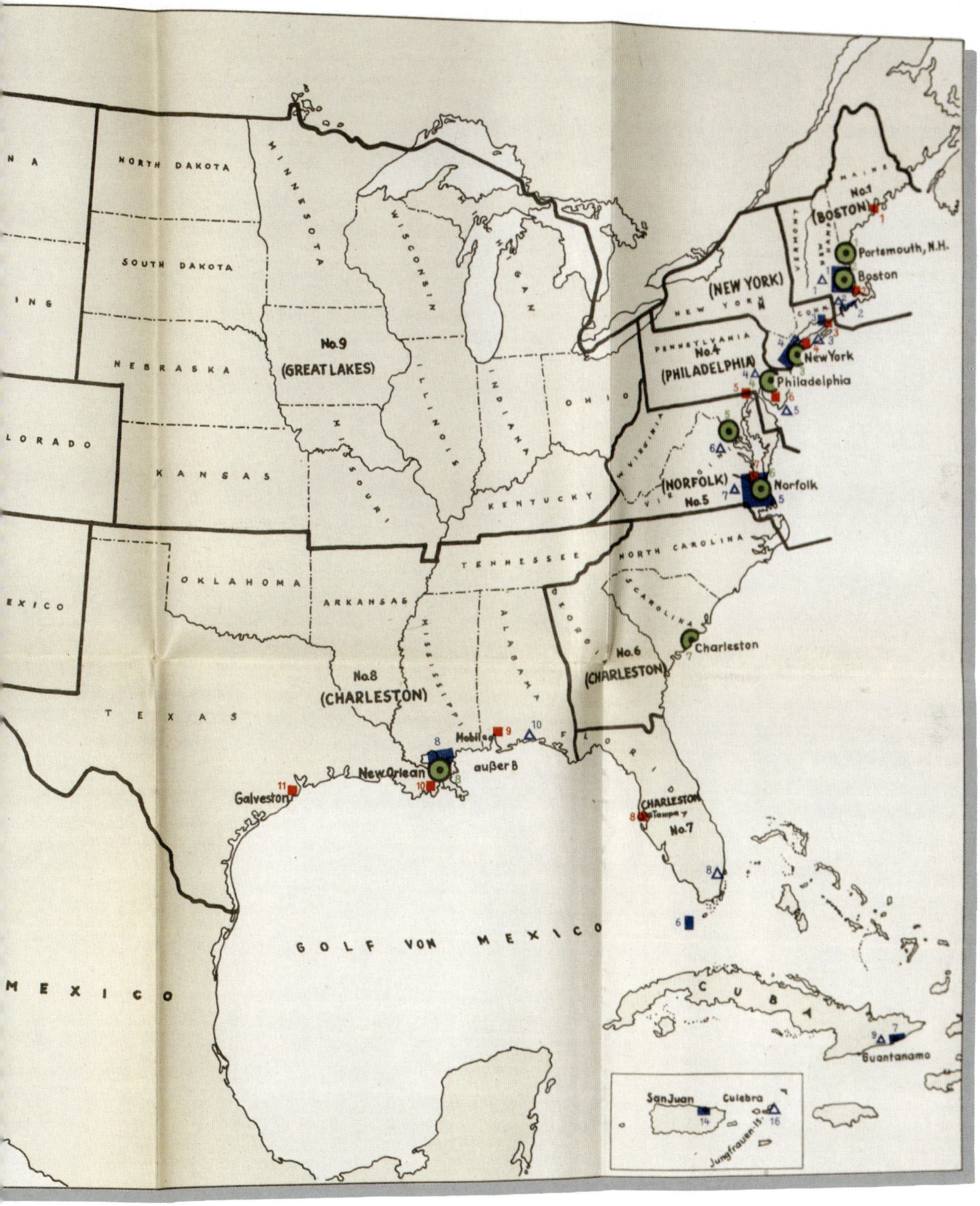
NORTH DAKOTA
SOUTH DAKOTA
NEBRASKA
KANSAS
OKLAHOMA
TEXAS
MINNESOTA
WISCONSIN
MICHIGAN
ILLINOIS
INDIANA
OHIO
KENTUCKY
TENNESSEE
MISSOURI
ARKANSAS
MISSISSIPPI
ALABAMA
GEORGIA
FLORIDA
NORTH CAROLINA
S. CAROLINA
VIRGINIA
W. VIRGINIA
PENNSYLVANIA
NEW YORK
VERMONT
MAINE
No.1
(BOSTON)
Portsmouth, N.H.
Boston
(NEW YORK)
New York
No.4
(PHILADELPHIA)
Philadelphia
(NORFOLK)
No.5
Norfolk
No.6
(CHARLESTON)
Charleston
No.7
CHARLESTON
No.8
(CHARLESTON)
No.9
(GREAT LAKES)
Mobile
New Orlean
außer B
Galveston
GOLF VON MEXICO
MEXICO
CUBA
Guantanamo
San Juan
Culebra
Jungfrauen-I.

East Coast of North America, Watch Hill Until Monmouth Beach: Important Defense Facilities U-boat Map

Map Index in order:

- Station Command
- 1st Order Naval Port
- 2nd Order Naval Port
- Fleet Training Areas
- Destroyer Base
- Section Base
- Auxiliary Naval Base
- Sea Pilot Training Area
- Private Shipyard
- Torpedo Station
- Torpedo Storage
- Ammunition Storage
- Barrier Weapons Depot
- Fuel Storage
- Radio Direction Finding Station
- Signal Station
- Submarine Base
- Sea Aviation Base
- Naval Arsenal
- Radio Station
- State Shipyard
- Coast Guard Station
- Coast Guard District
- Sea Flight Facilities

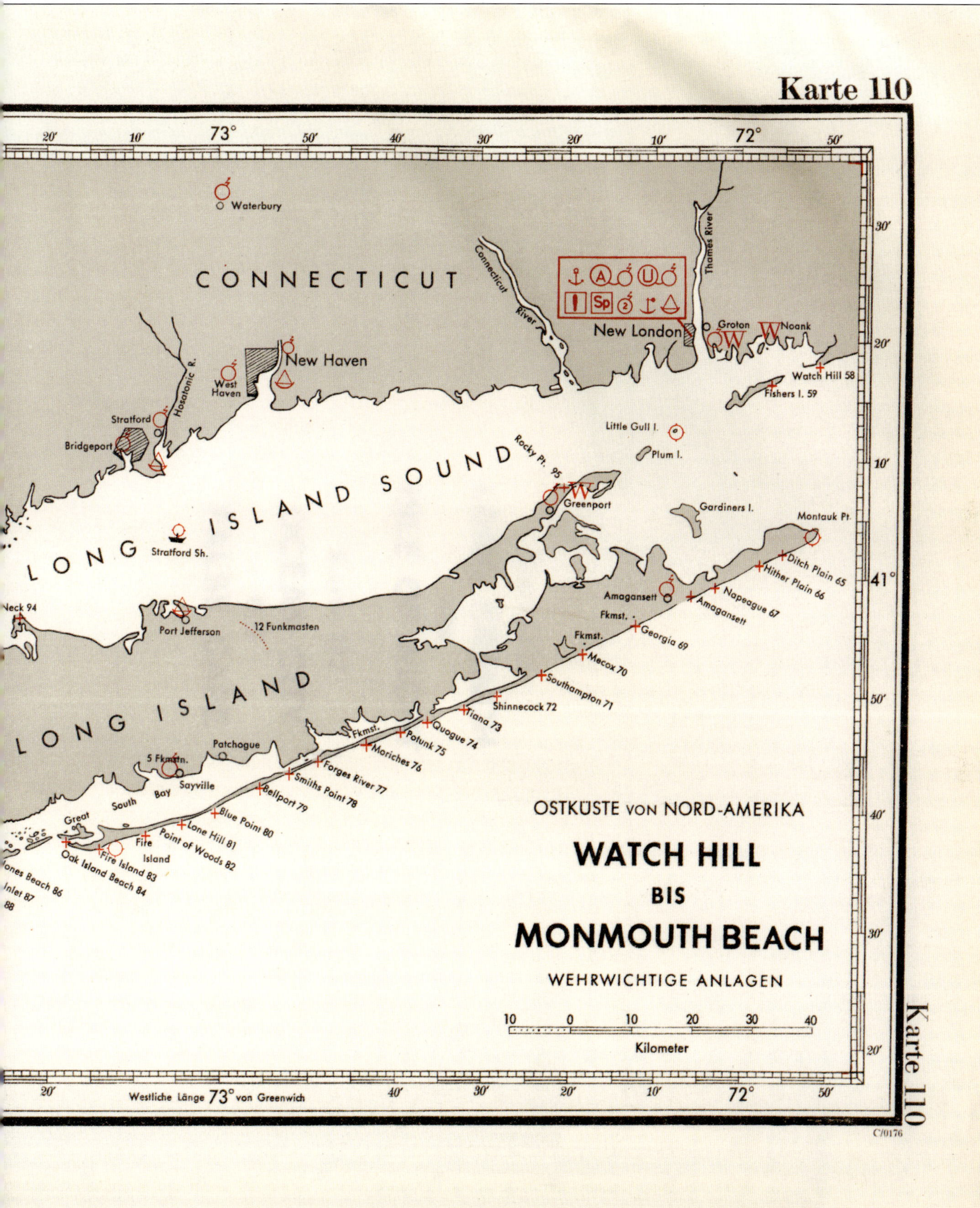
Karte 110
73°
72°
Waterbury
CONNECTICUT
Connecticut River
Thames River
New London
Groton
Noank
New Haven
West Haven
Housatonic R.
Stratford
Bridgeport
Watch Hill 58
Fishers I. 59
Little Gull I.
Plum I.
Rocky Pt. 95
Greenport
Gardiners I.
Montauk Pt.
LONG ISLAND SOUND
Stratford Sh.
Neck 94
Port Jefferson
12 Funkmasten
Ditch Plain 65
Hither Plain 66
Napeague 67
Amagansett
Fkmst.
Georgia 69
Mecox 70
Southampton 71
Shinnecock 72
Tiana 73
Quogue 74
Potunk 75
Moriches 76
Forges River 77
Smiths Point 78
Bellport 79
Blue Point 80
Lone Hill 81
Point of Woods 82
Fire Island 83
Oak Island Beach 84
Jones Beach 86
Inlet 87
88
LONG ISLAND
Patchogue
5 Fkmstn.
Sayville
South Bay
Great South Bay
Fire Island
41°
OSTKÜSTE VON NORD-AMERIKA
WATCH HILL
BIS
MONMOUTH BEACH
WEHRWICHTIGE ANLAGEN
10 0 10 20 30 40
Kilometer
Westliche Länge 73° von Greenwich
C/0176

St. Lorenz and Surrounding Area U-boat Map

This Kriegsmarine navigation map highlights the various coastal locations of importance in and around the Gulf of St. Lawrence and St. Lawrence River all the way to Quebec City. U-boats were most successful when they preyed on the weak and unprotected. Beginning in 1942, U-boats entered the Gulf of St. Lawrence and St. Lawrence River in pursuit of unescorted shipping. In total, 23 merchant and warships would be lost before The Gulf Escort Force was organized in June. This example was recovered from *U-190* after it surrendered in May 1945.

Map index in order:

- Planned coastal fortifications
- Coastal fortifications
- Coastal radio station
- Signal point
- Planned air base
- Civil airport
- Civilian transport

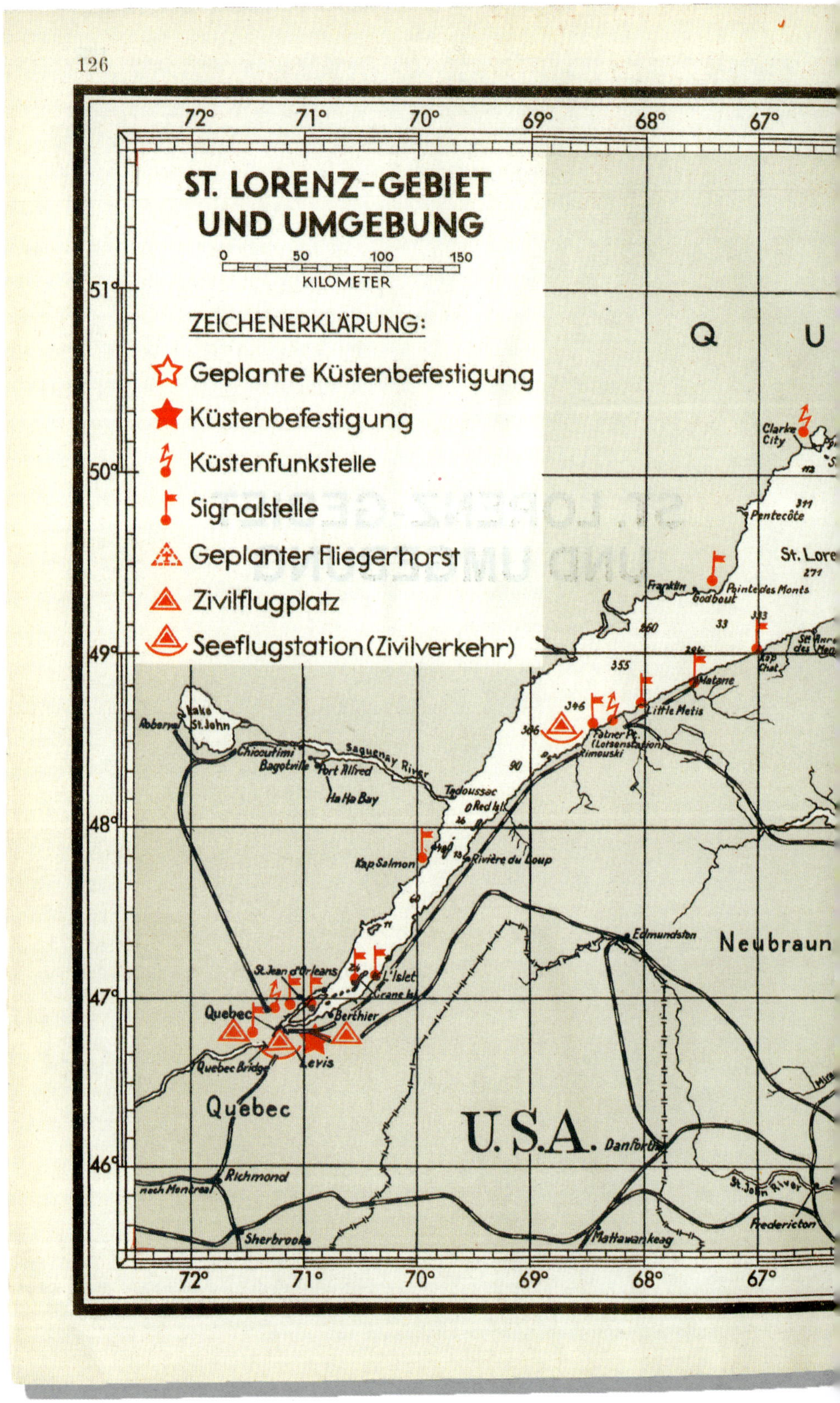

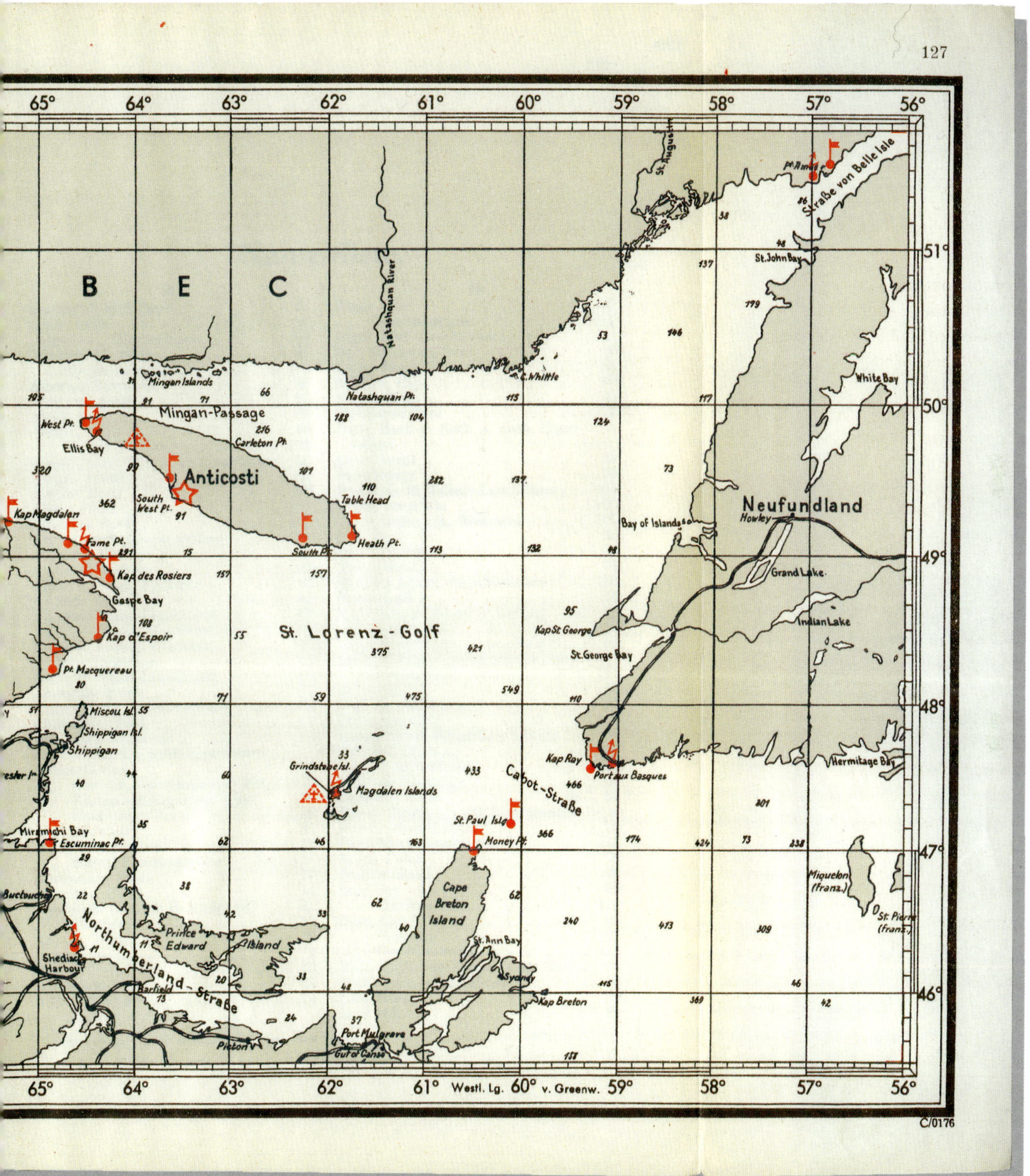
127
B E C
Mingan Islands
Mingan-Passage
Anticosti
West Pt.
Ellis Bay
South West Pt.
Carleton Pt.
Table Head
South Pt.
Heath Pt.
Natashquan River
Natashquan Pt.
C. Whittle
Kap Magdalen
Fame Pt.
Kap des Rosiers
Gaspe Bay
Kap d'Espoir
Pt. Macquereau
St. Lorenz - Golf
Miscou Isl.
Shippigan Isl.
Shippigan
Grindstone Isl.
Magdalen Islands
Cabot-Straße
St. Paul Isl.
Money Pt.
Miramichi Bay
Escuminac Pt.
Buctouche
Shediac Harbour
Northumberland-Straße
Prince Edward Island
Barfield
Pictou
Cape Breton Island
St. Ann Bay
Sydney
Kap Breton
Port Mulgrave
Gut of Canso
Straße von Belle Isle
Pt. Amour
St. John Bay
White Bay
Neufundland
Howley
Bay of Islands
Grand Lake
Indian Lake
Kap St. George
St. George Bay
Kap Ray
Port aux Basques
Hermitage Bay
Miquelon (franz.)
St. Pierre (franz.)
Westl. Lg. v. Greenw.
C/0176

Ventilation Section III-X, Upper Decks on the Heavy Cruiser *Prinz Eugen*

The *Prinz Eugen* was a *Hipper*-class heavy cruiser and was armed with a main battery of eight 203 mm guns in four twin-turrets and a secondary armament of 12 twin-mounted 105 mm guns. Like all major warships, ventilation was a critical function for the efficiency of the crew, engines and other heat-generating mechanicals. A good ventilations system must provide a continuous renewal of fresh air to the various spaces of the ship. It must also remove the products of combustion and the gaseous materials thrown off by the occupants and the stores of the vessel.

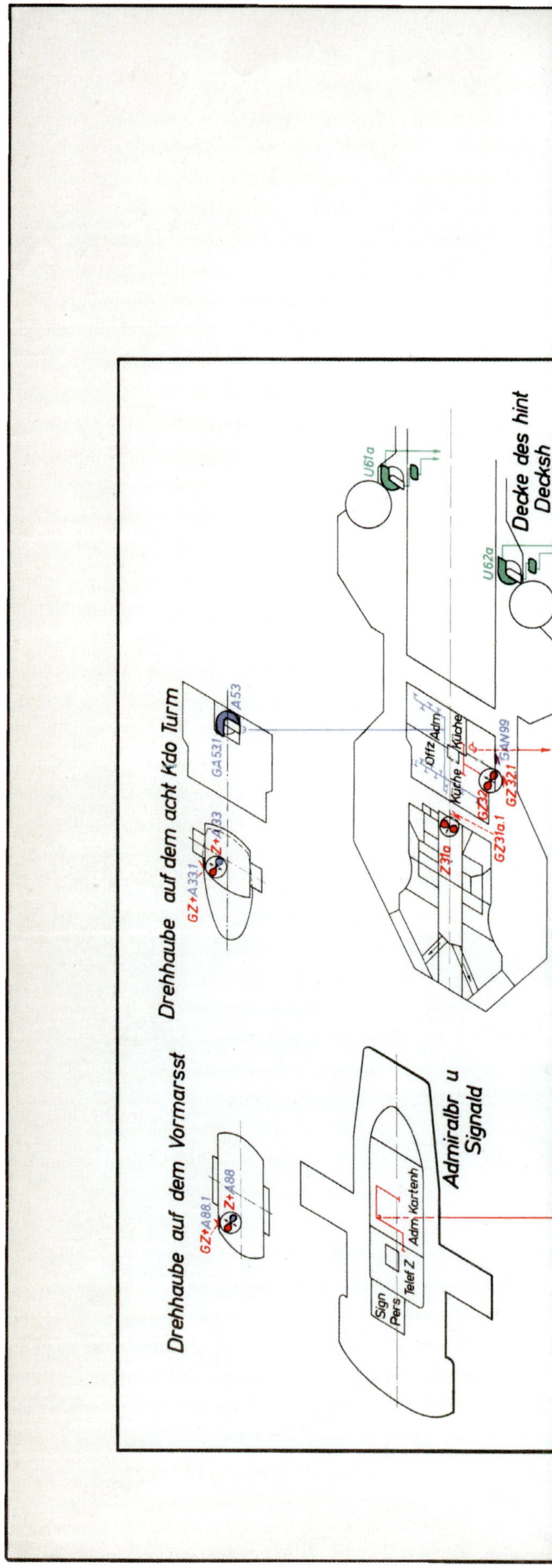

Kreuzer „Prinz Eugen"	Lüftung Abt. III—X obere Decks	11
Beschreibung und Betriebsvorschrift		

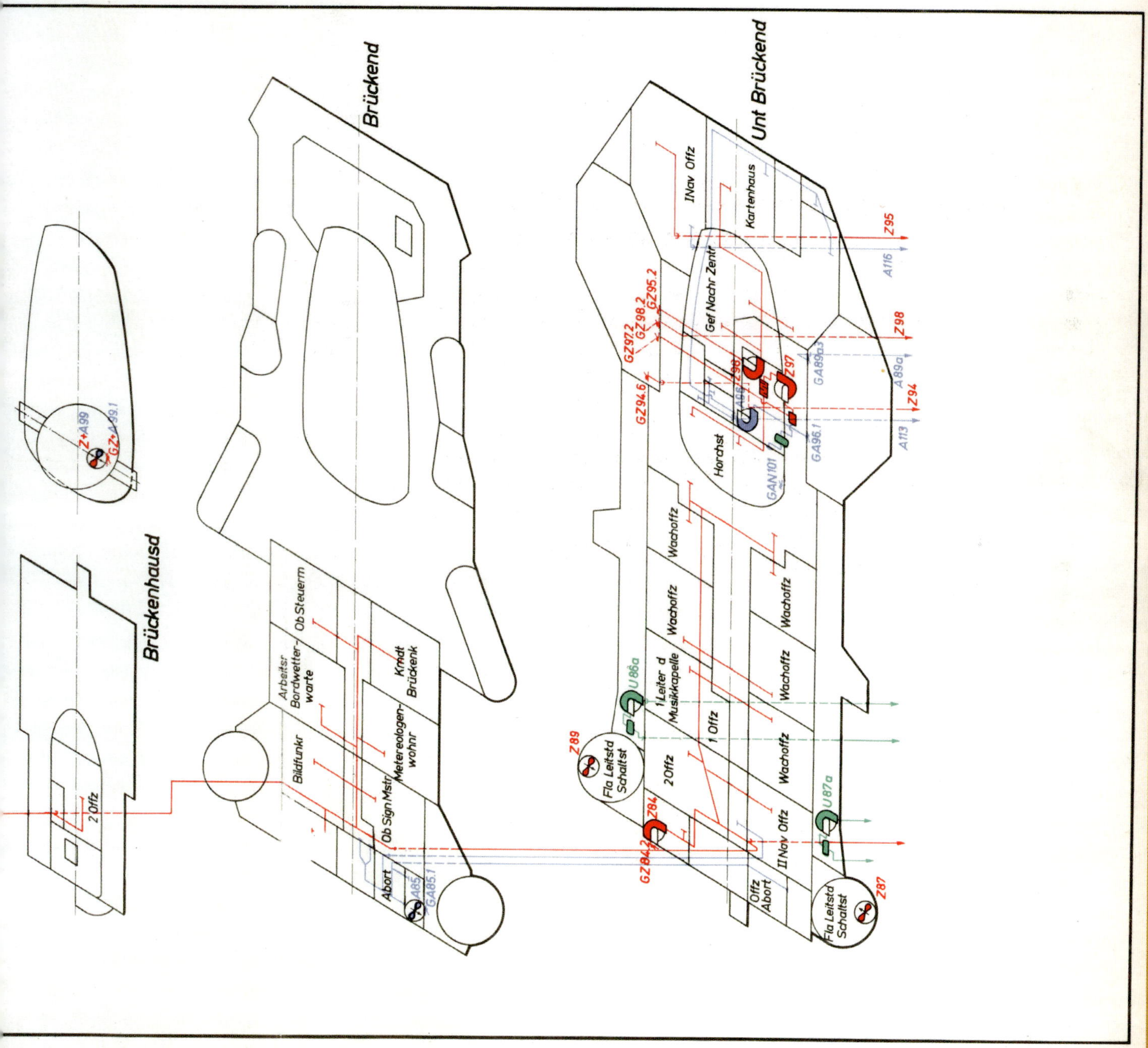

Kreuzer „Prinz Eugen" Lüftung Abt. III—X obere Decks 11

Routes of the USA, Upper Sea Merchant Shipping, August 1939

This Kriegsmarine map details the main shipping routes of American shipping companies prior to the outbreak of war in Europe. The heaviest traffic is along the American eastern seaboard and Caribbean, followed by the North Atlantic. On May 27, 1941, the U.S. Navy established the Neutrality Patrol (the sea lines between Iceland and the Atlantic Seaboard) to aid Britain and excluded all German and Italian warships and aircraft from that zone. That put the U.S. on a war footing, and on September 4, 1941, the destroyer USS *Greer* exchanged fire with *U-562*, a Type VIIC U-boat.

16 Lykes Bros.-Ripley Steamship Co.
Atlantik, Pazifik, Golf v. Mexiko, Ostsee, Mittelländ. Meer
17 Matson Line
Nord-Pazifik
18 Mobile Oceanic Line (Waterman)
Nord-Atlantik, Golf von Mexiko
19 N. Y. & Cuba Mail S. S. Co (A. G. W. I.)
Nord-Atlantik, Golf von Mexiko, Caraibisches Meer
20 American Hawaiian Steamship Co.
Nord- u. Süd-Pazifik
21 Pacifik Argentine Brazil Line (Mc Cormick)
Nord- u. Süd-Atlantik, Pazifik
22 Panama R. R. Steamship Line
Nord-Atlantik, Caraibisches Meer
23 Porto Rico Line (A. G. W. I.)
Nord-Atlantik, Golf von Mexiko, Caraibisches Meer
24 Robin Line
Nord- u. Süd-Atlantik, Indischer Ozean
25 South Atlantic S. S. Line
Nord-Atlantik
26 United Fruit Co.
Nord-Atlantik, Nord-Pazifik, Caraibisches Meer
27 United States Lines
Nord-Atlantik
28 Waterman Line
Golf von Mexiko, Caraibisches Meer
29 Oriole Lines (Southgate Nelson)
Nord-Atlantik
EUROPA
ASIEN
AFRIKA
SÜD-AMERIKA
AUSTRALIEN
Grönland
Grönland-See

Englische und franzosische Kriegsmarined August 1940 (English and French navies, August 1940)

These British ship identification drawings are taken from the Kriegsmarine's 'English and French Warship Appendix, August 1940.' At the time the German Luftwaffe and Royal Air Force were fighting the Battle of Britain over the English Channel and southern England. The Germans were planning a seaborne invasion of Britain, but it was highly unlikely. At the time the Kriegsmarine had just one heavy cruiser (*Admiral Hipper*) two light cruisers, seven destroyers and 22 U-boats for the planned invasion. In response the Royal Navy had five battleships, two carriers (many detailed here), 13 cruisers and 69 destroyers ready to interdict any invasion attempt. The RN ship identification silhouettes include HMS *Nelson*, *Warspite*, *Ramilies*, *Repulse*, *Hood*, *Ark Royal*, *Furious*, *York* and *Devonshire*.

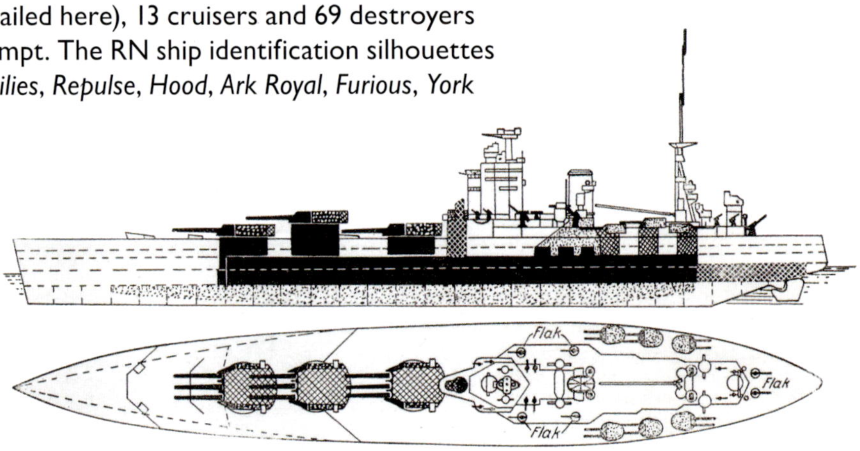

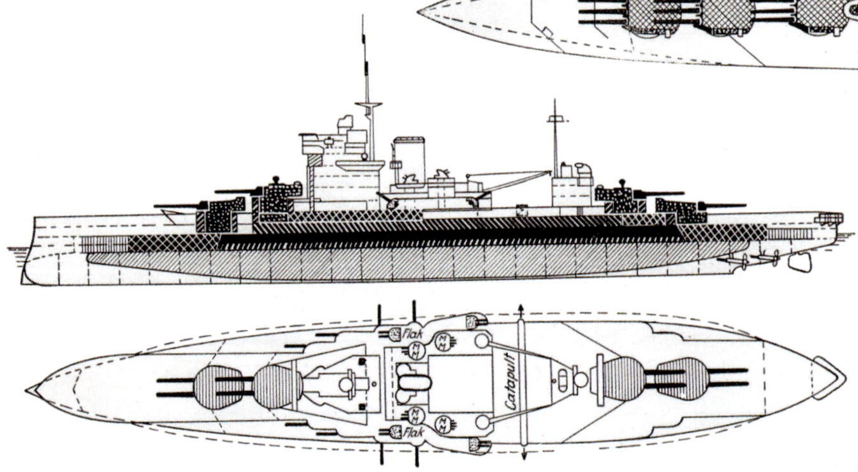

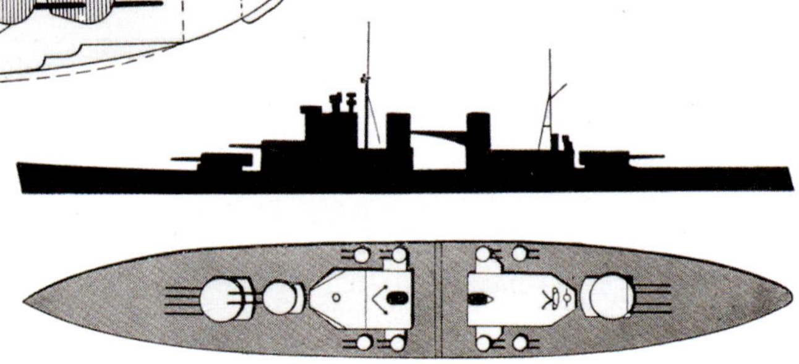

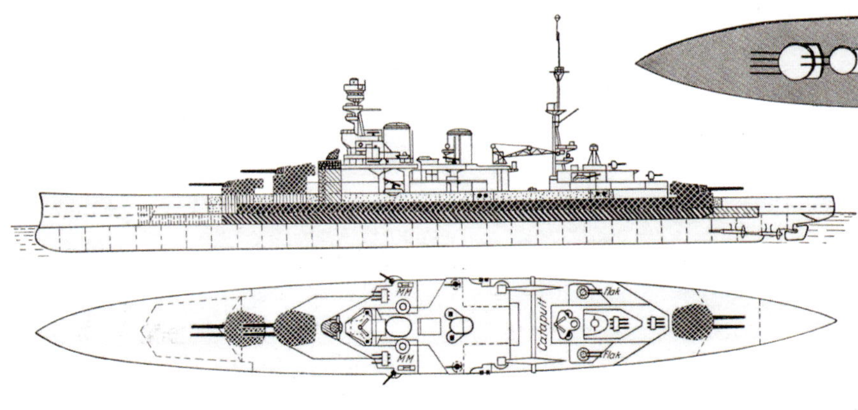

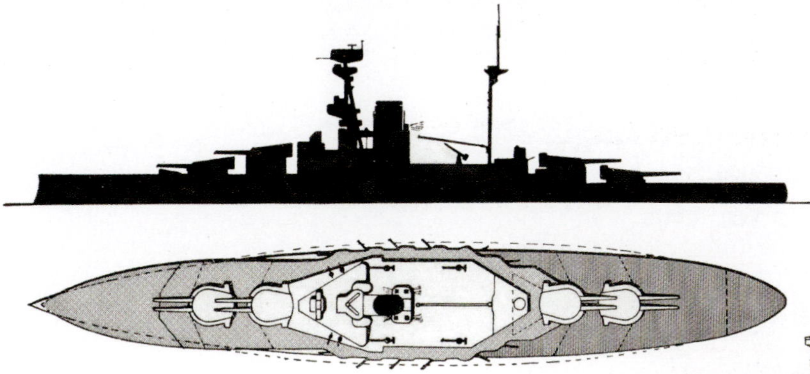

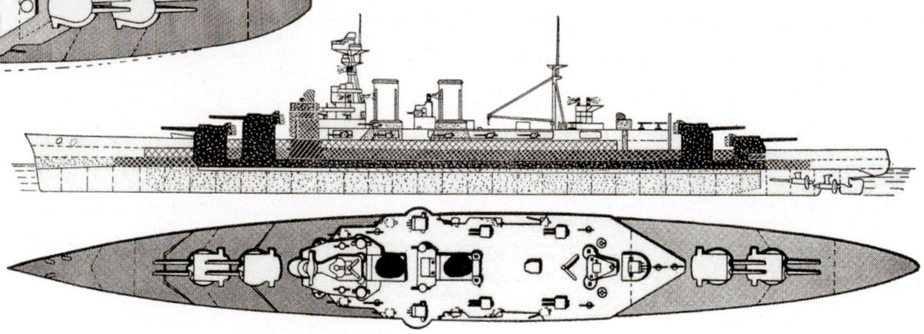

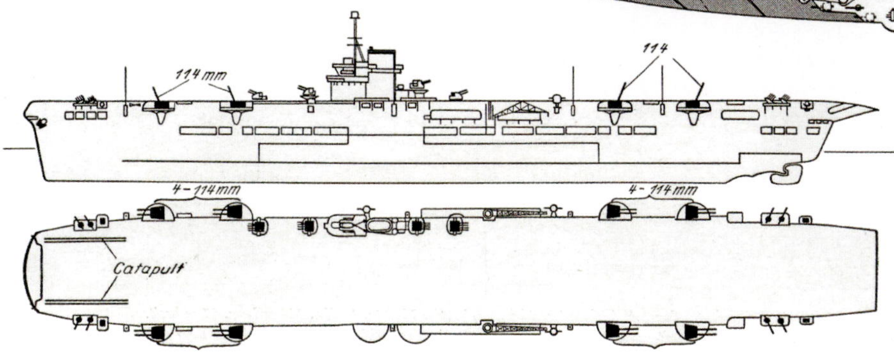
114 mm
114
4-114mm
4-114mm
Catapult

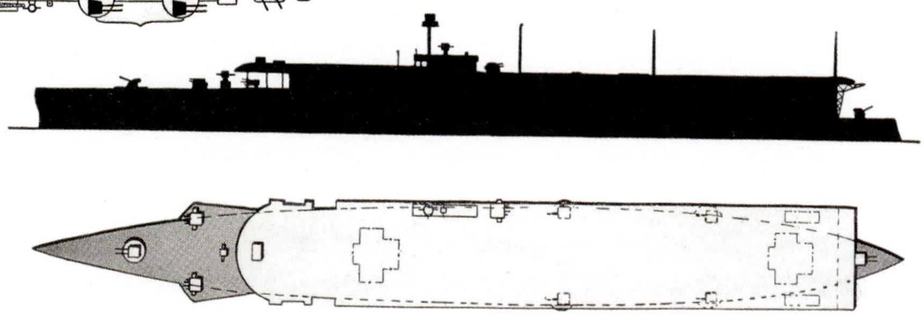

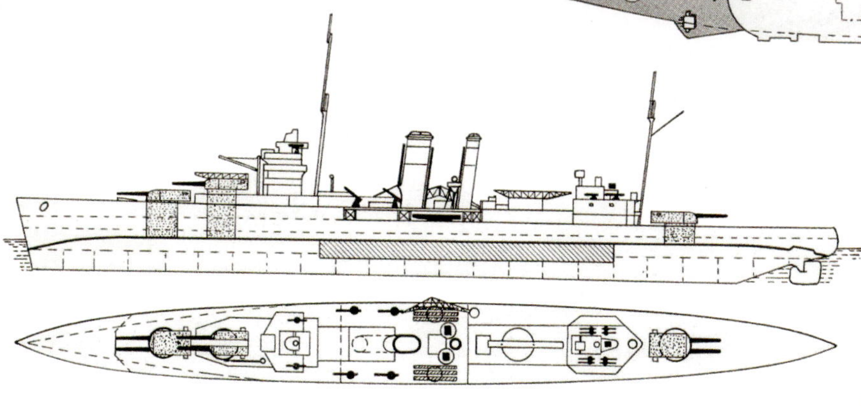

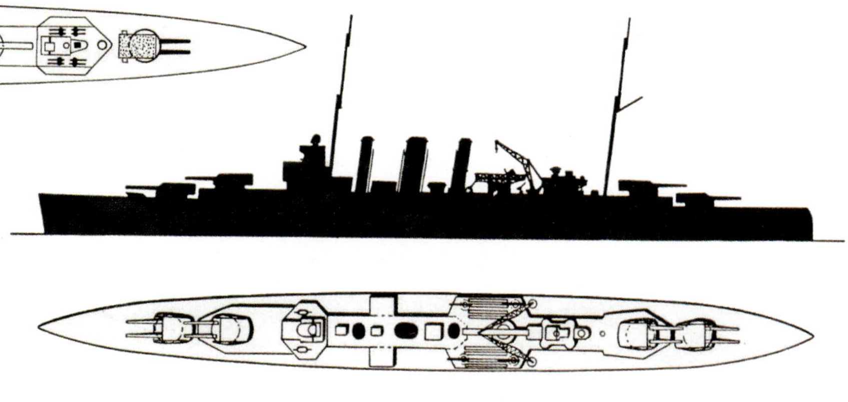

Munitionsborfchriften fur die Kriegsmarine Artillerie (Ammunition documents for the Kriegsmarine artillery No. 149)

The 10.5 cm gun was used primarily as an AA weapon on Kriegsmarine capitol ships and cruisers. It was also used on the Type IX U-boat. It fired both high-explosive shells with instantaneous impact fuses and with AA time fuses.

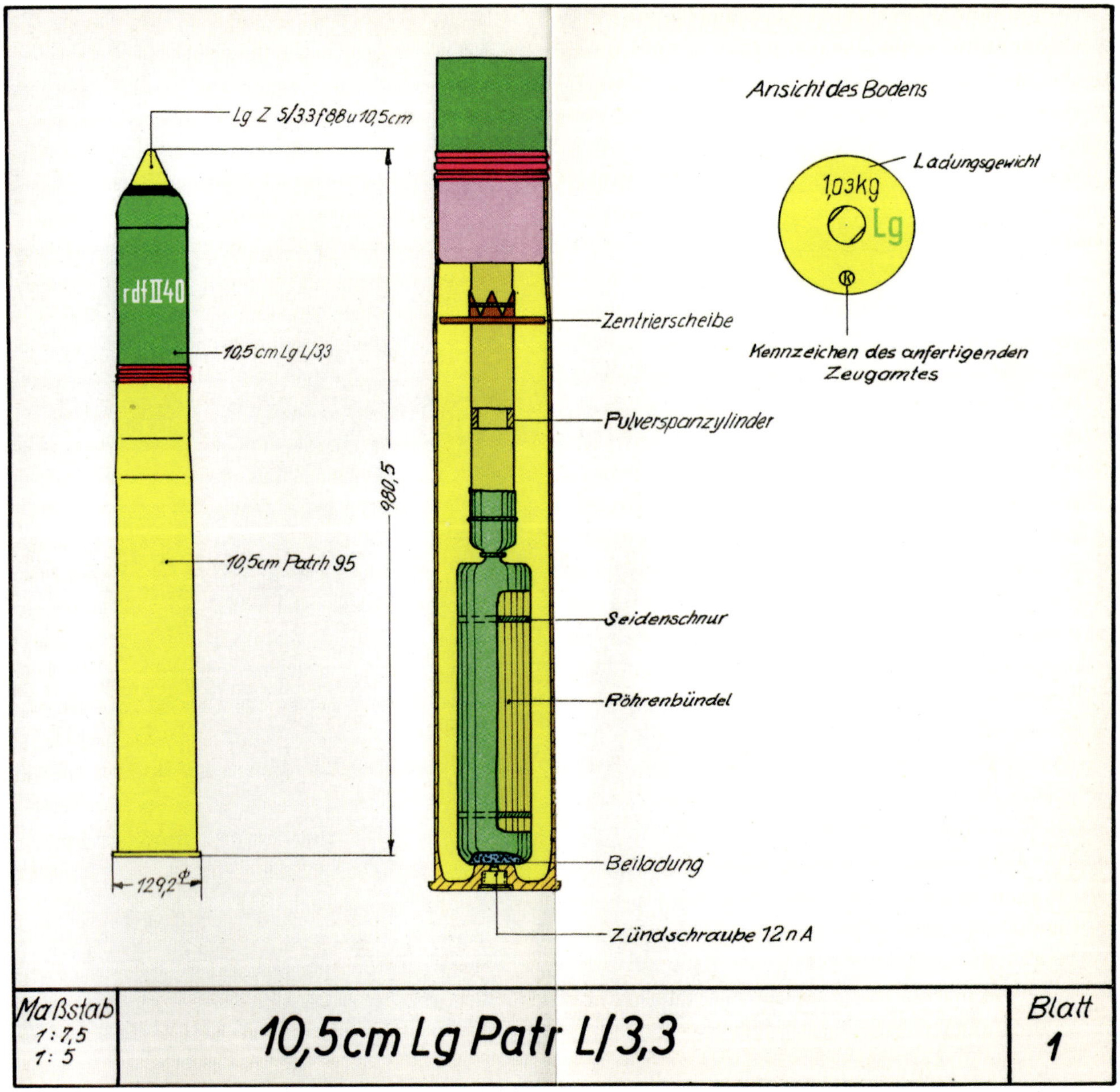

Munitionsborfchriften fur die Kriegsmarine Artillerie (Ammunition documents for the Kriegsmarine artillery No. 149)

One of the most widely produced artillery shells used by the German armed forces was the 8.8 cm round. It was used by the Luftwaffe for AA defence, the Wehrmacht in the anti-tank and artillery role and Kriegsmarine as a U-boat deck gun. The Type VII U-boat was armed with one 8.8 cm deck gun and carried 220 rounds.

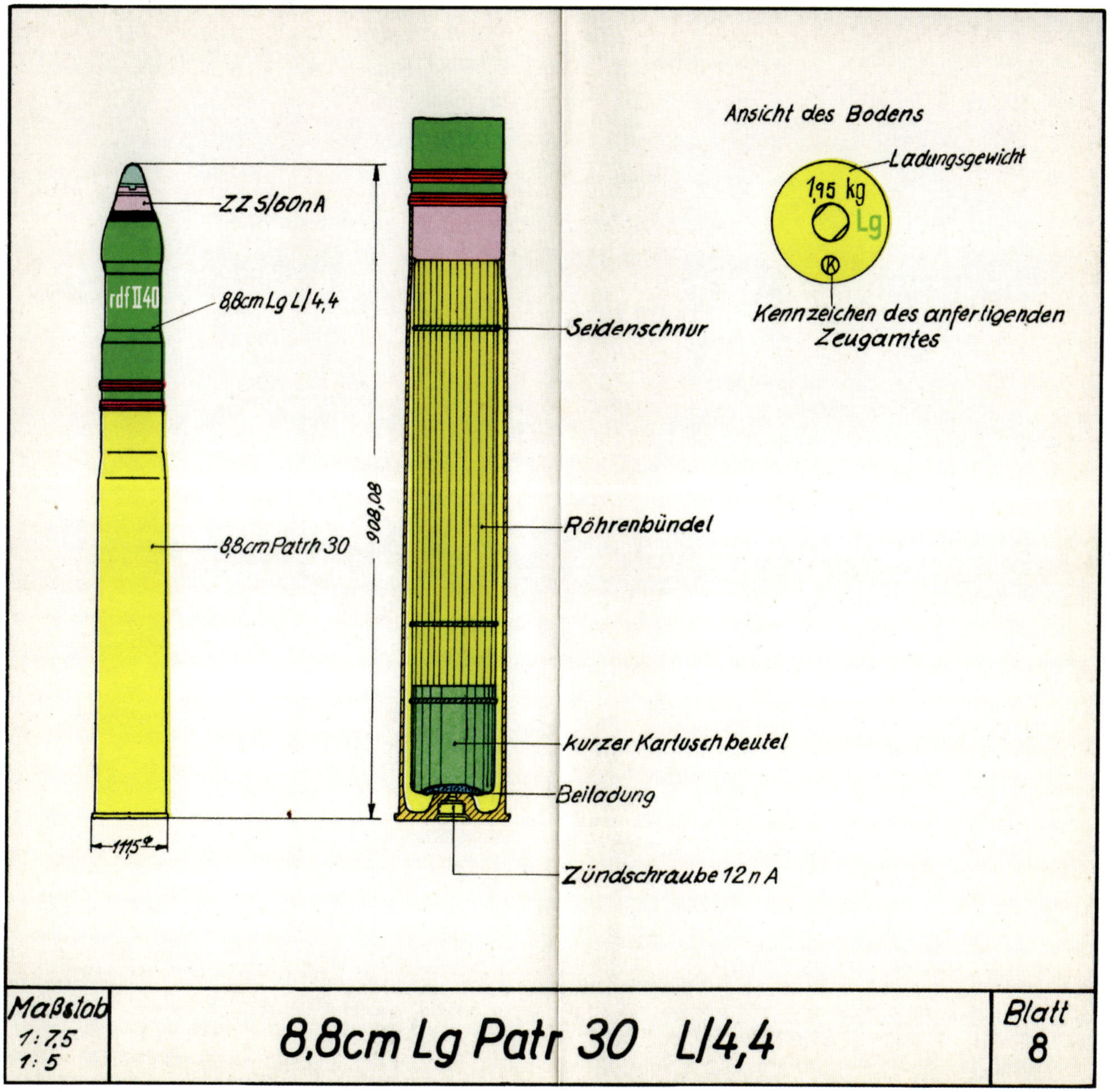

Bibliography

Bekker, Cajus, *Hitler's Naval War*, London (1974)

B.R.224/45, *The Gunnery Pocketbook 1945* (Gunnery Branch, Admiralty, London, June 1945)

Bishop, Patrick, *Target Tirpitz: The Epic Quest to Destroy Hitler's Mightiest Warship*, London (2012)

Beaver, Paul, *The British Aircraft Carrier*, Patrick Stephens, London (1982)

Brown, J. David, *Carrier Operations in World War II: Vol. 1*, Ian Allan, London (1974)

Burt, R.A. *British Battleships 1919–1945*. Annapolis, MD: Naval Institute Press. (2012)

Campbell, John, *Naval Weapons of World War Two* (Naval Institute Press, Annapolis, 2002)

Chesneau, Roger, *Aircraft Carriers of the World, 1914 to the Present: An Illustrated Encyclopaedia*, London (1992)

Friedman, Norman, *U.S. Submarines Through 1945*, Naval Institute Press, Annapolis, (1995)

Friedman, Norman (2008). *Naval Firepower: Battleship Guns and Gunnery on the Battleship Era*. Annapolis, MD: Naval Institute Press.

Friedman, Norman, *Naval Anti-Aircraft Guns and Gunnery* (Seaforth Publishing, Barnsley, 2013)

Friedman, Norman, *U.S. Aircraft Carriers*, Naval Institute Press (Annapolis, Maryland, 1983)

Herder, Brian, World War II Fast Carriers Task Force Tactics 1943–45 (Osprey 2020)

Hobbs, David, *British Aircraft Carriers – Design, Development and Service Histories* (Seaforth Publishing, Barnsley, 2017)

Konstam, Angus, Sink the Tirpitz 1942-44 The RAF and Fleet Air Arm Duel with Germany's Mighty Battleship (Osprey 2018)

Lardas, Mark, US Destroyers vs German U-Boats the Atlantic 1941–45 (Osprey 2023)

Lavery, Brian. *Churchill's Navy: The Ships, Men and Organisation 1939–1945*. London: Conway. (2006)

Lenton, H.T., *German Warships of the Second World War* (New York: Arco Publishing Co., Inc., 1976).

Llewellyn-Jones, Malcolm (ed.), *The Royal Navy and the Arctic Convoys: A Naval Staff History*, Abingdon (2007)

Mallmann Showell, Jak P., *Hitler's Navy: A Reference Guide to the Kriegsmarine, 1935–1945*, Barnsley (2009)

Mallman Showell, Jak P., *The German Navy in World War Two: A Reference Guide to the Kriegsmarine, 1935–1945* (Annapolis, MD: Naval Institute Press, 1979).

Stille, Mark, British Battleship vs Italian Battleship the Mediterranean 1940–41 (Osprey 2021)

Stille, Mark, USN Battleship vs IJN Battleship the Pacific 1942–44 (Osprey 2017)

Stille, Mark, USN Destroyer vs IJN Destoryer The Pacific 1943 (Osprey 2012)

Stille, Mark, USN Fleet Destroyer vs IJN Fleet Submarine the Pacific 1941–42 (Osprey 2018)

Stille, Mark, USN Submarine vs IJN Antisubmarine Escort the Pacific 1941–45 (Osprey 2022)

United States Navy, *The Bluejackets' Manual 1940, Tenth Edition*, United States Naval Institute, Annapolis, MD, 1940

Whitley, M.J., *Battleships of World War Two: An International Encyclopaedia*, London (1998)

Whitley, M.J. *Destroyers of World War Two*. Annapolis, MD: Naval Institute Press. (1988)

Williamson, Gordon, *German Seaman 1939–45*, (Osprey 2009)

Websites:

www.ibiblio.org/hyperwar

www. Navsourcce.org

www.pwencycl.kgbudge.com

www.armouredcarriers.com

www.history.navy.mil

www.martime.org

www.hmshood.org.uk

www.navweaps.com

Photo Credits

Author's Collection 17T, 17B, 41B, 42, 90, 114, 116, 164, 200, 204, 222, 226, 228, 230, 232, 234, 236, 238, 240, 241, 256T, 256B, 258, 260, 265, 280, 281

Canadian War Museum 24, 26, 30, 46, 48, 50, 52, 54, 56, 58, 60, 61, 62, 63, 64, 65, 66, 67, 68, 69, 70, 71, 72, 73, 74, 75, 76, 77, 78, 79, 80, 86, 88, 89, 92, 93, 150, 153, 180, 181, 182, 190, 191, 206, 207, 223, 224, 225, 244, 245

Hoover Collection 16T, 16B

Kartengruppe.it 276, 278, 279

U.S. Library of Congress 176, 177, 196, 197, 250, 251

maritime.org 106, 107, 165, 246, 247

NARA 22, 37, 43T, 122, 124, 126, 128, 130, 132, 134, 142, 144, 148, 149, 151, 152, 154, 155, 156, 158, 160, 161, 162, 170, 174, 178, 186, 187, 188, 198, 203, 252, 254

National Naval Aviation Museum 192, 193

RAF Museum 8, 108, 110, 112, 113

The D-Day Story 18, 19, 21

The National Museum of the Royal Navy 94, 96, 98, 100, 102, 104

U.S. Naval Historical Center 10, 15, 23, 25, 28, 29, 31, 33, 35, 36, 38, 41T, 43B, 136, 138, 139, 140, 146, 166, 168, 172, 183, 210T, 212, 218

U.S. Naval Museum 14, 27, 39, 40, 120, 184, 185, 194, 195, 202, 208, 209, 210B, 214, 216, 219, 220, 242, 262, 263, 264, 266, 268, 270, 272, 274

University of Glasgow 82, 83, 84

Index

V

W

Y